About

Rebecca Winters lives in Salt Lake City, Utah. With canyons and high alpine meadows full of wildflowers, she never runs out of places to explore. They, plus her favourite holiday spots in Europe, often end up as backgrounds for her romance novels because writing is her passion, along with her family and church. Rebecca loves to hear from readers. If you wish to email her, please visit her website at cleanromances.net

Anne Oliver lives in Adelaide, South Australia. She is an avid romance reader, and after eight years of writing her own stories, Mills & Boon offered her publication in 2005. Her first two published novels won the Romance Writers of Australia's Romantic Book of the Year Award in 2007 and 2008. She was a finalist again in 2012 and 2013. Visit her website anne-oliver.com

Since 2006, *New York Times* bestseller Donna Alward has enchanted readers with stories of happy endings and homecomings that have won several awards and been translated into over a dozen languages. She's worked as an administrative assistant, teaching assistant, in retail and as a stay-at-home-mum, but always knew her degree in English Literature would pay off, as she is now happy to be a full-time writer. Her new historical fiction tales blend her love of history with characters who step beyond their biggest fears to claim the lives they desire. Donna currently lives in Nova Scotia, Canada, with her husband and two cats. You can often find her near the water, either kayaking on the lake or walking the sandy beaches to refill her creative well.

A Mistletoe Chance Encounter

REBECCA WINTERS

ANNE OLIVER

DONNA ALWARD

MILLS & BOON

First Published in Great Britain 2024
by Mills & Boon, an imprint of HarperCollins*Publishers* Ltd,
1 London Bridge Street, London, SE1 9GF

www.harpercollins.co.uk

HarperCollins*Publishers*
Macken House, 39/40 Mayor Street Upper,
Dublin 1, D01 C9W8, Ireland

ISBN: 978-0-263-39668-3

MIX
Paper | Supporting
responsible forestry
FSC
www.fsc.org
FSC™ C007454

This book contains FSC™ certified paper and other controlled sources to ensure responsible forest management.

For more information visit: www.harpercollins.co.uk/green

Printed and Bound in the UK using 100% Renewable Electricity at CPI Group (UK) Ltd, Croydon, CR0 4YY

MARRY ME UNDER THE MISTLETOE

REBECCA WINTERS

To Lib.

What would our youth have been like without each other?

I don't even want to think about it.

CHAPTER ONE

JUST TWO WEEKS until Christmas and so-o much to do.

The latest merchandise from suppliers needed to be put in the window. The Hansel and Gretel shop located on Lemon Street in downtown Providence, Rhode Island, was a favorite place all year long for customers wanting imported hand-painted wooden gifts, nutcrackers, little girls' Bavarian dirndls and little boys' Tyrolean hats. But especially at Christmas.

Andrea Fleming finished her morning coffee, then quickly dressed in a navy wool skirt and a long-sleeved navy pullover with Snoopy on the front wearing a Santa's hat. After running a brush through her shoulder-length gilt-blond hair, she slipped into her comfortable wedgies and hurried downstairs to the shop below.

She'd been living here since her husband's death fourteen months ago. They'd been married only three weeks and had been staying with his parents in Braunschweig, Germany, when they'd been in a car accident and he was killed outright. She'd survived, but had been forced to stay in hospital following an operation.

Her mother had been there to help her recover enough so that she could board a plane. When she returned home it was without her husband and no hope of ever having children.

Though her divorced mom wanted Andrea to live at home with her, she'd preferred to renovate the loft above the shop so she could stay there. She felt closer to Gunter somehow in the store she'd always felt was enchanted.

She'd been twenty-three when he'd first brought merchandise to her family's store in place of his father. His grandparents were the original creators of the world-famous Braunschweig nutcrackers and wooden pyramids. His dark blond good looks and blue eyes had captivated her and they'd fallen in love. Within the year they were married.

They'd had a wedding reception here in Providence with all her family and friends. His family had held another one for them in Germany. It had been a picture-perfect wedding for both sets of families.

No one could have foreseen the crash that took Andrea's husband. In one moment she'd lost him as well as her ability to conceive. Never would she have a child with him. Never would she have a child of her own body. A sob escaped her.

Don't dwell on that right now, Andrea.

After checking the thermostat to make sure the shop was warm enough, she walked out back to start unpacking the boxes from their suppliers that had arrived yesterday afternoon. In the first one she discovered an exquisitely made Braunschweig wooden rocking chair and put the price tag on it.

Without hesitation she carried it through the shop

to the window and set it next to the decorated Christmas tree that was part of the Santa's workshop display. The chair needed something special. She had dozens of dolls, floppy elves and Christmas angels. Any one of them would look cute sitting in it. She would have to think about it while she finished unpacking.

"Oh!" she cried when she opened the last box and found a three-foot-tall gingerbread boy. It was made of dark chocolate-colored dotted Swiss fabric. A red, green and gold plaid ribbon was tied around his neck at a jaunty angle with a little golden bell hanging down.

He had large, shiny blue buttons for eyes, round pink felt cheeks and an impish smiley mouth done in red ribbon as if to say, "You can run and run as fast as you can, but you can't catch me. I'm the gingerbread man." The body was outlined in white bric-a-brac trim.

"You're so perfect I can't believe it!" She attached the price tag to it. "If Gunter hadn't had that accident, we'd have a little boy or girl who would love you as much as I do." Tears stung her eyes as sorrow overwhelmed her.

Surrounded by many items meant for a child, she knew this shop was a constant reminder of her loss. But the store was also a family treasure and legacy she loved, and of course there was the comfort and joy of working alongside her mother, who'd done everything to help her overcome her grief.

Andrea thought she'd been doing a little better, but for some reason this gingerbread man spoke to her inner heart. It was at bittersweet times like this that she had to fight against succumbing to the terrible pain of knowing she'd never have her own baby.

Though her mom gently reminded her that one day she'd meet another man and there was always adoption, Andrea couldn't imagine it. What man, when given a choice, would want an infertile widow?

After hugging the gingerbread man to her chest until the painful moment passed, she walked over to the window and placed it in the new chair. Once she'd added the latest set of nutcrackers from the Bavarian kings collection to the others, she flipped the switch on the wall and the window display came alive with colored lights and sounds.

On the floor around the tree loaded with wooden ornaments she'd placed an animated elf band with drums, cymbals and horns. Children and adults alike always stopped to watch their antics. Usually it brought people inside to buy an identical set and they ended up going home with more gifts.

On impulse she pulled the smartphone from her pocket and stepped inside the display area to take a couple of pictures. Wait till she sent them to the gingerbread girls. That was the nickname for her and her best friends Emily and Casey. Recently they'd lost Melissa, the other member of their special group.

They'd all met years ago on summer vacation at the Gingerbread Inn in Massachusetts and the nickname had stuck. Their families had continued to meet there every summer and the girls had become fast friends, a bond that had lasted to this day. But with Melissa gone, Andrea couldn't handle any more sadness thinking about that.

Instead she concentrated on getting the small shop ready for customers. Her mom would be over later in the day to help. Throughout the holidays Andrea opened up at nine-thirty rather than ten, and closed at eight rather than six. It was almost opening time now.

She ran the vacuum over the carpet and watered the pots of red poinsettias placed around the room among all the wooden objects displayed. The thoughtful manager of the floral shop next door had sent a centerpiece featuring white Asiatic lilies and red roses. Andrea set it on the counter. With the profusion of lights and decorations, she had to admit it looked like a fairyland.

Before she unlocked the front door, she went into the office in back and checked her emails on the computer. To her astonishment she saw a message from gingerbread3. That was Casey Caravetta's user name. Since Andrea was the youngest, her email was gingerbread4, Emily was 1, and Melissa's had been 2.

What a coincidence! She'd just been thinking about her friends. Andrea prayed this was good news, the kind she wanted to hear from Casey, who'd lived through a broken engagement a year ago and was still down from it. Andrea opened the message.

Hey, Andrea, it's moi. Could you possibly drop things and drive over to the Gingerbread Inn today? I've got to talk to you.

Oh, no. Things didn't sound any better for Casey since the last time they'd talked.

One of my issues is I'm up in the air about Christmas and the problems with my family (as always).

Casey was at the inn now? In winter?

I came to our favorite place because it seemed to work such magic for Emily, but I can't believe what it's like here. You should see how run-down it is. I could cry.

The three of them had suffered thinking of it gradually deteriorating.

As you know, Carol's always been like a mother to all of us and is taking great care of me. She's such a sweetheart. So's Harper, who lies at my feet and looks up at me with those soulful puppy eyes.

Warm memories of bygone days flooded Andrea. Throughout their youth they'd had marvelous times together with no hint of what lay in store for them beyond the horizon of Barrow's Lake.

I'd give anything if you'd join me. You're not that far away from Barrow's Cove. I realize how busy you are at the shop this time of year, but I need you and your wisdom, especially after what you've been through.

Andrea didn't have any wisdom. She was an empty vessel.

Let me know if you can make it, even if it's only for

one night. Remember when we talked about giving a party at the inn on Christmas Eve so Emily and Cole can renew their wedding vows? This would be the perfect time to formalize our plans. So see what you can do to get away.

Love ya, Casey.

Andrea closed the message and left the office to open the door to the shop. She glanced at the Advent calendar hanging on the wall, one of several dozen with chocolate tokens in each window. Luckily it was Wednesday—not the weekend, which was their busiest time.

The inn on Barrow's Lake outside Barrow's Cove, Massachusetts, was only an hour away from Providence. If she left after her mother came over, she could spend the night with Casey and drive home tomorrow in time to relieve her mom by afternoon.

She checked the weather app on her phone. No new storm systems right now. Though they'd had snow in the Northeast, most of the main roads had been plowed. It wouldn't take any time to pack for one overnight.

Andrea had already decided which nutcrackers she would give her friends for Christmas. All she had to do was wrap them and take them with her. She could give them out at the party on Christmas Eve.

During her musings an elderly gentleman walked into the store. It activated some Christmas chimes. When he said he wanted to browse, she used that time to phone her mom. As soon as she told her about the email, her mom told her to go for several days if she wanted, accusing her of never taking a vacation.

Andrea loved her mother, but told her she needed only one night. In truth she didn't like being away from the shop. It kept her going. Too much free time and she started to think about things that dragged her down to despair. None of that this year!

She got back on the computer and sent Casey a message that she was coming. Then she gift wrapped a smoker for her customer. After taking his credit card information, she handed him his package. That was when she saw a tall, striking male, maybe thirtyish, standing outside the window wearing a bomber jacket. He was carrying a blonde girl of five or six in his arms so she could see everything.

Loving the girl's animation, Andrea walked over to the window to watch. The child was pointing at the gingerbread boy, her face and eyes beguiled by him. Closer now, Andrea could see she wore a pink parka with a hood lined in fur. It had fallen back to reveal her soft golden curls that fell to her shoulders.

Against the bright pink color, the man's short cropped jet-black hair stood out. With brows the same color, he was darkly attractive. His lean chiseled jaw had that five-o'clock shadow that looked good only on a certain type of male.

When the little girl laughed at the antics of the drummer elf, the lines of his hard mouth broke into a half smile, causing Andrea's breath to catch. She had the strongest suspicion he didn't laugh often. Suddenly his gaze shifted to Andrea's, as if he could read her mind and didn't like it.

Completely embarrassed and shaken to be caught

staring at him, she walked back to the counter. That was the first time anything like that had happened since Gunter's death. There'd been plenty of attractive men coming in and out of the shop since her return from Germany, but they weren't in this man's class.

A second later she heard the chimes again before the charismatic man approached her. The girl walked at his side, clinging to his hand. With those light green eyes, they had to be father and daughter, although his were more hazel in color and a deeper hue.

"Good morning. May I help you?"

"I hope so," Rick Jenner said to the blonde saleswoman. "Do you have a set of animated elves like the one in the window?"

"Right over here on this table." She walked to it and picked up a box.

When she put it on the counter, his daughter stared at him with imploring eyes. "Will you ask her if I can hold the gingerbread man, Daddy?"

"No, Tessa. It's too expensive."

"What's expensive?"

"It costs too much," he said and pulled the credit card from his wallet to pay for the elves.

"I wish I could look at it." Tears welled in her eyes. If he had a dollar for every time she wished she could have something...

The clerk ringing up the sale took one look at those eyes and said, "Stay right there and I'll bring it to you." After handing him back his card and purchase, she walked around the counter and hurried over to the display window to pluck the gingerbread man and rocking chair from the case.

Good grief. His daughter was a little manipulator, a talent she'd learned from his deceased wife, who'd been indulged in turn by her own well-meaning parents, especially her mother, Nancy. He'd loved his wife and they'd had a good marriage, but she'd been high maintenance, which had caused minor strains and at times a few major ones. Rick was determined his daughter would learn she couldn't have everything she wanted.

When the clerk walked over to them, he became aware of her enticing fragrance, a light floral one. "If you'll sit down, you can hold him."

Rick wished she hadn't gone to the trouble, but it was too late now.

"Oh—" Tessa crooned after taking it in her arms. His daughter's happiness almost blinded him. "He's so cute." In a perfectly natural gesture, she kissed the cheeks just the way a mother would kiss her baby. Then she held it tight and with eyes closed started rocking.

The sight caused Rick's throat to swell. He was in luck. Only the first day of shopping to get an idea of what Tessa wanted and already he knew *this* would be the present Santa left under the tree. When he got home, he would ask his housekeeper to come in and buy it for him so it could be a surprise.

"We have to leave now, Tessa. We've got more shopping to do before I take you to kindergarten. Thank the nice lady for letting you hold him."

Tessa stared at the saleswoman. "Thank you."

"You're welcome."

He helped her off the chair and set the gingerbread man inside it.

Tessa's lower lip trembled. "Can't I have him, Daddy?"

"I'm afraid not."

"Please?"

"Tessa—that's enough."

"I'll sell it to you at half price," the woman said under her breath. He lifted his head and found himself gazing into the sapphire-blue eyes that had unexpectedly caught his attention through the display window.

"Thank you, but no."

On cue his daughter broke into tears. The clerk bent over her. "Have you written to Santa Claus yet?"

"Yes. My grandma helped me, b-but I didn't ask for the gingerbread man." Her voice wobbled.

"I'm sure your father will help you write another letter and ask Santa to bring you a gingerbread man." She flicked him a hopeful glance as she said it.

"This one?" Tessa pointed to the chair.

"Yes."

Rick blinked. *Yes?* The clerk's no doubt well-meaning intervention irritated the hell out of him. Worse, she'd played right into his daughter's hands.

Tessa sniffed. "Do you think Santa will know that my gingerbread man is in this store?"

An impish smile broke the corner of the clerk's mouth, drawing his unwilling attention to its provocative shape. "Yes."

"Promise?"

"I promise."

"Come on, Tessa." He picked up his daughter, who still wasn't in control of her tears.

"Have a merry Christmas!" The woman just kept it up.

Rick flashed her a brief glance. "Merry Christmas. Thank you for indulging her." With his daughter in one arm and his package in the other, he left the shop in a few long, swift strides.

Was that a little sarcasm Andrea had heard?

She bristled, realizing that he hadn't wanted his daughter indulged and didn't appreciate in the least what Andrea had done.

But maybe he couldn't afford it because he was out of work. He *had* told his daughter it cost too much. If that was the case, then she felt bad for putting him on the spot, and she decided she would grant his little girl her wish by Christmas.

Andrea knew exactly where to send the gingerbread man and the chair. The credit card listed him as Richard Jenner on Rose Drive in Elmhurst, a nice neighborhood. It was Christmas, a time for giving.

This could be her own little sub-for-Santa project. Every year at the church they had a list of families who needed help, and everyone who could contribute did so. This was one time when Andrea knew her present would bring happiness.

Picking up one of the big floppy elves, she took him over by the tree and put him in place of the gingerbread man and the rocker. Those items she took up the back stairs to the loft. Once she got everything gift wrapped and packed, then she'd send it to the Jenner residence. On the outside of the box she'd print "To Tessa from Santa."

With that accomplished she went back downstairs to face a steady stream of customers until her mother arrived so she could leave for Barrow's Lake.

During the late-afternoon drive her mind played over the incident in the store. What she'd give to have a child she could indulge. With those cherubic features, Tessa Jenner was absolutely adorable.

When she reached the Gingerbread Inn, she saw the state it was in and realized that Casey's email hadn't exaggerated. Despite some cosmetic fix-ups by Emily and her husband, Cole Watson, it was obvious the Gingerbread Inn had fallen on hard times. Despite all the inn owner's big dreams, Carol Parsons had lost her husband and couldn't keep everything going anymore.

In the kitchen, the heart of the once-fabulous two-story Georgian inn, Andrea looked around. Everything needed refurbishing. She longed to get rid of the dilapidated sunflower wallpaper and worn white vinyl flooring and make it all fresh again.

But Andrea was grateful for one thing that hadn't changed. She and Casey, her exotic-looking friend with the dark wild hair, were sitting at the very same long maple table where the girls had enjoyed many a meal day or night in past summers.

"Do you two want another cup of cocoa?"

Andrea jumped up from the chair and gave Carol another hug. The tiny gray-haired widow and sole owner was in her fifties and still looked great wearing a pale blue T-shirt and jeans. Best of all, she had a heart as big as the outdoors.

To the amusement of all, Harper, the golden retriever of uncertain mix, ran around sniffing everyone, hoping for crumbs from Carol's homemade coffee cake fresh from the oven.

"Don't you know you've done enough? It's after midnight. You should be in bed. Casey and I will be headed there ourselves pretty soon."

"No, you won't." She laughed. "I know you girls. Once you get talking, there's no stopping you. Since you have to get back to Providence tomorrow, I'm going to leave you two alone so you can catch up. In the morning I'll make scones."

"Those are to die for," the girls said in a collective voice.

Carol laughed. "Come on, Harper." The dog made a yapping sound and scrambled out the door after her.

Andrea and Casey were finally alone, surrounded by six empty chairs. One of them would never see Melissa again. Once upon a time they'd been filled with people and laughter and great happiness. Andrea wondered if she'd ever know real happiness again. Her hurt went so deep she couldn't fathom experiencing it again, let alone joy.

Casey studied her for a minute through dark brown eyes. "I know what you're thinking."

Andrea nodded. "Life has changed for all of us. Remember that horrid expression, 'Life is what happens when you had other plans'?"

"Oh, yeah. I could have written it."

"I think Eve probably coined the expression," Andrea murmured.

"Except I think things might be changing for Carol."

"Really?"

She smiled. "Cole hired a handyman to help around here. His name is Martin Johnson. He's been a widower for ten years and from what I can tell, he and Carol are getting along better than you'd believe. Having been a carpenter, he can fix anything."

"What's he like?"

"Tall and blue-eyed with the greatest shock of white hair."

"Wouldn't it be something if a romance blossomed around here?"

Casey nodded as they stared at each other for a long serious moment. "It's so good to see you and I'm so-o glad you came. I'm feeling alone and maybe more than a tad envious of Emily, who's off on her second honeymoon with Cole."

"I feel the same way, so let's get busy planning what we're going to do with this place to turn it into a winter wonderland for their vow-renewal ceremony."

Once they'd worked it all out Andrea said, "Tell me what's hanging so heavily on you right now."

"Oh, Andrea, I just feel like I don't want to be filled with self-pity around you when you've experienced so much loss. I guess I hoped to recapture some of that girlish wonder we had for so many years. But we can't turn back the clock. When I think about you and Gunter…I don't know how you're dealing with your life. It's all so unfair."

Andrea had known this conversation would leap to her own problems. "Let's agree the word *fair* should be stricken from the language. Luckily his parents have three other children and four grandchildren to dote on, and I have my mom and the shop."

"I'm glad about that. I know how much work is saving your life right now. But forgive me for asking another question. How will you ever move on if everywhere you turn, you see him?"

A weary sigh escaped her lips. "Mom has begged me to move back to the house with her for that very reason, but I'm not ready yet and don't know if I ever will be. She belongs to a church group that meets every few weeks. There's a widower I know she's interested in, but he's been on vacation. I'm hoping that when he gets back, he'll sweep her off her feet. If I'm not living there, it'll make his path easier."

"I love your mom. Any man would be lucky to find a woman like her. But I want to see you fall in love like that again."

"The chances against that happening are astronomical, Casey."

"Surely not. I predict some gorgeous guy is going to come along and you won't know what hit you. Maybe this fantastic man will see you in the shop and find you absolutely irresistible the way Gunter did."

"Maybe."

Heat rushed into her cheeks as a vision of Tessa's father filled her mind. He *was* fantastic looking, but if anything, she knew he'd felt like swatting her away from him rather than sweeping her off her feet. The encounter had disturbed her more than she wanted to admit.

Mr. Jenner had a daughter, for heaven's sake. Though he didn't wear a wedding ring—Andrea blushed to realize she had noticed—he was probably in an intimate relationship with a woman, so there was no point in wasting energy discussing him. The last person he'd be interested in was a widow who couldn't give a man more children.

Though she was tempted to tell Casey about the incident, she held back, needing to concentrate on anything that didn't have to do with the ache inside her. Andrea had her sister-in-law when she really needed to talk. With Marie she could open up. She'd been there right after the accident. They'd become close after Andrea had met Gunter, and they needed each other now that he was gone so they could mourn together.

"It has to happen one day, Andrea. You're too young and beautiful."

"And unable to conceive, don't forget."

"There's always adoption."

"That's what Mom says, but it's ludicrous to go there. I just don't want to think about it."

"Understood."

Feeling at a complete loose end, Andrea got to her feet and did the dishes. Once the kitchen was cleaned up, she took a deep breath. "You know what? It's late. Why don't we go to bed, and tomorrow we'll get up and drink hot chocolate, take a walk to the lake and think about Emily and Cole having a baby and how wonderful life can be. I've never been here in the snow."

"Nor I. If circumstances were different for you and me, this could be a very romantic winter getaway."

"*If* being the operative word," Andrea added wryly to cover her troubled emotions.

At least their plans for the wedding-renewal vows on Christmas Eve had been made. But much as she was thrilled to see Casey and leave the nutcrackers for everyone, their conversation had opened up her wounds and she was bleeding all over the place. This bleakness in her heart threatened to overwhelm her. She needed to get back to work where she wouldn't think. "Casey—"

"I know what you're going to say," Casey interrupted. They read each other's minds quite easily. "You're restless as a cat wanting out of a cage."

"The inn is hardly a cage."

"It is when you're needing other things to occupy your mind. Go on back to Providence after breakfast. To be honest, I'm afraid I'm suffering from the same problem. I'll probably head back when you do. I've got a project going for Emily's baby on my quilting frame at home. I'm making her a special quilt with a picture of the Gingerbread Inn in the center."

"Oh, how darling!" Andrea cried. "You've just given me an idea for a gift that will look perfect in her nursery." When more rocking chairs and gingerbread men arrived, she'd put a set away for Emily. On the way back to Providence, she'd put in a big order for both items.

In her mind's eye Andrea kept remembering Tessa rocking back and forth with her prize in her arms.... Oh, how she'd love to see that precious girl on Christmas morning when she ran to find out what Santa had brought her. To give birth to a daughter like Tessa Jenner would be joy beyond measure. But it wasn't meant to be. The sooner she got that child off her mind, the better.

She turned out the lights and they went up to bed. Clearly Casey was in so much turmoil herself, she didn't press Andrea to stay longer. They'd said all there was to say for the time being. Now they both needed their own caves to lick their wounds while they struggled to survive.

CHAPTER TWO

"LADDER 1 RESPOND to art-gallery fire on Lemon Street and Sixth."

The dispatcher's voice over the gong galvanized everyone into action. Hearing the address, Rick felt his adrenaline kick in. *Lemon Street?* After parking his car, he'd walked by that gallery earlier in the morning with Tessa. Only a florist shop separated it from the Hansel and Gretel shop.

He didn't plan to go there again and had planned to send his housekeeper to buy the gingerbread man for him. Not only did he have time constraints, he preferred to avoid a good-looking woman like the salesclerk who wore no ring. After losing his wife, he wanted to spare himself and Tessa that kind of pain ever again. Another romantic relationship was out of the question for him.

Unfortunately if the fire spread, that shop's inventory, including the gingerbread man, might go up in smoke before the night was over. The clock said 9:55 p.m. Hopefully the woman had long since gone home from work. He broke out in a cold sweat just thinking about her getting overcome by fumes or worse. Rick knew firsthand what that was like; as a child he'd almost died in a fire. That experience had changed the direction of his life.

"Let's go!" he called to his crew as he grabbed his turnout gear and headed for the engine. Arney drove them out of the truck bay to the downtown area. Rick got on the phone to the battalion chief discussing methods to proceed when he saw smoke pouring out of the third-story window of the art gallery. Engine 2 was first in, but the alarm had sounded for more help.

"Mel? You work with Arney. Jose? You're with me." Out of the corner of his eye Rick saw another ladder truck pull up to the fire ground. Already a couple of men from the engine truck had gone into the building with the hoses.

"Ready, Jose?"

He gave the sign and together they placed the ladder in an alley that gave access to the building and set it against the wall. After putting on their masks, they ascended. Their job was to hunt for any injured or unconscious people trapped in there.

The smoke continued to pour out the third-story window. Everything was black by the time he climbed inside the frame where the glass had blown out. Ladder 2 down the alley was having trouble opening up the side of the building to ventilate. The smoke was really heavy now. Rick's intuition was that the hoses had extinguished most of the fire and what was left was smoke from the burned electrical insulation.

He and Jose crawled in on their bellies, but after a few minutes of going from room to room, they were satisfied no one was inside except the fire crews. The smoke started to be drawn off, which meant the ventilation was finally working.

Dozens of charred canvases lay in heaps in one of the rooms on the top floor. Something about the arrangement of them didn't look right—strange even. He had a gut feeling the fire had been started there on purpose. After more probing he knew they had to have been placed in a pile like that.

When he got back to the station he would tell Benton Ames, the head of the arson squad and Rick's best friend. After more inspection, he made his way down the watery, debris-filled stairway.

Once outside, he pulled off his mask. Thank goodness the fire hadn't spread. It had mostly been contained on the third floor. The Hansel and Gretel shop was still standing. With a sense of relief that both it and the florist shop had been spared, he helped Jose bring down the extension. Soon they'd done their cleanup, and they rode back to the station. His ten-hour shift was at an end and he could go home.

The battalion chief got him on the phone. "When you report to the station tomorrow, take the truck to Lemon Street on your way to training exercises. I want you and your crew to talk to the businesses on either side and across from the art gallery. Get a report if they sustained any smoke damage of significance."

Another rush of adrenaline charged his body. That meant he might be seeing *her* again. Just the thought of it raised his blood pressure. Somehow her appeal had slipped past his defenses. He couldn't figure it out.

"Yes, sir."

Fifteen minutes later he pulled into the driveway of his house and let himself in the front door. Sharon Milne, his live-in housekeeper, would have put Tessa to bed at eight-thirty. His daughter had made him promise he'd help her write a letter to Santa in the morning.

Rick went to the kitchen and drank from the tap until he'd quenched his thirst, then he headed for his bedroom. After a shower and shave, he put on a robe and walked down the hall to Tessa's room.

He tiptoed inside and sat on the side of the bed to look at her. In sleep her profile reminded him a lot of his deceased wife, Tina. She'd been gone a year. They'd lost her to leukemia a month before Christmas after a year's fight against the disease. This was the hardest time for both of them.

Tessa had been very upset with him when he'd dropped her off at kindergarten today. She'd wanted to know why they couldn't go back and get the gingerbread man.

There'd been several reasons. Once again Rick had given her another talk about being grateful for the things she had and not to expect to be appeased at every turn. After Tina's death he'd done his share of giving their daughter things to comfort her in their grief, but it hadn't taken long before he'd realized it was the wrong thing to do.

She expected everyone to satisfy her slightest wish. His wife and her family had done too much of that in the past. Before Tina's passing, Tessa had already felt entitled. He smoothed the blond hair off her forehead.

Rick didn't want his daughter growing up with a princess complex.

But there was more bothering him. How could he explain to a five-year-old how he'd felt when he saw the clerk looking at him through the shop window with those brilliant blue eyes? She was the kind of woman the guys at the station would call a real stunner—blonde and curvaceous with classic features. Most likely she was married with children. Her response to Tessa had seemed very natural. It meant his thoughts should stop right there. The absence of a wedding ring didn't always prove anything.

Rick had felt dead inside for so long, he was shocked to discover he could have an emotional response to the looks of a beautiful woman again. The psychiatrist provided by the department had talked to him at length about dealing with his grief. He'd told Rick that one day he'd start to feel alive again, but there was no set time when it would happen.

Rick certainly hadn't expected the first signs of it to happen this morning. Part of the anger he'd felt masked guilt, because it seemed as if he was being disloyal to Tina even to notice another woman so soon after her death. The psychiatrist had warned him about that, too. He'd said it was perfectly natural to feel guilt, and he might feel it for a long time. If it went on too long, however, then he wanted to see him back in his office.

After the clerk had waited on him, his anger had grown worse because she'd been so incredibly nice and tuned in to Tessa's feelings. He didn't want her doing either of them any favors. For one thing, Tessa was *his* daughter.

The woman obviously thought he didn't have enough money to pay for the gingerbread man, so she'd lowered the price. He had to admit it had injured his pride. But after having a whole day to think about it, he recognized what he'd really been feeling.

The last thing he wanted was to feel beholden to her or any woman. Sharon, the housekeeper, was different in her caretaker role.

Face it, Jenner. You resent being attracted to her.

That was the truth of it. He supposed the fact that she was the first person since Tina's death to take his mind off his wife for a few minutes made him feel vulnerable. But for her to play Santa hadn't sat well with him. So many emotions had bombarded him, he hadn't been able to get out of the shop fast enough.

No one could take Tina's place as Tessa's mother. He couldn't trust another woman with that job. Rick didn't want another woman in his life. He didn't want to have those kinds of feelings ever again. It had hurt so much to lose Tina. He couldn't live through pain like that a second time. Once was enough for him and Tessa. He'd do whatever he could to protect both of them from more suffering.

Frustrated as hell because he would have to go by her business tomorrow, he leaned over to kiss his daughter's forehead before leaving to go to his own room. Maybe he'd get one of the crew to do it. Either way, it would be a short visit and that would be the end of it.

Before he went to bed he made a detour to the living room and set up the elf band beneath the Christmas tree they'd bought and decorated last night. When Tessa got up in the morning, she'd run in here to find out what the noise was and be delighted.

Now, if he could just get the woman out of his head so he could go to sleep… But that was a joke, because she'd been flitting through his mind—all the amazing parts of her, starting with her smile and the way her blue eyes shimmered.

At ten the next morning Arney pulled the fire truck in front of the scarred top half of the art gallery. An inspection team from the arson squad was walking around.

When Rick saw Benton, he climbed down from the truck in his gear and walked over to his sandy-haired friend. He and his wife, Deanna, an attractive brunette, had two children, one of whom was Tessa's friend Julie at kindergarten. They'd all become close during Tina's illness.

Benton patted him on the shoulder. "Thanks to your tip, we know this is the work of the same arsonist who started that department-store blaze three weeks ago. Underneath that pile of canvases, he'd filled a plastic milk carton with gasoline and made a wick with a piece of shirt. It was a slow burner, but did enough damage to ignite the whole thing."

"He probably used the fire escape here to knock out that third-story window we climbed into. I thought it had been blown out by the fire."

"Let's hope he's caught soon. In the meantime I've

spoken to the police chief. They're going to keep this downtown area under heavy surveillance 24/7 until after the holidays."

"That's good." If Benton hadn't mentioned it, Rick would have.

"How's it going?"

Rick didn't have to pretend around him. "Don't ask."

"That's what I thought. Deanna and I are having a little party on Saturday night. We want you to come. Susie Anderson from Engine 3 will be coming along with some of the others. She specifically asked if you'd be there." He put his hand up. "I know what you're going to say about that, but at least promise me you'll think about it."

"Susie's a good firefighter and nice in her own way, but she's been a part of the landscape for too long a time. She's just one of the guys to me, Benton. Everyone's been trying to line me up, but I just can't do it. I don't feel the spark. Without that…"

"Then bring a friend, so Susie won't get any ideas. If it's your housekeeper's night off, then bring Tessa. She and Julie can play."

Rick was aware the guys were waiting for him. He turned to his crew, having made a certain decision. "Mel? You and Arney cover the florist and the Hansel and Gretel shop. Jose? Go talk to the cleaners across the street. I'll take the print shop."

Once the men took off, he eyed Benton and gave him a clap on the shoulder. "Thanks for the invite. I promise I'll think about it."

His friend winked. "Good."

Before Rick walked across the street, his gaze wandered to the display window of the shop. Yesterday he'd looked into a pair of blue eyes in an angel face with a golden halo of hair. It had felt as if a thunderbolt had passed through him.

But neither the gingerbread man nor the little rocking chair was there now. That meant she'd pulled the items after he'd left the store. Hopefully they'd be in the back. Maybe another employee was on duty today. He'd asked Mel and Arney to find out. If so, Rick would go in and buy them.

With clipboard in hand, he walked across the street and interviewed the manager of the print shop. The smell of smoke still hung around, but he learned they hadn't been affected by the fire. He returned to the truck where the guys were waiting.

None of the people interviewed could give any information regarding a possible arsonist. All had been gone from their stores when the fire broke out. The florist was still using one of the department fans.

Rick collected their reports and read Arney's, absorbing the information on the Hansel and Gretel shop like a sponge.

Owner of the shop was Mrs. Valerie Bernard, fifty-three, who lived in College Hill, the most affluent neighborhood in Providence. Judging by the expensive items displayed, he wasn't surprised. She was also the person Arney had talked to, because it was her signature on the bottom of the form.

The report stated there'd been no damage, but the smell of smoke still lingered. She didn't think a fan was necessary. He called out to Arney. "Did you speak to any employees besides Mrs. Bernard?"

"No. She was the only one there."

That made his mind up for him. "Give me a minute. The smoke smell is stronger on this side of the street. I want to check her place again. She might need a fan anyway."

"Okay."

He headed for the shop. When he entered, the Christmas chimes sounded. It was déjà vu. An attractive older woman with short blond hair stylishly cut who looked vaguely familiar to him was waiting on a customer, but she smiled at Rick.

He walked around, deciding the smell of smoke wasn't that bad. As soon as the customer left with a package, he approached her. "Sorry to bother you again. I'm Captain Jenner of Ladder 1. I wanted to make sure you hadn't changed your mind about wanting a fan."

She gave him a pleasant smile. "No. It's not necessary, but I have to tell you I'm mighty thankful you got that fire out in time to save the rest of us. Some of my inventory is irreplaceable. Even with the insurance, there are several dozen pyramids and signed nutcrackers that are original pieces, and priceless. They're made in Germany."

"I'm aware of that. I came in here yesterday with my daughter. She saw the gingerbread man in the window. While I'm here, I'd like to buy it for her."

The woman frowned. "A gingerbread man?"

"Yes." He described it. "It was sitting in a little rocking chair. I'd like to buy the chair, too. Maybe the items got sold. Then again, it's possible one of your employees put those items away for some reason."

"The only other person who works here is my daughter, Andrea." Blood pounded in his ears. *That's why the owner looked familiar.* He'd wondered. The more he looked at her, the more he saw the resemblance in the shape of her face and body. "She must have unpacked those items while I was gone. Give me time to check in back."

She returned in a few minutes looking at a loss. "My daughter went out of town yesterday." *With her husband or a fiancé, maybe?* Why in blazes did he care? "She'll be able to explain. I'm expecting her back this afternoon. When she comes in, I'll ask her what happened. If you call the shop after two, you'll be able to talk to her."

Rick knew exactly what had happened. She was planning to give them to Tessa for Christmas because she believed he couldn't afford it. No doubt she'd hidden them away somewhere. "I'm afraid I'll be on duty until seven. When I next have time off, I'll call around. Thank you for your help. I'm glad your shop was saved, Mrs. Bernard. It's a delightful place."

"Thank you. It's been in our family seventy-five years." She walked him to the door. "If it weren't for brave men like you, I wouldn't have had a shop to open this morning. I'm very grateful and know the neighbors around here are, too. It was a pleasure to meet you."

Now Rick knew why Andrea was so nice. *Damn.* "The pleasure's mine, Mrs. Bernard. Have a good day."

* * *

Andrea drove down the alley and parked the car next to her mom's at the rear of the shop. She was glad to be home, even if it was closer to an hour later than she'd planned. There'd been a ten-car pileup on the freeway because of black ice. No one had been injured, thank heaven, but as a result the cars were lined up several miles waiting to get around the accident scene.

She'd also stopped at her favorite bookstore and picked up a copy of a gingerbread-man book with terrific illustrations. She'd loved it as a child. Another gift from Santa.

Pressing the remote that opened the back door, she entered and could immediately smell smoke. Her heart rate picked up speed. After putting down her overnight bag, she hurried through the office to the front of the shop. Her mom saw her and smiled. She was waiting on two teens buying some hand-painted wooden ornaments.

Until they left she couldn't talk to her mom, so she went back to the office and sent an email to Casey. She'd promised to let her and Carol know she'd gotten home safely. There were several emails waiting for her to open, all of them from Gunter's family.

Andrea decided to read them later except for one from Marie, whom she missed horribly. They were close to the same age and had a lot in common besides the fact that they'd both adored Gunter.

Her email was inviting Andrea to meet her and her husband, Rolfe, in the south of Spain after Christmas and vacation until the New Year. Would she please come? They would pay for her flight and would be staying with Rolfe's friend at his villa.

While Andrea stood there contemplating the generous offer and idea, she could still smell smoke, and she lifted her head. Where had it come from? She was dying to know, but a steady stream of customers kept both her and her mother busy for a couple of hours. Finally they had a break. As soon as the front door closed, Andrea gave her mother a fierce hug.

"What was that all about, darling?"

"Because I love you. Because Casey and I had a long talk, and it made me appreciate you all over again for being the best mother in the world."

"I could say the same thing about my daughter. I'm glad you got back safely."

"Me, too. Now tell me what's happened. Why is there that smoke smell?"

"The art gallery caught fire last night around ten when everyone had gone home."

"You're kidding!"

"I wish I were. There's a possibility of arson. I was talking to Wally earlier. He said the firefighters saved as many paintings as they could, but some of the ones in storage on the third floor didn't make it. We're very blessed they got here in time to save the rest of the surrounding stores, including ours."

Andrea shuddered. "When I think of the years you've put into this shop, and then to imagine a fire threatening everything... I'm sorry I wasn't here for you."

"Don't be silly. There wasn't anything anyone could do. Life is a risk."

Yes. But she'd never thought about it until she and Gunter had been broadsided by a man who was drunk. In a flash her husband had been snuffed out. "Casey and I came to that same conclusion last night."

"Did you have a wonderful time?"

She bit her lip. "It was good to see her and Carol again, and we were able to make plans for the party on Christmas Eve, but the inn is up for sale, and Casey is very low right now. She hasn't really gotten over her broken engagement. So to answer your question honestly, I've come home a bit depressed, but it will pass."

"That settles it. After we close up tonight, you're coming home with me, and no buts."

"I'd like that," Andrea said without reservation.

"Oh—before more customers walk in, I need to ask you about a gingerbread man and a chair, neither of which I've seen. Apparently you put them in the front window display, but when the man who'd seen them before came in today to buy them, they were gone and I couldn't help him."

Andrea's heart gave a kick. "Do you remember his name?"

"He introduced himself as Captain Jenner." *Captain?* "It was his crew of firefighters along with two other crews who contained the blaze last night and put it out. This morning he came by with his men to see if I needed a fan."

Tessa's daddy was a firefighter? Here Andrea had thought he might be out of work and was too proud to accept charity. Instead while he was on duty he'd come to the shop to buy everything without Tessa knowing.

Andrea didn't know whether to laugh or cry at her false assumption. The man's aloof behavior had been a disturbing mystery to her.

Her mother eyed her curiously. "Why are you so quiet?"

Just then they had another customer. "I'll tell you in a minute."

A minute turned into another hour before Andrea was able to relate the substance of what had happened, but she didn't tell her mother certain details. How could she when she didn't know what she was feeling herself? "I made a false assumption that he couldn't afford to buy the chair and the gingerbread man. His little girl was so cute and wanted it so much, I wanted to help, I guess."

Her mom nodded. "I could tell he was disappointed the items were gone. Why don't you run them to him at the fire station right now and make things right? It's only six blocks from here and will save him another trip to the shop. It'll help you feel better, too. After their heroic service, it's the least we can do for him, don't you think? But before you leave, I'd like to see that gingerbread man. Who sent it?"

"Our wholesaler in the Adirondacks. It's a sample of the new product they're introducing. I'll bring it down with the rocking chair."

Andrea went to the back room and dashed up the stairs to her bedroom. She brought down both items. While her mom was busy with another customer, Andrea placed the chair and gingerbread man next to the table with one of their three-tiered pyramids.

In a minute her mother started walking to the counter carrying a dirndl for the lady following her, but she stopped midstride when she saw it. "Oh, Andrea—without a doubt that's the most appealing craft item I've ever seen!"

"I totally agree. On the drive home from Barrow's Lake I ordered more of them and the rocking chairs."

The customer walked over and picked it up to examine it. "I'd like to buy this. My four-year-old granddaughter will go crazy over it. The rocking chair is superb, too. I think I have to have both."

"I'm sorry." Andrea spoke up. "They've already been sold, but leave us your name and number. When more come in, one of us will call you."

"Can they be here before Christmas? My friend Renee will want both for her little niece, too."

"I'll put a rush on it, but you never know."

Andrea eyed her mom before hurrying to the rear to pack up the treasures in one crate and gift wrap it. When she'd loaded it into the trunk of her car, she went back upstairs to shower and change into something fresh.

Several of her outfits had been purchased in Germany. After giving it some thought, she pulled out her cherry-red two-piece loden wool suit. She'd bought it the day Marie had gone shopping with her. Gunter had said it looked perfect on her.

Dark green braid lined the round neck and the front of the jacket. Eight ornate silver buttons the size of quarters ran down the middle to the hem at the waist. She loved this suit with its slightly flared skirt. It was reminiscent of the old-world items in the shop, but she'd worn it only once while she was still in Germany.

Chances were Captain Jenner wouldn't even be there, but she had to make the effort...because her mom had asked this favor of her. Because she realized she needed to start making an effort to get on with her life. Taking an interest in herself and caring about what she wore was a first step.

Much as she'd enjoyed seeing Casey, her overnight trip hadn't helped her spirits. It had been all talk about loss and unfulfilled lives. She'd come home actually alarmed over her depressed state of mind.

Two more hours before Rick's shift was over. While he was fueling the truck, he heard Cabrera's voice calling out, "Eighty-six! Eighty-six!" It was code that meant a woman had entered the station, but not just any woman. She had to be a total knockout. After dealing with life-and-death situations 24/7, there was nothing like hearing an "eighty-six" to set the place humming.

He watched in amusement as one by one the guys left their housekeeping duties to get a glimpse of the supposed femme fatale who'd set foot on the premises. In a minute Arney came running to the bay. He might be married with two children, but his blue eyes were all lit up and he wore a knowing grin on his face.

"There's a female here to see *you*." Rick blinked. "The guys have gone nuts. She brought a giant Christmas present all wrapped up in blue foil with a gold ribbon."

His adrenaline surged. Andrea was back from wherever. After hearing from her mother, she'd obviously come here. For some reason she'd been determined his daughter would receive the gingerbread man, even if it meant Santa came to the station in person to deliver it.

"I'd say she looks like a Christmas present herself, if you know what I mean." Rick knew exactly what he meant. Beautiful didn't adequately describe her. The expression "she looked good enough to eat" was more like it.

Arney nudged his shoulder. "You've been holding out on us big-time, boss. I'll finish the fueling while you…take care of business?"

Rick couldn't get mad at the guys for wanting him to meet another woman and start living again. No one had better friends, and they couldn't have tried harder to help him through the dark period of the past two years. They were his other family, the best of the best, but they didn't understand.

So far none of his close friends had lost a spouse. They didn't know what it was like to think of starting all over again with someone else. It took years to get to know another person, to put up with their flaws, to know their demons and still love them.

He hated being single again, coming home with no wife to hold him. He hated his empty bed, hated the loss of sharing. But he groaned at the thought of having to date again to regain that sense of completeness. As far as he was concerned, a widower was in a no-win situation.

Besides it being a new voyage of discovery that he had no interest in, it would have to involve Tessa. He had zero hope of finding another woman who would be right for him and his daughter. Would she be able to mother Tessa the way she needed it? Could he trust her with his daughter while he was out fighting fires?

It still tore him apart remembering the nights Tessa had sobbed herself to sleep in his arms. She didn't do it quite so much now, but there were still those moments.

What if a new relationship didn't work out? Where would that leave Tessa if he had to tell her he wouldn't be seeing the new woman again? How much should he allow his daughter to get involved so she wouldn't suffer a second time? Rick had no answers, no map to help him navigate through such a treacherous sea. Better to remain single now that he was getting used to it. Be the best father he could be to Tessa.

"Thanks, old man." He let Arney do the rest of the refueling while he made his way to the front of the station. En route he was aware of the guys watching him, with the same grin as Arney on their faces.

She was in his line of vision when he rounded the corner. For the second time in two days he was knocked sideways, only this was much worse. In a word she looked so adorable in that outfit, she might be one of those hand-painted imported wooden ornaments come to life.

"You wanted to see me?"

He heard a small cry escape her lips when she saw him. The way her chest moved beneath that fetching jacket, he had an idea she felt breathless, too. "I didn't know if you would be here. Mother told me you'd come by to purchase those gifts for your daughter. I'm so

sorry she couldn't find them. I'd taken them upstairs
to my apartment."

"You live above the shop?" Good grief. He swallowed hard. If that fire had spread and she'd been in
there asleep…

"Yes."

"Alone?"

She nodded, answering one question for him. "I had
the loft renovated after…after my last trip to Germany."
Why the hesitation?

"I'm glad I found you here," she continued. "I should
have realized right away you wanted to get them without her knowing about it. Since I made a promise to
her, please accept this as a gift from Santa. I wrote 'To
Tessa from Santa' on the box."

He reached into the pocket of his uniform for his
wallet. "Let me pay you."

"No, don't! My payment was watching your little
girl have one of those magical moments every child
should experience. To take your money would ruin that
memory for me."

Her features had hardened slightly, letting him know
she meant every word.

Rick put the wallet back and moved the box behind the desk. "I'm assuming you thought I was out
of work?"

"With this economy, it crossed my mind. Forgive
me. I shouldn't have jumped to conclusions. I'm afraid
I was putting myself in your daughter's place. I could
see how much she wanted it. I was a little girl once and
still know how it feels to want something more than

anything." Yup. That described his Tessa. "But then Mother told me about the fire and that you and your crew had come to the shop."

"You weren't so far off the track. A firefighter's pay leaves a lot to be desired."

"Maybe so, but if it helps, just know our world couldn't get along without you. My mother sends her warmest regards."

His black brows rose. "It was her idea that you come here?"

After a slight hesitation she said, "I was glad she suggested it. We wanted to be able to pay you back for containing that fire."

Her answer deflated him despite the fact that he had no intention of getting to know her better. "I understand you went out of town."

"Yes."

"With a friend?"

"No. To see one."

That still didn't answer his question and she wasn't about to give him one. *In other words, mind your own business, Jenner.*

He'd been wrong in his assessment of her show of interest. It was evident she had no intention of getting to know him better and was simply playing Santa's helper in a way that left him humbled by her generosity. Wasn't that what he wanted? No involvement? So how come he felt more irritated than ever?

As fate would have it, he heard the gong sound. "Ladder 1. Respond to Cheshire Hotel kitchen fire on Lemon and Weybosset."

Lemon again? Her eyes widened to hear the address, too. "That fire's not far from the art-gallery fire!"

"You're right." The arsonist was on the loose again, creating mayhem, which was likely part of his intention. Another part was the euphoria a firebug felt to watch something burn that he'd set. It was a definite sickness. Rick longed to catch him and put him away.

"Duty calls. Believe me when I say Tessa and I thank you for the gifts," he called over his broad shoulder.

CHAPTER THREE

RICK WHEELED AWAY, leaving Andrea too fast for any conversation to continue, but she'd felt his sincerity and was glad of it. The man was off to save buildings and lives without a thought for himself. She admired him terribly for putting himself in harm's way.

She heard the siren and watched the fire truck pull out onto the street. His daughter could have no idea how lucky she was that her daddy was still alive to be in her life. Every time he left for a fire, there was the possibility he wouldn't come back. She knew what that was like.

Now that her mission was accomplished, there was nothing more to do but go back to work. Taking a deep breath, she left the station feeling oddly let down and walked to the parking area around the side where she'd left her car.

On the way back she passed the intersection of the hotel fire. The police had cordoned off the area. She saw three fire trucks where the men were doing their jobs with calm, methodical precision. So far she couldn't see any flames. With all their gear and helmets, it was too difficult to distinguish faces, but one of the taller firefighters could have been Captain Jenner. Much as she wanted to pull to the side and watch, she didn't dare. Maybe he'd thought she was coming on to him, that that was the reason she'd gone to the station, using his daughter as the excuse. He was so attractive she could believe other women might have tried that tactic.

But for her to show up while he was fighting a fire now would convince him she had an agenda, and he'd be justified in thinking it. Impatient with herself, she drove on and parked around the back of the shop just three blocks away.

She used the remote to go inside and found her mom was out on the floor with a young couple. They were trying to decide on the right nutcracker for his father, but were having problems. From her mother's expression, it looked as if they'd been in here a long time and she could use some help. Andrea picked up one of her favorites on the shelf and took it over to them.

"This is King Richard. If I were a man, this one would appeal to me. He has such a proud countenance and bearing."

Their response was all she could hope for and her mother rang up the sale. After they left the shop she hugged Andrea. "Oh, I'm so glad you walked in when you did."

"After taking over since yesterday, you're tired, Mom. I want you to go home now, and I'll join you after I close up."

"I won't say no to that. Are you in the mood for an omelet and salad?"

"A light dinner sounds perfect."

She eyed her curiously. "Were you able to deliver your gift?"

"Yes. The captain thanked me and wanted to pay for it, but I wouldn't let him. No sooner did he take the box than he was off to another fire. And now it's time for you to leave before you drop."

"I'm going. You look lovely, by the way. I haven't seen you in that suit for a long time."

"I think of it as my Christmas suit."

They hugged again. "I'll be waiting for you."

After she left, Andrea spent the next half hour unpacking more merchandise. Once she was through setting things out on the floor, she stood at the counter. While she waited for another customer, she read the emails from Gunter's family.

Andrea loved her mother-in-law's newsy epistles. Apparently their oldest daughter, Lisa, was expecting her third baby at the end of May.

Emily was expecting, too.

The whole world seemed to be expecting....

Though this would be as good a time as any to reply, her mind was on the hotel fire. Putting off a response until later, she turned on the radio behind the counter. The talk show station she often listened to gave local updates every twenty minutes. They were coming up on the seven-forty news. Maybe there'd be some information.

But just as it came on, she had another customer and almost fainted when she saw who it was. Captain Jenner had changed out of his uniform. Beneath his bomber jacket he wore a dark blue turtleneck and jeans. He looked amazing in and out of uniform.

In the background they could both hear the news about the three-alarm fire. She hadn't been able to get him off her mind after leaving the fire station. He and his colleagues were incredibly brave. Andrea couldn't imagine facing an inferno the way he did every time their station got the call.

"You'd never know you'd been fighting that fire they were reporting on the news."

His half smile had pretty devastating appeal. "It was put out too fast to turn into a disaster, and now I'm off duty. I'm glad to say I'll live to see another day."

She hurriedly turned off the radio. "Your family must breathe a sigh of relief every time you come home from work." How did they stand it?

"According to statistics, firefighting is only the thirteenth most dangerous job in the world."

Andrea couldn't prevent a small smile of her own, though inside she couldn't understand how he could be so glib. "Only? If you thought that would make me feel better…"

He laughed. A deep male laugh she didn't expect. One she felt warm her insides.

"Seriously, how does your wife handle it?"

"Tina didn't like it," he said without taking a breath. "The great irony is that she died of leukemia a year ago. After all the years we were married while she worried about me, her time clock was running out along with our plans to enlarge our family. We wanted to give Tessa a brother or sister, but it wasn't meant to be."

The end of dreams. Andrea knew all about that. She'd never give birth to a child of her own, and she felt as if her heart had just been squeezed by a giant hand. "I'm so sorry."

He cocked his head, continuing to stare at her. "It's life."

"I know." Her voice had an awful tremor. Time to change the subject. "How can I help you?"

"Tessa and I talked about a special gift to give my housekeeper for Christmas." Naturally he hadn't brought his daughter with him. The last thing he would want would be to get her excited all over again about the gingerbread man. "Mrs. Milne is the widow of an army officer—she came to us before my wife died."

Another widow who'd been married to a man in a dangerous career.

"Tessa loves her, so it has to be the perfect present. That's one of the reasons I've come to your shop."

"That's nice to hear. Do you think she'd like a nut-cracker or a pyramid?"

"A nutcracker. Tessa was enchanted with the ones she saw in the window."

Andrea had been enchanted by his precious child. "We have a wonderful assortment of soldiers. The big ones are right over here. Maybe you'll see one that appeals to you the most."

He followed her over to the table. "They're all fabulous."

"What was her husband like?"

"She's mentioned several times he looked splendid in his uniform."

So had the man standing next to her when she'd gone to the station.

"Splendid… Hmm…" Andrea's keen eye landed on her favorite soldier, who stood fifteen inches high. She picked him up. "Meet the major general. He served in the French Napoleonic cavalry from 1804 to 1815, the most powerful branch of the *grande armée*. Fourteen hundred officers like this one performed with great gallantry."

Their hands brushed as she handed it to him. The contact sent a warm sensation through her body. His eyes held hers for a moment before he examined the nutcracker.

"I—I love this one." Her voice faltered in reaction to his nearness. "This white uniform makes him stand out. It's an exact replica of the uniforms they wore, down to the black hat and green-and-gold trim on the cuffs and bottom of the jacket."

"It's exactly what Tessa would want to give her." His husky tone set her pulse racing. "I'll take it."

"Good. I'll find the box for it in the back and wrap it for you. Be sure to keep the box. These signed nut-crackers become a collector's item and are more valu-able if you have the same box they came in."

"I didn't realize that."

She couldn't breathe until she was away from him. Good grief. She'd always heard about widow's hor-mones, but had never given it any thought until now. If a doctor were to examine her, he'd declare she had palsy.

After finding the box in question, she returned to

the counter with it. "If you'll notice, there's a piece of parchment inside that tells you about the major."

"She'll love it."

Andrea's hands were unsteady as she wrapped the gift in green foil with a red ribbon. He gave her his credit card. She put the receipt in the sack before handing him everything.

"Mom and I appreciate your business." She flashed him a smile. "Merry Christmas. Since I'm closing up, I'll walk you to the door."

Andrea knew she was being obvious, but she wanted him to leave and never come back. It was the exact opposite of her experience with him the first time he'd come into the shop. She couldn't afford to make more of a fool of herself than she already had. He could have no idea that seeing him again had been very hard on her.

Oddly enough, she sensed he wasn't ready to go yet. If he knew she was a widow, he wouldn't be able to leave fast enough, but he hadn't asked.

A tiny nerve pulsed at the side of his hard mouth before he opened the door. "Thank you again for your generosity to my daughter. Merry Christmas." He hesitated a moment, then left.

The second his hard-muscled frame disappeared, she locked up and hurried to her bedroom to pack for her overnight with her mother. Once back downstairs, she turned off the lights, set the electronic locks and slipped out to her car.

On purpose she drove past the hotel where he'd fought the blaze earlier. Like pressing on a sore tooth that increased the pain, she needed to remember what he did for a living. There was no point in getting interested in him. After losing Gunter, she didn't want to go through another horrific loss again.

If he could be killed in a freak car accident, what chance did Rick Jenner have of surviving his world much longer? He willingly put himself in danger every time he climbed onto that truck.

To her chagrin Andrea was strongly attracted to him. His sensual appeal reached down to the deepest part of her, bringing her alive again after more than a year. She was so vulnerable right now, it was frightening. If he came near her again, intuition told her a man like him could become an addiction.

But what could be worse than getting into a relationship with a firefighter? She'd wait for him to come back to her after his shift was over, fearing that if he was late, she'd learn he'd died.

The fact that she'd turned on the radio to find out about the fire proved how anxious she was about his welfare already. He'd admitted his wife hadn't liked it. What wife could, unless she were a police officer or a firefighter herself?

Memories of the accident assailed her. *We're sorry, Mrs. Fleming. Your husband didn't make it.*

Andrea was sorry she'd met Captain Jenner, and prayed she'd never see him again. By the time she reached the house, she was convulsed in tears that made no sense. For months now she'd been trying to build a new life. Now suddenly *he'd* come along with that darling daughter of his, reminding her of what she'd lost and what she could never have. It was his fault she was falling apart.

Rick had promised to watch the Christmas special with Tessa as soon as he got home. Wishing his mind wasn't still on Andrea, he entered his house and added his gift for Sharon to the growing pile of presents beneath the tree.

Tina's parents had brought their gifts over early. Too many gifts. His own parents' presents would come later, in moderation. Tessa looked at the wrapped presents every day while she waited impatiently for Santa to come. Rick had hidden any gifts he'd bought for her in the basement along with the big present. They'd come out of hiding on Christmas morning.

He would have to work the afternoon shift that day, but the following day he had off to spend the day with Tina's parents, who lived in Providence, and then they would all be getting together. His parents and one of his married brothers who lived in nearby Cranston would drop by and then spend New Year's with him and Tessa at the house.

"Rick? Is that you?"

Sharon always said that. She had radar for ears, which was a good thing to keep them all safe. Rick thought of her as the rock who stabilized his world and Tessa's. There was no finer woman anywhere. What would he have done without her?

"I'm home. Where's the cutest little girl in the entire world?"

"I'm here, Daddy." She came running into the living

room in her princess pajamas and dived into his arms, smelling sweet from her bath. He kissed her, loving this child who made his life worth living. "I've been waiting for you. Come in the family room. We're watching *Charlie Brown's Christmas*. Sharon made us popcorn."

"I can't wait!" He carried her through and sat down on the couch in front of the TV. Rick kept her on his lap while they munched and laughed. There was something touching about Charlie Brown, who'd picked out the only real tree for their Christmas play. But the dog's crazy antics as he danced on the piano brought down the house for his daughter.

"He's so funny. I wish I had a Snoopy shirt like that lady at the shop."

Rick remembered the way she'd looked in it. Tonight he'd gone back to get Sharon's gift. And to take another look at Andrea. If he hadn't given in to temptation, he might have been all right.

Who are you kidding, Jenner?

The whole time he was telling himself to stay away, he found himself entering her shop so he could feast his eyes on her in that stunning outfit she'd worn to the station. She'd produced such a sensation with the guys, he was afraid he'd never hear the end of it.

He moaned inwardly as memories of Tina passed through his mind to conflict him. But not enough to stop him from wanting to see her.

The inevitable guilt had passed. If he had to see the psychiatrist again, it would be for some other problem, because Rick had gone back to the shop when it hadn't been necessary. He'd needed to see her again and had used any excuse to drop by.

"Before I forget, Deanna called here today and has invited you to a Christmas party on Saturday night after you get off work."

"Benton mentioned it to me at the fire scene. It will all depend on my shift ending on time." He really didn't want to go. "Right now it's time for this young lady to get to bed. Let's go get your teeth brushed, then I'll read you a Mrs. Piggle Wiggle story."

Between Tina and Rick, they must have read the little stories to her a hundred times. Tina's mother had given the books to Tessa. He knew it made Tessa feel closer to her mother.

"Good night, Sharon."

"Good night, cutie."

"Thanks for everything," Rick murmured. "I couldn't do this without you."

"Sure you could." But she said it with misty eyes.

"Mom?" Andrea had just finished putting some more inventory out on the floor. "What are you doing here this morning?"

"I thought I'd get to work on the bills. Come in the back and have a bagel when you get a minute."

"I'm through now. You're a lifesaver!" The weather had turned freezing and gloomy. She was glad for the company. To her shock she'd been brooding over the firefighter who refused to leave her thoughts day or night.

Furious with herself for being this vulnerable, Andrea sat down with her mother, who'd made them coffee, too. "I'm afraid this cold front is keeping the customers away till later in the day."

"It felt like Siberia on the way over here."

She eyed her mom. "I can tell something's on your mind. What is it?"

"Your father called me late last night."

"Don't tell me Monica has left him again."

Her mother nodded.

"Didn't she do this last Christmas?"

They both chuckled. "Yes." Thank goodness her mom could laugh about it. She'd fallen out of love years ago. For a long time Andrea had prayed her mother would meet someone wonderful and worthy of her. He would have to be terrific.

"I hope you got off the phone fast."

"I did. He's driving in to Providence and wants to see you."

"Thank you for warning me, but what do you bet he doesn't?" Following her remark, they both heard the Christmas chimes.

"Maybe that's your father now."

"I don't think so. He'd call first." She got up from the desk. "I can't believe anyone ventured out in this." As she walked into the front of the store, Tessa Jenner came in accompanied by an older woman.

Andrea was delighted to see her. "Hello, Tessa."

"Hello." Her cheeks were rosy from the cold.

"What can I do for you on this wintry morning?"

A pair of green eyes looked up at her, reminding Andrea of Tessa's father. "We came to buy Daddy a Christmas present before I have to go to school. It's a secret."

"Well, how exciting!"

The older woman smiled. "I'm Mrs. Milne. I take care of Tessa."

"It's nice to meet you. I'm Andrea."

"Tessa begged me to bring her here," the older woman explained.

"I see. What kind of present are you looking for?"

Tessa pointed. "I want to buy that nutcracker over there on the shelf."

"Which one? There are five of them."

"The one with the gold crown and the cape. He has black hair and looks like Daddy."

Tessa had to have noticed him the first time she came into the shop. Andrea reached for the sixteen-inch-tall nutcracker and brought it down. "Do you know something? You're right. He does kind of look like your daddy. This one is King Arthur. A great king. Come over to the counter. I'll get a box and wrap it for you."

"Thanks."

While Mrs. Milne handed her a credit card, those innocent eyes staring out of an angelic face looked up at Andrea. "Where's my gingerbread man? He's not in the window. Can I hold him again?"

Uh-oh. "He's not here anymore, remember?" She smiled at her.

But Tessa's lower lip started to quiver. She was about to cry. "Where is he?"

It appeared Tessa hadn't understood what Andrea meant.

Was this the real reason the little girl had asked the housekeeper to bring her to the shop? Her heart had been set on him. Andrea had to think fast as she handed the woman her package and credit card. "One of Santa's elves came for it." That was as much as she dared tell her.

She expected a smile, but Tessa's face screwed up in pain. "No, he didn't." Her response took Andrea back. "My daddy didn't mail my letter to Santa yet. It's still home. My gingerbread man is gone! You promised Santa would bring it to me for Christmas!" She broke down in heart-wrenching tears and hugged Mrs. Milne's legs. Andrea felt as if she'd been stabbed in the heart.

"I'm sorry." Andrea mouthed the words to the other woman, feeling helpless to do anything.

The housekeeper nodded in understanding. "We'd better go." She led a desolate Tessa out the door.

After they left the shop, Andrea looked at her mother in anguish. "I didn't know what to say to her. Mr. Jenner is giving it to her for Christmas. I already made one mistake with him and didn't want to make another for fear I'd give away his surprise."

"Don't worry about it. She'll get over it when she finds it on Christmas morning. I must say she's about the cutest little girl I ever saw in my life. Except for you," she added. "No wonder you wanted her to have that gingerbread man. It was meant for a child like that."

"I agree, but she was really devastated."

"When you were her age, you had a few meltdowns, too."

"I probably did, but this seemed different. She believes I lied to her."

"Honey, you know children."

"Actually I don't, Mom. I won't ever know them, since I can't have one of my own. After this incident it's probably just as well, since it appears I'm not so great in that department."

"Andrea—"

"It's true."

Her hope for a family wasn't meant to be. She wasn't destined to be a wife and mother, and she needed to get over her self-pity. Thankfully more customers entered the store, keeping her too distracted to wallow in her deepest emotional wants for the time being.

After lunch Andrea was showing her newest customer a music box when the chimes sounded. As she glanced up and saw Tessa's striking father, she clung to the edge of the display table for support. He wore a forest-green crewneck sweater beneath his black bomber jacket. The lines bracketing his hard mouth led her to believe he was upset. It enlarged the pit in her stomach left from his distraught daughter's visit earlier in the day.

He wandered around the shop inspecting the merchandise until she was alone once more, then approached her. "I heard what happened here this morning," he said without preamble. "Sharon admitted she'd brought Tessa to the shop to get me a gift—she'd had no idea what was going to happen."

Andrea took a quick breath. "Is Tessa all right now?"

"She's fine. I had a talk with her and explained Santa already knew what she wanted without a letter."

"Did that satisfy her?"

"Enough for her to go to school this afternoon. I'm sorry she made things uncomfortable for you."

"*She* was the one who was upset. I didn't want her to think I'd lied to her."

"I appreciate you keeping my secret. Sadly, Tessa has gotten her way too often when she wants something. It's a habit I'm trying to curtail."

Andrea shook her head. "I didn't help when I took matters into my own hands the other day to grant her wish. Forgive me. It'll teach me not to do anything like that again."

His dark brows rose. "You couldn't have known the struggle I've been having, and it *is* Christmas after all, as you reminded me that first day." His comment relieved her. "Right after Tina died, I'm afraid I indulged her too much. So did both sides of the family, but my wife's in particular."

"Naturally everyone is still grieving."

"True, but I finally recognized that giving in to her at every turn wouldn't make the pain go away and was setting a negative precedent for the future."

"You sound like a very responsible parent doing the job of two on your own."

"I'm trying, but I learned quickly that I can't be the mom." *No. That job was given out to the very luckiest of women.* "My housekeeper helps with that."

Andrea smiled. "While I floundered, she handled Tessa very well at the shop."

"Sharon said she was impressed you thought of the elf idea."

"It was a stretch."

Stillness enveloped them both while he studied her intently. "I don't see a ring on your finger, so I presume you're single."

"Yes." She fought not to show emotion. "My husband was killed in a car accident fourteen months ago. Like you and your wife, we thought we had a whole lifetime together."

More silence, then, "That's tragic." The compassion in his voice got to her.

"Yes," she said, followed by the first thing that came into her mind. "If you've come by to pay me for those gifts, your effort has been in vain."

"I already got that message at the station," he said in a grating voice. "One of my reasons for being here is to thank you properly. You've convinced me there really is a Santa Claus."

"If I could do that to a man of your age, then I'm convinced miracles really do happen."

His dark brows quirked. "A man of *my* age?"

"You're older than ten, right?" He chuckled. "What's the other reason you came in?"

He shifted his weight. "My closest friends have invited me to a Christmas get-together tomorrow night. If you're not busy after work, would you like to come with me?"

His invitation excited and dismayed her at the same time. "I'm afraid I can't, but thank you."

"You already have plans with the person who took you out of town?"

Her mother must have told him. "That's not it. I went to visit one of my best girlfriends at Barrow's Lake.

She's been having a bad time lately. We're planning a Christmas Eve party for our other friend who's on her second honeymoon right now. When she gets back, they're going to renew their wedding vows. I was hoping that in making plans, it would cheer up my friend."

"Did it help?"

"I don't think so." And all the trip had done for Andrea was make her realize she was in a depression and needed to climb out of it.

"I used to water-ski there from time to time when I was in my teens. As I recall, there was an inn."

"Yes. The Gingerbread Inn. My family went there every summer for years. Casey is staying there right now. It's where we're planning the party."

"I see. You made a quick trip."

He was too observant for words. "Yes. I didn't want to leave my mother alone too long."

"She's charming."

"I'll tell her." Andrea wished he would leave.

"Is there someone else in your life, then? If so, just tell me."

His persistence surprised her. "No. I mean, there isn't anyone else."

"But you're still turning me down."

"Yes," she answered in a quiet voice.

"Is it because it's too soon for you?"

"Yes." Another monosyllable. She grabbed at the excuse, which wasn't far from the truth.

"I'm a grown man, as you reminded me earlier, so I'm going to be blunt. If I were to call you up in say a month and ask you out, do you think you would go?"

She sustained his gaze. "I'm afraid not." Andrea could be blunt, too. She had to be to protect her heart from this man whose chosen career could be cut short in a fire. She couldn't handle that kind of anguish a second time. She wouldn't.

"I have to admit it's refreshing to meet a woman who speaks her mind, even if I don't like the answer. Maybe we'll see each other again, Mrs...."

"Fleming."

If she wasn't mistaken, she saw a hint of satisfaction light up his eyes. "Even if you didn't want to know, my friends call me Rick."

After he left the shop, Andrea was so out of sorts she couldn't calm down. Once she'd closed up, she made a sandwich and watched TV to get her mind off him, but it didn't work.

After a restless night in bed she was a wreck. But by morning she refused to feel any more guilt over the way she'd let Rick Jenner know she didn't intend to go out with him in the future. His dangerous line of work loomed too negatively on the horizon for her to consider getting to know him better.

Andrea was thankful for a busy day that kept her and her mom going nonstop. But when it got to be seven o'clock, she marched her mother to the back door. "You'll be late for your party at the church if you don't leave now. I'm sure Rex Medors will be there if he's back from California." Andrea so wanted her mother to find someone to share her life.

"I hope so. Now, promise me you'll come to the

house in the morning. We'll fix a big breakfast and talk."

"As long as it's not about Captain Jenner." Andrea had confided the situation to her mother, who admitted she understood Andrea's fears. Her mom had agreed that firefighting was a terribly dangerous profession, so enough said about him. "Have a good time with your group."

By ten to eight there weren't any more customers. Andrea decided to close the shop for the night, and she dimmed the lights. But before she set the electronic locks, a tall, dark figure swept through the front door. *Rick!*

Beneath his bomber jacket he was dressed in a silky black shirt and gray trousers. Her mouth went dry just watching those long powerful legs stride toward her. His chiseled male features stood out in the soft glow of the Christmas lights. He was an incredible-looking man whose male scent, combined with the soap he used in the shower, assailed her.

His veiled eyes traveled over her. "Good evening. It looks like I got here just in time. As you can see, I decided not to wait a month to see you again."

Her breath caught. "I—I wish you hadn't come."

"So do I." His deep voice resonated inside her. "I didn't like being rejected twice yesterday, so I have to ask you a question. Have you been out with another man since your husband died?"

"No. I guess it's obvious."

"I haven't been with another woman since Tina's passing either."

She wished he hadn't told her that. His admission made everything way too personal.

"To be honest, Mrs. Fleming, I don't like this attraction any more than you do. Maybe if you come to the party with me, we'll both get this out of our system and it won't seem so important."

Maybe for him... But Andrea knew herself too well. This man already did stand out in her mind. She averted her eyes, unable to think clearly with him so darkly attractive and disturbing.

"I already took Tessa over there to be with Julie, because my housekeeper needed to visit her brother tonight. Under the circumstances I don't expect to make it a late night."

"Even so, I'm not ready to go anywhere with you."

"I'll wait while you change."

"No— I meant—"

"I know what you meant. What will an hour out of your life hurt?"

More than he could possibly know. She should refuse him, but at the last moment she caved like a fool. "Will there be other children there besides your daughter and her friend?"

"Just Matt, Julie's younger brother. He's four. Why do you ask?"

"Because it's Christmastime and I feel like I should take something for the family, to be polite."

"They don't expect anything."

"Maybe not, but I couldn't go empty-handed. Give me a few minutes to pick something out." Normally when she was invited to a party, she took the hostess a gift, but in this case she'd give the children a present.

Aware of his haunting presence, she walked over to the rack on the side wall and sorted through the dirndls that would fit a six-year-old. They were all darling. Andrea picked two and then reached for a child's dark green Tyrol hat.

"You're being too generous," he commented as she wrapped each gift in different colored foil paper and ribbon.

She flashed him a quick smile. "Christmas is for children. I can't resist."

Charged with adrenaline, she hurried upstairs. After a quick shower she put on lipstick and ran a brush through her hair. She left it loose without a part. Her choice of outfit was easy. He'd already seen her in her Christmas suit and would realize she hadn't gone to any extra trouble for him. Her hair swished against the collar of her camel hair coat when she put it on.

After grabbing her purse, she went back downstairs for the gifts and set the locks. Rick cupped her elbow during the short walk to his red Toyota parked down the street.

"Busy day?"

"Yes. And you? How many fires did you have to put out today?"

"Only four."

Her body shuddered of its own volition. "Have they proved arson on the art-gallery fire?"

"Yes, but catching the culprit is something else again.

The last notorious one in Providence set over 150 fires before he was caught."

"That's horrifying!"

"Agreed, but let's not talk about work tonight."

No. Let's not. What he did for a living kept her awake at night.

He made desultory conversation with her about the weather as they drove to Duncan Circle, an area not that far from downtown. The five houses on the circle were lit up for Christmas. One of the yards had a full manger display. Half a dozen cars had parked near number 42. He pulled behind another car and parked.

Rick escorted her inside the foyer and helped her off with her coat before removing his. People had congregated in the living room, which had been beautifully decorated for the holidays.

While Rick introduced her to Deanna and Benton Ames, two excited little girls came running up to him with a younger boy trailing them.

"Daddy!" Tessa hugged him.

"Hi, sweetheart."

"Come in the family room. We're watching the Grinch."

"I will in a minute. Tessa? You remember Andrea. I invited her to the party. Andrea? These are Deanna and Benton's children, Julie and Matt."

"Hello." Andrea smiled at them.

"Hi," the two children said, but Tessa gave her only a brief, cool glance.

It crushed Andrea, who was instantly aware Rick's daughter wasn't happy to see her. Hopefully she could get her to warm up. "It's so nice to meet your friends, Tessa. Are you having a wonderful time?"

The others nodded, but Tessa only stared at her. On impulse Andrea decided to give the presents out now. "I brought each of you an early gift for Christmas."

Once she'd handed them over, Julie's eyes shone like stars. "Do we have to wait till Christmas to open them?"

Andrea smiled. "No. You can do it now."

"Is it okay?" Julie looked to her parents for permission.

Benton winked. "Go ahead. I'm curious to see myself."

His children tore off the wrappings, but it took some urging from Rick before his daughter undid her gift. Julie squealed in delight as she held up her dress. Matt had already put the hat on his head.

Deanna picked up the wrapping paper. "I believe you've made our children's Christmas, Andrea. Thank you for being so thoughtful and generous."

Rick nodded. "I've been telling her she needs to be careful or she's going to give away all her shop's profits."

"Where children are concerned, it's worth it."

"Agreed," Deanna murmured. "What do you all say to Andrea?"

"Thank you, Andrea." This from Matt.

"I love my dress," Julie said.

There was nothing more than a mumble from Tessa, who held the dirndl in her hand.

"Why don't you girls go in the bedroom and put on your new dresses for us to see."

"Come on, Tessa." Julie started running and Rick's daughter followed her down the hall. Matt trailed after them.

A frown marred Rick's handsome features. "I'm sorry about that, Andrea. I don't know what's gotten into my daughter."

Andrea could tell her appearance had been a huge shock to Tessa. To see her daddy with another woman at a party like this changed her happy child's world. That was what had caused her to dart away unable to appreciate the gift. But what she said aloud was, "I think she's still upset about the gingerbread man missing from the shop."

He rubbed the back of his neck. "I can't believe she behaved so badly."

"It's all right. Please don't worry about it."

Deanna gave them an understanding glance. "She'll get over what's wrong before long. In the meantime I have to tell you that your red suit is incredible. Where on earth did you get it?"

"In Germany."

"I thought it had to be an import. I wish they made clothes like that here. Except you have to look perfect in it the way you do."

"Thank you, Deanna."

"I couldn't agree more." Benton grinned.

"You're making her blush," Rick teased. He was wrong. Rick was the reason she was blushing, because he hadn't taken his eyes off her. "Come on, Andrea. I'll introduce you to the others."

From what she could tell, all of them were colleagues

associated with the work Rick and Benton did. They talked shop, laughing and joking at the same time. One of them was a female firefighter named Susie Anderson. The attractive redheaded woman couldn't take her eyes off Rick.

Andrea understood. In her life she'd met her share of good-looking men, but few came close to Rick with his dark, almost brooding looks. Gunter's blond, blue-eyed coloring had given her husband a different kind of appeal.

While Rick was discussing the recent rash of fires in the area with Benton and the others, Andrea turned to Susie, who seemed very friendly. "How long have you been a firefighter?"

"Eight years."

Andrea couldn't imagine it. "I guess everyone asks you how you got into it."

The other woman smiled. "I come from a family of firefighters starting with my grandfather, then my father and all my brothers. I was the youngest of five children and the only girl. It's the only world I ever knew and I became one as soon as I could qualify, to prove to my brothers I could do it, too."

Laughter escaped Andrea's lips. "You're a real heroine to me."

"In my family I had to fight for my place, and I guess it rubbed off."

"I know I'd be terrified to enter a burning building. I honestly don't know how you find the courage to do it."

"You get used to it. I'd go crazy if I had to sit at a desk all day."

"I wouldn't like that either."

"Of course, I'd give it up if the right man came along and we had children, but until that day comes…"

Sometimes the children don't come. But Andrea didn't dare tell Susie that.

"I'm sorry to hear about your husband, Andrea. I can't imagine anything worse than losing a spouse."

Her throat tightened. "It was an awful period in my life, but it's behind me now and life has to go on."

"That's so true. My grandfather died in a fire, but my grandmother was amazing about it. She's my idol."

Andrea shuddered. She couldn't handle the conversation any longer. As if Rick had picked up on her thoughts, he walked over and supplied her with some more eggnog and hors d'oeuvres. Soon the children came into the living room once more.

A subdued Tessa walked over to her daddy looking absolutely precious in her outfit. "Aren't you coming to watch the movie?"

"Not yet."

Julie stared up at Andrea. "This is my favorite dress in the whole world!"

"You look adorable in it. So do you, Tessa. Those dresses are called dirndls. Years ago the children in Germany used to wear them all the time."

"Do you have one, too?"

"Yes. I have several. The first present my husband ever gave to me at the shop before we were married was one that looked a lot like yours."

"Is he from Germany?" Julie wanted to know.

"Yes."

"How come he didn't come to the party?"

"He died a year ago."

"Oh. So now he's in heaven." She looked crestfallen. "Do you miss him a lot?"

Andrea's heartbeat sped up. "Yes."

"My grandma died. She's in heaven, too."

Tessa's silence over her own mother's death caused Andrea's eyelids to sting. This conversation had to be terribly painful for Rick, as well.

"Your dress is really pretty. Did it come from Germany?"

"That's right, Julie."

"Are *you* from Germany?"

"No. I live here in Providence."

"She runs the Hansel and Gretel shop." Rick intervened. "They sell nutcrackers and music boxes."

"I want to see it!"

"Ask your parents to take you."

To Andrea's relief, Deanna came over to join them. It seemed as if the more Julie talked, the more Tessa clung to Rick. "You children come with me. I've got *A Charlie Brown Christmas* for you to watch."

"Daddy and I already saw it."

"Then we'll watch Rudolph. We've got a lot of fun Christmas videos."

Rick put a hand on his daughter's shoulder. "Tessa, go with Deanna."

"But—"

"No buts." He spoke firmly. "This is a party and Andrea hasn't finished talking with everyone yet."

Those green eyes glazed over with tears. "Will you come in the other room later? You promised."

"I know I did, and I will in a while."

When they were out of sight Andrea turned to Rick, sick with worry. "I think this would be the perfect time for me to leave. My father's in town and expects to see me tonight." It was the truth, but even if her father didn't make it, Rick wouldn't know that. "Will you explain to Deanna and Benton? If Tessa doesn't see me leave, it will be better. I'm sure as her father you understand what I mean."

His eyelids drooped, veiling his expression. "Of course. I'll get your coat. Deanna will watch Tessa until I get back."

"I hope your friends won't think I'm very rude for leaving."

"No. Deanna could see how Tessa was behaving and will understand better than anyone why we left. Don't you be concerned about it."

"I wouldn't hurt your daughter for anything in the world."

"You think I don't know that?" He sounded disturbed. "Until tonight I had no idea she could behave like that to you of all people. I'm sorry, Andrea."

"Please don't be. The little darling has been used to it being just the two of you. Tonight she felt her bond with you was threatened."

As a first date, it had bombed completely in ways Andrea hadn't foreseen. But it had served as a wake-up call why a relationship with Rick wouldn't work.

She saw him say something to Benton before he returned with two coats. He helped her into hers and she felt his hands tighten a little on her upper arms. It sent curling warmth through her body.

"Don't look now, but there's sprig of mistletoe above the door. All's fair," he said before pulling her close so he could press a warm, firm kiss to her lips. It caught her totally by surprise.

"Rick—" She let out a quiet gasp.

His eyes seemed to smolder in the twinkling lights. "I've been wanting to do that since we got here, and I refuse to apologize."

After he shrugged into his jacket, they left the house and walked to the car without speaking.

While her pulse still raced from that kiss, he drove quickly but expertly to her apartment, slowing down as he entered the alley. He parked outside the back entrance.

Without more words he got out of the car and came around to open her door. "Before I leave you for the night, I'm coming inside with you."

Her heart thudded. "I'm not up to company."

"This isn't in the nature of a social call. Benton has a theory about this arsonist, that this lunatic might be back to do more damage along this street, and I'm inclined to agree with him. I want to come in and check your place out thoroughly."

"You mean upstairs, too?"

"That's the part I need to see. The art-gallery fire was set on the third floor. Is your father here already?"

"Not yet, or his Blazer would be here." She felt panicky to think of him checking out her apartment. It was kind of messy, but her real concern was the fact that she'd thought she'd seen the last of him. Now he was going to invade her private space, putting them on a more intimate footing. "What about Tessa?"

"She'll sleep there tonight. Right now I want to concentrate on your shop. With all its wooden inventory, it would appeal to this pyro. You can be certain he's cased it pretty thoroughly. I know I've alarmed you, but it's better to be on the alert. It won't take me long."

Andrea pressed the remote so they could go inside. "We have the most up-to-date security system installed. The fire department did a safety check here in October."

"That's good to hear, but some arsonists have an inside track to avoid getting caught. Just so you know, the police are patrolling this area 24/7, especially after dark, so you should feel safe."

"Why do people set fires?"

He gave his shoulders an elegant shrug. "What's wrong with anyone who goes berserk in our culture? In their case they start fires to cover up a crime or pay someone back for a wrong. But I've a gut feeling this one loves to light fires for the fun of it. He wants notoriety and is the worst kind. It won't take me long to check out the ground floor, then I'll come up."

Leaving him to his work, she ran up the stairs. The shop had been so busy she hadn't had time to straighten the living room of her apartment. After hanging up her coat, she picked up some odds and ends and hurried into the kitchen to put things into the dishwasher. Once that was done, she raced to the bedroom to make her bed. He'd think she was a sloppy housekeeper.

While she was tucking the quilt beneath her pillow, he walked in. She saw his glance touch on the bed, then the eight-by-ten picture of Gunter on her bedside table. No doubt he had a similar one of his wife in his bedroom.

First he checked out her bathroom, then walked over to the bedroom window. After opening it, he looked out. When he reshut it he turned to her. "I'm glad to see the fire escape leads down from your kitchen window. A would-be intruder couldn't get in this window unless he had James Bond's scaling equipment."

"That's reassuring."

"But as an extra precaution you need dowels for all the windows upstairs and down. It'll make more trouble for him or any intruder and buy you a little time if someone wants in. What do you have for personal protection?"

"I carry pepper mace on my key chain and keep bear spray in the drawer." She indicated the bedside table.

He nodded. "Do you have a gun?"

"No. I'd rather use spray."

Without any more questions, he walked back out to her sitting room. She had no Christmas decorations upstairs. Until now she hadn't even thought about doing her own decorating, because her emotions had been in deep freeze.

But no longer. Her pulse raced just looking at him.

"You have a lovely modern apartment here. In an older building like this, it's a surprise."

"I know. Before my marriage I lived with Mom. Gunter and I were going to buy a house here, but he died too soon for us to decide on one. The loft seemed the perfect choice to remodel so I'd be close to my work."

His hands went to his hips in a purely masculine gesture. "I would have sold my house to help let go of memories if I didn't have Tessa, but any more changes to her life would have been disastrous at the time."

"They already are."

He shot her a probing glance. "What do you mean?"

"She didn't like me the other day, and likes me less after seeing me with you tonight."

Lines bracketed his mouth. "Don't read so much into everything, Andrea."

Andrea didn't want to go down this road, but tonight's experience had left her with no other choice. "Your daughter doesn't want to share you with anyone else."

He took a deep breath. "She has to share me every day when I go to work. Between all the love from her grandmothers, aunts, Sharon—from my colleagues' wives and her kindergarten teacher, she's learning to adapt."

"That's not the same thing, and you know it. When she looked up and realized I was with you, she shut down. She feels a child's jealousy that you would give personal attention to another woman besides her. *I* don't want to be that woman."

She noticed his chest rise and fall from a tumult of emotions. "This phase will pass."

"Sometimes that phase lasts years."

His eyes narrowed. "What else is going on inside you?"

Andrea tossed her head back. "Isn't Tessa's nega-tive reaction enough to let you know this wasn't a good idea? She's so precious and you're her whole world. Your daughter needs more time."

His features hardened. "You didn't answer my ques-tion," he said, ignoring her comments. "I know for a fact you feel something for me, but you're doing your damnedest to pretend otherwise. Why?"

At his question she backed away from him. "I ap-preciate your checking out my apartment, but if you're through here, you ought to go back to the Ameses' house to be with your daughter. It will reassure her she hasn't lost you."

He moved closer. "I'll take your advice under con-sideration, but not before I get the truth from you. They say it makes you free. Do me that favor and I swear I'll never darken your doorstep again."

She wouldn't look at him. "Tonight we got this out of our system and your daughter had to pay the price. More than ever I'm not interested in a relationship."

Rick reached out and grasped her upper arms. "You're lying or you wouldn't have come to the party with me, and I can prove it." Before she could cry out, he lowered his dark head and covered her mouth unerr-ingly with his own. There was a hunger in his kiss that ignited her desire in spite of everything she'd tried to do to stop it. Without being able to help it, her mouth opened to the seductive pressure of his.

He was right. This was what she'd been waiting for. A moan of pure pleasure escaped her throat, one she knew he heard. In the next instant he crushed her against his hard body until there was no space between them. She felt feverish as one exploratory kiss grew into another, then five, ten, twenty until she lost count. He was insatiable. So was she. It was shocking how much she wanted this ecstasy to go on and on.

"I didn't know a woman like you existed. In a matter of days you've managed to turn me inside out. Give me a chance to let me love you, Andrea."

If the buzzer outside the downstairs rear door hadn't sounded, she had no idea how long she would have clung to him, kissing him back again and again as if he were life to her. What really terrified her was that for these moments in his arms, he *was* life to her.

CHAPTER FOUR

Rick hadn't imagined that buzzing sound. With the greatest of reluctance he allowed her to tear her mouth from his without pulling her back. "Your father?" Both of them were out of breath.

"I'm sure it is."

"This late?" It was after ten.

"Yes. He drifts in and out at will."

The buzzer went off again. Her parent sounded impatient. "You'd better answer."

"I know, but I need to freshen up for a minute."

Rick studied her features and glazed eyes. Her lips looked swollen and his five-o'clock shadow had put a rash on her face. All in all she looked slightly ravished for a first kiss, but he felt no shame. On the contrary...

"Would you like me to go down and let him in while you repair the damage?"

She blushed. "If you wouldn't mind."

"It would be my pleasure." With his body throbbing from unassuaged longings, he went back downstairs and undid the lock. He'd met her mother. Now was his chance to meet Andrea's father.

To say her graying parent in his North Face parka

was shocked to see Rick standing there was an understatement. He gave him the once-over with dark blue eyes reminiscent of Andrea's. "I thought one of Andrea's friends was parked outside. Who are you?" he asked, sounding a bit territorial for the father of a grown woman.

"I'm Captain Jenner of Ladder 1 at the downtown fire station. You must be Mr. Bernard. Your daughter will be right down. Come in."

Once he was inside, Rick shut the door. Her father looked around the office. "I can smell smoke."

"That's right. There was a fire in the art gallery two shops up the street the other night, set by an arsonist. I just got off duty and came by to let your daughter know the police will be patrolling this area more heavily until January. But she needs to pay special heed when she's here alone."

"I never liked the idea of her living upstairs, but would she listen to her own father? Andrea's mother always let her be too independent, so what can you expect?"

As Rick grimaced, he heard footsteps on the stairs. "Hi, Dad. Mom said you'd be coming by."

Andrea came down in jeans and a T-shirt. Everything she wore she filled out to perfection, but that was a quick change, he thought. Rick had the strongest suspicion she didn't want her father to know anything about their evening, especially the passion they'd just shared.

She gave her dad a kiss. "You've met Captain Jenner. His crew put out that fire he was talking about. He's been making an inspection of the buildings around here and checked my fire escape to see what kind of access it has to the upstairs. He was just leaving."

Rick glanced at him. "It was nice to meet you, Mr. Bernard."

"I appreciate you keeping my little girl safe. She shouldn't be living here on her own. Did she tell you about the bear spray?"

"Yes."

"It's good stuff. Go for the eyes."

Rick flicked his gaze to Andrea. "Be sure to get those dowels put in the windows. Good night. I'll let myself out."

After having to prematurely relinquish Andrea, whose incredible response had set him on fire, Rick had been forced to pull himself together to let her father in the door. But he'd been reeling from the taste and feel of Andrea, so that the meeting with her parent had barely scratched the surface of his mind.

However, now that he was on his way back to the party, he had time to reflect and couldn't help wondering about the relationship between her and her father. She was such a warm, demonstrative woman, but she'd controlled that emotion around him. Andrea had lived through her parents' divorce and had obviously been affected by the pain.

There was so much Rick didn't know about her, but he planned to find out. One truth was perfectly clear. When they'd heard the buzzer a few minutes ago, she hadn't been ready to let him go. Her desire was every bit as explosive as his. Both of them had experienced a moment of sheer ecstasy, and it was going to grow stronger no matter how much she might want to fight it.

But she was right about his daughter. Tessa had been jealous of his attention to Andrea. He could see that he would have to be extra careful and realized he needed to follow Andrea's advice and take Tessa home. There'd be other nights for sleepovers.

Deep in thought, he drove back to the party. Being a good friend, Deanna didn't ask any probing questions about Andrea's quick departure. He talked to everyone for a while, noticing that Susie had already left.

Rick was glad Susie had seen Andrea involved with him, in order to end any speculation or hope that he might be interested. Before he took Tessa home he sought out Benton, who was in the kitchen on the phone.

After he hung up, Benton motioned Rick over to the counter with a scowl on his face. "There's a certain pattern our fire starter has been following. One of my sources believes he's a colleague working among us. He's too good at what he does. These fires have been done by an insider."

Rick groaned. He thought of the guys assigned to Ladder 1 and couldn't imagine them going berserk. Two of them were here tonight with their wives. The thought of having to be suspicious of any of them tore him up inside. "It wouldn't be the first time one of our own turned bad."

"Nope. Watch your back, Rick. If it's true, then this guy not only likes setting fires, he's got a vendetta. I've got my guys going through every history to find out who might have it in for the department or one person in particular."

Rick let out a low whistle. "I know one firefighter who pretty well hates my guts, but I haven't worked with him for at least a year."

"Who's that?"

"Chase Hayward. When we have more time, I'll tell you about him."

Benton frowned. "That's a place to start. Let me know when you come up with any other names."

"You can count on it. Thanks for the party. Sorry Andrea had to leave so fast. Her father came into town and she had to go home."

"No problem, as long as it didn't spoil your evening."

"Not spoil. Just…complicate things a little." The result had left him breathless and wanting more of the same excitement only she could engender. "Talk to you later."

He gathered up his daughter, who'd fallen asleep on the family-room couch. She wakened enough to smile as he slipped on her parka. After he carried her out to the car and strapped her in the back car seat for the ride home she fell asleep again.

While he put her to bed, his thoughts were on Andrea. His teeth snapped together when he thought of her father showing up when he did. One taste of Andrea hadn't been nearly enough. Rick had only half believed her excuse that she'd needed to leave to get home to see him.

Trying to tamp down his charged body, he turned out the lights and shut Tessa's door. As he walked through the house, it felt like the night before Christmas. The words floated through his mind—"not a creature was stirring, not even a mouse." He couldn't believe it, but the darkness of his life seemed to have lifted and a new sense of purpose had taken over. Like it or not, Andrea Fleming was responsible for this metamorphosis.

When morning came, Tessa ran into his room to hug him. But the first words out of her mouth brought bad weather for the rest of the day. "Daddy? I wish you hadn't brought Andrea to the party."

Startled, he sat up. "Why not?" He knew the answer, but he needed to let her talk this out.

"I don't like her," she said in a tremulous voice.

"Can you tell me why?"

"Julie said she might be my new mommy and I don't want a new one." On that note she buried her face in his chest and sobbed.

Rick rocked her in his arms. What to say that would comfort this child he loved more than life itself? For the past year his heart had cried out that he didn't want another woman in his life either. But he hadn't counted on Andrea....

At this juncture he didn't dare lie to Tessa, who took everything so literally. But at the same time, he wasn't about to stop seeing Andrea. He had no idea where things were headed with her. Possibly nowhere, except that deep inside he didn't believe that.

"Right now Andrea is a friend I've met. She's been very sad."

That brought Tessa's head up. "How come?"

"A year ago she was with her husband in Germany when they were in an accident and he died."

He could hear his daughter's mind ticking over. "And now he's in heaven like Mommy?"

"Exactly."

She wiped her eyes. "I bet she cries a lot."

Rick groaned inwardly. "I'm sure she does."

Tessa touched his cheek, reminding him he needed a shave. "You used to cry."

His throat practically closed up from emotion. "We all had to cry so we'd feel better."

"Do you feel better?" she asked in all earnestness.

"Better than I did."

"Me, too."

"Then let's go eat and then we'll build a snowman in the backyard." From the window he could see snow had fallen during the night. Not a lot, but just enough to blanket everything in white. He had some shoveling to do. "I'll make us Mickey Mouse chocolate chip pancakes."

"Can I put in the chips?"

He smiled, thankful that so far they'd gotten through this tense moment in one piece. "That's your job."

Half an hour later he'd showered and shaved and they were just finishing their pancakes and bacon when he heard his cell phone ring. He checked the caller ID and saw that it was the battalion chief calling. He frowned before clicking on. "Hey, Rob—what's up?"

"Plenty. I know it's your day off, but we need all the extra help we can get. A couple of guys are out with stomach flu, one from your ladder. Just a minute ago there was a big explosion at the downtown furniture mart. We're calling in help from all over the city."

That sprawling monster? "Say no more. I'll be at the station as soon as I can." He hung up with a grimace. "Sweetheart, I hate to do this, but there's an emergency at work. Go tell Sharon I have to leave."

"Dad? Do you want more scrambled eggs?"

"No. I think I'm done, but I could use some more coffee."

Andrea poured another cup for him. He'd slept on the couch and had opened his Christmas present early because he'd be gone hunting over Christmas. She'd listened to him rant about the numskulls at his work.

While he'd turned on the TV and was grazing the channels for the news, Andrea had slipped into the bedroom to phone her mom. To her delight she found out that Rex was taking her to dinner that evening. Then the subject changed to Rick Jenner and the scene with Tessa.

"But I can't talk about that right now, Mom. I'll call you later once Dad's gone."

After she came out of her bedroom, she saw breaking news flash across the TV screen. "…case you just joined us, we're in downtown Providence on the scene of a raging nine-alarm fire that is engulfing the old furniture mart." *Nine?*

Her father whistled. "That's one mean fireball. I'd hate to be the firefighter I met last night."

Andrea was already quaking in her boots over Rick. Today was supposed to be his day off. She'd heard one of the firefighters say they could all stay up late for the party and sleep in. But word of a fire of this magnitude would reach every firefighter in the city. She hadn't known Rick long, but she knew he wouldn't stay in bed once he heard the news. Her stomach muscles tensed.

"The recent rash of fires in the downtown area seems to indicate an arsonist might be involved."

Andrea remembered what Rick had said. *I've a gut feeling this one loves to light fires for the fun of it. He wants notoriety and is the worst kind.*

When her father turned off the television, she wished he hadn't. Now that she'd seen the fire, she couldn't think about anything else. "I'd better head home to make things right with Monica."

Andrea pretended she didn't know anything about their troubled marriage. "What happened?"

"I told her when I married her I didn't want to get involved with her kids."

No. Andrea's father could hardly handle having one child of his own. What a blow it must have been to her mother when she discovered the kind of man she'd married. The difference between him and someone like Rick Jenner, who adored his daughter and was devoted to her, was too astounding to contemplate. She found his parka and helped him put it on.

"It's good to see my little girl." After putting a new can of bear mace on the coffee table as his contribution to her Christmas, he gave her a hug. He'd always had trouble parting with his money unless it was for more ammunition or a new scope for his rifle. She thanked him and hugged him back before going downstairs with him.

"It's a fine day now that it's snowed," he exclaimed after opening the door to the alley. "But I'd rather be up in Alaska."

That was his mantra. "Drive safely."

The second he took off, she raced upstairs to grab her things, then ran down and got into her car. Once out on the street she could see the dark plumes of smoke over the downtown area, making her feel sicker as she listened to the radio report. Without conscious thought she drove to the fire station. If she saw Rick's Toyota there, then she'd know he'd been called in to help fight the blaze.

After turning into the driveway to the station parking lot, she spotted it with several other cars and broke out in perspiration. But maybe he was inside the station. She had to find out, and she went in. To her consternation she discovered there was only a skeleton crew on duty. Captain Jenner had been called to the downtown fire.

It was too late to remember that someone on duty would tell him she'd been by. So much for her avowal that she wasn't interested in any kind of a relationship with him. She wasn't, but she feared the danger of a fire of that magnitude. Her thoughts leaped to Tessa. The idea of her daddy not making it back home was too ghastly to contemplate.

She called her mother again. "Have you seen the news about the fire on TV?"

"Yes. I've been watching, and I thought immediately of Captain Jenner."

"I was fixing Dad's breakfast when he turned on the news."

"Where's your father now?"

"He's gone back home. I'll come over later, but there are some things I need to do first."

"All right, darling."

Andrea headed to the hardware store. When she came out the smoke in the sky wasn't as black as before. Part of her wanted to drive down by the fire, but another part preferred to stay in denial about him fighting the fire, so she headed for the shop.

While she listened to the news she kept busy placing the dowels and cleaning up after her father. By now the fire was 95 percent contained, but there'd been injuries. A number of firefighters had been taken to Providence general hospital. One had died on the way after a wall had collapsed on him, but no names were being given out yet.

Andrea cried out in anguish. It could be Rick, or one of his friends at the party. She couldn't breathe until she knew the truth. Without hesitation she drove to the hospital. The main streets en route had been plowed. Andrea parked underground and followed the signs to Emergency.

When she saw Rick's name on the wall chart, her heart thudded like the striking of an anvil. After inquiring at triage, she was told he was in cubicle eight and she could go back. Behind the blue curtain she found him.

To her everlasting surprise and gratitude, he was sitting on the end of the hospital bed in his uniform, breathing oxygen. As far as she could tell, nothing else was wrong with him. When he saw her walk in, his eyes suddenly gleamed a brighter green. Surrounding him were three of the foulest-smelling, grubby-looking firefighters she'd ever seen.

Arney and Jose she recognized from last night's party. "Hey, Andrea," they said in unison with a decided grin. "You're one sight for sore eyes. How did the boss find you and how come he's so lucky?"

A smile broke out on her face. "I must say you guys looked a little better last night," she teased, ignoring their questions.

"Yeah, well, now you're seeing the real us."

"Whoa—" the other firefighter exclaimed. "I know I've never seen you before." His blue eyes studied her in a way she found too bold. "Someone introduce me."

Jose smiled. "Andrea? As you can see, Chase is dying to make your acquaintance. Andrea runs the Hansel and Gretel shop downtown."

"Is that so? Well, I'm just going to have to drop by, then."

Andrea hoped he wouldn't.

"Chase swung in from another station to assist," Arney explained.

Thankfully the attending physician came in and took Rick's vital signs, preventing her from having to make a comment. Something about the other firefighter's attitude was borderline obnoxious to her.

"Can he drive back to the station with us, Doc?"

"I can't release him for an hour. Just so you know, your captain won't be going to work tomorrow. For the time being it's home and total bed rest. Follow my advice and you shouldn't have any lasting effects."

The guys didn't sound happy about it, but Andrea rejoiced that the doctor had taken charge. For the rest of today and tomorrow he'd be safe!

After the doctor left the cubicle, Rick pulled down his mask, still staring at her. "All right, you guys. Get out of here."

Andrea thought he sounded slightly hoarse but completely like his confident self. She sent up a silent prayer of thanksgiving that Tessa's daddy had been spared to live another day.

"We're going." Arney grinned and punched him on the shoulder. One way or another the guys managed to give a physical manifestation of their affection and relief by a nudge or some other gesture.

Their camaraderie revealed they were a close-knit family of which she wasn't a part. This was Rick's element, a whole other world, and he was happy in it. She could see that. They belonged to a special club, unconsciously making her feel excluded.

Chase filed out last, not paying attention to Rick. He gave her a look that made her uncomfortable. "I'll be getting in touch with you." She wanted to call back, "Please don't."

When they were alone she urged Rick to lie back down, but he ignored her. Maybe she was wrong, but something about the other firefighter seemed to have made him tense. His next question was unrelated. "How did you know I was here?"

She told him the sequence of events, starting with her father sleeping over. Through narrowed lids he appeared to digest everything she said. "I thought you didn't want anything more to do with me."

"I don't, but the nine-alarm fire was on every channel."

"You knew it was my day off."

"True—however, it was such a huge fire I figured you'd be called in. When I drove to the fire station and saw your car in the parking area, then I knew you'd gone on duty."

"You actually drove there to see?" A glint of satisfaction entered his eyes.

"Yes. I was concerned when I found out there were injuries…and a death."

He nodded gravely. "A father of four."

"I heard. It's so tragic." Her voice shook. "Thank heaven it wasn't you. Tessa wouldn't be able to handle it."

"I don't plan to die on her if I can help it." He bit out the words.

"I realize that."

"Now that you're here, would you be willing to wait long enough to drive me to the station for my car when I'm released?"

"I'll drive you home first," she said without hesitation. "Doctor's orders. We'll arrange for your car later. Don't talk anymore, Rick. Give your throat and lungs a rest. If you'll give me your housekeeper's phone number, I'll let her know you'll be home in another hour."

Andrea knew she shouldn't be overjoyed that he wanted her help to get home. But if he hadn't asked her, she would have worried that much more about him.

* * *

When the nurse pushed Rick outside the hospital in the wheelchair, Andrea was waiting right there in her car. The woman was tying him up in knots. He climbed inside and fastened the seat belt before they took off. If it had taken him breathing too much smoke to see her again, he wasn't complaining.

The doctor had said his heart rate was a little high. What the medic didn't know was that moments before, Andrea had walked into the cubicle. After figuring he'd never see her again unless he made it happen, he knew the shock of realizing she'd come to see him on her own had played havoc with his vital organ.

A lot could happen in twenty-four hours. He planned to use every one of them wisely.

"Are you feeling terrible?" Andrea sounded anxious.

"I'm fine."

"No, you're not."

He looked over at her lovely profile. "I'm sorry that the death of one of my colleagues alarmed you enough to bring you to the hospital. I'm sure it was a reminder of what happened to your husband. I wish you could have been spared. Tell me. What did you do with your day after your father left?"

"Besides worry about you, I bought some dowels and put them in the windows."

"I'm glad you took my advice."

"If they'll act as a deterrent, then I'm indebted to you." He noticed her hands grip the wheel a little tighter. "Was the furniture mart a set fire?"

"Benton thinks so, but it'll take a day to find the proof."

She flashed him a glance. "What's your opinion?"

"I think this particular pyro is having a field day."

"Tell me about your friend who died. How old are his children?"

"He has two teenagers and two in their twenties." Rick saw telltale tears trickle from her eyes. "Becoming a firefighter is a lot like joining the military. Everyone knows there's going to be risk."

"I'm sure they do."

He wanted to get off that subject to talk about something more important. "Is your father going to be in town for the week?"

"No. When he comes two or three times a year, he's always just passing through."

"It's obvious you're very close to your mother."

"As opposed to my father, who was never a family man, but I'm sure you already figured that out even before you met him."

"It's his great loss for not spending time with you. He told me he doesn't like you living on your own."

"He said that because the loft is small and I don't have a guest room for him."

"Andrea? Be serious."

"I am. He hates my couch."

Rick shuddered to think what kind of father hers had been. All the lost opportunities.

Andrea pulled into his driveway, where she parked to the side to leave room for another car. He gave her a covert glance. "What are your plans for the rest of the day?"

But he didn't hear her response because he'd already opened the passenger door and Tessa had come running out of the house without boots or a parka. "Daddy—" She sounded ecstatic and flew into his arms.

After giving him a hard hug, she stared at Andrea. While his mind sought an explanation his daughter could handle, Andrea spoke up. "Hi, Tessa. Your daddy needed a ride home because he was so excited to see you. Now *I'm* going home."

His little girl shifted her gaze back to him. "Sharon said you breathed too much smoke, Daddy. I'm going to take care of you because Mommy told me to." She pulled on his hand to get him out of the car.

His daughter's sweetness made his heart quake. "You always take perfect care of me."

"See you," Andrea called to them before backing out of the driveway. Helpless to do anything else at the moment, Rick had to let her go. The last thing he saw was the sheen of her wet blue eyes before she drove off.

Tessa helped him inside the house. "Sharon says you have to take a shower and go straight to bed."

His housekeeper met him in the foyer. "We're glad you're home. I'll bring you dinner when you're ready."

Rick was so drowsy from whatever had been put into his IV, he barely made it to his bedroom. After he collapsed on the bed to get his second wind, he knew nothing more until thirst brought him out of a deep sleep. He reached for his water and drank until he'd emptied the glass.

When he opened his eyes, he discovered it was quarter after nine. That was the time he'd gone to his room last night. It meant he'd slept twelve hours! The last thing he remembered was being ordered to bed.

He rolled off the mattress, aware he was breathing more easily. He didn't feel he needed the inhaler. But once on his feet, he still felt weak. Some breakfast would make all the difference.

After a visit to the bathroom, he left for the kitchen in his sweats and T-shirt, expecting to see Sharon and Tessa, but they weren't there. He checked the note on the fridge under the magnet.

Nancy came over this morning and took Tessa home with her so you could sleep. She'll bring her back this afternoon. I'll be home from the grocery store shortly. Your friends brought your car home from the station, so don't worry about a thing.

He drank a quart of milk and munched on a banana and a couple of peanut butter sandwiches before checking his phone messages. There were half a dozen, but of course nothing from Andrea. She didn't have his cell phone number, but he *had* given her the land line number so she could call Sharon. But when he checked those messages, there still wasn't one from her.

Remembering the tears in her eyes before she'd backed down the drive, he realized she'd heard Tessa and didn't want to say or do anything to upset his daughter more. Though touched by her sensitivity, he didn't want Andrea distancing herself because of it. He'd find a middle ground for them no matter how long it took.

As he walked down the hall, he heard the sounds of the animated elf band he'd set up around the Christmas tree. He frowned. That was odd. He hadn't remembered hearing it on his way to the kitchen.

Clearly mystified, he headed for the living room and collided with a heavenly female form just coming down the hall in jeans and a melon-colored cotton sweater.

Andrea, as he lived and breathed.

A cry escaped her throat. "I thought I heard you in the kitchen."

"I needed food."

She bit her lip. "In case you weren't dressed, I didn't want to surprise you, so I turned on the elf band."

His hands shot out to steady her. Sharon must have let her in this morning. "How long have you been here?"

"Not long."

"What a welcome surprise," he murmured in a gravelly voice. Maybe he was dreaming. All he knew was that he had to taste her mouth again. He'd been hungering for it since the other night.

"No, Rick—" she begged. "This isn't why I came over." But it was too late. He'd already stifled most of the sound. In the next instant he pressed her against the wall in the hall and found himself devouring her, bite by delicious bite. What made everything more miraculous was that she was giving him breathtaking permission.

Between the flowery scent of her hair and the warmth of her luscious body, he felt transported. He forgot the time as his hands roamed over her back and hips. Being with her like this made him feel young and alive again. She clung to him in a way that told him she was experiencing ecstasy, too.

"Why do you say no when you mean yes? You're torturing me."

"It's not on purpose," she whispered against the side of his neck.

"Yes, it is. Do you have any idea how beautiful you are? How exciting?" He kissed her scented throat. "Ever since I saw you through the display window, I fought not to want you, but it happened anyway."

"I know," she admitted, sounding breathless. "I never thought I could feel this way again and I didn't want to either. I still don't." She eventually tore herself from his arms. "This couldn't be good for you. I came to find out if you were all right. How are you feeling?"

Andrea could ask him a question like that after what they'd been doing in the hallway? "Would that I could wake up every morning feeling this...marvelous." If he wasn't mistaken, she blushed. "But I need a minute to shower. Promise me you won't leave, or you'll have to put up with a grubby firefighter whose beard must be two inches long."

Her eyes studied his features. "Maybe an inch," she teased.

"By what miracle are you here?"

"I called to see how you were. Sharon said you were still sleeping and Tessa had gone out with her grandmother. When I asked if there was anything I could do, she said I could babysit while she went shopping. Since I promised to stay till she came back, you have my word I won't leave. But after your shower, you need to lie down, Rick. Doctor's orders."

He grinned. "Yes, nurse." Rick pressed a hot kiss to her mouth before disappearing, but knowing she was waiting for him, he decided it was going to be the fastest shower and shave in history.

CHAPTER FIVE

RICK MIGHT BE recovering from smoke inhalation, but the way he'd kissed her in the hallway just now, she still hadn't recovered from what she considered a more serious problem. Andrea sat down on the couch and had to acknowledge she was crazy about him.

To be alone with him for any length of time could be disastrous if she didn't want to end up in his bed. Hopefully Sharon would return soon. Rick seemed to have this power over her. When she was near him, rational thought ceased and only desire remained. Deep down she'd known from the first he could become an addiction. He already *was* her addiction. The only way to break it was to go cold turkey.

"Andrea?"

She hurried into the hallway. "Yes?"

"I'm waiting for you. It's the last door on the right."

Since she'd told him to lie down, she couldn't very well tell him it wouldn't be a good idea to join him. Her stomach got flutters when she found him clean shaven and stretched out on top of his bed in a different pair of sweats and T-shirt. He was gorgeous no matter his physical condition.

"What took you so long?" he asked in a deep voice that sent delicious chills through her body. "Come and sit by me." He patted the place next to him.

Since he didn't have a chair, Andrea chose to sit near his feet. His half smile turned her heart over. With charm like that he could get her to do whatever he wanted. "Can I bring you something to drink?"

"I'm not hungry or thirsty. What I want is to talk to you. Without Tessa, it's the perfect time to get some matters straight with us."

Andrea took a shuddering breath. "I agree, but doesn't your throat still hurt?"

"No. That long sleep did me a world of good. Finding you here has made my day."

Finding you alive yesterday made mine.

"I have a confession. On my way home from Barrow's Cove, I bought a book for Tessa. I was going to send it to her from me, but everything has changed since then. Since I agree she needs the emotional love that gifts can't give her, I thought maybe you could slip it in with her toys from Santa. It's in my purse in the living room."

He leaned forward with a concerned expression in his eyes. "I'm sorry I came across so heavy-handed with you in the beginning, Andrea."

"But I understand why you did."

"You're an amazingly forgiving, generous person. You need to know I'm no longer going to tiptoe around Tessa where you're concerned. You shouldn't have to either, because I intend to go on seeing you. Yesterday

I told her you're my friend. It gave her a lot to think about."

Andrea stood up in panic. "We can't be friends, let alone anything more. It won't work."

His handsome face darkened with lines. "Why not?"

"You *know* why."

"Because of Tessa?"

"That's a part of it."

He got to his feet. Suddenly the bedroom seemed so small. "What's the other part?"

"I meant what I said before. I don't want to get into another relationship if that's where this is headed. Just a few minutes ago you admitted you fought your initial attraction to me, too. It's because in the end I can't give you what you want any more than you can satisfy my needs. We're better off parting company for good today."

A dark brooding look descended. "How can you be so cold-blooded when just a few minutes ago we were communicating in the most elemental of ways and didn't want to stop?"

She lifted her chin. "That's called chemistry, but it doesn't supply all the other things needed to make up a relationship that will last forever."

"You and I have both learned the brutal lesson that nothing can be counted on to last forever, but a fire's been lit and it's not going to go away any time soon."

"It will if we don't see or talk to each other again," she responded emotionally.

"You think it's that easy to douse the flames licking at us? I fight fires every day. Some become fully involved. That's what has happened to us."

Andrea shook her head. "I don't believe it can't be put out. I met that attractive female firefighter Susie at the party. Deanna told me she's single. During the time I was there, she didn't take her eyes off you. A woman with interests like yours would be a great match for you."

His mouth thinned. "What interests?"

"You both fight fires. It's who you are and what you do."

"If I'd been interested in Susie, I would have taken her to the party." His voice grated.

"Fine. All I'm saying is, there's a whole world of wonderful women out there who, given the chance, would love you and your daughter and want to start a new family with you."

"But you're not one of them."

"I can't be."

His dark expression grew forbidding. "You're keeping something from me, and I mean to find out what it is."

"Yoo-hoo, Rick."

Mrs. Milne couldn't have chosen a better moment to return. "I have to leave now." Andrea started down the hall to the living room. Rick was right behind her.

"If you want me to fix you and Andrea something to eat, just tell me," his housekeeper called from the kitchen.

"Thanks, Sharon, but we're fine right now."

Andrea hurried over to the couch to get her purse.

Just as she pulled out the gift-wrapped book to give to him, Tessa came running into the house straight past Andrea. "Do you feel better now, Daddy?"

"I sure do." He lifted her in the air and kissed her. "Where's your grandmother?"

"She had to go to the dentist."

"Did you have a nice time?"

"Yes, but I wanted to stay home with you. You slept a long time," she said. Then her glance fastened on the Christmas present in Andrea's hand and she looked at her. "Did you bring that to Daddy?"

Finally a connection. Since her talk with Rick, Andrea felt she had permission to do what came next, but her heart was pounding too fast. "No. I brought it for you."

"But it's not Christmas yet."

"I thought you might like it now." She handed it to her.

"What is it?"

Rick lowered her to the floor. "Why don't you open it and find out?"

Tessa quickly tore off the paper. "Look, Daddy— it's the gingerbread man!" she cried. For the first time since the disaster at the shop, Rick's daughter looked up at her with a smile.

"I promise that Santa will bring you your gingerbread man. But while you're waiting for Christmas morning, this will be fun to read. It was one of my favorite stories growing up."

"Mine is Mrs. Piggle Wiggle."

Andrea's heart melted. "I loved those stories, too."

"My favorite's about the boy who wouldn't clean up his room."

"That's a really good one. My mother used to read them to me. I think my favorite was the Slow-Eater-Tiny-Bite-Taker Cure. But the really funny one was about the Radish Cure."

A giggle escaped. "I know. Will you read the gingerbread man to me?"

Andrea's gaze darted to Rick, whose eyes glowed with a warmth she could feel permeate her body. "I'd love to. Come and sit down on the couch by me."

Together they went through every page identifying all the characters while she read the story. Tessa was totally engrossed.

Andrea would always treasure this moment, but now it was time to go while she could leave with a good feeling. She closed the book and put it in Tessa's hands. "That was fun. Thank you for letting me read it to you. Now I have to leave."

"You do?" Andrea heard a slightly wistful tone. *Well, what do you know?* she thought.

"Yes, but I bet your daddy would love to read it to you. He's been waiting for you to come home and needs to get back to bed." Andrea's gaze flew to Rick's. "Get better soon. I'll see myself out."

To her shocked surprise, Tessa followed her to the door. "I love my book."

"I'm glad, darling. Bye." She left the house, closing the door behind her. This was the best way to end things. Cold turkey.

Before long she pulled into her mother's driveway. "Mom?" she called out when she entered the house.

"In the kitchen."

Andrea found her making the fondant for the pecan rolls she gave to her friends at Christmas. "How soon will Rex be over?"

"Not for a couple of hours. I want to hear more about you and Tessa's father."

"I left the party early to get home because of Dad. Rick insisted on doing an inspection of the shop and the loft. He said there's a firebug on the loose. On his suggestion I bought some dowels and put them in the windows."

"That's a good idea, honey. I'm worried about you staying there."

"I'll be fine, Mom."

"Then why are you so tense?"

"Is it that obvious?" She averted her eyes.

"I'm your mother."

"I made a huge mistake. He…kissed me and I let him."

"Was it a terrible experience?"

Andrea could hardly swallow remembering the rapture she'd felt. "No, of course not."

"But?"

"I didn't want it to happen."

"That's not really true—otherwise you would have stopped him. I'm glad this happened. Darling—Gunter's been gone fourteen months. You're free to look at another man and to care about one again. I have eyes and can see how attractive Captain Jenner is. You wouldn't be a woman if you didn't notice him."

"But there's a big problem, because he's *too* gorgeous!"

Her mother laughed out loud before she poured the hot fondant onto a buttered marble slab. "Well, you'll have to blame his genes for that. Andrea, you're so young, with a whole life ahead of you. You knew someone else had to come along one day.

"Why does the idea of getting to know this man cause you so much angst? Don't let guilt that you might be betraying Gunter's memory prevent you from getting to know him or any man better."

"It's not guilt, Mom. Trust me."

"I'm glad to hear it. So what's wrong?"

"I told you before. After losing Gunter, I don't want to care for a man whose chances of dying on the job climb astronomically because of his profession."

Her mother studied her for a long moment. "You really mean that, don't you?"

"Yes. I feel doubly sorry for Tessa. She lost her mom. One of these days she could lose him, too. That poor little girl will spend her whole life worrying about him. You should have seen her earlier. She'd been with her grandmother, but she came running into Rick's house like a rocket to hug him. It caught at my heart. Rick admitted his late wife didn't like his job either."

"Well, you have to look at it this way. He's one of those selfless men who loves what he does for a living. What would we do without his kind? In caveman days he would be the one who went out to hunt for meat to bring back for everyone," she teased. "Seriously, some men are made that way. You can only admire them."

"I do, and I've always asked myself how they can do it, but now it has hit home to me in a more personal way. Yesterday should have been his day off, yet there he was in the heart of some holocaust with no one to save him."

"I understand they work on the buddy system."

"Even so, they can die. One did yesterday."

Her mom let out a troubled sigh. "What are you going to do?"

"I have no intention of going out with him again."

By now her mom was spreading the pecans on the paper. "Did you tell him that before or after he kissed you?"

Andrea's cheeks filled with heat. "Before."

"I must say he lives up to his reputation for living dangerously. I wish I could help you with your dilemma. If you truly mean what you say and don't want to see him again, you could be missing out on a great love affair."

"Not if it's cut short." *Not when I can't give him or any man a baby.* He'd told her Tessa needed a sibling. With the right woman, Rick could have several more children.

"I'm going back to the loft. I need to clean and do a wash before work in the morning. I hope you and Rex have a great evening. I can't wait to hear about it tomorrow."

As soon as Andrea got home she lit into her house-cleaning until she was ready to drop. But she still spent a restless night dreaming about Rick, and she got up early the next morning to put more merchandise out on the floor. Her mother joined her in time to wait on a steady stream of customers. The weather had warmed up, bringing in shoppers.

The chimes sounded again. She happened to glance toward the entrance and found herself staring into the blue eyes of the firefighter she'd met at the hospital. He'd warned her he'd look her up, but she really resented it when he knew she'd been at the hospital to see Rick. "Andrea Fleming. I was hoping I'd find you here. Remember me? I'm Chase Hayward, from the hospital. How's the invalid?"

He was attractive in his own way, but he had an aggressive nature she hadn't liked at the hospital, and liked less now.

"I would imagine he's still recuperating. This is my mother, Mrs. Bernard. Mom? This is one of the firefighters who came to the hospital to see Tessa's father."

"How do you do?"

His smile widened. "Now I know where Andrea gets her looks."

"Thank you. If you two will excuse me, I have some business in the back."

She wished her mom hadn't left her alone with him. "Are you looking for a special gift? We have nutcrackers and pyramids."

"No. I didn't come to buy anything. I wanted to ask you out to dinner this evening, unless you and the captain are an item."

This man would be the last person she'd ever want

to go out with, but how to do this tactfully so as not to offend him or affect his relationship with Rick? "I'm friends with the captain's daughter and haven't been out with another man since my husband passed away. I still miss him terribly." Though it was the truth, she'd gotten past the pain since meeting Rick.

"I'm sorry you lost your husband."

Andrea had nothing more to say to him. "So am I. If you'll excuse me, I have more customers waiting."

"Andrea?" Her mother walked up to her with a serious expression. "You're wanted on the phone. I'll take over for you." Andrea had the impression it was Rick, and she went to the back of the shop. Unfortunately she was breathless when she picked up. "Hello?"

"I'm sorry if I'm getting you at a bad time, but this couldn't wait."

"What's wrong?"

"Yesterday you walked out on me and Tessa. After you left, she told me she wished you had stayed to read some more books to her. There's been a breakthrough."

"That makes me happy. She's very precious," Andrea said in a shaky voice, "but I'm afraid I can't talk any longer." Thrilling as those words were, it didn't change her decision.

"Don't hang up. Your mother just told me Chase Hayward was in the shop."

She blinked. "Yes?"

"Is he still there?"

"I don't know."

"What did he want?"

There was no use lying to Rick, who sounded so

terse. "He said he didn't come to buy anything—he wanted to invite me out to dinner."

"What did you tell him?" His voice sounded an octave lower.

"That I'm still mourning my husband. Then Mom told me I was wanted on the phone. What's wrong?"

"Do me a favor and drive over to my house as soon as you can get here. Ask your mom if she'll take over while you're gone. This is important, Andrea."

"Rick—"

"Just do it!" He sounded fierce before she heard the click and the dial tone.

Stunned by the call, Andrea found her mother on the shop floor and told her Rick needed to see her right away. "It sounded like an emergency."

"Then go, and don't worry about me."

Andrea grabbed her purse and coat before flying out the back door. She couldn't imagine what was going on, but knew it had to do with the other firefighter. During the drive she reflected on the scene at the hospital and Chase's cocky behavior. Andrea felt as if he couldn't have cared less about Rick's condition. He hadn't acted the same as Rick's other friends and colleagues.

To her surprise Rick came outside when he saw her drive up. His long, well-honed body was clothed in jeans and a polo shirt, drawing her gaze. Andrea parked behind his car. He walked over to help her out. "Thank you for getting here so fast."

"It sounded urgent."

"I know I frightened the hell out of you, but I had

to do something to get your attention." He cupped her elbow as they walked into the house.

"Where's Tessa?"

"Sharon's gone to pick up her and Julie at school. Let's go in the kitchen where we can talk."

"You sound much better today."

"I'm fully recovered." In the next breath he pulled her into his arms and gave her a long, hungry kiss. To her shame it went on and on and left her gasping for breath once he relinquished her mouth. "I had to do that before we talk about Chase Hayward."

She saw his lips tighten. So she hadn't imagined tension between them at the hospital. "I hope you know I'm not interested in him." Andrea decided to tell him everything. "I'm sorry to say I didn't like him. Among other things he has an attitude problem."

"There's a lot more wrong with him than you can imagine." At this point the glaze of desire in Rick's eyes had vanished, to be replaced by the dangerous glittering look he'd given her in the shop that first morning. He let go of her arms so she could sit down at the table.

"I take it you're not friends."

"Anything but." His hands went to his hips in a totally masculine gesture. "We joined the department at the same time eight years ago and worked at the same station for three years. He always saw everything as a competition. After his divorce, he got worse. When I was promoted to captain of my own ladder truck and transferred to the station I'm in now, it was a great relief.

"A year later I learned he'd made captain at our original station. On the rare occasion when we were fighting the same fire, he was openly hostile to me when the other guys couldn't hear him. Arney confided that Chase was jealous of me because not only had I been promoted earlier than him, but I'd made captain of the ladder truck in the downtown station."

"Why would he care?"

"Because our station fights the most dangerous fires. It's a matter of pride with him."

With those words it felt as if a bomb had exploded inside her. Rick had just given her more reason to walk away from him as soon as Sharon got back.

"That had to have been a wound to his colossal ego," she murmured.

"You could say that. He was the only firefighter I knew who didn't come to my wife's funeral. As Benton said, he was conspicuous by his absence."

In a fraternity like theirs, Andrea realized any absence would be noticed. "Then I don't understand why he came to the hospital with the other guys to see you."

"I've been asking myself the same thing, but I think I know now." His hands gripped the back of one of the chairs. "How long was he there at the shop?"

"I don't know. I left first."

"Let's call your mother and find out. Ask if he ever went into the back area. Put it on speakerphone."

Rick had a definite reason for asking that question. Andrea was positive it had nothing to do with her. She reached into her purse for the phone and made the call. When her mom answered, she asked about the firefighter who'd been in the store earlier. Andrea explained this call was at Rick's request.

"Well, he wandered around the shop for about five minutes looking at all the merchandise while I waited on some other customers. He eventually picked out a smoker and paid for it. Then he thanked me and left."

"Rick wants to know if he went in the back."

"No."

"Thanks, Mom. I'll explain later."

She clicked off and looked up at Rick, who'd started pacing. "Tell me what you're thinking." His grim expression made her nervous. "Obviously something is very wrong."

He came to a standstill. "Didn't Hayward tell you he wasn't there to buy anything?"

"Yes."

"But in the end, he bought something from your mother." Lines marred his handsome features. "I don't want him harassing you again."

"After what I told him, I'm sure he won't."

Rick averted his eyes. "Excuse me for a minute while I make a phone call. Don't move." He gave her a long, hungry kiss that left her thoroughly shaken and trembling before he let her go and walked out of the kitchen.

While she sat there dazed, Tessa came running into the kitchen from the door leading into the garage. She was carrying a packet and Sharon was right behind her. "Hi, Andrea!"

What a change in her! Andrea thought. "Hi yourself!"

"Where's Daddy?"

"He's on the phone in the other room."

"Is he still in bed?"

"No."

"That's good. I want him to get well really fast."

"So do I. How was class today?"

"Rodney Carr threw up by the teacher's desk. He ate corn dogs for lunch. Everybody ran out in the hall."

"Oh, dear."

"His mom had to come and get him. Mrs. Riley said the flu is going around. If we start to feel sick to our stomachs, she doesn't want us to come to class."

Amazed at all the information pouring out of her, Andrea tried to stifle her laughter. Wait till she told Rick. "Did you like the corn dogs?"

"No. They're yucky."

"Then I bet you're hungry," Mrs. Milne interjected.

"Yes. What are we going to have for dinner?"

"I thought I'd make tacos."

"Um. Daddy and I love those. He's always hungry and eats anything."

That child had worked her way into Andrea's heart. "Well, that's lucky. Somewhere I read that a firefighter consumes a lot of calories when he's on duty." She was still trying to stifle her laughter.

Sharon rolled her eyes. "That makes it easy for me. My husband was a picky eater."

"So's my father," Andrea admitted.

"Tessa? Go find your daddy and wash your hands while I fix you some apple dippers."

"Okay. I'll be right back."

A few seconds later she could hear voices in the hallway. When Rick's deep, male belly laugh resounded in the air she knew Tessa had told him about what had happened at school. After his dark mood, the happy sound was a revelation.

CHAPTER SIX

RICK WALKED TESSA back to the kitchen and beckoned to Andrea from the doorway. "Sharon? Benton just arrived. The three of us will be in the den until dinner."

She nodded. "Tessa's going to help me grate the cheese."

"Hurry, Daddy."

"We won't be long," he promised.

When they reached the hallway, Rick pressed a swift kiss to Andrea's unsuspecting lips. "I'm in agony waiting to be alone with you, but Benton wants to talk to you first."

She blinked. "Why?"

"I'd rather he told you. While you were driving over here, I phoned him and told him about Chase. He said he'd be right over."

When they walked into the den, Benton greeted Andrea and told her to sit down. Rick sat in the chair next to her. "I'm glad you came so quickly. As Rick has indicated to you before today, someone has deliberately been setting fires in the downtown area. We suspect Chase Hayward is responsible."

A gasp escaped her throat. Her anxious eyes searched Rick's. "You think our shop is next?"

"Since he saw you in my hospital room and found out it's your shop, I'm positive."

Benton nodded. "I've been on the phone with your mother. At this point she's very concerned, especially for you."

"That shop has been in the family for years. I had no idea you'd been talking to her."

Benton cocked his head. "It pleased Hayward to find out Rick had been injured in the fire. That's why he came to the E.R. He needed to inspect the damage. That's what arsonists do. But he failed to snuff him out, so he's unlikely to quit."

Andrea lost color. "That's so sick."

"You're right. When he set the art-gallery fire, he would have cased the outside of the buildings, front and back, on the street. This afternoon he cased the downstairs of your shop. By now he's done his research and has probably found out that you live upstairs. He's probably come by Rick's house and seen your car in the driveway."

Rick felt her shudder, even though they weren't touching.

"Since he visited your shop this afternoon, we're fairly certain he would enjoy it if you got hurt—or worse—in the fire he plans to set. It would be his ultimate revenge against Rick."

Her head jerked in Rick's direction. "That's horrifying. How have you stood working around someone that mental?"

Rick reached out to give her arm a reassuring squeeze. "As I told you earlier, we don't bump into each other that often. But the point is, nothing's going to happen to you or your mother. I swear it."

"I know that."

Benton said, "We've set up a sting operation using help from the parcel service that delivers freight to you. If Hayward doesn't start a fire tonight, then we'll have a trap set for tomorrow night or any night in the near future. With your cooperation, we'll catch him."

"We want to help!" she assured him. "I can't bear for that man to destroy more businesses and lives."

"Amen," Rick muttered.

"Naturally we hope he'll show up tonight. Of course you won't be there. But if he decides to wait until another night, here's the plan. In the morning we want you and your mother to drive to work together. While she's out on the floor, we'd like you to answer the buzzer. One of my men will come to your back door disguised as a parcel service employee. He'll bring in the freight.

"Once inside, he'll take off his uniform and you'll put it on. He'll be wearing a wool hat. It's the key. Make sure none of your hair is showing. While your mom shows him upstairs, you'll hurry out to the truck and the driver will take you to an undisclosed location, where one of our men will drive you to your mother's house. We already have police surveillance on your mother's home 24/7 to keep both of you safe."

Rick could feel her trembling. Just when he felt he'd been making real progress with her and Tessa, Hayward had chosen this moment to get his revenge. Rick hated it that because of his association with Andrea, she and her shop were being targeted by that maniac.

"Tomorrow your mother will work until she decides to close," Benton explained, "then drive home to be with you. One of my men will hide in your apartment for as long as it takes to capture Hayward. In the meantime you'll stay at your mother's and the two of you will continue doing business as usual. Do you think you can handle this?"

Andrea nodded.

"Good." He got up from the table. "Sorry this is such an ugly business, but it should be over soon."

"Stay in here, Andrea," Rick whispered before he walked Benton to the front door. The second he left, Rick returned to the den and found her with her head buried in her hands.

He knelt and covered her hands with his own. "*Andrea*...I know this terrifies you."

Slowly she lifted a tearstained face. "I have to admit I don't like the idea of Mom being involved. If anything happened to her, I don't know what I'd do."

Rick kissed her wet cheeks. "I promise that neither you nor your mother will get hurt. I swear it."

"I believe in you." Her voice trembled. "That's part of what's wrong. Chase is after you. It's horrible and so strange because it's one nightmare I hadn't thought of."

"What do you mean?"

Andrea wiped her eyes and sat all the way up. In the soft light of the room her hair fell in waves around her shoulders like spun gold. The contrast with her brilliant blue eyes set in an oval face was stunning. His gaze traveled to the passionate curve of her mouth. He could never get enough of it, not in a lifetime.

"I don't know where to start."

He shook his head. "You puzzle me, Andrea. I never know where I am with you. How about a little honesty over what is really going on with you? I take it you were very much in love with your husband."

"Yes."

"So was I with my wife. Meeting you has come as a shock. I'm feeling and thinking things I never expected to experience again. I can see it's the same for you."

"You know it is." She half moaned the words. "It seems way too soon to experience emotions this strong."

"Is guilt the reason you keep pulling away?"

"No," she answered truthfully. "Like you, I'm over-whelmed with feelings I thought had died with Gunter. But you have a child and I don't want to hurt her. She's too important."

"Why would you hurt her?"

"If I see you any more, then she'll grow more attached. I mustn't let that happen."

"In other words, you intend to carry out your plan to stop seeing me."

"I can't go on like this."

He breathed in sharply, because she sounded as if she meant it. "In the name of heaven, why not?"

"Because...you're a firefighter."

Rick shot to his feet. "*That's* the real reason?"

She reared her head, causing her golden hair to swish against her cheeks. "It's the most important one."

"So there are other reasons, too?"

"Let's just say that your line of work trumps every-thing else. I couldn't stand to get into a relationship with a man who puts himself in harm's way every time the truck leaves the station. I'm not made of the same stuff as your late wife. I'm a coward."

"That's an excuse for what you're not telling me."

Her eyes searched his. "Why don't you humor me and tell me why you became a firefighter. What is it about the job that sends you into a raging fire time after time? Are you going to tell me you come from a long line of firefighters?"

Interesting it had taken this long before she asked. "Nothing of the sort. One grandfather was a college professor, the other worked for a newspaper. My father is a chemical engineer who heads projects for a gold refining company in Cranston, where I grew up. My elder brother is a dentist.

"Though I started out in engineering in college, I'm afraid my heart wasn't in it. During my last year I dropped out and became a firefighter. I knew it would be a disappointment to my family, so I never talked about it. But from the time I was ten, I always wanted to be one."

He'd finally captured her attention. "What happened when you were ten?"

"I was at a neighbor's house, upstairs with my friend Denny. It was a summer afternoon. We were playing with my dog, Shep, and teaching him tricks. His mom was downstairs cooking dinner. I learned later that the deep fat fryer caught on fire and it set the whole kitchen ablaze. We didn't know anything was wrong until we were both enveloped in suffocating black smoke and couldn't see our way to the stairs."

Andrea covered her mouth in horror.

"We opened the windows to get out, but there was nowhere to climb down. I heard the fire engines coming and screamed to them for help, but the smoke was so thick I knew I was going to die. I couldn't see or hear Denny or my dog. All I remember after that was someone grabbing me and carrying me down a ladder to the ground."

"Thank heaven—" In the next breath Andrea threw her arms around him, almost strongly enough to knock the wind out of him.

"I told him my friend and my dog were still up there. In a minute both were brought down unconscious, but one of the firefighters put oxygen masks on Denny and Shep and saved them. Denny's mom was hysterical until she realized we'd made it out alive.

"Later in the week our two families went to the fire station to thank the two firefighters who saved our lives. Denny and I decided they were gods and we wanted to be just like them."

"I can understand that." Her voice shook. "Did he become a firefighter, too?"

He hugged her tighter. "No. He went into the military and has made it his career."

"One way or the other, you're both saving people, but I can't imagine going through such a horrendous ordeal."

"It was awful. I had nightmares about it for years

until I started fighting fires and helping people trapped in an inferno. Now I don't have those bad dreams anymore."

"I'm so glad of that." Andrea sobbed quietly. "Forgive me for getting upset over your work. I haven't meant to judge you. What you do is so heroic. You save lives every day. You saved a lot of the art gallery and prevented our shop from burning. There are no words to tell you what I really think of you."

"If that's the case, I'll ask you this again. Do you wish we hadn't met?"

"Yes."

"Surely you can't mean that."

"But I do. I may feel a strong attraction to you, but it doesn't follow that I could handle a permanent relationship. As you can see, I can't." He heard the tremor in her voice. "In just a week's time you've been in the hospital with a problem that could have injured you forever, and it's Chase's fault. Someone died in that fire, a man with a family.

"I can't stand it that there's a guy out there from your own profession trying to kill you. Even if he's caught, you'll be out fighting fires again and could perish like your colleague. I don't want to be around when that happens, because one day *it will*."

Rick ground his teeth. "Did you ever get professional help after Gunter died?"

She stirred restlessly and pulled away. "No."

He studied her features. "Have you considered that this fear of yours stems from his sudden death?"

Andrea had to be disturbed by his questions, because she moistened her lips nervously. "I'm sure his death plays a part in my fear, but it goes much deeper than that."

"Then explain it to me. Help me to understand."

She hugged her arms to her waist. "You don't want to hear it."

"Let me be the judge of that. We're talking about our lives here. Our happiness. I've just met this incredible woman and already you're distancing yourself from me. Help me understand."

He had to wait a minute for an answer.

"My first recollections of life were of a loving mother and an absentee father. He lived to go hunting. If he wasn't at work, he was out at the shooting range with his best friend Frank, who was also a hunter. I hardly saw him from season to season and hated it every time he walked out the door with his rifle.

"Frank was married, and he abandoned his family to hunt, too. I knew people got killed hunting and begged my dad not to go. He'd just pat my head and tell me to be a nice girl for Mommy. After he'd leave, I'd run to my room and pray and pray he wouldn't die."

"Andrea—" Rick was devastated.

"One day my fears came true. He and Frank got shot by accident. Frank died and Dad was hospitalized for a gunshot wound in the arm. While he was recovering, that was the longest time he ever spent at home. But it wasn't a happy time for me or Mom, because that's when he started drinking."

Rick grimaced, imagining her pain.

"He cried for his friend all the time. It felt like he

loved Frank more than he loved me and Mom. When he got better, he didn't stop hunting. He went again and again with hunting friends. Every time he walked out the front door, my heart died a little more, but I knew my pleas would never stop him.

"By my teens I realized he didn't love us like he loved hunting. He provided for us, but with insight I saw that he was so selfish, he always put us last. Mom did the only thing that made sense and divorced him. She'd always had the shop to run, and that was her solace. We had peace after he left.

"The only reason I had a visit from him the other night was because he needed a place to stay and didn't want to pay money to go to a hotel. His third wife doesn't like his hunting either.

"You know what he left me for a Christmas present? Another can of bear mace."

What Rick was listening to made him ill.

"When I met Gunter and fell in love, I was so glad he didn't hunt or do any dangerous sports. I knew my marriage would be ideal because he'd always be there and always come home to me and the family we planned to have. But he died, too," she said in a pained voice that ripped up Rick's insides.

On a groan he reached for her. After wrapping his arms around her, he rocked her for a long time, never wanting to let her go. But slowly she eased away from him and wiped her eyes.

"I've had enough of death and the pain of worrying. Meeting you has proven to me there are other men out there who can attract me. Perhaps one will become special, but he won't do any of those thirteen most dangerous jobs you talked about, maybe not even the first thirty.

"When I see how well Tessa handles your work, I marvel. Maybe being born into a firefighter's family makes all the difference. More important, she knows she comes first in your heart and is loved beyond everything. She's very lucky. I'm quite crazy about her. That makes this extra hard, because she's at the age where she wants and needs a mommy, but I can't allow her to become attached to me.

"So, as much as I'd like to lie in your arms and feel alive again, I know of the terrible price that will have to be paid the first time I learn you're off to another fire. I simply wouldn't be able to handle it."

He shook her gently. "There has to be a way for us to work this out, Andrea." Rick couldn't conceive of not being with her. After hearing about her father, all he wanted to do was love her.

She shook her head. "You know there isn't. Admit that having felt the sparks with me, you'll meet another woman out there who makes you happy again. She'll love you without fear of how you make your living and she'll love your daughter. Best of all, she'll give you more children."

Rick moaned, trying like the devil to process everything she was telling him, but something still wasn't connecting.

"I happen to know she'll consider it a privilege to be loved by you. You're a remarkable man, Captain Jenner. Fearless. Honorable."

"Don't set me up to be something I'm not."

She laughed sadly. "Tell that to the birds. I'm going to try to forget you, but it may not be possible. Nevertheless I intend to go my own way once Chase Hayward is caught in the act. Now I'm going to slip out your front door and meet Mother at the house. You need to eat and sleep. Tell Tessa my mommy needs me and I had to leave. She'll understand that."

Andrea kissed his jaw and left the den. He followed her to the front door and watched her drive away. Rick could have gone after her, but knew this wasn't the right moment. There was a fight going on inside her. He needed to give her more time, but one thing was certain. No way was he going to let her walk out of his life.

Hours later he put Tessa to bed, then lay down on his own waiting for Benton to phone and tell him that the Hansel and Gretel shop had a nocturnal visitor. But the call never came. It meant Chase had something else in mind. For the rest of the night Rick wrestled with his thoughts, wondering what his next move might be.

The man had hated Rick for years. For him to go to the shop and ask Andrea on a date was a premeditated move on his part to bait Rick. The lowlife had probably been stalking her every move.

Rick's gut told him Chase meant to harm her. Maybe he didn't plan to set the shop on fire, but this night would have given him the perfect opportunity. He'd been in the cubicle of the E.R. when the doctor had told Rick he wouldn't be able to go back to work for a couple of days.

Armed with that knowledge, Chase probably had something much more evil in mind while he assumed Rick was still out of commission. The fear of what he might be planning brought him to his feet in a cold sweat.

He checked his watch. Five-thirty a.m. Without hesitation he phoned Benton with his newest suspicions. After they made a plan, he hung up and got dressed, opting for his hiking boots and parka. He left Sharon the message that he'd had to leave early for work.

One way or another he was going to beat Chase at his own game. It was only a matter of time.... He'd promised Andrea he would protect her and her mother. He wouldn't be able to breathe until Chase had been caught and put away.

Instinct prompted him to drive over to Mrs. Bernard's home, but he parked alongside a group of cars three blocks away at an all-night shopping center. The streets were dry. Armed with his licensed concealed weapon and binoculars, he stole through a series of people's backyards, some with snow, others where the snow had melted.

He climbed a leafless tree in order to keep watch without being detected. Someone intentionally looking for him might see him, but that was a chance he had to take. Rick braced himself against a sturdy limb and ate a couple of granola bars while he waited.

After a nearly sleepless night, Andrea and her mom left the house at nine in her mom's car. Andrea left hers in the garage. Since she would be putting on a parcel service uniform later, she'd dressed in jeans and a sweater she could wear under it without problem.

She knew that if Chase Hayward had tried to get into the shop last night, Rick would have notified her by now. She was thankful he hadn't yet tried to burn their business down.

En route they stopped for bagels and coffee before they let themselves in the back door. Over breakfast Andrea eyed her mother through tears. "If anything happened to you..." She couldn't finish the thought. "You're the bravest person I know, Mom. I'm practically falling apart over this situation, but you remain fearless. How do you do it?"

"I'm as nervous as you are deep down."

"To think that firefighter would hate Rick enough to want him dead." Her voice shook. "I can't bear it."

"Chase's jealousy of Rick is a terrible thing now that it's out of control. But the police and the fire department are all working on this case. I have faith he'll be caught. Don't you?"

Andrea couldn't swallow the rest of her bagel. "Yes, but it's all so hideous. Rick risks his life every day, and now he has to worry that someone's after him with a vengeance. Now it's put him and the shop in danger, including my mother."

"We're being protected, honey, but none of us is exempt from the ugliness of this world."

"I know, but this must be so awful for him. I don't know how he goes on." She jumped up from her chair. "What if he dies?"

Her mother stood and put an arm around her. "I have

a feeling you're remembering that agonizing time when you were in the accident. Such deep-seated pain can color your emotions for a long time. Just remember you're not in that situation now and Rick is very much alive. Hold on to that thought."

"I'm trying." She sniffed. "Tell me about Rex."

"We're going to dinner and the ballet tonight."

"I know. I guess what I'm asking is, how do you feel about him?"

Her mom smiled at her. "I like him a lot. We're going out tomorrow night, too."

"*And* Saturday night?"

"Yes."

"I'm so pleased for you, Mom," Andrea said with a slight glistening in her eyes.

"Oh, darling, it will happen for you, too," replied her mom.

Minute by minute the neighborhood came to life—people leaving for work, other people out walking their dogs, kids headed to school. By eight-thirty he noticed more traffic. Several vans for satellite TV, a moving van.

His pulse raced the moment he saw Andrea and her mother leave the house by the front door. The binoculars hanging around his neck gave him a close-up of the woman who'd turned his life upside down over the past week. This morning she'd dressed in a parka over her jeans. Her gilt hair gleamed in the sun.

Andrea's mother backed them out of the driveway and they drove down the street. Once they were gone, he figured Chase would come now if he was going to.

But if Rick was wrong, then he'd revert to plan B and start stalking him.

When ten more minutes had passed, Rick decided he'd made a miscalculation. After tucking the binoculars inside his parka he was getting ready to descend when he saw a work truck pull up in the driveway. His adrenaline kicked in and he pulled out his field glasses. "Bailey's Garage Door Service."

A man in a work uniform and a blue cap got out with a satchel, but Rick recognized his height and build immediately. *I've got you, Hayward.* His profile met the criteria of the sociopath, particularly in the areas of no remorse and illusions of grandeur.

While he got busy opening the garage door, Rick made his descent. When he'd disappeared inside, Rick sprinted across the yard and over a fence. With stealth he approached the small window on the side of the garage.

Chase was hunkered down by the driver's side of the car. Sure enough, he was planting an explosive device that would kill the person who opened the car door. He'd left the garage door open so he could get out fast and then close it before driving off.

Rick stole to the opening, then crept up behind him. Close enough now, he put an arm around his neck and squeezed until Chase was forced to let go of the device. The next thing Rick knew it detonated in a burst of flame. At that point the garage filled with police and he was hauled into an ambulance, where the paramedics got to work checking him out.

Benton climbed inside and rode to the hospital with

him. "Hey, buddy. Nice work. You've caught our fire-bug, who took the hit with his own bomb. Thank goodness you got off light. Just some hair was singed."

"What about Chase?"

"I'd say he was burned over a third of his body, including his hands. If he'd been farther inside the car, there'd be nothing left of him."

Thank goodness. He'd never be able to hurt Andrea again.

Andrea and her mother both heard the Christmas chimes at the same time, cutting off further conversation.

"I'll go wait on our customer while you watch for the truck. It should be here any minute. Are you still nervous?"

"I'm more angry than anything else right now. I want Chase in jail."

Andrea felt a moment of shock when she realized the man coming into the shop was Benton. Alarm bells went off in her head and her heart began to race. Something must have gone wrong, and Andrea found she could barely draw breath.

"What's happened? Is Rick all right?"

"He's fine. Our arsonist made his near fatal move."

Andrea gasped. "Where? You mean he's been caught?"

"Caught and in the hospital under guard. He broke in to your mother's garage after the two of you left for work this morning. He was planting a bomb in your car when Rick surprised him. In the struggle, it detonated too soon and Chase received burns over a third of his body."

Her mind reeled. For a minute she couldn't breathe. "But Rick was supposed to be home resting under doctor's orders!" she cried. "How could he be at my mom's?"

"I'll let him explain after he's released from the hospital."

"He's in the hospital, too?" she cried in absolute panic.

"Not in the way you're imagining. He's only there to be checked out and give our team information."

Tears had pooled in her eyes. "How bad is he, Benton? I want the truth!"

"A little singed hair and eyelashes. He's fine, Andrea. I promise you."

She groaned aloud. "He's still supposed to be in bed recovering from smoke inhalation!"

"Let's be thankful he followed his instincts and figured out what Chase had in mind before it was too late. Rick is never wrong. He'll receive another citation for this."

"I'm not surprised, but it doesn't take away from the fact that he could have died!"

"But he didn't—you can't think that way, Andrea. Between you and me I'm thankful things turned out as they did. Otherwise I shudder to imagine what would have happened to you the next time you got in your car."

Rick... He'd put himself in jeopardy to save her life. It was too much.

"Our city of Providence is safe from who knows how many fires he would have set off until he was caught."

"C-can I go visit him?" Her teeth had started to chatter.

"Rick's at an undisclosed hospital with police officials while they wind up this arson case. He'll phone you later. You and your mother can go home at any time, but the garage is still a crime scene. Your mother will have to park out in front.

"When all the damages are assessed, we'll let you know how soon your car can be restored to you. I'm sure your insurance company will give you a loaner car."

"Thank you for telling me that," she said, but her mind was on someone else. "What about Tessa?"

"She doesn't have any idea what's gone on. My wife will be driving her and Julie to school and picking her up at the end of the day. Stop worrying."

Benton could say that because he was a man who, according to Rick, had been a firefighter first. Men thought differently than women, especially these heroic men. "I wish I could."

He put a hand on her shoulder. "The menace is over, and I happen to know Rick's fine, because I've seen him and I've been on the phone with him."

"You have?"

"I wouldn't lie to you. He'll get in touch with you when he can. We're all breathing a sigh of relief that you and your shop are safe."

"You're very kind, Benton. I appreciate everything you've done to keep us safe." She looked over to her mother.

"Oh, Andrea—" Her mother hugged her hard. "Thank heaven Rick stopped that horrible man before he could hurt anyone else."

She shook her head. "I can hardly comprehend it. He doesn't care about himself."

"Of course he does! But it's his job!"

Andrea's anger suddenly got the better of her. "He could have died this morning, Mom!"

"*You* might have died if Rick hadn't intervened when he did."

"I don't want to talk about it. Let's get back to work. We have a lot to do."

Rick was finishing a cup of coffee in the loft's kitchen when he heard Andrea's footsteps on the stairs. Benton would have apprised her of the facts. In order not to alarm her, Rick walked over to the doorway so she'd notice him right away.

But maybe his surprise visit hadn't been such a good idea, he thought. The second those soulful blue eyes saw him, the color left her face. He knew about her fear. Because of that, he'd driven his car straight here from the hospital to reassure her nothing was wrong with him.

"Easy, Andrea."

Before she fainted, he picked her up in his arms and carried her through to the bedroom, where he laid her on the bed. She stared up at him. "I—I thought you were still at the hospital," she whispered.

He leaned over her, smoothing some gold strands from her forehead. "Just long enough to be checked out and released." She was so enticing, he found her mouth and kissed her until she clung to him because she couldn't help herself.

When they came up for air, one of her hands strayed to his face. "Benton said the fire singed your hair and eyelashes, but it's not nearly as bad as I had imagined."

Rick kissed the palm. "I'm glad to hear it. You think Tessa will notice?"

"Yes. She notices everything. Little girls who love their fathers are like that." Tears trickled out of the corners of her eyes. "Thank goodness you weren't killed, Rick."

He lowered his mouth to hers in a gentler kiss. "It didn't come to that."

"How did you know what Chase was going to do?"

"Instead of dragging you back into the house and my bed last night, I used all my energy to concentrate on that devious mind of his. By coming to your shop, he made it too obvious he planned to set it on fire. Since he knew I was home recovering, what better time for him to do something to throw us off the track and plant a device in your car? Firebugs like to set cars on fire."

She clutched his hand. "You saved my life." Her voice shook. "How can I ever repay you?"

He studied the mouth he'd been devouring. This was where he wanted to stay for the rest of his life. "By stopping your worry. I've been told I can't report to work until Thursday, so I've decided a mini vacation is in order. Do you think the Gingerbread Inn would have rooms for us?"

Andrea sat up looking totally shocked. "It has a lot of rooms, but I couldn't possibly go there with you."

"Why not? Tessa can miss a day of school. Do you think your mother could spare you for that long? With the sun shining, we should take advantage of it and celebrate the good news about Chase's capture. We'll take turns driving to give both of us a rest. Along the way we'll stop for meals and return tomorrow."

When she averted her eyes, he got off the bed. "I know you planned never to see me again once this business was over. But I don't think going on a little outing with Tessa will do irreparable damage."

Andrea rolled onto her side and slid off the bed. "You're wrong, Rick. No one is more thrilled than I that you're safe, but I never plan to go through this experience again, and you know why."

There was still something she hadn't told him—his instincts sensed it.

"Obviously your answer is no, but that isn't a problem. It was just an idea. I can see your fear is debilitating and I put you on the spot without meaning to, so I'll say merry Christmas to you now and wish you a wonderful trip."

"What trip?"

"The one you're going to take to the south of Spain after Christmas. I hear it's warm and beautiful there this time of year."

"Mom told you?"

"She happened to be on the phone with your sister-in-law when I entered the shop. I understand you've been invited to join her and her husband after Christmas. After you've gone, I have relatives coming for New Year's. Tessa's world will be full of excitement with her cousins. I promise you she'll be fine whether you come with us today or not. It's your call."

Her lack of response poleaxed him, but there was always the New Year when she got back from Europe, because he refused to give up. Struggling for control, he moved to the doorway. He'd made a decision and would stick to it.

Get out of here, Jenner.

"Goodbye, Andrea."

He raced down the steps and through the shop. Her mother was waiting on a customer. "Merry Christmas and happy New Year, Mrs. Bernard."

Her gaze darted to him in surprise. "The same to you, Captain Jenner. As I told you earlier, words can't express all our gratitude for what you've done for our family. We owe you everything."

"Say no more. It goes with the territory."

Once outside, he levered himself into the car and headed for Benton's house to pick up his daughter. He needed her. Whatever they ended up doing today, he didn't want to be alone with his thoughts. Andrea kept fighting him. He'd thought by now he would have broken her down, but such wasn't the case.

There was a reason she'd been invited to Spain. No doubt her late husband's sister had picked out a man she wanted her to meet. A European whose occupation wouldn't threaten her and who had the approval of the Fleming family. Someone safe.

Rick's hands gripped the steering wheel tightly. No

man could be immune to her beauty. The guys at the station couldn't stop talking about her. Neither could Benton. Chase had gotten sidetracked by it. Because of it he'd now be spending time in the hospital before he was sent to prison.

By the time he reached Benton's house it was noon. He went inside and discovered the children were finishing their lunch. After thanking Deanna profusely, he told her he was taking Tessa home with him for some daddy-daughter time. They went out to the car and he strapped her in before driving off.

"How come I don't have to go to school today, Daddy?"

"Because I miss you and want you home with me."

"I miss you *all* the time."

"You do?"

"Yes. Every time you go away, I'm afraid you won't come back."

Her words drove a pain deep into his gut. *Andrea's exact words about her father.*

When they reached the house and went inside, he carried her into the den and sat down with her. "Tessa? Will you tell me the truth about something?"

She gazed at him out of those beautiful green eyes, then touched his hair. "What happened? It looks funny right here."

Andrea had warned him his daughter would notice. "I got too close to a Christmas candle. It'll grow back."

His daughter's expression sobered. "Julie said you were in a bad fire and had to go to the hospital again. I was afraid you'd die like Mommy and I cried all morning."

Oh, hell. Benton's little girl had big ears and had probably listened in on her parents' conversations. Naturally she had told Tessa everything. "Well, as you can see, I'm fine."

"No, you're not. Your eyelashes look funny, too. I wish you didn't have to put out fires. Julie's daddy doesn't have to anymore. She says he's home a lot doing his work."

Tessa had never said these things to him before. "Does it worry you what I do, sweetheart?"

Her eyes filled with tears. Suddenly she slid off his lap and ran out of the room. Alarmed, he got up and followed her to the bedroom. She lay down on her stomach, parka and all. He watched her body heave with silent sobs.

"Tessa—look at me."

"I don't want to."

His dark brows furrowed. "Why?"

"Cos I'm afraid you're mad at me for saying that."

He knelt down. "I could never be mad at you. I love you."

"Promise?"

Heartsick over that question, he said, "Don't you know that already?"

She flung her body around and hugged his neck. "Please don't die, Daddy." Now her sobs were vocal. They held on to each other for a long time. Tessa clung to him until she'd cried out her tears and finally fell quiet.

His phone rang, disturbing the silence.

"Don't answer it, Daddy! Don't go to another fire!"

The anxiety in her voice was terrifying to him. After the talk with Andrea, he realized how deep-seated his own daughter's fear had become since losing her mother.

How could he not have known? Though Tina hadn't been thrilled about what he did for a living, she'd never let it become an issue. But maybe she and Tessa had talked about it in private and Tina's death had brought their daughter's fear to the surface.

"I'm off duty, sweetheart, so I'm not going anywhere. I'll just see who it is." He pulled the cell from his pocket. The blood pounded in his ears. *Andrea.*

Whatever was on her mind, he didn't want to talk to her in front of Tessa. His daughter was already too upset. He let it ring, deciding to call her back when Tessa got busy doing something else. "It's not an important call," he lied. "What would you like to do today? I'll let you choose."

More animated, she jumped off the bed. "Can we go to Andrea's shop and look at the nutcrackers?"

His heart thundered in his chest. All roads led to Andrea. His daughter had just given him an excuse to find out what Andrea wanted. So much for his decision to leave her alone. "Why don't I call her and see if it will be all right?"

CHAPTER SEVEN

"Thank you. I'll be by for it later today."

Andrea got off the phone with the car rental agency and started out of the bedroom. On the way downstairs her cell rang. She checked the caller ID and immediately clicked on. "Rick?"

She knew she sounded out of breath. It had been ten minutes since she'd phoned him. When he hadn't answered, she'd feared she'd angered him beyond forgiveness. Taking her silence as a firm goodbye, he'd left the loft like a shot and she'd wanted to die. He'd just saved her life, and she'd let him go without saying a word!

"Are you all right?"

I am now. "Yes. Thank you for calling me back. You're a much better person than I am."

"What can I do for you?"

He *was* upset.

She leaned against the stair railing for support. "I—I've been thinking about what you said…." Her voice faltered. "Tessa has a whole fulfilling life with you, so being around me for another day isn't going to be the end of the world for her. As you told her, you and I are friends. You were right about something else, too. After almost losing your life this morning, we should celebrate. If you still want to drive to Barrow's Cove, I'd love to go."

"If you're saying this because you feel you owe me, I'd rather not see you again." His borderline wintry tone gutted her.

"I want to be with you," she admitted on a whisper. He would never know how much.

"That's all I needed to hear. Tessa and I will be in the alley in half an hour."

Excitement almost caused her to crush the phone in her hand. "Honk when you've arrived and I'll come out."

After hanging up, she hurried downstairs to tell her mother what was going on. Under the circumstances her mom decided to close the store for the rest of the day and go home. It was music to Andrea's ears that Rex would be going over there to inspect the damage in the garage and take her out to dinner.

Once upstairs again, Andrea phoned the car rental agency and told them she wouldn't be picking it up until later the next afternoon. All she needed to do now was pack her overnight bag and winter clothing.

On impulse she phoned the inn and spoke to Carol, who sounded delighted they were coming and said she would get a couple of rooms ready for them. When she asked who the man was, Andrea told her it was a friend. Carol let it go at that.

When Andrea heard the honk, she grabbed the pecan roll her mother had brought her and hurried out the door. Rick got out of the driver's seat at the same time. Their eyes met for a breathtaking moment before he put her things into the trunk. He'd forgiven her this time, but she knew her behavior could destroy any feelings he might have for her if she kept this up.

"Andrea—"

She knew that voice, and she climbed into the front seat before turning to his daughter. "Tessa—how are you, darling?"

"I'm glad you could come on a trip with us."

"So am I. It's kind of fun to miss a day of school."

She giggled for happiness. "Daddy says we're going to a lake where he used to water-ski."

"I used to go there, too. We'd boat and swim and have a wonderful time, but it's too cold to do that in winter. Years ago there was a place that took people sleigh riding around the lake in the snow. I've never done it, but maybe we could do it today before dinner."

"You mean like in Santa's sleigh?"

Rick darted Andrea a smiling glance.

"Exactly like that."

"With reindeer?"

He burst into deep laughter. "I think horses, sweetheart."

"We'll eat treats and see what kind of birds and little animals we can spot. There'll be a lot of them around the inn where we'll be staying."

"What's an inn?"

"It's another word for a hotel. My family used to spend our summers there. That's where I met my best friends. After we get settled, we'll go for a walk while your daddy takes a nap."

"He needs one. Did you know his hair got burned in the fire?"

"It did?" She pretended to know nothing.

"Yes, and his eyelashes."

She looked over at him. "He still looks good to me," she said to hide her emotions. Whether injured, sleep deprived or unshaven, Rick was still the most striking male anywhere around, bar none.

He grinned. "I think I like the sound of that."

Without snow or ice on the freeway, they made good time. When they came to the outskirts of Barrow's Cove, Rick pulled into a family restaurant. "I feel like some hot chili. Do I hear any takers?"

Andrea nodded. "That sounds delicious."

"I want a hot dog and a hot chocolate," Tessa proclaimed.

Before long they'd eaten and were on the road again. This made twice in one week Andrea had come here, but being with Rick and Tessa this time was so different and thrilling, she had to pinch herself to believe this was real.

Soon the small hand-painted sign with a wooden arrow pointing up the hill announcing the inn came into view. There'd been no snowplows here. Part snow, part slush covered the gravel drive. Tessa was all eyes as Rick pulled to a stop near the sagging front wraparound porch.

"Is this a haunted house?"

Both Rick and Andrea burst into laughter. Trying to view the dilapidation and snow-covered tree limbs from a child's vantage point, she knew it did look forlorn with only Carol's pickup parked at the side.

"No, darling. It's a place loaded with happy memories. But the owner can't take care of it anymore and is trying to sell it, so that's why it looks a little sad. But you'll find it cozy and charming inside."

Rick got the bags out and they climbed the porch stairs. To Tessa's delight the golden retriever came running out the front door and started sniffing her. "This is Harper, Carol's dog. She's very friendly."

Carol met them in the foyer and hugged her. "How lucky am I to see you again so soon!"

"I feel the same way. Carol Parsons, I want you to meet two very important people. Rick Jenner and his daughter, Tessa, from Providence. She's in kindergarten and Rick is a firefighter for the Providence Fire Department."

The older woman beamed at them. "You can climb up the ladder to my window any time," she teased, causing him to laugh. "Young lady? Did you know you're my first customers today, but I'm expecting some more guests later. Welcome to the Gingerbread Inn!"

"Gingerbread?" Tessa's squeal reverberated through the hallway, causing the three of them to chuckle. "Does the Gingerbread Man live here?"

Rick tousled her blond curls. His dashing smile turned Andrea's heart over. "Who knows? After he ran away, maybe the fox didn't eat him after all and he decided to hide here."

"Daddy...you're funny."

"When the inn was built, they called it that to let guests know it was children friendly."

"It was always a magical place to me, Carol."

Tessa's green eyes twinkled. "Santa Claus is going to bring me a gingerbread man."

"He is?" Carol clapped her hands together. "That's right! Christmas will be here before we know it. Do you want to follow me up the stairs to your rooms?"

"Come on, Daddy." While Tessa trudged on up the old-fashioned staircase with Carol and the dog, Andrea reached for her overnight bag. Rick brought the rest.

"I've put you in the rose room and the Jenners are across the hall in the lilac room." Each room had two double beds, all of them four-posters with chintz quilts.

Tessa walked in to look around. "Did you used to sleep in here, Andrea?"

"With Casey, Melissa and Emily. We had a slumber party every night."

"I don't think they slept much," Carol said with a laugh. "They stayed up half the night gabbing." Rick sent her another private, heart-grabbing smile.

"We're going on a sleigh ride!"

Carol eyed Tessa ruefully. "If you're talking about Sterling's, they're not doing that sleigh ride anymore. It's a shame, but these are hard times."

Andrea's spirits plummeted for Tessa's sake. "Oh well, we're going to have lots of fun anyway, aren't we, Tessa?"

She nodded her cute blond head. The dog had engaged her attention, which was a good thing. Clearly

Tessa was so happy being out with her daddy, nothing else mattered to her.

"Make yourselves comfortable. If there's anything you need, come and find me in the kitchen. I've got fresh coffee and coffee cake for you. If you get hungry in the night, just rummage in the kitchen all you want."

"You're too good to be true, Mrs. Parsons."

"Call me Carol."

Andrea hugged her. "You're an angel."

After she disappeared, Andrea walked across the worn carpet to the other bedroom. "I bet your father is sleepy. Shall we let him lie down while you and I take a walk around the inn?"

"Yes. You go to bed, Daddy. You need your sleep."

Rick didn't put up a fight. After what he'd lived through over the past few days, Andrea knew he needed rest more than anything. "Thank you." He mouthed the words to her before she left with Tessa.

Andrea could see his exhaustion was so great, he might sleep longer than a few hours. In anticipation, she talked to Tessa about going for a long walk by the lake instead. His daughter was willing to go along with anything.

As it turned out, Rick didn't wake up till the next morning. After their walk with Harper, Andrea and Tessa ate dinner in the kitchen with Carol. They talked about the plans for the wedding-vows party and how they would decorate. Then they sat in front of the fire to eat coffee cake for dessert. Carol brought out an old puzzle, which they all worked on until it was time to go to bed. Andrea kept Tessa in her own room so Rick wouldn't be disturbed.

* * *

At four in the morning, Rick came wide awake. He raised himself up in bed and saw that Tessa's bed hadn't been slept in. Once again he'd slept a solid twelve hours.

Unable to lie there anymore, he got up to shower and shave. The long uninterrupted sleep had made him feel like a new man. If he didn't suspect his daughter was asleep in Andrea's room, he'd go in and make love to the beautiful woman—the woman who had stolen his heart—until the sun streamed through the windows.

Barring that, he had to do something with all this energy. He decided to take Carol up on her offer and raid the kitchen before he took a walk outside in the snow. Between heavy conversations with Andrea and Tessa, he had a lot of serious thinking to do about his life and where he wanted to go from here.

One thing he knew beyond all else. He couldn't imagine a life that didn't include Andrea. The idea of her leaving for Spain after Christmas was unthinkable to him.

It was six-thirty when he returned to the inn and went up the stairs. After removing his boots and parka, he slipped across the hall to Andrea's room. The two people he loved most in the world were still sleeping peacefully. He hunkered down at the side of the bed.

"Andrea?" he whispered.

She stirred and opened her eyes. Heavens, she was beautiful. Then she sat up in alarm. "Rick—is something wrong with Tessa?"

It thrilled him that her concern for his daughter was

at the forefront of her mind. He couldn't fall in love with a woman who didn't love his daughter as much as possible. He knew Andrea did.

Taking precautions, he put a finger to her lips. "She's still out for the count. I need to talk to you alone. This is important. Come across to my room. We'll leave both doors open. If she wakes up, she'll know where we are."

Her eyes wandered over him. "You're already dressed."

"I woke up early and took a walk outside."

She took an audible breath. "I need to put on some clothes."

"I'll wait for you in my room." Rick pressed a kiss to the base of her throat before he left. He stood at his window and looked out at the lake until she joined him wearing jeans and a becoming plum-colored sweater. With her golden hair, she looked fantastic in everything. "Come over here by me."

"I'm afraid to."

"That's honest. By now you know I'd like to eat you alive, and that's just for starters."

She stayed where she was in the center of the room, rubbing her palms against womanly hips. "You sound like you must be feeling better."

"I feel reborn."

"I wish twelve hours' sleep would do the same thing for me."

"Frankly it wasn't the sleep that turned me around. Although I admit I needed it and appreciate you taking care of Tessa."

"She's a joy. To be truthful, she took care of me."

"Tina and I often remarked she was going to make a good little mother one day." He eyed her for a long moment. "You're going to be a wonderful mother in the future, too. I can imagine your children decked out in little alpine outfits." He'd almost said *our* children. "It's no secret Tessa likes you more and more every day. What would it take to prevent you from going on that trip to Spain?"

Maybe it was a trick of light, but he thought she paled a little. "Why do you ask?"

"I thought the reason was obvious."

She clutched the back of the nearest chair. "I've already told you this little celebration outing has to be the end for me."

"I can't accept that. The last thing I want is for you to leave Providence." He moved closer. "If I had my way, we'd spend every moment together with no separations."

She lifted her chin. "Except for when you're fighting fires, or recovering in the hospital, *or* sleeping twelve hours at a time to recuperate before you tempt death again. I care for you very much, Rick, and care what happens to you. In fact, there are no words to tell you what I really think of you."

"Then show me instead," he begged as his mouth descended. He needed her kiss more than he needed breath.

"Rick—" she cried against his lips before she began kissing him back with an urgency that set him on fire. He drew them over to the bed and followed her down, desperately hungry for her. They lay entwined, trying without success to subdue the desire exploding inside them.

"I want you in my life, Andrea. Can't you see I've fallen in love with you?" He looked down at her, cupping her hot cheeks. "Admit you've fallen in love with me, too."

A moan escaped her lips. "I don't dare."

"That's because you *are* in love. Don't be cruel and shut me out. I couldn't take it."

She rolled her head away from him. "But I couldn't take living in fear again like I did throughout my childhood."

"You don't have to."

Her head jerked back. With blazing eyes she looked up at him. "What are you saying?"

He kissed her lips quiet. "I've made a decision that will put you and Tessa out of your misery."

She frowned. "I—I don't understand," she stammered. "Why do you mention Tessa in the same breath?"

"Yesterday my daughter and I had a heart-to-heart. You told me she would notice my singed hair and lashes. You were right. Then she bared her soul to me. I learned she's been living in fear of what I do for a living every time I walk out the door. I heard *you* in her, Andrea."

"Oh, no—"

"It was a revelation. I saw and felt it, and I was devastated. One day I live in fear that she'll accuse me of loving my work more than I love her."

Andrea caressed his cheek. "She would never do that, because she knows how much you love her. You're devoted to her every second that you're home. That wasn't the case with my father. He didn't like to be home and didn't want me. Don't ever compare yourself to him."

Pained, yet loving her for saying that, he pressed another kiss to her luscious mouth before he sat up. "But maybe love isn't enough if her fear grows too great. I've thought about nothing else since she told me."

"Has she asked you to stop?"

"Not in those words. What she did say was, 'Please don't die, Daddy.'"

Andrea sat up and looped her arms around his neck. "That must have killed you."

He rubbed her back, pulling her closer. "It did. I always thought Tina was straight up with me. We got lined up on a blind date after I became a firefighter. She knew why I wanted to be one, but I think deep inside she must have hated it, too, and somehow Tessa picked up on it. All this time she has held back…until yesterday."

"The little darling."

"While I was outside walking earlier, I had an epiphany. You wouldn't know, but for the last year Benton has been asking me to consider coming to work for the arson squad."

"That goes along with what he said," she murmured.

"What do you mean?"

"Yesterday he told me you had remarkable, exceptional instincts for that kind of work. Does this mean you'd give up firefighting altogether?"

Rick shouldn't have been surprised at the wonder in her expression. "Yes, but it would still let me be a part of a world I love—just a different aspect of it."

"What would you actually do?"

"As you found out with Chase, a fire that is caused deliberately with malicious intent to cover up another crime, or to collect insurance money on the property, is arson. I would become an arson investigator and inspect fire sites full-time to determine what exactly caused the fire, and if the fire was set intentionally. If it appears to be arson rather than an accident, my job will be to figure out where in the house or building the fire started and what was used to start it."

"Then there's no danger involved?"

"None at all. You gather evidence, communicate with law enforcement, write reports and testify in court as a witness."

"You'll still be helping people."

"Yes." He kissed her mouth again.

"But it won't be like fighting fires, something you've always wanted to do." Her eyes bored deep into his soul. "Would it be hard for you to give it up? I know why you fight fires, and it might be asking too much of you."

"Not when in exchange I'm going to make you and my daughter happy. That means more to me than anything else."

She bowed her head. "When are you going to tell Tessa?"

"After I've spoken to Benton and turned in my resignation."

"Your superiors are going to mourn their loss."

"My leaving will give some other guy a chance to do what he loves."

"How soon will you speak to them?"

"I'll phone Benton today to get the process started.

I'm fully aware Tessa needs to hear my decision right away so she can stop worrying."

"Your news will change her whole life."

"And what about your life?" He smoothed the hair off her cheek. "I want to know how *you* feel about what I've just told you."

Andrea eased off the bed. The act itself caused him some consternation. "My feelings shouldn't matter, Rick. I don't want to be one of the reasons you're considering making this huge career move. I feel so responsible already, I think I'm frightened."

Rick's brows knit together. He got to his feet. "Something's wrong. What aren't you telling me?"

She clasped her hands nervously. "If I weren't in the picture—if I hadn't told you about my fears because of my father—would you honestly be reading this much into Tessa's fear? Maybe with some therapy she could go on handling what you do."

Her reaction was the last thing Rick had anticipated. Perplexed, he rubbed the back of his neck. "I thought you and I were in the same place emotionally, but I sense that we're not. Even having told you what I'm prepared to do, your reaction leaves me baffled. What I'm concluding is that all along things have been sketchy with you and they still are. I can see our relationship has been too much for you this soon after Gunter."

"No, Rick—that's not true." She sounded panicked.

"I think it is. I went through my mourning for a long time while Tina was still alive and am evidently ready to move on. But you lost your husband in an accident and are still grieving because it happened so quickly. I've been trying to make something work between us you're not ready for. Maybe you never will be."

She let out a sigh of exasperation. "If I didn't feel something powerful for you, do you think I would have gone to the hospital to see if you were all right?"

"I think you were acting on hormones that had suddenly kicked in. As you said, physical attraction can be very strong without involving the emotions. You've been missing your husband and wanted to feel alive again after so much pain. But it's evident you can't make a move that will constitute a commitment of any kind yet. You're simply not there."

"Rick—please listen to me."

"It's not your fault." He bit out the words. "It's mine for wanting something so badly. I'll get over it, but let's not drag this out."

"Don't you know you're going to meet other wom—"

"Spare me the speech." He cut her off. "I don't want to hear about some fictitious female who's going to come into my life and transform it and how we'll be perfect for each other. I've had enough of that from friends and family. But I don't want to hear it from you of all people."

Before he lost it completely, he moved past her to go wake up his daughter. Andrea hurried after him. When they reached the hall, she grasped his arm. "You've got things wrong."

Rick spun around, forcing her to let go. "No. Otherwise you'd be telling me what I want to hear. Let's agree you're taking this trip to Spain to get away from me. Though it isn't necessary, because I don't intend to be with you again after today. I can see that's why you're leaving. I should have known something this marvelous was too good to be true."

As he turned, he was shocked to discover Tessa standing in the doorway to her room, still in her nightgown. She was all eyes. "What's wrong, Daddy?"

"Nothing, sweetheart. We were just talking." He gave her a kiss.

"But you said Andrea was going away."

The truth, Jenner. "Not today. Later on she's going to spend some time with her husband's family."

"When are you going to leave?"

"After Christmas," he answered for her. "Come on. Let's get you dressed. After we eat breakfast we're going to go back and see the ice sculptures at the university on the way home. I understand they have some Disney characters you'll love."

To his relief Andrea had disappeared for the moment to give them some private time. But Tessa wasn't listening to him. She'd focused on Andrea and wouldn't let go. "I don't want her to go."

"I'm sorry." He walked her into the room to help her get dressed. "But we're going to have your grandma and grandpa at our house. And Uncle John's family and your cousins Lizzy and Jake."

Her lower lip quivered, a dead giveaway she was on the verge of tears. After she put on her pants and top, he helped her on with her boots. "Listen to me, Tessa. She's been our friend and we've been having a great time. But she misses her husband's sister and this is her chance to visit her."

"What if she doesn't come back?"

Her question acted like a vise squeezing his lungs. "Of course she'll come back. She works in the shop with her mother. Tessa, let's just be happy she's spending today with us. It won't be long before I have to drop her off at work and take you to school."

"I don't want to go to kindergarten today."

"But you missed yesterday." He finished packing up her things. "Julie will be glad you're back. No tears, now." He picked her up. "If you'll give me a kiss, I'll tell you a secret."

Though his sweet little girl was unhappy, she gave him a big one on the cheek. "What is it?"

This couldn't wait. He was desperate to help her out of her pain. "I'm not going to be a firefighter anymore."

She stared at him for the longest time. "You're not?"

"No. When we go home I'm telling Benton that I'm going to work with him on the arson squad. I won't be riding a truck anymore, so you don't ever have to worry about me again. But you can't tell anyone yet. Not even Julie."

Tears of joy welled in her big green eyes. She wrapped her arms around his neck so hard she almost cut off his breathing. Andrea had done the same thing to him earlier, though not for the same reason.

"Can I tell Andrea?"

"She already knows." But for some underlying reason he didn't understand, his decision had made no difference to her.

Once Rick had paid the bill and Andrea had thanked Carol for everything, they took off. Andrea offered to drive, but he told her he felt rested and wanted to do it, so she didn't insist. Tessa asked a lot of questions about her upcoming trip to Spain until he turned on the radio to a station that played Christmas music.

He drove them past the amazing sculptures and stopped for lunch, after which he headed for the shop. When he parked in the alley, Andrea got out and opened the back door to say goodbye to Tessa.

"I hope you had as wonderful a time as I did. I'll be thinking of you-know-what on Christmas morning."

In the rearview mirror he could see his daughter's green eyes. They stayed dry. She was being the best little soldier in the world and he was proud of her. As for Rick, he was the one who was dying inside.

"Do you promise Santa will bring me the gingerbread man?"

"I know he will. Now, have a lovely day at school." She leaned in to give her a kiss on the cheek. "Oh, I forgot." She reached into her purse. "This is some candy my mother made for you and your daddy. It's really good." Andrea handed it to her. "Merry Christmas."

As she stood up, Rick was there with her overnight bag. She reached for the remote on her keys to open the back door. He followed her inside. Her mother was probably out on the floor. There was no sign of her. Andrea turned to him.

She couldn't look him in the eye. "Thank you for the outing. Thank you for everything…for saving my life," she whispered.

"Anytime. Have a safe flight to Spain."

He was out the door before he made the grave mistake of crushing her in his arms one more time.

CHAPTER EIGHT

SEVERAL DAYS LATER Andrea got her sister-in-law on the phone. *Please answer.*

"Marie?"

"Andrea—it's wonderful to hear your voice. I can't wait for you to come to Spain with us so we can have a long talk."

She gripped her phone tighter. "That's why I'm calling. I—I can't come." Her voice faltered.

"What's wrong?"

"I hope this won't come as a shock to you, but I've met a man."

"It's about time," Marie responded without hesitation. "I hope you're going to tell me you're in love."

Tears welled in her eyes. "I am. Terribly."

"I've prayed this would happen to you."

"He's not like Gunter. Rick's a firefighter who lost his wife. His little daughter, Tessa, has captured my heart, but there's one big problem."

"Has he asked you to marry him?"

"Yes. He even said he was giving up firefighting for me and Tessa so we wouldn't worry about him anymore. But just a little while ago I ended it with him."

"Why?"

"He doesn't know I can't have children."

"If you truly love him, then you have to go to him and face your demons. Talk to him about what happened to you in the accident. It's not up to you to decide how he'll react and feel. You're so certain he'll reject you for being unable to have children. But don't you see you're denying him his agency to choose what he wants for himself? That's wrong!"

"Mother told me virtually the same thing." *You could be passing up a great love affair out of fear.*

"Let's put this another way. What if Rick wouldn't commit to you because he couldn't give you a child? Consider how you feel about him right now. If he avoided being with you for the same reason, how would you react?"

"But it's not the same thing!"

"Of course it is! How can you say that?"

"Because he had plans to enlarge his family and deserves to find a woman who can give him another child."

"Just listen to yourself, Andrea. He may have had plans, but his wife died. *You* had plans, too, but Gunter died. It's life! If both of you want children, then adoption would be the route to go. At least give him the chance to tell you whether it's what he wants or not. He's already told you he's going to give up firefighting to win your love."

"But—"

"But what? Are you really afraid he'll reject you? He's not your father, Andrea," she inserted quietly.

"What do you mean?"

"Gunter once confided in me about him and how much damage he did to you. I can see you're afraid that in the end, Rick won't want you enough."

Andrea closed her eyes for a moment. Marie had hit on the crux of her greatest fear.

"If I were you, I'd prove myself right or wrong. But if you can't, then maybe you should get professional help. Otherwise you'll go through this every time you meet a man who wants a relationship with you. If that happens, you'll be single all your life. Is that what you really want—because that's where you're headed. Gunter would say the same thing, and you know it."

Marie was so right about everything, Andrea couldn't find the words. "Thank you for being my dearest friend and setting me straight. I'll love you forever. Take care of yourself. I promise I'll call and let you know what happens."

"I'll be waiting."

After Andrea hung up, she started rehearsing what she'd say to Rick. There was only one more call to make. The most important one of her life.

What if he didn't want to see or talk to her again? She was terrified of his response. When she called his house, Sharon answered and said he'd gone downtown to a special meeting, but she'd make sure he got the message that she'd called.

When Rick left department headquarters, Benton was waiting for him outside the public safety building in downtown Providence. The chief and battalion commander had held an impromptu goodbye party for him. Some of the guys had come in and there'd been a lot of laughs, but now it was over.

"Ready to go home? There's more partying to be had at my house."

Rick eyed his best friend. "I know."

"Tessa's one happy little girl."

Yes. She's happy except for one thing. After losing her mother, she was suffering over a second loss.

"How does it feel to be a free man?"

As of today he was no longer a firefighter. "First tell me I have a job with you, then I'll respond."

"Was there ever any doubt?" He squeezed his shoulder. "Welcome to the dark side." Benton could be a tease. The ironic term had been coined because it was the arson squad that unearthed the dark matter after a fire to learn the cause. "I'm having your name printed on the door of your new office." It would take Rick a while to get used to it. "You don't have to start until January 2."

"I owe you for so many things, Benton, I hardly know where to start."

"Don't go sappy on me now. I seem to recall an incident five years ago where you saved my life before I was promoted to the arson unit. Deanna still cries about it. Sometimes I think she loves you more than she loves me."

"You're full of it."

"I just wanted you to remember I've owed you for a long time."

They walked to the parking lot. Rick had left his car

at the Ames house and ridden downtown with Benton. Because of his change of career, his plans had changed. He'd decided to take advantage of the next ten days off and spend them with his family in Cranston. He and Tessa would stay at his parents' home while Sharon got a well-earned rest at her brother's.

Tonight after Tessa went to bed he'd load all the presents into the car. In the morning they'd drive over to see Tina's parents and spend some time with them. Later in the day they'd head out for Cranston. With four cousins under the age of eight, his daughter would have a whole week to enjoy them. Hopefully in that amount of time she'd be able to face going to school again.

Tessa had become attached to Andrea and it showed. Maybe being with family would make a difference.

From the entrance to the circle Rick could see at least a dozen cars parked. A little closer and he glimpsed the painted banner across the front of Benton's house. "Congratulations on your promotion, Investigator Jenner!"

His eyes smarted.

Before Benton had pulled up in the driveway, the children came running outside. Rick jumped from the car as soon as he could and swept his daughter into his arms.

"Are you all through fighting fires, Daddy?"

"All through, sweetheart."

All through.

They went inside, where he was besieged by more congratulations from the men and families with whom he'd worked the most closely over the years. The celebrating continued until nine-thirty when Rick could see his daughter was conking out fast. With his plan to drive to Cranston tomorrow, he decided he needed to get her home to bed. He still had a lot to do after she fell asleep.

With profuse thanks to Benton and Deanna for all they had done, he gathered Tessa and they drove home. For once she fell asleep the moment her head touched the pillow. The knowledge that he wouldn't be fighting any more fires had something to do with her being able to relax. But twice during the party she'd mentioned that she wished Andrea had been there with them.

Andrea was never out of his daughter's mind. *Or his.*

After getting half a dozen big garbage bags from the kitchen pantry, he packed up the presents under the tree and went out to the garage to fill the trunk. Everyone had gone overboard out of love for his daughter, but there was an indecent amount of gifts.

In a few minutes he headed for the basement to bring up the presents he'd hidden from her. Those he put on the backseat of the car and covered with some blankets. All that was left was the big carton from Santa Claus, which he brought upstairs to the kitchen. He hoped it would fit in the backseat with the rest of the gifts; otherwise he'd have to open it.

Rick hated undoing it, because Andrea had wrapped it so beautifully. The vision of how she'd looked at the station when she'd delivered it had never left his mind. While he stood there aching for her, he spotted the note Sharon had left under the fridge magnet before she'd gone to her brother's house.

Hardly able to breathe, he pulled out his cell and phoned Andrea.

"Rick?"

His heart almost failed him. "I just got Sharon's message."

"Forgive me for calling. I-if you don't want to talk to me, just hang up and I'll never bother you again. I swear it."

A surge of adrenaline charged his body. "Where are you?"

"Home."

He gripped the phone tighter. "What's wrong?"

"Look, if this is a bad time, please tell me. I realize I could be interrupting anything. If Tessa is nearby, I don't want her to know I'm on the phone."

"I put her to bed a half hour ago," he answered, still in a daze.

"I need to talk to you, th-that is if you're willing."

His heart was getting the workout of its life. "Are you at your mother's or the apartment?"

"The apartment."

"I'd come over there, but Sharon has gone to her brother's until after New Year's."

"Does that mean you're leaving Providence?" Unless he was mistaken, she didn't sound happy about it.

"Tomorrow we're headed for my parents in Cranston to stay the week."

"Then this is a bad time to be calling. We can talk again after you're back from your trip. Your family must be thrilled you're coming." The throb in her voice was telling.

"I don't want to wait ten days to see you. Why don't you drive over here now?"

"You're one man who needs his sleep, Rick."

"But you're no longer speaking to Captain Jenner who has just come off shift and needs twelve hours to restore him."

A small cry escaped on the other end. "What are you saying?"

"What do you think?"

"So you really resigned? It's all over?"

He took a fortifying breath. "As of today I'm officially known as Investigator Jenner of the Providence Arson Squad. Benton is already having my name put on the door of my new office in the department of public safety building." Might as well tell her everything right now.

"From now on I work several ten-hour shifts in one week, then I have two weeks off to do follow-up and paper work. One week I'm on call to do investigations. All of it safe."

"Oh, Rick—" Her cry resounded over the phone line. That was pure happiness he heard in her voice. "Tessa must be overjoyed."

"Yes." At least in that regard his daughter was at peace. As for himself, he would be a walking time bomb until he heard what she had to say. "Can you drive over right now?"

"But aren't you getting ready for bed?"

"Do you honestly think I could sleep after hearing your voice, knowing you're home?"

"What were you doing when I phoned?"

"Loading the ton of gifts for Tessa in my car. I'm still wondering how to get the big gift from Santa Claus inside. It might not fit. Come and help me."

"If you're sure."

His breath caught. "Why don't you come and find out?"

"I—I'll leave now." She sounded jittery. "I'm driving a rental car."

"I'll watch for you. For your information, I checked on your car. It's all repaired and ready for you to pick up at your convenience."

"That's great news. Thank you. I'll see you shortly."

"Drive carefully."

"You don't have to tell me that." Her voice sounded unusually shaky.

He'd said it automatically, but then he remembered her husband's fatal car accident.

Rick was on the porch waiting for Andrea when she pulled into his driveway. In the light she could see he was wearing a navy crewneck sweater with jeans. His tall, dark, handsome looks worked like an assault on her senses. It seemed like years since she'd last seen him. The pain of longing to be in his arms again reached the palms of her hands.

As he walked toward her, she realized he truly was the most wonderful, marvelous man alive. More than ever she dreaded what she had to tell him. But as Marie had said, Andrea needed to hear his response—otherwise she'd remain in a frozen state for the rest of her life, unable to go forward.

She got out of the car before he could help her. Andrea didn't want him touching her yet. As soon as she got inside the house, she took off her coat and put it on one of the living-room chairs.

He shut the door and walked slowly toward her, his hands in his pockets. Between his fire-singed black lashes, his hazel gaze traveled over her. After a shower at the apartment she'd decided to wear a new outfit he hadn't seen before—a lighter aqua top shot with gold threads and push-up sleeves to the elbow. The darker aqua skirt was made of the same silk jersey fabric.

"Did you know in the lights from the Christmas tree your hair gleams like the gold in your top? You look fabulous, Andrea."

"You look good, too. Rested."

Rick cocked his head and stood with his powerful legs slightly apart. "I take it something has happened you felt you had to discuss with me, if only for Tessa's sake. So tell me what it is, because I can't take the suspense any longer. I've never been a patient man."

Rick looked dark and dangerous right now, as if all his energy was barely sheathed. It sent shivers through her body.

"Let's sit down." She purposely chose one of the upholstered chairs.

He studied her for an overly long moment before he lounged against the arm of the couch. "Go on. This had better be important, after telling me you didn't intend to see me again." His voice sounded deeper than usual, almost gravelly.

"It is. Very." *Just say it, Andrea.* She was keeping

him up and it wasn't fair to him, but the blood pounded in her ears. She couldn't sit still and jumped up. "I need to tell you about Gunter's accident."

Lines suddenly marred his striking features. He watched her pace until she stopped. His black brows rose. "Are you sure you want to talk about this?"

"I *have* to. H-he wasn't the only person in it."

His hands came out of his pockets. "Did another family member die, too?"

She shook her head. "*I* was the other person in the crash."

His sharp intake of breath resounded in the room. "You never told me that."

"I'm sorry I couldn't talk about it until now. I don't remember it, but I was told that another car on the freeway came at us out of nowhere. Apparently the police thought I was dead, because they had to pry me out to get to me."

Rick's color seemed to go gray. *"Andrea—"*

"When I woke up in a hospital room, I thought I had to be dreaming. IVs were hooked up to me. I remember Gunter's whole family surrounding me. His parents were too devastated to talk. It was Marie who told me we'd been in a bad accident and my husband had been killed outright.

"At first I couldn't comprehend it because I was so drugged. Mother arrived. It was then I realized I was awake and had lived through a horror story. But there was more. After a few days when I could get up and walk, Mom told me that the accident had caused internal injuries to my pelvis."

She swallowed hard before she admitted the one thing she feared telling Rick. "Mom told me I was operated on and would never be able to have children. That blow on top of losing my beloved husband was like being given a death sentence. I wanted to die, but of course I didn't."

Rick's face was a study in pain before he wrapped his arms around her. He held her for a long time before she lifted her head. "Would you believe that when my father called several weeks after I'd been home, he said that unlike Frank I'd dodged a bullet and was lucky I could walk. So I should get over it. At the time I hated him for it, but with hindsight it's probably the only good piece of advice he ever gave me."

"Andrea," he whispered in a pained voice against her neck before pressing kisses all over her face and hair.

"On some level I realized he was right. I was still alive and I needed to live for my mother's sake. Before long I discovered I needed to live for my own. That's when I decided to have the upstairs of the shop remodeled into an apartment and move in. My friends came to see me and I started getting out.

"I'd been doing pretty well until the day I saw you in front of the shop window holding Tessa. She was so dear, I moved closer to get a good look. Your daughter was the living version of my fantasy child I'd hoped to have one day with Gunter.

"You were so sweet to her as you both looked at everything. I thought then what a remarkable daddy you were to take her shopping, something my father never did with me. I saw this tall, attractive man enjoying a day out with his daughter and wondered what it would be like to get to know you. I couldn't stop staring. That's when you suddenly noticed me. Then your demeanor changed."

Rick molded her shoulders with his hands before he moved her far enough so he could look into her eyes. "That morning I was at my lowest ebb after doing all right for a long time. But the display had drawn me in, reminding me of happier times.

"When I saw this beautiful blonde woman watching us through the glass, instead of ignoring you I wanted to go on staring. At that moment I felt such a strong attraction, it angered me. Here I'd been thinking about Tina, and all of a sudden I was thinking about you. That hadn't happened to me since her death."

"We both had similar guilt reactions, Rick, and my feelings for you continued to grow despite any pitiful efforts on my part to avoid you. If anything, all I did was pursue you. I'm ashamed of myself when I look back."

His hands tightened on her upper arms. "Ashamed?"

"Well, embarrassed anyway."

"That makes two of us. On the day of the fire inspection, I sent Jose into your shop, but I couldn't stay away and went in there myself afterward. Your mother looked familiar to me and I discovered why when I found out you were her daughter. At that point, I couldn't stay away any longer.

"The truth is, I fell hard for you, Andrea Fleming. So did my daughter. I'm glad you've told me everything. So now does this mean you're going to marry me? I want you for my wife more than anything in this world."

With the mention of that word she eased away from him and moved over to the chair to steady herself. "Didn't you hear what I told you?"

He frowned. "I heard everything."

"But if we were to get married, I couldn't give you a child. Not ever."

"Are you saying we couldn't have a sex life?"

Heat rushed into her cheeks. "No. But I no longer have a uterus."

"We don't need it. I'll be able to make love to you morning, noon and night and never worry about your getting pregnant. Do you know how heavenly that sounds?"

She laughed in spite of the seriousness of the situation. "Darling—"

"Ah…I've been waiting for you to call me that. Every time you say it to Tessa I get jealous. Speaking of my daughter, we already have a child. She loves you, Andrea," he said calmly. "As for more children, when we want more, we'll put in for adoption so Tessa doesn't grow up a spoiled, pampered only child. I know a person at the state agency who can help us when the time comes."

Her eyes glazed over. "Be serious, Rick."

He rubbed the back of his neck, something he did when he was in deep thought. "Is this the reason you left? You thought I wouldn't want you?"

She twisted her hands. "I didn't know."

"You can't be serious. It's *you* I want to spend the rest of my life with." His eyes glittered with desire. "There's a hell of a lot you still don't know about me.

Come here." She needed no urging as he pulled her to the couch and lay down with her.

"How about a proper greeting for a man who's been dying of love for you?"

Time faded away as they gave in to their needs and began giving each other pleasure beyond imagining.

Some time later he whispered, "Admit your sister-in-law planned to introduce you to some man while you were gone."

She kissed his jaw. "That's absurd. There is no other man and never will be again."

"Thank heaven you said that. Now that I've got you exactly where I want you, I need to make total love to you, darling. But not where Tessa could walk in on us. You *are* going to marry me?"

"Yes!"

"Good. Now that we've got that out of the way, it had better be soon. I don't care about convention. I'd marry you tonight if we could."

"So would I, but I thought you'd never ask."

"*Now* she tells me." He barked with laughter.

"I needed to hear it because no other woman is going to get a chance to snare you. You're mine."

"I don't want another woman." His smile melted her bones. "Santa brought me what I wanted for Christmas. Give me your mouth, Andrea. It's life to me, just as you are."

CHAPTER NINE

RICK WOKE UP at six with Andrea half lying on top of him, her head nestled beneath his chin. With her return he'd gotten his Christmas present early.

She was still sound asleep. He studied every beautiful feature. Her skin showed a tiny rash from his beard. He loved the way her hair fanned out like spun gold against the cushion. While she slept, he had an idea. Easing away from her, he crept over to the fireplace. After opening the flue, he put a match to the newspaper and kindling. Pretty soon they'd have a roaring fire to warm up the living room for her.

No telling when Tessa would wake up. Before she came running in, he went out to the kitchen and brought Andrea's gift for her into the living room. He set it right in front of the tree. It was conspicuous any time, but especially so without the other presents.

So far, so good.

He slipped his shoes back on and walked down the hall to his bedroom. He pulled a little wrapped package out of the drawer, along with another small ring box, and put them in his pocket. Then he tiptoed into Tessa's bedroom. This was going to be fun. The most fun he'd had since before Tina had been diagnosed with her fatal illness.

Unable to wait any longer, he sat down on the side of her bed and kissed her cheek. She stirred and opened her eyes. "Daddy!"

"Good morning, sweetheart."

She sat right up. A couple of blond curls flounced over her eyes. "Is it time to go to Cranston?"

"Not for a while. I came in here to tell you that we had a very special visitor come down the chimney last night."

Her eyes widened. "But it's not Christmas!"

"That's true, but when Santa Claus found out we wouldn't be here on Christmas, he came early to bring you your presents."

He heard her suck in her breath. "My gingerbread man?"

"I don't know. You'll have to open your present first."

She scrambled out of bed in her nightgown and ran through the hall to the living room. "How did he get such a big box down the chimney?" She hadn't seen Andrea yet. He'd placed the couch facing the fire.

Rick grinned. "He has his magic ways."

On the periphery he saw Andrea stir and sit up to see what was going on. Beneath her disheveled gold hair, her eyes dazzled like blue jewels. They exchanged a private glance. He put a finger to his lips. She smiled and waited.

"Go ahead and open it."

Having been given permission, she undid the ribbon

and tore the paper. It took her a minute to get the job done. "I can't undo the lid, Daddy."

"I'll help you."

Winking at Andrea, he leaned over and pulled off the top. Both presents were wrapped in green and red tissue paper. Andrea had gone all out. He pulled out the chair first and set it down on the carpet. Tessa was jumping up and down with excitement.

"There. Now you can open it."

His daughter peeled away the paper, and there sat the carved rocking chair she'd sat in at the shop. "Get out the other present, Daddy. Hurry!"

With a deep chuckle, he pulled it out. She tore off the paper faster than a whirlwind could do it. "He brought me my gingerbread man!" She squealed in such delight it brought tears to his eyes. "Andrea promised he would."

When he looked at the woman responsible for such happiness, tears were running down her cheeks. Together they watched his daughter sit down in the chair and cuddle her gift as if it were the most precious baby on earth.

"Santa Claus brought you something else, too."

The rocking stopped and she looked up at him. "What?"

"Do you remember what you said during your prayers last night? You wished Andrea weren't going away?"

"Yes?"

"Why don't you look over on the couch?"

Tessa got up with her treasure to see. "Andrea— you came back!"

"Yes, darling."

All the joy in the world exploded from his daughter. She ran over and flung herself into Andrea's arms, gingerbread man and all. Quickly before he broke down from too much emotion, Rick pulled out his phone and took a picture of the two of them embracing like mother and daughter. Before much longer, they *would* be.

"I'm going to get my gingerbread book." She dashed out of the room and was back in another instant. "Here it is."

"Shall we read it?"

"Yes."

"Then sit right down in the rocking chair and hold him tight."

Rick snapped more pictures of the two of them as Andrea began to read, making the fairy tale come alive once more. When she'd finished, Tessa ran over and they cuddled for a long time while he got more pictures.

"I have some presents, too," he interjected. "One for you, Tessa, and one for Andrea."

He pulled the little packages out of his pocket. Rick started with Tessa first. "I didn't wrap this one because it's a present that was always yours, but I needed to wait for the right moment."

She took it from him, recognizing it immediately. "This is Mommy's ring."

"Yes. I gave that to her when I asked her to marry me. We both decided that one day we'd give it to you to remember her by. We'll keep it in my drawer and you can look at it and wear it whenever you want."

Tessa took it out of the box. "I love you, Daddy!"

"I love you. It's yours, sweetheart."

"What's your present for Andrea?"

"I don't know. Shall we see what I'm going to give her?"

"Yes, Daddy. Hurry!"

With a smile because she was so predictable, he handed it to the woman he loved, but Andrea's fingers were trembling. When she removed the paper and opened the velvet-lined box, she gasped.

"That diamond is the color of your eyes, Andrea. They're heavenly, just like you. I bought it a few days ago because there was no way I was ever going to let you go." He reached in and put it on her ring finger before he looked at Tessa. "Do you know what this means, sweetheart?"

His daughter was a quick study, because she said, "Did you ask her to marry you yet?"

Rick roared with laughter.

"He did." Andrea spoke for him with her eyes more dazzling than the blue diamond set in the gold band. "And I said *yes*."

"It means Andrea has consented to be my wife and your new mommy."

Her face lit up. "You're going to get married and live here with us forever?"

"That's the idea." He leaned between them to kiss Andrea long and hard in front of his cherub. "I love you," he whispered fiercely.

Andrea threw her arms around his neck. "I love you until it hurts, Rick. I'm not afraid anymore. My mother is going to be overjoyed, because she loves you, too.

You've made a brand-new woman out of me. I'm going to take your love and run with it for as long as we're granted life, because you and Tessa *are* my life and this is just the beginning."

* * * * *

MISTLETOE NOT REQUIRED

ANNE OLIVER

This book is dedicated to anyone whose lives have been touched by breast cancer – mums, daughters, sisters, aunts, grandmothers. And the men who support them. That's pretty much everyone, really.

With thanks to Wendy for making my time in beautiful Tasmania even more enjoyable.

With thanks to my editor, Suzanne Clarke, for putting the hard word on my hero.

CHAPTER ONE

OLIVIA WISHART SLICKED ruby gloss on her lips, then checked her strapless cocktail dress in the mirror and frowned. 'Red lips, red dress, red hair.' She reached for her standby little black dress. 'I don't care if everyone's decked to the halls in Christmas finery, it's—'

'Lovely, but not for tonight.' Her best friend, Breanna Black, whipped the garment from her hand. 'And not another word—you look sensational.' She eyed the cleavage on display and nodded. 'Wise choice—men will look.'

'So long as they listen.' Olivia wasn't a fancy dress fan but the opportunity to talk up her charity to her fellow competitors in this year's Sydney to Hobart Yacht Race was too good to pass up. And a little flesh never failed to get attention.

'Try to remember, it *is* Christmas.' Brie shimmied into a short mulberry all-in-one playsuit with a fur-trim neckline then tossed Olivia a white feather boa. 'Here. It'll put you in the mood.'

Olivia's lips twitched as she slung the silky feathers around her neck. 'I assume you're referring to the *festive* mood.'

'That'd be a start,' Brie suggested, brightly.

Raising the Pink Snowflake Foundation's profile was the reason for Olivia's entry into the race. Being invited by yachting royalty to celebrate the festive season at the mega-million-dollar mansion overlooking Sydney Harbour was a bonus, but anything else…well, it wasn't going to happen.

Brie unravelled a luscious strand of silver tinsel. 'You're sure you don't mind if Jett shares our suite?' she asked for the umpteenth time.

'This mysterious brother you've managed to keep out of the way for— How long's it been?' Stepping into red stiletto sandals, Olivia reassured her, 'I told you I don't mind. I'm interested to meet him actually.'

Brie paused in her task of twisting the tinsel into her hair. '*Half*-brother. And it's a slow, fraught process. Jett's a hard guy to get to know. I'm not sure he even likes me.'

Olivia smiled. 'What's not to like? And he accepted your invitation, didn't he?'

'Only because his initial plans fell through.'

'You don't know that for sure.' But Olivia was pretty sure *she* did. Classic irresponsible, egocentric male behaviour. Yes, she was absolutely interested to meet him, even if it was only to make certain he knew how much he meant to Brie.

Sighing, Brie flipped her reef of long black hair over her shoulder. 'It makes me feel bad that I'm going away for New Year's Eve now, but he told me not to alter my plans on his account.'

'And why should you? If you're right about *his* plans, he's the one who changed his mind and decided to come at the last minute.'

It was obvious Brie cared but apparently the lost sibling she'd spent three years looking for didn't give a toss. Even though they were as close as sisters, Olivia had decided it was a sensitive issue and none of her business unless Brie opened up to her. 'When's his flight due in?'

'Any time. I'll let the front desk know to expect him before I leave—' Brie's mobile buzzed and she checked caller ID. 'That's him now. Hi, Jett…'

Olivia saw her friend's smile fade, and the temptation to snatch the phone and give him a piece of her mind was overwhelming. She had to turn away. *None of your business, remember.*

'Oh… Uh-huh. Okay. You've got the party's address? I'll meet you there. Text me when you're here,' Olivia heard her say before she disconnected. 'His flight's been delayed. Christmas rush; he hasn't even left Melbourne yet.' She flicked through the contacts on her phone, her smile returning. 'Which gives *me* a spare couple of hours to meet the *Horizon Three*'s sexy skipper for a drink downstairs at the bar after all.'

'Good for you,' Olivia enthused, reserving judgement on Jett—for now. She slipped a wad of business cards into her evening purse, handing one to Brie. 'Give him this and highlight our cause. And just remember, sexy skipper or not, he's the enemy come Boxing Day.'

Brie nodded, mobile attached to her ear, obviously waiting for Mr Sexy Skipper to pick up. 'Don't get smashed or pick up any strange men before I get there.'

As if. Olivia preferred to wake up with a clear head and no regrets. Brie, not so much. Differences aside, they made a good team, trusted and looked out for each other. She flipped the end of the boa over her shoulder. 'I promise not to get smashed.'

'And…?'

'Hey, it's a party for yachties, there'll be men. And I don't care if they're strange so long as they're rich and I can persuade them to part with large sums of money. It's Christmas Eve and I'm hopeful.'

'Good luck, then, and be careful, okay? Hi, Liam…' Brie's voice instantly switched to smooth sensuality.

'Back at you,' Olivia murmured as she slipped out of their

suite and headed downstairs to summon the driver they'd organised exclusively for the entire evening.

As the chauffeured vehicle made its way across the bridge, Olivia's thoughts weren't so much on the harbour's glittering light show, but on the session she'd attended as a mandatory part of the genetics testing she'd undergone last week.

Her counsellor had said it could take weeks before she had the results. A chill ran deep through her bones. She'd never have taken the test if her mother hadn't made her *promise* to have it before her twenty-sixth birthday—the age her maternal grandmother had been when she'd been diagnosed with breast cancer.

So she'd done it. Two months late, but she'd done it. Fulfilled her mother's death-bed request. She'd been so busy, it had been easy to push aside her own needs—or as Brie had said, to bury her head in the sand—but now it was real and she could no longer deny the probability that she'd inherited the same mutant gene.

She wrapped her boa tighter around her shoulders. At least the result, whatever the verdict, would bring relief from the uncertainty she'd lived with as long as she could remember. And she'd deal with it in her own way—she had control of that at least.

Until then she refused to think about it. It was Christmas, she had a yacht race to win, a charity to run.

A life to live.

He was late but Jett Davies skirted the massive gold Christmas tree dominating the black marble foyer as he made his way up yet another sweeping staircase. The third level was an outdoor entertainment area and he caught a waft of briny harbour and freshly mown grass. Winking party lights cast a muted kaleidoscopic blush over the elite guests wearing anything and everything from a token nod to the festive season to the full Christmas get-up.

The guest list included the Who's Who of the yachting world from all over the globe, along with their glammed-up wives, lovers and/or mistresses. Seemed anyone with money to throw at Australia's prestigious Sydney to Hobart, one of the world's top and most difficult off-shore yacht races, was partaking of the evening's merrymaking.

A force-field of inquisitive eyes found him as he took a beer from a circulating waiter's tray. Eyes dead ahead, he cut straight to an antique spiral staircase he'd spotted in the corner. He hoped its steep and winding steps would discourage stiletto-heeled females from venturing up. He wasn't looking for an available woman. He was looking for his sister. Or had been until she'd texted him ten minutes ago to say she'd been caught up. Car problems, she'd told him—she'd let him know when she was on her way.

The stairs opened up onto a small viewing platform above the main outdoor entertainment area. Deserted—the way he liked it. Leaning on the rail, he watched the ferries track across the twinkling harbour.

Car problems. Breanna. He didn't know her well but he knew her well enough—there *was* no car and a man was definitely involved. He chugged back on his beer. Perhaps they had more in common than he'd thought.

The band below fired off a set of rocking Christmas tunes and his head throbbed. He didn't do the festive season—all that Kris Kringle nonsense, mistletoe madness and nostalgia.

So why had he agreed with Breanna's suggestion to meet her here instead of the hotel bar? Or *them* as it happened, because Breanna was sharing the suite with a girlfriend. Which had him wondering about the wearer of the strawberry lace panties and matching D-cups hanging over the shower rosette in the second bathroom…

Don't even think about it. He shook trouble away, checked the time. *Ten more minutes, Breanna, and I'm gone.*

Guests were starting to leave when Olivia finally found a moment alone and a semi-secluded spot to sit. She sucked on the straw of her Christmas Jones cocktail—her first alcoholic beverage for the evening—and leaned towards the balcony watching the incandescent candles amongst the garden shrubbery.

Hurry up, Brie.

She'd networked all evening to promote Snowflake and was delighted with the responses and promises for donations. But she and her crew had just come off five days' intensive training on the harbour, her feet were killing her and she was ready for some shut-eye.

Except Brie wasn't answering her phone—but she'd texted a winky face.

Did that mean she'd forgotten their arrangement to be there for each other at the end of the evening or what? Pushing up from her plastic party chair, she considered texting a response to say she was leaving but they'd made a promise to watch out for each other years ago and that had never changed.

Then, as if fate stepped in, her eyes snagged on the lower half of a man descending a pretty spiral staircase that she'd not noticed earlier. Even if men weren't a priority for Olivia, a little blip of pleasure registered on her radar. Black trousers covered legs that went all the way up—and up—the fabric lovingly clasped around muscled thighs, a firm, rounded, superhero-in-tights butt. Nice. A girl deserved a little lust blip every now and then and this blip was brightening by the second.

He reached the bottom step and the full-frontal, full impact hit with a *wow*. It was as if a flashbulb went off and Olivia blinked. There he was. A fully formed, three-dimensional, reach-out-with-both-hands-and-touch example of prime masculinity.

The stranger she'd *not* promised Brie she'd stay away from.

A mouth-watering stranger with bronzed olive skin that tempted any woman with a pulse to lick her way across that shadowed chin and linger awhile at the perfectly sculpted mouth.

His gaze met hers as if she'd summoned him to look her way. And he didn't look pleased about that. His eyebrows lowered, his mouth firmed and a muscle clenched in his jaw.

He looked kind of familiar but she'd totally have remembered a guy like him. She'd revelled in that initial instant of feminine power but now somehow he'd reversed the situation and that cool control she could always count on, and was so proud of, was disappearing like ice on a barbecue grill.

Steely black eyes with the power to tempt. To persuade. A shiver rippled down her spine. The power to take her will and flex it between his long slender fingers like so much overcooked spaghetti.

And Olivia felt hot, as she did when standing on the steaming deck of her yacht on a midsummer's day in Barbados. In the eye of a tropical storm even, because her usually strong sea legs were wobbly.

She was still looking at him and he was still looking at her and she swore she saw him mouth, 'Trouble'.

Oh yeah, absolutely. Double trouble in flashing neon lights. She'd never met a man who'd affected her this way—this hot, itchy, melty way. Not that they'd met… Had they?

Her pulse took off and her heart raced to catch up. He'd moved so subtly she hadn't noticed that he stood between her and the only route to the lower levels via the marble staircase. Intentional or not—she couldn't be sure and the anticipation hummed through her body like a build-up of static electricity.

Fight or flight? In yachting there was only one option. Unexpected and dangerous situations were dealt with in a calm, rational manner. Dealing with men was no different. Whatever happened, she would *not* run away.

With feigned indifference, she tossed her bedraggled twist of feathers over one shoulder, a silky strand catching on her lip as she drew in a wheezy breath to say, 'Hi.'

Jett knew it was time to leave when Trouble with the most eye-catching, reddest hair he'd ever seen spoke to him in that husky, breathless voice. But he couldn't tear his eyes away from the feather stuck to her pouty lower lip as she made little *puh-puh* noises to try and blow it off. He had the weirdest image of her blowing those little noises on his belly while her fingernails raked over his nipples and her hands swirled over his chest, his hips. Lower.

Damn.

Just say hi back and walk away. Fast. But his feet obeyed only that rapidly hardening part of his anatomy, and before he knew it he'd crossed the space between them, reached out and plucked the feather from what was a very pretty mouth. He felt a sensation of warm static before he snatched his fingers back.

'Thanks.' Eyes the colour of his signature Blue Mint Lagoon cocktail sparkled.

He curled tingling fingers into a fist. Another damn. Trouble with a sense of humour.

He saw…something…behind the fun and she looked away quickly, as if she hadn't meant to share. Her gaze flicked upwards and behind him. 'Anything interesting up there?'

There could be—if you want. 'Nope.'

'There has to be *something*, or why the staircase?'

He shrugged at her logic, stuck his hands in his trouser pockets. 'Just a couple of telescopes.'

'Really? I love stargazing.'

Even in the dimness he could see the fairy lines fanning out from the corners of her eyes and a splash of freckles over her nose. She enjoyed the outdoors whereas he rarely had the time for such indulgence. No doubt another spoiled socialite with plenty of time to waste. 'Too much light pollution in the city,' he told her, rocking back on his heels. 'I'd say they're for watching the harbour.'

'Oh, yes, why didn't I think of that?'

She walked to the bottom of the spiral stairs and peered up, one slender hand on the rail. Sun-kissed skin. Neat unvarnished nails. A nice flash of abundant cleavage. Man, he had to stop staring like some pre-pubescent teenager—

'Did you sneak a peek?'

'What?' His guilty gaze shot somewhere over her shoulder, then he realised she was talking about *telescopes*. 'Ah… no.'

She cast him an unreadable look then started up. 'Why not?'

'Because— Hey, you won't want to go up like that.' In one stride he was there, his fingers closing firmly over hers. The contact sent a zing up his forearm. All that static build-up discharged in one hit.

She must have felt it too because her eyes widened and her mouth dropped open. 'Like…what?'

He yanked his hand away. 'Those heels—you'll break your neck.'

'Only if I—' On cue, one stiletto slipped and caught in the iron lace doyley tread. She yanked it free. 'Cripes. I see your point.'

He shook his head. 'Why don't you—?'

'Okay…' On the third tread, she toed off her shoes. And

groaned lustily—a sound that did dangerous things to his already wide-awake libido. 'Relief at last. Why didn't I think of that earlier?' She handed them to him over the rail, avoiding skin contact. 'Hold these till I get back.'

'I…' Siren-red patent, they were warm from her feet and smelled of new leather. Dangling them from one hand, he watched her climb, toenails painted to match, strong toned calves. Smooth, golden thighs disappeared beneath the shadows of her dress's short hemline. She moved fast and without effort, as if she worked out a lot. A yachtie's woman?

If Jett were the skipper, he'd keep her below decks and all to himself for the entire journey. Yep, naked and barefoot—he could get creative with feet, a little warm brandy and sweet ripe apricots—

Hell. He shook his head to clear it. Now was *not* the time to be coming up with new recipes.

He wasn't looking for a woman, dammit. He had to remind himself again because his mind seemed to have forgotten. He was waiting for Breanna, half-sister, who was doing whatever, with whomever. Everything, it seemed, except checking in with him. He should go back to the hotel, catch up on some sleep. Away from trouble in a red dress.

But he had her shoes. He could hardly just abandon them here. And he didn't want to leave without one more glimpse of her. Which wasn't quite true because he wanted more than a glimpse. A lot more.

He placed one foot on the bottom step and made an instant decision. Forget Breanna; she hadn't answered his call. Instead, a little up-close and personal might just be on the menu for tonight. No trouble, he assured himself; he didn't want or need to know who she was. A hot lick of anticipation stroked down his body and his steps quickened while his stomach tightened and his mouth watered. One sweet taste. The perfect dessert to end the evening.

* * *

Olivia hoped the sound of her heart pounding its way out of her chest wasn't audible. Hearing his footsteps on the metal treads, she turned as the guy appeared on the platform behind her. And was blown away again by the sight of all that blatant masculinity. Which was unsettling because she'd relegated men to the bottom of her list of priorities a long time ago.

Determined not to let him see how much he was affecting her, she moved to the larger telescope and adjusted it for a view of the party-goers milling around Circular Quay to distract herself and give her time to think what to do next.

She could feel his gaze stroking heat down her spine and the backs of her thighs. His musky masculine scent wafted her way. As diversions went, the impromptu viewing idea was an epic fail—she had no idea if the lens was in focus or not. As for coming up with what to do next, heck, all she could think was how his lips would taste… 'Amazing,' she murmured.

'Have to agree with you there.'

She turned to him but he wasn't looking at the twinkling carpet of lights on the harbour, he was watching her and screwing with her equilibrium again. She deflected with, 'Are you sailing in the race?'

'Not me.'

She noticed he didn't ask the same of her. No doubt the women he associated with were willowy, fragile types who were afraid of breaking a fingernail or a sweat. 'Sailing's not your thing?'

He shrugged, his hands in his trouser pockets. 'In case you're wondering, I'm here for the free food.'

She laughed spontaneously. 'Ah, it was you who demolished all the prawns.' She gestured to the crowd on the dance floor below who were swaying their hips and waving their little gold bells to 'Jingle Bell Rock'. 'So, were you getting your groove on down there on the dance floor tonight?'

He shook his head, a smile on his lips. 'I'm not the prawn thief and since you didn't ask me to dance, no, I wasn't.' And oh, my, in the shadowy light, the cutest, *innocent-little-boy* dimples flirted at the corners of his mouth. It kick-started some sort of weird maternal instinct when what it should have been doing was to warn her to run in the opposite direction.

Between talking up Snowflake to anyone who'd listen, she'd danced her feet to death—*and* had continued to promote Snowflake while bopping. 'I didn't see you…' Men never joked with her, but this one was—at least she *thought* he was—and she trailed off, feeling awkward.

'Haven't been here long,' he told her at last. 'Anyway the Macarena's not really my thing.'

'Not even the Christmas Macarena with the jingle bells and reindeer antlers to wiggle along with?'

'I don't do Christmas.' He walked to the railing, gazed at the harbour.

'No?' she said to his back. 'What, like, you don't do the whole mistletoe, eggnog, Secret Santa thing—or is it a personal belief?'

'Two words: Christmas commercialism.' When he turned to her, his eyes had lost their spark.

She wasn't buying it—something had happened in his past that had nothing to do with Christmas commercialism.

'It doesn't have to be,' she said. 'Unless you let it.'

He shrugged. 'Anyway, who needs mistletoe? If you want to kiss someone you should go ahead and kiss them, wouldn't you agree?' He seemed to lean towards her. 'Why wait for Christmas?'

Why, indeed? He *had* leaned towards her. 'It depends on whether that person wants to be kissed.' She told herself she didn't. She *wished* she didn't but, oh, she really did. Every muscle in her body tightened and softened and her lips were practically puckering up in anticipation. 'But a little festive smooch beneath the mistletoe's always fun.' *And infinitely safer than shadowed, secluded corners.*

Dark brows rose. 'Always?' Somehow, as if she'd willed it, he was within touching distance. She could feel the heat radiating from his body, like runaway power from a nuclear reactor. His eyes seared her with dark intensity.

'Usually,' she amended with a laugh that sounded nervous to her own ears. 'With a few Christmas drinks under one's belt and everyone bursting with good cheer, it's harmless enough.' Unlike that nuclear reaction approaching critical mass in the narrowing space between them.

Had she said *harmless*? It was a foregone conclusion; this virtual stranger was going to kiss her and she was going to let him and excitement tingled through her body like a swarm of hungry fire ants.

'So convince me Christmas is worth all the fuss,' he murmured, reaching out and fingering the ends of her hair.

She wondered that she couldn't smell the singe in the air and had to fight for her composure again. 'Where do you want me to begin?'

'Refresh my memory and run that Secret Santa bit by me again. Is it the same as Kris Kringle?'

'Not necessarily,' she decided, and ventured into uncharted waters. 'First off...' she reached up on tiptoe, slid her boa around his neck then stepped backwards, letting it slide through her fingers until she was holding the very ends '...and most importantly...' she met his eyes boldly even though her legs felt as though they were stumbling through sand '...it has to be a secret.'

'Trust me, I won't tell a soul.' His voice was silk seduc-

tion, sliding over her and all but stealing away any sense
she might have had.

'Trust you? Where are my shoes, by the way?'

'Safe.' He glanced down between their bodies then back
to her face. 'I like you barefoot.'

'So do I, it's so liberating, don't you think?' Something
danced behind his smouldering gaze and her feet tickled—
as if he were sucking them right into his mouth. One toe at
a time. 'You'd be my Secret Santa?'

'For you…' he ran one lazy fingertip over her left collarbone, making her shiver '…I could be persuaded. Are you
sleeping with anyone?'

The question came out of nowhere and he spoke casually,
as if he were asking whether she liked sugar in her coffee.
A tugging sensation she'd never experienced unfurled low
in her belly and her cheeks burned with fire. 'Not that it's
any of your business.' Confusion warred with irritation at
his smooth, almost lazy arrogance.

'It is if I'm going to kiss you the way I want to kiss you.'
His fingertip moved from her collarbone to skim across
her lower lip.

Her lips burned and the low tugging sensation pulled into
a tight knot. Her habitual defensiveness evaporated. What
was it about this man that she'd throw away any sense of
caution?

She'd obviously been struck by some random insanity.

Over the years, she'd grown accustomed to guys accusing her of being intimidating or closed off. Snowflake and
her studies had taken her focus and consumed her energy
for so long it hadn't left time for anything else, particularly
any fleeting and indulgent liaisons with the opposite sex.
She had more important things on her agenda, such as making a difference for people with serious and terminal illness.

But it was Christmas Eve and random insanity had indeed

struck because right now on the top of this year's Christmas list was his lips on hers. Her Secret Santa—dark as midnight, and an exciting mystery to unravel and enjoy. Just for tonight.

He watched her, reading her thoughts. Knowing she was going to say yes. But then he said, 'When a woman tells me it's none of my business, it's usually because she wants me to kiss her regardless of the man she's sleeping with.'

Oh, he was cocky, arrogant, full of himself. An irate breath caught in her throat. 'Of course I'm not sleeping with anyone or I wouldn't be standing here with you.' She drew herself up tall. 'And if you think I'm that kind of woman then you have very poor taste and we have nothing in common.'

'On the contrary, I have very discerning taste when it comes to women. If I thought you were lying you wouldn't see me for dust.'

She relaxed a bit, if you could call letting out a slow breath and sucking in another relaxing. 'Good, then. Because…because I want you to kiss me…that way.'

His mouth quirked and he touched the ends of her hair again as the band struck up their version of 'All I Want for Christmas'. 'Glad we cleared that up.'

'Me too.'

'Now, where were we?'

She licked dry lips. 'Secret Santa.'

'Ah…' The devil with a smile lurked in his black eyes as his hands slid up her bare arms to her shoulders.

The hairs on her arms rose in response and she shivered and met his gaze. 'Except you look like more of a sinner than a Santa.'

He pulled the top half of her body into stunning and breath-stealing contact, his lips tantalisingly close to hers. 'Which do you want me to be?'

CHAPTER TWO

OF COURSE THE GUY was a mind-reader as well because he knew her instant preference for sin over safe and his body hardened against hers and his fingers tightened on her arms. Up close Olivia could see gold stardust in his irises and her own desire reflected back.

And heaven help her, wild and wicked was exactly what she needed tonight. She wanted to lose herself to oblivion. To dive headlong into those dark depths and surrender to the promised pleasure she saw there—

Except...this whole scenario was straight out of her private fantasies but now it was real and happening and moving too fast and she couldn't catch her breath.

'Wait.' She dragged a hand up between them, pushed it against his chest. Hard as concrete. But warm and sculpted, and to her dismay her fingers spread over the undulating surface of their own volition. 'Just. Wait.'

'Are you okay?' He loosened his hold and leaned back. 'Because if you're not s—'

'I'm fine.' She sucked in air. 'Absolutely fine.' Or would be if she could establish the same footing with this godlike, devilishly attractive being in front of her. *Not* surrender, she told herself. Equality.

'Tell you what,' he said, slowly. 'Why don't we—?'

'Yes. Why don't we?' And before she changed her mind

again she wound her fingers around the ends of her boa for a firm hold. Here was a rare chance to grab life and living with both hands and reel him in. She saw the glimpse of surprise in his dark eyes as she reached up on tiptoe, yanked him close and planted her mouth on his.

And oh, this man didn't disappoint. As their lips connected she was sure she heard a hiss. More of a sizzle, actually. Heat met heat and that smouldering spark that had been arcing between them since they'd first laid eyes on each other ignited. She felt it catch, deep down inside, sending showers of sparkles to every extremity.

He pulled back a fraction. 'Is control your thing, darling?' A rogue's smile danced over his lips and his eyes lit with amusement.

In a different situation his condescending *darling* would have annoyed her, but she didn't have time to be annoyed because he was already moving his lips over hers once more and playing the game—his way. He was mayhem and magic and completely irresistible.

Determined to keep up, she matched his enthusiasm, leaning in and arching her body against his. Their lips softened and parted. Merged. His flavour invaded her mouth as breath mingled, tongues met and entwined.

She tasted wealth and power and persuasion. Danger in a will that matched her own. And for the first time in her life she wondered if a man—specifically, *this* man—might be more than she could handle.

But this was just a little harmless flirtation on a balcony. And Christmas Eve was about midnight madness and whimsical delights.

With eager hands she acquainted herself with his body. Hard slabs of muscle, the soft indent below his Adam's apple. The springy masculine hair that sprouted from the V of his open-necked shirt. He was a gift and she was a kid on Christmas morning.

His hands were busy too, warm and firm on her shoulders, beneath her hair, down her back, toying with the top of her zipper. She gave an involuntary shiver—the tiny metal teeth were the only things holding up her dress and preventing her from standing here in nothing but red lace bikini panties.

On a balcony metres away from a hundred or more guests.

With a man she didn't know.

Someone had so spiked that cocktail.

Or maybe it was time to live on the edge for once.

Damn. Jett managed, with difficulty, to pry his lips from hers. 'I knew it.' He leaned back and searched her face through a fog of lust. 'Was that a *fun* shiver of delight and anticipation or do we need the festive foliage?'

'Definitely fun.' She smiled, those effervescent starlight eyes sparkling. 'No mistletoe required.'

'Thank God for that, then; I've no idea where to find any.'

'What did you mean by: *you knew it*?' she asked.

He hadn't intended to say it aloud and blamed it on working all day after last night's all-hours drink-fest. He slid his hands over lush feminine curves, lingering on her hips. 'That you'd be a refreshing surprise at the end of a very ordinary day.'

Her hands covered his. 'Not trouble?'

He touched his nose to hers. 'You're big trouble.'

'I can live with that.' Unrepentant, she entwined their fingers and rubbed her lips over his. 'How about you?'

He sucked her sweet taste from his lips. 'Mmm…' Strawberries and pineapple with a dash of vodka. 'So can I,' he murmured before leaning down for a second helping.

More of this out-of-control feeling he'd not experienced

since his teens. His erection throbbed and ached and burned as if it were his first time. His head spun with the fragrance of her skin, her hair and the way she shifted against him—breasts, belly, thighs all aligned perfectly, as if she'd been made to order. It wasn't his lack of sleep sending him slightly insane—it was her.

Crazy was good—so were her lips: warm and pliant and mobile. He'd been working manic hours for months now; he needed a change of pace and didn't everyone need a bit of wholesome crazy now and then? As she said, it was Christmas. It wasn't called the silly season for nothing. 'Maybe there's something in this Secret Santa business after all,' he murmured into her ear.

Her cheek lifted into a smile against his. 'Definitely,' she agreed, winding slender arms that smelled of sun-warmed apricots and cool cucumber around his neck.

With a growl, he walked her backwards until she butted up against the wall. He might have stopped a moment to admire the Titian-haired picture of perfection before him but patience had never been one of his strengths when it came to beautiful, willing women. He ground his pelvis against her and was rewarded when she arched her hips in response and sent up a little whimper of longing and capitulation. Her fingernails dug into his shoulders and she moaned.

'Yes, darling, I've got what you want.' One hand cupped the back of her head to hold her in place while he continued to savour the sweet delight of her mouth, the other glided over a breast, finding a taut little bead that hardened instantly beneath his touch.

He rolled it between his fingers through the fabric and she moaned again—the soft yielding sound compelling him to put his lips there. His teeth. To nip at the silk, to close his mouth over the bud and suck. To soothe her while he tortured himself with what he couldn't do. At least, not here.

But the sounds of the party below seemed muted and irrelevant in the shadows. He looked into her desire-drenched eyes while he smoothed his palms over her dress, sliding the skin-warmed silk up her thighs. Up, over her hips. 'You like what I'm doing to you.'

She pressed her lips together but a little mewing sound escaped.

'There's more,' he promised, his fingers finding and exploring the smooth flesh of her inner thighs. Her head rolled back against the wall and her eyes darted towards the stairs. 'No one's going to come up here,' he reassured her in his best persuasive tone. 'Trust me.'

Wide-eyed, she looked back at him, disbelief etched between her slim brows. Her arms slid down to her sides, apparently incapable of holding on any longer.

Satisfaction rolled through him. She was his. Or would be, before the night was done.

'Hey,' he murmured, inching his hand higher, drawing tiny circles with his fingertips and feeling her legs start to tremble. 'You chose sinner over Santa, work with me here.'

She shook her head. 'I...'

'A good choice.' His fingers found satin and lace. *Hot and damp* satin and lace, and he knew they were halfway to where they both wanted to go.

But then she tensed. Sucked on her bottom lip.

'Hey, it's Christmas,' he teased gently.

'But—'

He cut off her protest with a slow, soothing kiss until he felt her soften once more. 'Okay, forget sinner,' he said against her lips. 'We'll play Secret Santa instead, and he won't do anything you don't want him to. You're in the driver's seat, and a few dozen guests within earshot over the balcony will tell you the same.'

In the driver's seat? Olivia might have laughed but she

was half out of her mind. Delirious and blinded by a desire and an urgency she'd never experienced.

A mistake, that cocktail, because she should have been able to resist. She'd never had a problem resisting men. But this man wasn't just any man. He was wicked and persuasive and clever, and his hand was *inside* her panties, touching her—thrilling her—with just one flick of his finger over her most sensitive place and any second now she was going to shatter into a million pieces and she knew she'd never be the same ever again.

'Come for me.' The voice at her ear transported her to undiscovered realms, lifting her higher to some pinnacle just beyond her reach—

The distinctive beat of Coldplay jolted her back to some vague resemblance of reality. *Brie.* With trembling fingers she yanked her phone from the jewelled bag slung over one shoulder. Brie's picture smiled at her. She glared back, found her voice. '*Now* you call.'

His fingers stilled but his hand remained, hot and arousing and slippery, inside her panties. 'Is it an emergency?'

'I don't think so, b—'

'Then get rid of whoever it is.'

His dictatorial tone irritated. 'No.' However tempting, she couldn't—*wouldn't*—ignore her friend until she knew she was okay. 'I have to get this.'

Reluctantly, she tried to push his hand away. It didn't budge. In the end she had no choice but to answer—breathlessly. 'Hi…' She closed her eyes as if not seeing him would somehow make him disappear. Resisted squirming against his fingers—for all of three seconds or so. 'You all right?'

'I'm great. Fabulous. What took you so long to answer?'

Brie wasn't the only one feeling fabulous. 'I'm…' what the hell, Brie would be happy for her '…being seduced by a man in black. He's my Secret Sinner-Santa.'

'Believe it,' he whispered into her ear.

She pressed her lips together to stop the urge to smile and squeal at the same time and felt the scrape of his bristled jaw against her neck.

Pause at the other end of the phone. 'Oh. Okay. Sorry I'm late but I'm here now. Are you still at the party? I've looked everywhere.'

Not quite everywhere, Brie. 'Yes…' *Omigod*… His thumb was doing something amazing. How could she think, let alone carry on any semblance of intelligent conversation while he manipulated her with such devastating expertise? Darts of pleasure were shooting through her body and lights were coalescing and swirling in front of her eyes. 'Still… here. Already told you…'

'Where?' Irritated impatience.

'I'm…not…good company right now.'

'I disagree,' murmured the muffled voice, this time against the top of her breasts.

'What?' Brie's voice, confused. 'Is there someone with you?'

'Must be…the hand—*the band*.' A breeze with scent of summer and sex cooled the raging inferno in her cheeks while Secret Sinner-Santa assumed control and drove her to a rising crescendo of delight and desire and sheer desperation with every manic beat of her pulse.

'And what do you mean *not good company*? Ken's waiting, stay right where you are, wherever it is, I'm coming to get you.'

'No… *I'm* coming…'

And she was. Right now. Right here. Awareness narrowed down to a pinpoint of sparkling sensation and the hand holding her phone slid from her ear as the world receded like the tide before a tsunami.

She heard the disembodied moan—part plea, all pleasure—sprint up her throat as the crescendo peaked and rolled, sending her tumbling over the silvery crest and showering her body with gold.

A slow sigh escaped her lips. Sweet, sugar-coated bliss. Sagging against his hard-packed stomach and an impressive erection, she floated down, her feet still not quite touching the ground. She wasn't exactly a virgin but no guy had ever done it for her the way he had. Now she understood how sinfully, devastatingly irresistible the right man's touch could be.

On the downside, it reduced even the most rational, self-disciplined person to a quivering, mindless mass. It had changed a sane sensible woman with a mind and opinion of her own—and an ability to say no—to someone she didn't recognise.

She flopped her head back against the wall and looked up at him, committing his face to memory, then kissed her fingers and pressed them to his lips. 'Merry Christmas.'

From somewhere near her left elbow, she heard Brie's voice. 'Olivia, are you *drunk*?'

'No.' Just not herself. Without taking her eyes off him— the way a sailor wouldn't take her eyes off an approaching storm front—she raised the phone to her ear. 'Meet you on the driveway. Two minutes.'

She disconnected and began sidestepping along the wall. Away. Now she'd had a moment to come to her senses, all she wanted was to be by herself and think about what she'd done. What *he'd* done. *Oh my God.* Her inner muscles clenched in fond remembrance. Casual sex on a balcony was *not* who she was. She didn't know what to say, so she went with, 'Thanks.'

He caught her arm, his dark, almost familiar eyes a cool shade of cynical. 'So that's it? *Thanks?*'

'Yes. What else do you want me to say?'

His nostrils flared and a muscle twitched along his jaw. 'We haven't finished.'

Oh. She couldn't help it; her gaze flicked down between them and her whole body felt weak and fizzy at the tempting display of manly magnificence outlined in fine black fabric. Pity she wasn't going to see it in all its glory. 'Sorry. I am, truly.' *You'll never know how much.* 'But my friend's waiting.'

He remained where he was, expression dangerously impassive. 'Better hurry, then. And watch your step.'

A shiver ran down her spine but she realised he hadn't meant it as a threat but a warning to take care on the stairs. Hiding his annoyance that she was running off without so much as a name uttered between them. Or was he relieved, as she was, that this had just been a little harmless Christmas Eve flirtation? No, she very much doubted he felt relieved.

Coldplay started up again, making her jump. 'Thirty seconds, Brie, and I'm there,' she said to the phone. 'Have you met up with Jett yet?' She was proud of her casual question and breezy voice as she all but stumbled to the stairs, scrambling for the handrail and tripping over her feet on her way down, a pair of eyes following her every move. She could feel them, dark and intense down her spine.

'Forget Jett,' Brie told her in a tight-lipped voice. 'He's obviously forgotten *me*. He can damn well find his own way back.'

Olivia slowed her mad dash when she saw Brie pacing the circular drive beside their chauffeured car. But not soon enough, because Brie had caught sight of her first. One slim eyebrow hiked and a smile played around her lips. Taking in Olivia's no-doubt ravished and guilty-as-sin appearance.

'Let's go,' Olivia said, pulling her evening bag off her shoulder and crushing it between her fingers.

Brie didn't move. '*Sinner-Santa*, Liv. You weren't kidding after all.'

'It's Christmas.' The car was idling, the door was open and Olivia moved fast. 'What are we waiting for?'

'Such a hurry.' Brie stepped into her path, sharp eyes scanning Olivia's bare feet. 'Cinderella only lost one shoe.'

Oh. *Crap.* 'Never mind.' She darted around Brie, muttering, 'Thanks, Ken,' and sweeping past their driver as if the hounds of hell were about to catch up with her. 'What's a pair of shoes?'

She piled into the back seat, her pesky observant friend settled in beside her, and Ken closed the door. Brie pressed a button and the privacy screen rose. As the vehicle progressed sedately towards the gates she picked a feather off Olivia's shoulder, held it up as evidence. 'And where's the rest of my boa?'

Leaning back against the head rest, Olivia closed her eyes, which only drew attention to the riot happening inside her. 'There was a wink in those words, Brie. And a nudge. And I'm warning you now they won't get you anywhere.'

She felt the seat dip as Brie shifted towards her. 'BFFs share.'

'There's nothing to share.' Blood rushed to Olivia's cheeks. 'Not a thing.'

'Well, fa-la-la-la-la!' She punctuated each meaningfully loaded syllable with an exclamation mark. 'Not a thing, hmm?'

She blew out a resigned breath. 'Okay, not quite not a thing.'

'Not quite?'

'No. Yes. No. Doesn't matter.'

'What's his name and are you seeing him again?'

'No to both.'

'Oh.' Brie sounded disappointed. Olivia's emotions were

so all over the place she didn't know how she herself felt. 'And if I did know his name, I wouldn't tell you. Big fat *huh* to BFFs. You haven't talked to me about Jett, so we're even.'

'Jett's my brother, not my lover, it's hardly the same. And if you must know, I haven't talked about Jett because he asked me not to.'

'Why? Oh, Brie, he's not done something, like, really bad, has he?' She remembered Brie talking about his reluctance to open up and dropped her voice to a whisper. 'Like, has he been in prison…?'

'No.' Brie laughed. 'Nothing like that. But he's in the media—'

'Famous?' Olivia nodded slowly. 'I'd know him.'

'Livvie, you've been so focused on your work and studies and getting Snowflake up and going these past few years, I doubt it. And you really know how to deflect the conversation away from you.'

'I told you. Okay, I didn't tell you.' She lowered the window to let the breeze cool her face. 'We didn't… But he… I…' She smiled—she couldn't help it. 'It truly was an orgasmic experience.'

'Wow.'

'Totally.' But Olivia's buoyancy faded and something not so cheerful hooked in her chest. She pushed it away hard and joked, 'Sinner-Santas are strictly for Christmas Eve. They disappear in a twinkle of Santa's sleigh bell at midnight. And…' she checked her watch '…Christmas Eve's over.'

It was officially Christmas Day. The two of them were supposed to be having Christmas lunch with the mysterious brother—if he bothered to turn up. And Boxing Day it was all hands on deck, meaning if he didn't show Brie wouldn't catch up with him for days. 'You've heard nothing from Jett?'

She gave a tight shrug. 'He texted he was on his way to the party. Since then, nothing.'

'He knows you're in the race, doesn't he?'

'Yeah. He was coming to Sydney anyway, so I suggested we could celebrate the festive day together. Maybe it wasn't a good idea.'

'He'll turn up, Brie. And I can't wait to meet him.'

Well, if that didn't take the celebration cake. Jett watched her flee, red hair flying, relieved he hadn't gone any further. Still, it could've been an even hotter night in the city—if he hadn't found out who she was. He shifted his stance to accommodate the swelling in his trousers that wasn't likely to subside any time soon.

Trouble in strawberry lace D-cups. In the flesh.

And there'd been an abundance of that. Smooth and creamy and *damn*. Dragging off the feathers she'd left around his neck, he stuffed them in his back pocket. He could smell her skin—apricots and cucumber.

He might have followed, if only to return her shoes—then persuade her that the festivities should be extended a few hours because it was still Christmas Eve somewhere in the world—until he'd heard her mention his name. *His* name.

He'd been fooling around with Breanna's friend.

A harsh bark of laughter escaped. What were the odds? Walking to the balcony, he searched out the driveway mostly hidden by a corner of the house. He caught sight of Breanna in the car's headlights. He didn't have to wait long to see a flash of red zip past her and disappear into the car.

The car accelerated down the drive and he turned away, facing into the breeze blowing up from the harbour. He needed to cool off. One minute without an audience—he shifted again—better make that five minutes. The excruciating pity of it all was she'd had no idea who he was and he might have enjoyed an evening—and a hell of a lot more—with someone who wasn't out for his name and fame.

Breanna's friend.

Sexy.

Available.

Not a good idea.

He scowled at the wall where she'd come apart beneath his hand, dress hiked, thighs quivering and her moans of pleasure sobbing on the air. The scent of her arousal lingered. Hell. He'd be lucky if he slept a wink tonight.

He'd known she was trouble the instant he'd clapped eyes on her.

But—he couldn't help but grin—trouble had never come in such a tempting package.

CHAPTER THREE

'THIS IS THE LIFE.'

After five days of hard slog on the harbour, Olivia was enjoying a traditional Christmas Day breakfast of champagne, strawberries and Danish pastries while a little light Christmas music played in the background. She wasn't accustomed to inactivity but two days of R and R were well deserved and a necessary break before the hard work, both mental and physical, that the next few days would demand of them.

Brie, looking as boneless as Olivia felt on the other recliner, studied the forest-green lacquered toenails as she wiggled them in front of her. 'This is so not the life; you'd be bored to distraction in a couple of days.'

'True. I should wander down to the gym in a bit.'

'Nuh-uh.' Brie nibbled on a croissant. 'No workouts allowed today.'

Olivia flopped back, almost relieved. She'd barely slept after all. 'If you say so.'

Jeez, she was so easily seduced. *Seduced. Workout...* Hot, steamy, sweaty— 'The pool, then. A quick twenty laps.'

Brie lifted her sunglasses off her nose to stare at her. 'After this feast? I don't think so. You're just feeling the twitchy after-effects of last night's indulgence with Secret Sinner-Santa.'

A shiver of remembered delight danced down her spine and settled low and warm between her thighs. 'You are so right. I never knew sinning was that much fun.'

'Woo-hoo, now you do.'

She'd been involved short-term with a guy a long time ago and it had been more about a loss of innocence than sinning— or even enjoyment, because with Jason there hadn't been much enjoyment, for her at least. But since she and Brie had met at the hospice where Brie's dad and Olivia's mum were dying, she'd been so focused on getting Pink Snowflake up and running and her plans for a retreat, she'd had no time for guys, relationships. Sex.

But last night... Olivia smiled. He'd whetted her appetite. It was as if that dormant part inside her had finally woken up and demanded breakfast.

'He was good, then?'

She sighed. 'The man had *the best* hands. *And* he knew how to use them.' She smiled, lost for an instant, reliving the pleasure. Heat spurted through her lower belly and she reached for her glass of sparkling mineral water. 'The fact that he was built like a god was a bonus. He had these eyes...' She blinked the images—him—away. He was long gone.

And switched topics. 'So Jett made it back here eventually.' She'd heard him come in after she and Brie had said goodnight and had been tempted to go pour herself a glass of water from the kitchenette, just to sneak a peek. But she'd changed her mind when she heard their muffled voices through her closed door. She'd not wanted to intrude. 'Was he lost?'

'I don't think so.' Brie stirred her coffee. 'What I can't work out is that he said he'd made it to the party late and all would become clear.'

'That's cryptic,' Olivia said.

'Good morning.'

The deep male voice had Olivia pushing upright and turning to the open doorway. 'Hi…' As she spoke her smile dropped away; her entire body started to dissolve.

How had he known where to find her? *What are you doing here?* But the words never passed her frozen lips because even as she asked the question she knew the answer.

Jett.

Her not-so-secret Sinner-Santa.

One and the same and ambling away from the door as if he'd been leaning casually against it. Listening in. Laughing at her. Looking so, so smug. Every indignant hair on the back of her neck rose and she pushed suddenly sweaty hands over her trembling thighs and down the skirt of her festive emerald-trimmed white sundress.

He wore khaki shorts and a white polo shirt and brown sandals. Plenty of bare leg sprinkled with dark masculine hair. Then she caught sight of a pair of red stiletto sandals set neatly on the floor beside the door frame.

Brie didn't notice the incriminating evidence and rose. 'Jett, glad to see you're awake at last. Did you sleep well?'

'Not bad.' His eyes flicked to Olivia. 'Considering.'

The eyes. Brie's eyes, Olivia realised, seeing the pair of them close together. How had she missed that? Both tall and equally stunning with their bronzed complexions and midnight gazes. Brie leaned in and pecked him on the cheek. 'Merry Christmas.' She turned to Olivia. 'Jett, I want you to meet my best friend, Olivia Wishart. Liv, this is Jett Davies. My brother.'

He nodded to Olivia and a corner of his mouth quirked. 'Already had the pleasure.'

At the mention of pleasure, fingers of guilty heat stroked her belly and lower. How outrageous and inappropriate of him to mention it. Aware of the height disadvantage, she forced herself to stand. *Almost* eye to eye. Give or take a good six inches. But her legs felt like wet seaweed and the sun shimmered on all that bronzed masculine skin. Sliding on her sunglasses, she snapped out, 'It's always helpful to put a name to the face.'

'You two know each other?' Brie's gaze darted between the two of them then settled on Olivia, puzzled.

'Last night.' Jett fired the two words across the patio like an accusation or a challenge, then reached down beside him and swung the shoes on two fingers. 'You left these behind. Cinderella.'

She watched, appalled. Those same fingers had wrought wicked and unimaginable pleasure on her most intimate and private parts. When Olivia made no attempt to step forward and take them, he set them back by the door with a lazy grin, his eyes stroking down her body as if reacquainting himself with her shape, stopping at her bare feet. 'I'm sorry, were these your only shoes?'

'No.' She drew in a breath, embarrassed beyond belief, furious at his attitude. If Brie hadn't been there Olivia would have told him exactly where to put those shoes. 'Of course they're not. It's easy to forget—I'm a barefoot tragic.'

His lips pulled wide at that as if enjoying some private joke. 'I'll keep that in mind.'

'Whatever for?' She clenched her hands behind her back so he wouldn't see how they shook. Those little-boy dimples mocked her. And annoyed her—she doubted he'd ever been innocent in his life. 'Why are you *smirking*?'

Still grinning, he shrugged, lifting his arms to waist height, palms up. 'Why are you so uptight?'

'Olivia?' Brie's voice broke into their conversation. 'Can you help me in the kitchen a moment?'

'We don't have a kitchen here,' she reminded her, not taking her eyes off Jett. 'We have a private butler.' *And a problem.* She snatched up the magazine she'd been intending to read. 'Why don't you two catch up? I'm going to take that dip in the pool, then I'm going to shower and get ready for our yummy traditional Christmas feast. I expect you're looking forward to sharing Christmas lunch with Brie, Jett, as much as she's looking forward to sharing it with you.'

The force of her killer glare and unsubtle reference to Christmas luncheon rocked Jett back on his heels. 'You bet.' Still grinning, he watched her pick up her shoes, enjoying the rear view of touchable bottom and lightly honeyed thighs as she bent over. She stepped past the glass doors, into the entertainment area, skirted a low table where she dropped her magazine beside her boa, which he'd left there, then crossed the room and disappeared from view.

Man, she was hot. 'I guess she's mad at me. Must be the Christmas thing.'

'Christmas thing?' Brie murmured, following his gaze. 'Oh, you mean Secret Sinner-Santa—she mentioned it.'

That too.

'You didn't introduce yourselves?'

'Why would we? It was just a...' He trailed off. Probably not the wisest thing to say to the best friend. 'Should I try to—?'

'No. Sinner-Santas are for Christmas Eve—so I heard. I think if I was her, I'd want a little alone time. How long were you standing there?'

'Long enough.'

'Okay, here's the thing, Jett.'

She got real serious. It was always an unnerving experience with Breanna to be looking at his own eyes, and right now his sister's were clear and cool.

'Olivia's my best friend. She's also the most generous, caring person I know. She's been too busy studying and setting up her own charity and a dozen other activities over the past few years to have any sort of social life—and goodness knows she needs it. I can't remember the last time she—'

'What we get up to is between me and Olivia.'

'And that's fine with me. You're my brother, Jett, and I care about you. Whether or not you believe it, whether or not you want it, it's there and it's unconditional. But I care about Livvie too. She's like a sister to me. So be careful, okay?'

He felt awkward around sentimental words when they were directed his way and shrugged them off. 'Hey, it's cool. I don't need your care and concern, but thanks anyway.'

Her expression switched instantly and regret brimmed in eyes that looked at him as if he were a sick puppy. 'I can't forgive Dad for what he did.'

Ah. No. No way in hell was he getting into deep and meaningfuls with Breanna about their shared parentage. 'Forget it,' he muttered. He strode to a table sheltered by an umbrella. Ice clinked as he picked up a jug of chilled water.

'So as part of our familial connection,' she continued, while he poured himself a tall glass, and another for Breanna, 'I keep up with the press goings-on and your social-media updates. I know your fast and loose reputation with sophisticated women who know what the game's all about. A girl in every port.'

He held out one glass to Breanna and threw the contents of the other down his suddenly dry throat. *She'd kept tabs on him for the past three years?* Hell. 'So?' he said, meeting her gaze.

'Olivia's not like that.'

'You saying last night she wasn't herself, then?'

She waved her hands about her, unsure. 'I don't know about last night, I wasn't there. I'm just telling you what I know about who she is. How she is. Usually.'

'She's hardly talking to me as it is. Don't worry, I won't lay a finger on her. Or anything else.'

Unless she asks me to. He grew hard just thinking about last night and where his fingers had been. He refilled his glass and sat on one of the recliners to hide the incriminating evidence building a bonfire in his shorts. Yeah, any glimmer of reciprocation on the best friend's part and all bets were off.

Breanna took the other recliner. 'I'm not saying don't have a good time, Jett. She deserves some fun. She's in *desperate need* of some fun. But…' She shrugged, seemed to consider. 'Fine. You're both adults, I'll leave it up to you. And her.'

He nodded. 'It'll be okay,' he reassured her. 'You're racing tomorrow. I take it she's sailing with you?'

'Livvie's the reason I'm going. We've sailed together heaps.' She hugged her shoulders and smiled. 'I can't wait. It's turning out to be such a great Christmas.'

'Yeah.' His gaze flicked to the harbour, filled with myriad different craft on the white-flecked water, some decked with tinsel or coloured streamers. He'd never tell his sister he always spent the twenty-fifth of December doing anything so long as it wasn't related to Christmas.

When his trip to Thailand with a couple of mates had been cancelled at the last minute, he'd decided, on the spur of the moment, to accept Breanna's invitation to meet up in Sydney. He'd not realised he'd accepted the full Christmas Day deal until too late. She'd sounded so damn thrilled about it, he just hadn't been able to bring himself to disappoint her.

But she looked as if she was settling in for a bit of a sisterly chat so he said, 'Reckon I'll lie here and snooze for a bit.' He closed his eyes. 'Didn't get much sleep last night.'

She cleared her throat. 'Right. I'm going to take a shower.'

'Okay.' Which reminded him he'd been disappointed the

pretty strawberry underwear had disappeared when he'd used the second bathroom this morning.

The air was warm and muggy and he was dozing within moments...

...*Hurry up, Mummy.* She was always late to pick him up from school. Jett had got himself there this morning because he hadn't been able to wake her up. Again. He'd been so hungry he'd asked his teacher if he could have a Vegemite sandwich from the canteen, cos they did that sometimes when his mum didn't give him food cos she'd run out of money.

But then strangers came and took him away to another house and told him his mum had passed away. He wasn't sure what that meant but he knew he wouldn't be seeing her again and he cried heaps cos she'd told him she loved him and promised him that one day they'd go and live with his father in a big house and there'd be everything he'd ever wanted.

The lady that had picked him up told him he'd be living with other kids like him and he'd have lots of fun and make new friends. And he tried. But he didn't have fun and they picked on him cos he was smaller. So he fought back. And then they told him he was a trouble-maker and moved him to another place, then another. Who needed dumb friends anyway? He was waiting for the day his father came to get him, then everything would be okay.

And while he waited he dreamed how it was going to be. His father would laugh and open his arms and fold Jett in close like his mum used to do on her good days and tell him he'd been waiting for this day too.

Then one day they said his father wanted him to come for Christmas Day. He was overcome with breathless anticipation. Filled with wonder and excitement; his first proper Christmas with a real turkey and a tree and presents and stuff. His father might've got him a bike and he'd take him outside after lunch to teach him how to ride it and then he'd tell him he loved him and wanted him to stay for ever and that he had his own bedroom with a pirate bed and a pirate night light, cos he really liked pirates.

But when he got there, the man he'd dreamed about had sad eyes and didn't smile like how he'd imagined. He took him inside and there was a lady there too. Jett didn't understand why the lady wouldn't look at him or why she left the room with wet eyes. Then his father showed him a tiny bundle of baby with dark hair and eyes just like his own and told him her name was Breanna. His very own sister. And he forgot the man had looked sad cos now he was smiling and he let Jett touch the baby's skin and it felt like his mum's silk pillow case that she used to let him sleep on sometimes, only even softer. Today was the best day in the world.

But then the lady came and took the baby out of the room and his father told him that Jett couldn't be a part of his new family. Ever.

Jett stirred, rasped a hand over his stubble but kept his eyes closed. Christmas—and the old bad still followed like a dark shadow.

But his sister—the baby who'd ousted him from his rightful place in the family—was a bright light and not what he'd expected. He was still amazed that Breanna had come looking for him after their father had died and she'd learned she had an older brother. She'd been the sole heir to their father's estate but didn't seem to want anything from him but his friendship.

'*You*,' muttered a curt female voice. Just sharp enough to cut through the air and ensure he was listening, followed by the sound of fingertips drumming impatiently on the balcony rail.

His lips curved but his eyes remained closed. 'Hello, Trouble. Taking a few moment's down-time. Didn't get much sleep last night.'

'It's not your sleeping habits I'm bothered about.'

Her fresh apricot and cucumber scent wafted to his nostrils and he cracked open one eye. She'd showered; her gloriously red hair was damp and kissed elegant bare shoulders. A short black-and-white geometrically patterned dress hugged her curves. Curves he'd been getting intimately acquainted with not twelve hours ago. Curves he might have got even more intimate with if Breanna hadn't phoned Olivia and cut his plans for the rest of the evening short.

Breanna had phoned him too. Checked up on him. Left messages of concern, then annoyance. Which he probably should have answered but simply hadn't got around to.

Who the hell ever checked up on Jett Davies?

He caught Olivia glancing at him from beneath auburn lashes. She turned a pretty shade of watermelon pink when she saw him admiring her physical assets, then looked away and became preoccupied with counting the vehicles crossing the Harbour Bridge.

'You sure about that?' he said to her profile, his smile widening when he saw the increasing tension in her shoulders. 'My sleeping habits could be a good conversation starter. Why don't you sit down and we can discuss them?'

He'd half expected her to decline but she took a chair opposite him. 'As I was saying…it's your typical irresponsible male behaviour.'

'I am male,' he pointed out. 'I thought you'd have noticed last night. And yes, I'm pretty sure it was typical male behaviour when in the company of a sexy woman who wants the same thing he does. What I'm not sure about is the word irresponsible. I *have* heard of safe sex.'

She inhaled sharply, poured herself a glass of water from

the table beside her. 'You really have no idea what I'm talking about, do you?'

'But you're going to tell me.'

'Last night...'

'Last night...' He trailed off suggestively and the sultry images hung heavy in the air between them. He had an erection most men would be jealous of and nowhere to use it—damned if he was going to make it easy for her.

She cleared her throat, downed half the contents of her glass. 'It never occurred to you that Brie would be waiting to hear if you were okay, did it.' It wasn't a question. 'You never bothered to ring and let her know where you were.'

He flipped a hand. 'See, that's exactly why I don't keep women around long-term.' But he had to admit he saw her point.

'Brie's not just any woman, she's your sister. And I don't care what you do with your groupies, but you told Brie you were on your way to the party and that's the last she heard. While you were getting it on with some random woman she was worried about what might have happened to you.'

His brows rose. 'That woman was you.'

'*And* she felt let down because she'd been looking forward to sharing the evening with her brother. The fact it was me is irrelevant, Jett. Just because you're a famous chef-slash-food-writer-slash-critic—yes, Brie filled me in moments ago, and no, I didn't recognise you, which must be a blow to your over-inflated ego—doesn't mean you treat people who care about you that way. Accountability's obviously not a word you're familiar with and—'

'You sure have a lot to say.' Crikey, she was red hot when she was mad. Fiery. Filled with a vibrant energy to rival his own. It matched her hair and made him want to reach up, wind it around his fingers and pull her down so he could put that tongue to better use.

'When necessary, yes.'

'I get it.' He clicked his fingers. 'You're feeling bitchy because I got inside your panties and you loved every delicious second of it and now it's all over because you've decided that somehow it's not politically correct to mess around with your best friend's brother.'

Olivia blinked, her cheeks on fire. Because he had it so right. And she'd let her tongue run away from her. 'I'm not going to respond to that.'

'What, nothing to say now?' His voice held both humour and frustration. 'Or maybe it's because you know what I said is true.'

Her chin lifted. 'Plenty to say, but I'm resisting.'

'Like you did last night?' His expression was pained. 'Do you have any idea how *I* feel?'

Hot as molten steel and hard as concrete? She kept her gaze well away from his shorts. 'I said I was sorry.'

He nodded slowly, stared out at the harbour view. 'I'll apologise to Breanna.'

She nodded. 'Good.' She started to move to the balcony's glass doors. 'I think lunch is about ready. I'll go and check.' Escape.

'Wait up,' he said, and his hand shot out, curling around her elbow before she could blink. 'We'll check it out together.' Still holding her, he rose, all long loose limbs and lazy grace.

She went to step back, away, but his grip held her in place. His chest grazed her breasts and her nipples tightened into hard little bullets. It felt as if he were pinching them between his fingers the way he had last night and she bit back a moan.

This wasn't going her way at all. *Control, Olivia.* But his gaze was full of heated promises and she was already a devotee. She drew in a breath, her will dissolving like jelly.

Racing heart, throbbing lips. Arousal like lava spurting

through her veins and lower. A little sound rose up her throat and her face lifted itself to his. Just a kiss, she told herself. She could allow him—just once more. It was Christmas...

'Trouble,' he muttered, his lips so close to hers she could almost taste him. But not quite.

And then he smiled his wicked Sinner-Santa smile and walked inside, leaving her to follow. Or not.

No! She wanted to scream the word—and a few more explicit ones besides. To reach out and haul him back by his collar and give him a taste of real trouble. But she refused to let her personal problem with him interfere with a rare and happy family lunch.

The nerve of the man grated on her already tense nerves. Who was he to call *her* trouble? And in that sexual drawl that conjured up memories of when he'd called her that last night. Still, she only had to put up with him for a few hours. *So be nice a little longer. For Brie's sake.* Tomorrow they'd be oceans away.

CHAPTER FOUR

'DOES THE PRIME rib beef with Yorkshire pud meet your professional standards?' Brie asked Jett as the three of them worked their way through the scrumptious four-course silver-service luncheon served in their suite overlooking the famous harbour view.

Light reflected off water and danced across the ceiling and over crystal; a soft breeze fluttered the tinsel on the table decoration. The balmy air smelled of salt and roast dinner.

He topped up their champagne. 'I'm on vacation. The beef's tender, the pudding's puffed, browned and crisp, that's all I need to know.'

'Surely your professional taste buds never take a holiday?' Olivia suggested.

'No, but on occasion I like to eat without having to do an in-depth analysis. Like today.'

'Makes sense.' She nodded. 'Just indulge, enjoy and appreciate.'

Instant heat spurted up her neck. Wrong choice of words. *Wrong, wrong, wrong.* She focused on the stem of her glass while she twirled it on the tablecloth, but she knew his gaze was stroking over her and that he was interpreting those words in the context of their recent up-close and personal. 'I'm enjoying my grilled salmon,' she managed, desperately, then turned to her friend. 'How's the duck, Brie?'

Brie slipped a delicate mouthful past her lips. 'Perfection.'

Olivia mentally mimicked Brie's indulgent sigh. The duck wasn't the only perfection around here.

But was she the only one feeling the sudden lapse in conversation? Was it because they were too busy eating? Or maybe it was because the CD she'd put on earlier for just this possibility had come to an end...

Forcing herself to meet Jett's eyes, she said, 'So in your professional chef's opinion what's your most popular dish?'

He chewed a moment before answering. 'My soufflé is to die for. So I've been told.'

By a woman, she'd bet, judging by the way his mouth quirked and the little lines around his eyes crinkled when he answered. Possibly being fed from his spoon or while flat on her back. Or both. Not a scenario she wanted to think about. But she couldn't stop the tall, dark and delicious image flirting with her consciousness.

'You like soufflé?' Jett's question, spoken in that deep husky voice, those midnight eyes focused on her as if he'd read her mind...

'I tried to make it once. But it failed.' Cooking was her weakest skill and least favourite thing to do.

'You only gave it one shot?'

'Once was more than enough.'

'Persistence, Olivia,' he told her with a wink in his eye. 'Perfect timing's the key to good soufflé.' He regarded them both in turn while he chewed but Olivia sensed he was talking to her specifically when he said, 'You'll have to try my amaretto soufflé some time,' in a subtle way that stroked over her nape like the warm liqueur it was named for.

Brie's fork stopped halfway to her mouth. 'You're going to give us the famous Jettsetter Chef recipe? It's not in his books,' she told Olivia.

'How about I come and cook it for you some time? Show you how it's done?'

How about you do that? Olivia swallowed, the response turning her cheeks hot.

She should have recognised him from the photo inside the dust cover of *Sundae Night*. How could she not have picked up on the perfect bone structure and classic dark handsomeness? 'Brie gave me one of your books last Christmas.' She'd thought it was Brie's way to inspire Olivia's interest in cookery—now she knew better. Her best friend had kept him a secret... She raised her champagne flute. 'Now I know why it was a signed copy.'

'Did you enjoy it?' He added another dollop of horseradish sauce to his plate.

'It's got some delicious desserts.' And the added bonus of some sexy photos of the chef at work, but nowhere near clear enough to recognise him in the flesh. 'I do have to admit, though, that I've only tried out a couple.' She studied him a moment over the crystal rim. 'Do you ever get tired of cooking?'

'We've just finished filming a TV series to be shown later in the year, and, with the restaurant critiques, it's been full-on. I'm looking at some time-out so I'm working on ideas for themed cookbooks. Planning to start in Tasmania after the Taste Festival.'

At his mention of Hobart's premier summer event on the historic docks where the yacht race ended, Olivia said, 'If anyone can appreciate that particular festival, it's a chef.'

'I hope so.'

'Where to, then?'

'I've booked accommodation at Cradle Mountain.'

'Admit it, you must have had at least one cooking disaster in your lifetime.'

His lips twitched in amusement and his sinner's eyes teased. 'I don't recall.'

'Tell me about it anyway.' Olivia smiled back, and, awkwardness forgotten for the moment, she barely noticed Brie excuse herself and head out to the balcony with her glass of champagne.

Despite her earlier antagonism, she found herself drawn to him. The way he laughed with his eyes, his smooth way of talking, his hands. She couldn't seem to take her eyes off his hands, especially when he absently toyed with a miniature glass angel from the table centre-piece and she imagined those fingers toying with her—

Stop. Now.

He wasn't here for her pleasure; he was here to see Brie and share Christmas.

Olivia's family had always celebrated the day at home, with a tree and silly hats and enough food to feed an entire naval fleet. Even last year after her mother had passed away, she'd ensured they had a traditional day—her and Brie and a couple of single girlfriends from the health centre where they worked.

'Are you into natural beauty therapy like Breanna?' Jett asked, glancing at Brie as she sauntered back to resume her seat at the table.

'I work in the field of natural medicine. I share a suite of rooms with Brie, a massage therapist and a kinesiologist. I've taken a month's leave to participate in the race and focus on our fundraising.'

'Livvie has an advanced diploma in Naturopathy,' Brie boasted before Olivia could get another word out. 'She's also got a degree in Health Science. Now she's halfway through a business course so she can set up a cancer retreat. *And* there's her charity foundation, and—'

'*Brie...*' Olivia felt herself flush at Brie's enthusiasm.

She'd learned that guys weren't interested in a woman whose academic achievements outstripped theirs. It had never bothered her before. It shouldn't bother her now, but, for some reason she couldn't figure out, it did. She wanted Jett to see her first and foremost as a woman. Which made no sense at all.

'…And we're going to be business partners when the centre's up and running.' Smiling, Brie sat back and crossed her arms.

Jett regarded Olivia a moment, thoughtful. 'Are you going to fill me in on your charity? Does it have a name?'

'You mean she hasn't told you?' Brie's voice rose in astonishment.

'We didn't get around to it,' he said, eyes still on Olivia.

'That must be a first.' Brie laughed. 'She lives to talk about her Pink Snowflake Foundation. Jett, you must be the only one she hasn't harassed—and I do mean that in the nicest possible way.' When Olivia turned, Brie's eyes were twinkling at her across the table.

Brie was right. Olivia had been so infatuated with Jett last night, she'd forgotten to talk his ear off about her work and convince him to contribute. 'My mother died of breast cancer and I'm working on building a retreat for cancer survivors and those undergoing therapy to recuperate. It's still not much more than a very expensive dream but we'll get there eventually. Mum and I set up the foundation five years ago after she got sick the first time.'

'She has an amazing vision,' Brie said. 'And I'm proud to say I'm going to be a part of it. *After* I survive the race.'

'That's the positive attitude I want to hear.' But Olivia's grin quickly sobered. She was honouring a pact she and her mum had made years ago—to race their yacht in the Sydney to Hobart. Not just in memory of her mother, but all the women in her family who'd died of breast cancer. All women with breast cancer.

'This time tomorrow we'll be heading down the New South Wales coast.' Excitement and nerves were building and tangling in her stomach.

'What's the name of the boat you're sailing on?' Jett leaned back as the wait staff appeared to whisk away the plates.

'Yacht,' Olivia corrected. '*Chasing Dawn.* She may be small but she's a real and classic beauty.' They'd bought the old sea-craft together when her mum had been in remission and there'd been hope.

His gaze flicked between them. 'So two females on the crew. Doesn't that bring some sort of bad luck—women and boats?'

Oh, for goodness' sake. 'What about Aussie Jessica Watson's record-breaking solo sail around the world at sixteen? And *did you know* that the only yacht to reach Hobart in 1946 was skippered by the first *woman* ever to take part? Would you call that *bad luck*?'

'Your skipper obviously doesn't mind the distraction,' he went on, as if Olivia hadn't spoken. 'Does he ever get a little too up-close-and-*nautical* with his crew?'

The way he said that…in an entirely sexual way…made her want to slap him.

She should have expected it: the cocky grin, the sexual spark in his eyes. His sheer masculine arrogance. And to think they'd been having an almost pleasant conversation moments ago. She kept her cool, took a long, calming swallow of iced water. 'Not at all. Everyone concentrates on their job. No one gets distracted.'

He raised his brows. 'I bet.'

'There are no *nauticals* on our yacht, *Mr* Davies. We're a team—we work as a team, everyone's equal.'

'I'd like to see that.'

How he'd meant it was anyone's guess but Olivia was inclined to think it wasn't in a flattering non-gender-biased way. 'Would you really?' She snipped the words as if she were dead-heading roses. 'I can easily accommodate you there.'

He grinned, even white teeth flashing like a toothpaste ad, anticipation in his eyes. 'Yeah? You going to invite me aboard?'

'Yeah.' A plan was coming together in her head and she felt a grin to rival his spread over her face. 'One of our crew had to pull out due to illness three days ago. And you would be the perfect person to fill the void. Snowflake needs publicity. A quick word to the media and you'd be doing me, us—my *foundation*—a huge, huge favour. Wouldn't he, Brie?'

She glanced at Brie, who'd not said a word but seemed to be enjoying the moment as much as Olivia. 'Yes,' she said, slowly. 'I reckon you're right.'

When Olivia looked back at Jett, she noticed a little of his smugness had slipped.

'On the boat?'

'*Yacht*. You'd love it, Jett.' Olivia lowered her voice an octave and added a husky purr. 'The entire crew is female. Imagine. All those bronzed beauties in bikinis.' Except they wouldn't be in bikinis, but the word image begged to be painted for him all the same. 'And I'm sure you'd enjoy hot-bunking.'

His eyes grew round, his brows raised. 'Hot-bunking?'

She nodded. 'You'll find out if you join us.'

'The entire crew? The skipper too?' His smugness seemed to have disappeared altogether.

She tipped an imaginary cap. 'Yours truly.'

'But…'

'I know. Unlucky for some, but *Chasing Dawn*'s had her fair share of women aboard and she's not sprung a leak yet.' She swore he blanched and she pressed her lips together to stop her enjoyment from showing too much. 'Come on, Jett. Say yes. Please. We need you.'

'Please, Jett,' Brie chimed in. 'It's for a good cause and we're having roast quail and veg on our first night at sea.'

Olivia knew they'd never win the race—it had never been about winning. The whole reason behind the motivation was to raise money and awareness, and a celebrity aboard would be just what they needed. A sexy celebrity chef even better.

A sexy celebrity chef out of his comfort zone the best of all—the media would *eat* it up.

Roast quail. Was that supposed to be a deal maker? Jett detected the tiniest twitch at the corner of Olivia's mouth and ground down on his back teeth. He'd been outmanoeuvred. His masculine pride was at stake, because he knew from bitter personal experience that seasickness could turn the toughest of the tough into a whimpering shipwreck of a man.

And that was before leaving the dock.

'You're right about the late notice. Too bad, I didn't bring the appropriate gear.'

'No worries.' Her reassuring tone did nothing to alleviate his quickly burgeoning discomfort. Already he could feel the roll and swell beneath his feet.

'We have caps and T-shirts with the foundation's logo left over from last year's charity run,' she told him. 'Rest assured, we'll find one to fit you. And we have abundant spray jackets and oilskins on hand for when it gets rough.'

When it gets rough. Her gaze drifted down his body as she spoke, raising goose-bumps and questions he wasn't game to ask. Like whether it was too late to check in. Or back out. Except quitting was never going to be an option.

'Think about it over dessert,' Brie suggested, giving him

time to digest this new twist as a traditional flaming plum pudding was carried in and set on the table.

He helped himself to a second slice a few moments later. Olivia surprised him. Her drive and enthusiasm for a cause she believed in. Other girls her age were self-absorbed party princesses. When he'd first seen her he'd thought she was the same, but now he knew differently. And he wanted to help her.

But did it have to be on a boat?

He was still digesting the idea when they'd scraped their bowls clean, licked the last of the brandy sauce from their spoons and Breanna said, 'Presents time,' and pushed up from the table.

An uncomfortable sensation slid down Jett's spine but Breanna was right behind him, her hands on his shoulders. 'Relax, bro.'

Slipping a hand around his arm, she steered him to the Christmas tree with its glossy wrapped parcels beneath.

He reached for the swing bag with its exclusive store logo etched in silver. 'This is for you.' He held it out to Brie. 'It's probably not the right sort for a beauty therapist…' He shrugged, feeling awkward.

She grinned. 'French label, are you kidding? I'll love it. Thank you.'

He turned to Olivia. 'I wasn't expecting you.' He realised he meant that in more ways than one as he handed her the tissue-wrapped crystal vase he'd purchased in the hotel's gift shop earlier this morning.

She met his gaze with a smile in her eyes that said she was as surprised as he. That maybe she'd forgiven him for the moment. 'It was all kind of last minute, wasn't it?'

'I've waited a long time to share Christmas with you,' Breanna said. 'So here you are.' She reached down, picked up a box, held it out. 'Merry Christmas.'

He took it from her hands but it felt weird. 'Thanks.'

'Merry Christmas, Jett.' Olivia held out a smaller packet.

'Hey, I didn't expect—'

'Why don't you sit on the couch and open them?' Breanna suggested, sitting down herself and patting the space beside her, then reaching into her swing bag. 'I can't wait to smell this perfume.'

He sat next to his sister. Since it was on top, he opened Olivia's gift first. A pair of soft kid gloves.

'For Melbourne's winter,' she told him. 'I hear it gets cold there.'

'Thanks. They're great.' He admired the deep charcoal colour, her thoughtfulness. 'You've never been to Melbourne, then?'

'Never got around to it.'

'Less than an hour's flight from Hobart?' He glanced at her, surprised, and caught a wistfulness in her eyes before she blinked it away.

'Never seem to get time to travel these days.'

'You'll have to visit some time. You'd love the boutique shopping. I—'

'Shopping's not one of my priorities.' Her voice was brisk. 'At least not the indulgent kind of shopping you're referring to.'

'You'd enjoy it anyway,' he assured her, turning his attention to Breanna's gift. He lifted the lid on the box. Inside was a home-made Christmas cake. The enticing aroma of brandied fruit filled his nostrils.

He nodded and said, 'Family recipe?' then wished he hadn't.

'No. One of your tropical fruit specialties, actually.' She rose and walked to the tree and picked up another box. 'One more.'

'Breanna. You shouldn't have.' Damn, he really meant

it. She had no idea how uncomfortable she made him feel, and with Olivia watching on, he just wanted to walk out and leave the pair of them to their sentimental traditions.

Beneath the wrapping paper he found a beautifully bound album. Old leather. The kind that might have been a photograph album a long time ago. Its pages were empty. 'What's this for?'

'I thought maybe if you had some old photos, you could put them in here with some of mine around the same time period. A kind of combined effort. And I'm hoping that we're going to make some memories together to fill the latter pages.'

'I don't have any photos.' Photos were memories and he didn't want them. He didn't do sentimental and nostalgia. Especially not for Christmas. 'Excuse me, I've remembered I've got to make a couple of business calls.' Pushing up, he strode to the door.

'Where are you going?' Olivia's voice. 'What about tomorrow? Are you in or out?'

He didn't turn around. 'Later.'

CHAPTER FIVE

'THAT DIDN'T GO so well.' Brie grabbed up a cushion and hugged it close. 'The album idea was a mistake. I didn't expect him to react that way.'

'Not a mistake. He's a chef—unpredictable—need we say more?' But Olivia didn't know his past so how could she judge? But business calls on Christmas Day? 'Give him time, Brie.' She sat next to her, smoothing the torn wrapping paper over her lap as she spoke. 'Why don't you give your sexy skipper a call and tell him you're cleared for the rest of the afternoon? He's single with an all-male crew, right? He'd probably love a bit of female company.'

Brie was slow in smiling but she unfolded herself and stood. 'I might just do that. If you're sure.'

'Of course I am. I'm going to check on our ride for tomorrow, make sure everything's okay, take a stroll around the harbour while I'm out.' Anything to soothe tomorrow's nervous anticipation. 'See you later.'

An hour later Olivia walked downstairs on her way to the marina, going over last-minute details in her head. And Jett's disappearance. This evening was the last chance for him and his sister to catch up before the race, and he'd walked out on her.

Following a hunch, she detoured via the bar and *bingo*—

she saw Jett propped on a bar stool, a beer in his hands. Chatting up the long tall brunette beside him who looked as if she'd been poured into her shimmery red sheath. Reindeer antlers bobbed on her head as she talked and smiled and pushed her boobs into his personal space.

She counted herself lucky she and Jett hadn't taken things further and watched the pair of them. On closer inspection, she noticed the brunette seemed to be doing most of the talking.

The woman he *should* have been talking with was Brie, but no. It just demonstrated oh-so-clearly that was how men were and why she didn't waste her time with them.

Like her father's decision to leave when Mum had got sick. Easier to walk away than to face the tough times. Like Brie's dad—Jett's father—who'd walked away from a child he'd made.

Jason who'd walked away because he didn't like her sexual inexperience.

Maybe Jett felt her silent criticism because he turned and looked right at her. *Déjà vu.* Last night all over again, except this time Olivia was ready for the delicious onslaught. She wouldn't be seduced a second time.

He slid off the stool without so much as a glance back at the woman he'd been talking with and headed Olivia's way. Her jaw firmed as painful memories scratched over old scars. Like father like son. Olivia's father hadn't looked back either.

She watched the confident way he approached her, his long strides closing the gap between them, an almost-lift at one corner of his mouth. As if this afternoon hadn't happened and he was ready to continue with Olivia where they'd left off last night.

She lifted both hands waist high, palms out in front of her.

'I want to talk to you,' she told him crisply across a couple or so metres of floor space.

'Olivia. Nice name, by the way. We never got as far as introducing ourselves last night.'

His voice was casual but when he reached her she realised he wasn't ready to carry her off and have his way with her after all. He had the attitude down pat, but the darker, almost distant glint in his already dark eyes told a different story. 'Can I buy you a drink?'

'What about your lady friend?' Olivia jutted her chin towards the bar.

'She's not with me. I was being polite.'

Frustration seethed in her blood and her voice gathered strength as it rose. 'You want to talk about polite?'

He took her arm, turned her around and steered her towards the door. 'Why don't we walk while we talk—unless you want an audience?'

'Fine. I'm headed to the marina to check on our yacht.' Then because she remembered telling Brie to give Jett time only an hour earlier, she injected a composure she didn't feel into her voice and asked, 'Would you care to join me?'

They hit the crowded, sun-baked footpath. Jett might have only just met Olivia but he'd known she'd hunt him down. He knew what she was going to say too, because he had to admit he'd been a bit of an ass. He was going to have to smooth things over.

Which was fine with him because he wanted to indulge his eyes awhile and see her again. He flicked his eyes her way and watched the sun tangle in her hair, setting it on fire. To breathe in that uniquely fragrant combination of warm and cool. To—

'Did you have to be so rude to Brie? That album idea meant a lot. What the hell's wrong with you?'

—And to watch the spark come alive while she told him what she thought of him.

He liked that spark. It seemed to light her from the inside and grew brighter with passion. It made him want to grab her right here, right now, and kiss the hell out of her and see if he couldn't steal a little of that light for himself. 'I'll talk to Breanna. Explain.'

'I hope so.'

As close as siblings, he thought. A childhood memory flitted darkly through his mind. His father telling Jett he couldn't live with him because Breanna had taken his place. 'Your loyalty's touching.'

'And your cynicism's showing.'

'Guess it is.' He lengthened his stride so that she had to hurry to keep up.

'Don't you understand loyalty?'

'Never had a reason to.' He understood independence and self-sufficiency. Responsibility and achievement. He answered to no one and he liked it that way.

'What about your staff?'

He frowned. 'What about them?'

'Don't you appreciate their loyalty?'

'I don't have staff. Not long term.'

'I wonder why,' she muttered almost to herself.

'Because I'm not in one place long enough.'

'What about friends? Or don't you have them either.' It wasn't a question.

'I have acquaintances. No point making friends.'

She stared at him, obviously missing his logic. 'Brie's not just a friend,' she pointed out. 'She's your sister. Blood. *Family.*'

Her impassioned words unsettled him. 'In the New Year. I'll work on it. Satisfied?'

'Guess I'll have to be.'

'Hey, it's Christmas, how about a truce?'

She skirted around a kid trying out his brand-new skateboard. 'Okay, truce. For now. I don't want your last night with Brie spoiled by our inability to understand one another.'

'So where is she?'

'Spending time with a guy since you walked out on her. She'll be back later.' They'd reached the marina where the yachts were moored. 'Let's talk about yachts instead,' she said, and stepped out of her shoes. 'Ever sailed in one of these?'

'Took the *Spirit of Tasmania* across Bass Strait once.' He spoke of the passenger and freight vessel linking Tasmania to the mainland.

'Enjoy it?'

He rubbed the heel of his hand over his belly in wretched remembrance. 'Even with a deluxe cabin it was eleven hours of pure hell.'

She nodded, swinging her shoes at her side. 'Bass Strait can get pretty rough.'

He didn't tell her they'd had smooth seas for the whole voyage. That he was no sailor in any way, shape or form.

They passed several magnificent craft while Olivia described each one in pretty impressive detail.

Then he saw *Chasing Dawn* bobbing gently on the water and his throat went dry. Was he actually considering—even remotely—going to sea in this child's bath toy?

She interpreted his expression correctly. 'She may be small but she's proud and every last inch of her is seaworthy.' On light feet, she almost skipped ahead and waved a hand towards it when he reached her. 'Come aboard.'

He gestured. 'After you.'

The deck tilted ever so slightly beneath him as he stepped on board behind her. He had an impression of ropes and canvas and an animated Olivia amidst the chaos.

'You're the first male to be invited aboard, so welcome. I hope that's not a bad omen.'

Making reference to his earlier gaff about women and boats. Should've kept his mouth shut.

'So do I.' He could tell she was determined to impress him with her baby. So far *not* good. 'Where's the rest of the boat?' he wanted to know, glancing at the end only a few metres away. Or was it called the stern? He was out of his depth.

'Down here...' Then she was descending through the hatch, leaving him to follow.

Humid, stuffy air met his nostrils.

He took in the surroundings—it didn't take long. What was virtually a narrow tube of polished wood, glimpses of laminate and aluminium. A few envelope-sized windows. Claustrophobic was an apt description. So much for any ideas about getting *nautical*. 'Do I get the grand tour?'

Olivia smiled, pride warming her all the way through. 'Of course.' A few moments later—because it really didn't take long to tour the *Chasing Dawn*—Olivia pulled two bottles of mineral water from the fridge. 'Have a seat.' She set them on the tiny table between them, unscrewed hers and raised it. 'Cheers.'

He did the same and they both drank.

Olivia hadn't realised how small and cramped the vessel was until Jett had come aboard. How he seemed to have sucked all the oxygen from the air. How his skin looked more swarthy down here, the stubble thicker, blacker. He reminded her of a romantic version of a pirate. Except she doubted even imaginary pirates smelled this good; his suave woodsy cologne enticed her to breathe more deeply.

'You're planning roast quail tomorrow night.' He gestured to below decks with his bottle. 'Here?'

Even his voice sounded too rich for the space. It seemed to reverberate across the short distance between them and brush up against her chest like a hand. 'That's what the microwave's for,' she said. 'Something special for our first night at sea.' She gave him a wry smile. 'Don't worry, I'm not cooking; I've had it specially prepared.'

'The skipper, eh.' He cast another look around the cabin. 'You're an experienced sailor, then.'

'My parents were dedicated yachts-people. I've sailed all my life.' She tilted the bottle towards him. 'You're safe with me.'

He glanced around them again. 'Safe from pirates?' He lowered his voice to a conspiratorial murmur and she leaned closer almost without thought.

'Pirates,' she joked. 'Off the coast of Tasmania. With helicopters and the press following our voyage?'

'Yeah. Captain Jack Sparrow and company. Ever see any?'

There'd been a time off Madagascar, she recalled, and rubbed the sudden shiver from her arms. 'They're bloody and vicious and these days they use rocket propelled grenades and automatic rifles rather than the cannon and cutlass.'

'You don't find the notion of pirates romantic, then.' He sounded almost disappointed.

'Not in the least,' she decided, brushing off her romantic vision of a piratical Jett. 'So you can forget any pirate ways and whatever else you may have had in mind.' She checked the time. 'We'd better get going.'

'Not yet. First we should discuss this attraction.'

Olivia almost choked on her water.

'This crazy thing between us,' he went on. 'It could be awkward—best friends and brother.'

'Very awkward. So we'll put last night behind us. Forget it.' Heat rose up her neck and into her cheeks and she glared at him, forced herself to hold his gaze. 'We don't need—'

'I've heard the sound you make when you come. That soft bitey noise between a sigh and a scream.'

Oh. My. God. 'I did *not*—'

'But you did.' His eyes crinkled, that delicious-looking mouth tilted up at the corners. 'What's more, I want to hear it again. You don't think we should discuss it?'

She tipped her bottle to her lips, gulped as if she were dying of dehydration then cleared her throat. 'Since a *discussion* involves two or more people, will you let me finish a sentence at least?' When he cocked his head to one side, she firmed her chin and said, 'We've acknowledged it and now we move on.'

'I've acknowledged it. I'm not so sure about you,' he said, tilting his bottle at her.

'Okay. Yes. I acknowledge it. Satisfied?'

'Not nearly.' But his eyes twinkled, his lips twitched. 'We need to get it out of the way if we're going to be in such close quarters for the next few days.'

Her heart leapt into her throat then took a giant tumble. 'You're coming with us?'

'Isn't that what you want?'

'No—yes… Um…'

'You've changed your mind?'

'No. No. Not at all. Brie'll be thrilled.'

'Not you?'

'Of course. I'm happy too. Very happy. For Brie's sake. And thank you,' she finished.

'Okay, I can live with that.' Jett didn't think he'd enjoyed anything more in a long time than watching a twitchy Olivia blush and stammer. It was almost worth taking this marine misadventure just to see her lost for words.

Almost.

She pushed her hair off her face, seemed to regain her composure and said, 'You'd better get a good night's rest, then, because you'll need to familiarise yourself with the safety aspect before we leave. We need Brie.' She tapped her phone. 'Brie? I need you down at the marina asap.' She smiled at something Breanna said. 'Jett's decided to join us.' Pause. 'No, I didn't talk him into it. Okay, see you…um… how long do you think you'll be?' Pause. 'Okay.'

She disconnected and pushed up. 'Brie's on her way. We rise at four a.m., race starts at one. I've got stuff to do.'

'Wait just a damn minute. We still haven't had our discussion.'

'I don't think we—'

'Neither do I, Trouble, but here we are.' If he was going to die at sea, he wanted to make sure it was worth it. He pushed up as well and stepped into her path at the edge of the table, and their bodies bumped.

He felt her breasts rise against his chest as she sucked in a breath and stared up at him. It wasn't the only body part rising—and she knew that too.

The sea lapped softly against the hull and cast the late afternoon's watery reflections across the boat's interior, bathing them both in a blinding crimson glow.

She didn't step back, nor did she encourage him. She simply continued watching him, expressionless but for the spark of heated arousal in her eyes that gave her away.

'I want you to think about this…' Contemplating, he slid his index finger along the top of her dress, his gaze following the freckled swells and the valley between.

She shifted restlessly against him. 'We can't…'

'So tell me to stop.' He lowered his head to nuzzle. Just a nip on that tender spot between shoulder and neck, a lingering taste where her fragrance bloomed with the heat of her skin.

She arched her neck, giving him better access, and murmured, 'St-o-p.'

'I'll stop when you mean it.' Sweeping her hair aside, he cruised his lips from the side of her neck to beneath her jaw to a neat little ear lobe. Greedy little bites that only whetted his appetite for more. 'You taste incredible.' He nibbled along her jawbone. 'I want to taste you all over,' he murmured and was rewarded with a little shiver. 'But I'm prepared to stop at a kiss.'

She didn't answer, obviously too turned on by his moves to speak.

'For now,' he finished. He smoothed her hair again, loving its silky feel and fascinated with the way the light played over its vibrant strands, turning them golden. He straightened and watched her face, animated with conflicting emotions.

'Jett, it won't make a scrap of difference.' She watched him, her chin firm, her eyes resolute. 'This race is too important on so many levels. I can't be distracted…'

He smiled and her almost appalled gaze dropped to his mouth. Banding his arms around her waist, he pulled her closer, explored the shell of her ear with his tongue and whispered, 'Wrong.'

She pushed at his chest. 'No, I—' He cut off her excuses with a kiss that started out to prove a point and quickly turned into something more.

Her mouth yielded and opened beneath his and he took instant advantage of the honeyed heat within, sliding his tongue against hers in a dance, a duel or a demand—he didn't know which. He didn't care. She was a feisty combination of strength and vulnerability, of seduction and naïvety, and he found her completely enchanting.

She didn't try to push him away again, nor did she reach for him, but the fury of her heartbeat thundering against his as their upper bodies touched was the answer he was looking for.

Gathering her loosely flowing hair, he wound it around both fists and tugged her head back the better to taste her. If he was looking for surrender, he didn't find it with Olivia. She met him will for will. Force for force. Passion for passion.

He could have her in that *aft berth* as she called it, in five seconds flat—she wouldn't refuse him and it would be fast and furious and mutually satisfying—but even in his lust-crazed state, he knew it would also be a mistake.

Breanna was on her way and there wasn't nearly enough time to do what he wanted to do.

With a good deal of reluctance and admirable restraint, he lifted his lips and drew back slowly, watching her. Huge glassy eyes watched him back. He was surprised to find himself as breathless as she. 'After the race, Trouble,' he promised, letting her hair slide through his fingers as he stepped away, 'we're going to finish this.'

She gave him no indication how she felt about his decision. Footsteps approaching had them drawing further apart. Olivia patted at her hair while Jett resumed his seat at the table for obvious reasons.

'Brie.' Olivia darted towards her as if she couldn't wait to get away. 'I've got a million things to do, so I'll leave Jett with you.'

She turned to him, not quite meeting his gaze, residual heat in her eyes, her cheeks a little too pink, her movements a little too jerky.

'I'll be attending a weather briefing in the morning so I won't see you till you board,' she told him. 'But Brie'll go over the safety procedures. She'll look after you, fill you in with what you need, get you up to speed until it's time to leave. The rest of your gear can go with ours; it'll be in Hobart when we arrive.'

Look after you? Screw that. He aimed a killer smile at her, just to watch that spark come to life again. 'Looking forward to it.'

CHAPTER SIX

SYDNEY HARBOUR'S DEEP blue was awash with vessels of every size and shape, ferrying binocular-wielding spectators. Pleasure craft bobbed on the water from a safe distance; colourful sails billowed in the stiff breeze.

Without a specific role other than to sit in a designated spot and 'look sexy for the cameras', Jett used the lead-up time to appreciate *Chasing Dawn*'s all-female crew as they went about their assigned tasks. He barely felt the rocking movement beneath his feet, refused to acknowledge the tiny curl of unease beneath his breastbone.

He found the helicopter-circling media's up-close and personal interest in the Jettsetter Chef over the top. He shrugged, uncomfortable in the neon-candy-pink T-shirt and cap, and gave a double thumbs-up to a TV crew above them. It was for a worthwhile cause, and their crew's flirtatious glances, the gentle teasing and admiration for his support made up for it.

All the crew, that was, except for their preoccupied skipper, who obviously had more important matters on her mind.

A monster yacht cruised by, its deck crawling with male-model types standing around looking like a shoot for a men's magazine.

If he had to be on a boat, this was the one to be on. In this case, size did not matter. Surrounded by super-fit, sun-bronzed beauties who'd each dropped by—Miranda, Flo and Samantha—and extended a personal invitation to show him the sights and tastes of Tassie. Samantha, the blue-eyed blonde, had explained how the six-person crew had been divided into watches called Wet and Wild. She'd told him he was on the Wild watch with her and Brie. She'd kind of winked when she'd said it.

He forced himself to relax and watched the action around him, cleavage, perfume, feminine voices. He loved women—loved their curves and silky skin, their scents and tastes. The way they insinuated themselves against him and made him feel like a king for however long it lasted—one night, a week. A month at most.

Five-minute warning shot. Twelve-knot breeze on the harbour. A gusty change expected later this evening.

The crew were in their positions. From his spot he got a glimpse of Olivia, her hair tucked beneath her cap, looking gloriously intense in her skimpy pink T-shirt that rode up at the back, giving him a tantalising view of flesh as she moved lightly across the deck. Her toned and tanned legs flashed in the sun and her feet were bare. He decided there was nothing sexier than a bare-footed skipper.

She'd offered him prescription-strength seasickness medication, which he'd waved away. He didn't tell her he'd purchased an over-the-counter generic brand from a nearby pharmacy last night. Apart from that time, he'd hardly laid eyes on her since that kiss in the galley late yesterday afternoon.

An urgent commotion broke out amongst the crew, catching his attention. He heard the words 'main power' and 'power winch' and a few sailor-worthy curses.

He half rose but he caught sight of Breanna sprinting across the deck already shaking her head as if she expected him to offer his expertise. 'Olivia knows what she's doing.'

Of course she did. Obviously a boat mechanic on top of everything else. Since he didn't have a clue about boat mechanics and he'd only be in the way in addition to showcasing his *lack* of expertise, he leaned back again and watched the crew work feverishly to fix whatever the problem was.

And it would be fixed, he had no doubt. Wonder Woman was in charge. Interesting. He'd never been remotely involved with a take-charge woman.

The girls returned to their positions, problem obviously sorted. Seconds later the starter pistol cracked the air and they were off, tacking against the north-easterly wind. As they rounded the marker outside Sydney Heads, the huge and distinctive pink spinnaker sail unfurled, accelerating them to a fast rate of knots in a southerly direction down the coast.

Smooth sailing on a sparkling blue sea, fresh sea air. Roast quail and veg for dinner tonight. A single male in a boatful of gorgeous girls.

They settled in, the rhythmic motion almost hypnotic, and his mind wandered. He envied Olivia her focus and drive and dedication. She had her plan, she'd charted a path for her life and nothing was going to divert her from it.

Whereas he was drifting. Career-wise he'd been restless and unsettled for a while. He needed a change of direction, something to bring back the zing in life, to motivate him. Even if it had nothing to do with career, this sailing-cum-fundraising opportunity was a new experience. He gazed at the tilting horizon. Out here on the endless Pacific Ocean he felt as if he was on the brink of something new, different, exciting.

He'd not felt so alive in a long time.

He wished he were dead.

On deck and huddled into a spray jacket over his hoodie, Jett stared listlessly at the night's stormy horizon lifting and sinking, up, down… Death was preferable to this washing machine on spin cycle. He swallowed several times as bile rose up his throat. Again. His quail dinner and worse—his pride—had disappeared overboard in spectacular fashion even before the change in weather had really shaken things up. He'd woken for his Wild watch and emerged from the sticky fume-filled cabin and into the fresh sea air and *bam*.

The watch was nearly over. Thirty more minutes. Then all he wanted was to be left alone to die in peace. A familiar figure emerged from below decks and began making her way towards him in the dimness. The sexy skipper. A hot tide of humiliation washed through him and he averted his eyes to the clouds scudding across the night sky. Neither wish was going to be granted, it seemed.

'I can take over here.' The voice of his mistletoe angel, barely audible in the bluster. Offering him the chance to slip into her still-warm bunk—the mysterious hot-bunking, she'd lured him in with—and grant his last wishes after all.

'I'm fine.' He huddled deeper into his hoodie, pulled it low over his sweat-damp brow to hide his malaise. 'Go away, it's not time yet.'

Unfazed by his curt demand, she sat down beside him. 'The weather's starting to ease up.'

He leaned away, super-aware that his Armani aftershave had been replaced by infinitely more unpleasant and pungent odours, and popped a peppermint in his mouth. 'Could've fooled me.'

'You're doing great, Jett.'

Her tone wasn't sympathetic, just matter-of-fact with an injection of humour. Even in his misery, he appreciated that. 'Glad the skipper thinks so.' He kept his gaze down, alongside him, and saw that her long legs were tightly encased in denim but those sexy feet of hers were still bare. If he could just be sure he wasn't going to spew in front of her…

He pressed his lips together. He didn't think he could ever face her again if that happened.

'Talking takes your mind off the queasiness.'

'Yeah, right.'

'Okay, go ahead, ask me something.'

'Why bare feet?'

She wiggled her toes like a kid in sand. 'For the grip when the deck's slippery. And bare toes can twist around ropes—I'm pretty good at that.'

Jeez, chirpy as a seagull with a hot chip. 'You're pretty good at a lot of things nautical.'

'I lived on-board a cruiser until I went to high school.'

He forgot his reluctance to look her in the eye and stared at her. 'Yeah?'

She laughed, a joyous sound, her face aglow even in the grey night. 'It was a large cruiser. I was an only child and my parents home-schooled me while we travelled the world. They called it a living education.'

'A fair description, I suppose.'

'Yes.' She pushed back her hood and smoothed her hair from her face and he realised the wind had lessened. 'But when I reached secondary-school age and my mum's sister was diagnosed with cancer, they sold the cruiser and bought a property out of Hobart to be near her.' She chuckled. 'High school was a learning curve for me; I'd never been around kids my own age before.'

She'd learned to be content with her own company. A bit like him, in a random kind of way. His gaze lifted and he saw a break in the clouds—he'd been so preoccupied he'd not noticed. 'When did your mother pass away?'

'Eighteen months ago.'

'What about your dad, does—?'

'I haven't seen or heard from him in years. He walked out on us when Mum got sick the first time.' She spoke without the emotion he read in her eyes, the dip he saw in her shoulders. 'She was in remission when we bought *Chasing Dawn* together. We had hope then, that she'd make it, and we set up Snowflake, but her condition deteriorated sooner than we expected.'

'You mentioned your aunt. Did she…?'

'Breast cancer runs in my family. My grandmother, my cousin, and great-grandmother too, they suspect.' She spoke matter-of-factly, her eyes on middle distance. Avoiding his.

He frowned. The familial link to the disease would surely be a concern for her, but she didn't elaborate and he didn't want to broach a delicate subject. 'Why a pink snowflake?'

'When individual ice crystals bump into others they grow into the stunning and unique shape of a snowflake. We think of ourselves as those individuals working together to create something worthwhile and beautiful. Pink because it's raising awareness for women's cancers.'

He looked up at the sky where a few stars peeked through and thought about what she'd said. How she'd turned something bad into something good. 'That's pretty special.' He admired her for it. It also made him question his own life's contributions—pretty damn ordinary.

'I like to think so,' she said on a note of cheer. 'Thank you again for sailing with us and helping make a difference.'

'I've not done much.' Except chuck all over your lovingly polished deck.

'Oh, but you have,' she reassured him with abundant enthusiasm. 'You've drawn attention to our foundation just by being here. I expect a huge influx of donations and sponsorships.' Her grin was full of fun. 'You can keep the T-shirt and cap as a thank-you.'

She turned to him at the same time he turned to look at her. She was sharing the humour, her eyes sparkling in the night's soft grey light, her bound hair coming adrift from its plait, tendrils spiralling behind her into the wind.

And there it was again. That flare of attraction. Hot, bright, bewitching. Reciprocated.

Despite his roiling stomach, lust smouldered along his veins. With her torso covered in a padded jacket, Jett's focus narrowed to her smiling lips—lusciously plump and unglossed.

They were still smiling when she said, 'Your support means a lot to Brie too when clearly sailing's not your thing.'

Nothing like mention of his sister and seasickness to douse the lust sparks. He raked fingers over his skull, discovered his hands were disgustingly shaky, like his gut. What the hell had he been thinking, telling her they were going to finish…whatever this thing was between them? He'd be lucky to get past the starting line. She valued commitment, loyalty. Stickability. Her focus and her priority were with other people.

He was a travelling one-man show.

She'd been trouble from that first glimpse. Trouble from that first kiss. Trouble from that first glide of his hand over silken female flesh.

Trouble.

So why the *hell* was he hung up on her?

'Leave you to it,' he muttered, pushing up and listing to one side as the boat pitched and rolled.

'Jett. Caref—'

'I'm f—' His stomach revolted and he waved her away, hauled himself to the railing and retched pitifully over the side.

Humiliation complete.

CHAPTER SEVEN

SINCE THEY WERE on different watches and Olivia was occupied with duties that included keeping them on course, she didn't see much of Jett. Still, there were four other women more than eager to see to his welfare. Cater to his every whim. In his current state of malaise she was pretty sure they were safe from his unique brand of charm. He was, to all intents and purposes, harmless.

On the following morning when she forced her gritty eyes open after a fitful two-hour doze, she heard the sounds of feminine laughter and Jett's low, husky rumble in the thick of it. Obviously seasickness was no longer such an issue.

She checked the time, pushed up, eyes narrowing as Miranda's laugh echoed with his. A mouth-watering aroma teased her nostrils as she reached the galley and her stomach gurgled.

The threesome were relaxed around the tiny table, sharing some joke she hadn't heard. The chick magnet working his irresistible charm.

Not so harmless.

Downright sexy, in fact, with one of the heavy vinyl aprons they used aboard moulded tight over his broad chest making him look disgustingly virile and domesticated at the same time.

He didn't notice her standing there practically salivating

until she said, 'Jett, I hate to spoil the party but isn't it your watch?' She lied—she didn't hate it at all.

Miranda and Flo paused at her no-nonsense tone, fluffy white scones with lashings of jam and cream halfway to their mouths. Flo looked apologetically flustered, straightened and pushed back from the table. 'Livvie, Brie said—'

'Breanna and Sam have it covered upstairs,' Jett told Olivia smoothly, staying right where he was and reaching for his bottle of ginger ale. 'My sister put me to work. Come and try them while they're hot, skipper. I was just going to see if you were awake and bring you a couple...'

Yeah, right. 'Let me guess, you were distracted.'

He shot her a raised-brow look, chugged back on his bottle.

'They're so-o good,' Miranda groaned, licking cream from her lips. 'I didn't know microwaved scones could turn out so delicious. Thanks, Jett,' she said in a wily feminine voice Olivia had never heard her use. She rose—reluctantly, Olivia noted—placing a few scones in a shallow plastic bowl and exchanging looks with Flo. 'Let's take some up for the others. You two stay here and relax.'

'So you're feeling lots better, then?' Olivia enquired sweetly after the girls had gone.

'Getting my sea legs,' he said. 'Isn't that what you call it?' But his complexion still had a greenish tinge and dark smudges lay beneath his eyes. 'The girls were complaining about the lack of comfort food on board.'

He wasn't eating, she noticed, and a twinge of sympathy stirred her enough to say, 'You didn't have to cook. Don't let *the girls* take advantage.'

He stood, cleared the crumbs from the table. 'And here I was expecting you to tell me off for taking advantage of *them.*'

Her lips twitched. 'Were you?'

He shot her a glance. 'There's only one girl I'm interested in on this boat.'

Her blood quickened through her veins. 'Yacht.'

'Whatever. Don't be shy.' When she just stared at him, he indicated the plate on the table with a jerk of his chin while he rinsed the utensils in the tiny sink.

Oh. Of course. She helped herself and bit in. They tasted like heaven. 'And you made them in that itty-bitty microwave?' The mystery was, *how*?

'Yep.' He moved to the pantry and began pulling out her basic supply of ingredients. 'I'm going to show you how to make simple muffins so next time you take this itty-bitty boat out, you can have some comfort food for the crew.'

Just her and him, in this itty-bitty space. She remembered too well the last time they'd been here. The way he'd kissed her. The way she'd responded. 'Oh. No, I—'

'We're both off duty.' He set the mixing bowl on the table, shook in flour. 'Would you rather put the time to a different kind of use?' His eyes burned into hers, turning her blood to syrup. 'Your choice.'

She looked away fast, reached for the spice rack. 'Okay, muffins.'

He held out the other vinyl apron. 'I'll mix the batter while I tell you how to make a perfect streusel topping.'

As instructed, she added the brown sugar, chopped nuts and spices to her bowl while he beat eggs and stirred them into the dry mix he'd prepared.

'Who taught you to cook?' she asked to distract her thoughts away from imagining him whipping the mix in *only* her vinyl apron. Geez, what was it with him? With *her*? She'd never objectified a man before. She pressed her lips together. She should be ashamed of herself.

'A foster carer's housekeeper. As a kid I was fascinated by chemical reactions. On a TV programme I discovered the pantry was filled with exciting opportunities, so after a spectacular volcano with some baking soda and vinegar that spread considerably further than I'd imagined, rather than risk me blowing up the place, Mrs Tracey put me to work. She gave me a love for cooking.' A fleeting smile touched his lips.

Olivia grinned, imagining the young Jett. 'Sounds like you two had lots of fun.'

The animation in his expression dropped away and his hand tightened briefly on the whisk. 'I was shifted elsewhere a few months later.'

'Why?' The word popped out in spite of telling herself she wasn't going to ask.

He shook his head, dipped a finger into the mix and touched it to her mouth. 'Why, indeed.' Dark eyes met hers. Challenging her. 'Taste.'

When she went totally still, he rubbed his finger sensuously along her lower lip. 'Come on, taste.'

Oh...my. Seduction by muffin mix. She closed her lips over his finger. The batter swirled sweetly over her tongue; a hint of masculine soap drifted to her nose. She swayed a bit to the rolling movement of the yacht beneath her feet as she sucked him in deeper and scraped her teeth over his finger. Watched the surprise in his gaze turn to red-hot desire. She drew back instantly, super-aware of their own highly volatile chemical reaction in progress.

Who had seduced whom? Even semi-incapacitated he lured her. His willingness—or was it sheer stubbornness?—to ignore his discomfort for the crew's sake. Wiping the back of her hand across her tingling lips, she stepped away. 'Leave you to it. I'll be on deck if you n... I'll be on deck.'

She heard him chuckle as she fled.

Late in the afternoon of the third day they were within hours of crossing the finish line. Olivia watched Tasmania's rugged coastline through misty eyes and her heart ached. *I know you're here somewhere, Mum. Sharing the dream we made together. And I've been good. Had the test as you requested.*

'Are you okay?' Brie murmured beside her.

Olivia startled. She was aware her eyes were stinging. 'I didn't hear you come up.' She sniffed, searched for that elusive tissue in her pocket, then blew her nose. 'Sea air,' she mumbled.

She knew Brie wasn't fooled. They both stared at the coast. 'Your mum would be proud.'

Olivia lifted her shoulders, hugged her arms, her eyes fixed dead ahead.

'*I'm* proud,' Brie continued. 'Not just of the race. I'm proud of you. Taking that test took guts.' Olivia felt her friend's gaze. 'And I'll be here for you whatever happens, you know that.'

Olivia rubbed at the ache in her chest, still watching the horizon. 'I know. I'll be back in a jiffy.'

'Take your time,' Brie told her. 'Everything's fine and you're dead on your feet. I'll let you know when to come up.'

'I won't be long.' Olivia made her way below deck and stretched out on the other berth for just a minute, the one blessedly free from any trace of masculine scents or clothing or reminders.

She'd hardly slept for the entire voyage, responsibility on her shoulders, and aware every moment that she was making this trip without the person who'd meant so much to her. 'Mum,' she whispered. 'You'd be impressed with what we've achieved.' Having Jett aboard had been an unexpected bonus, giving their Snowflake savings account a real boost.

But had her rash challenge to Jett been about the foundation? Or was it more about having him see her as strong and competent? To keep him around because she wanted to see more of him before he took off? And wasn't there also that sneaky itch to get back at him for mocking a female's expertise in a traditionally male-dominated role?

Yet he'd used his own expertise yesterday—in a traditionally female-dominated role—cooking up delicious treats for them when she'd known he was still under the weather. He'd kept a sense of humour about it all when he could have spent his free time sleeping it off.

The crew had loved it. They loved *him*—naturally. She'd never seen them go to such lengths to please and she was *not* jealous of the respect and attention he gave back to each crew member. Okay, she was. A little. But most of all, she admired his good-humoured participation. He'd gone above and beyond what she'd expected from a playboy chef suffering seasickness. He'd kept to his word and not distracted her during the trip—at least not intentionally.

Then last night when she'd come to switch watches, he'd stopped awhile to talk about her future fundraising plans. What she hoped to achieve. As if he was *interested*.

Then as he left, he'd mentioned their 'unfinished business'. Caught off guard, she'd told him again that the only important thing to her was the race and Snowflake. That she wasn't interested in anything more than his friendship.

He'd taken her at her word and disappeared down the hatch too damn quickly for her self-esteem.

A mistake, she'd decided. A no-strings fling with a gorgeous, intelligent and attentive guy was exactly what she needed right now.

Need.

A word she hated.

She rolled onto her back and stared at the overhead a few inches from her nose. She was *not* one of those needy women who required a man in their lives to make them feel complete. She was doing fine on her own, thanks very much. But distraction; she could have done with some of that… Her eyes drifted closed, the yacht's gentle motion carrying her away.

When she next opened her eyes, the flicker from a low-hung lantern cast a glow over the dim, wood-panelled cabin. She'd slept longer than she'd meant to. The air smelled oddly of old spices over the rich aroma of stewed meat.

'You're awake, my pretty.'

At the low growl of appreciation accompanying the words, she turned her head on the pillow and what she saw took her breath away. He was magnificent. Gloriously naked from the waist up, dark breeches riding low on lean hips, held there by a length of rope. The edge of a cutlass glinted beside one muscled thigh.

'Jett?'

He grinned. A sailor's grin. A sinner's grin. A grin that turned her inner thighs to jelly and made her woman's flesh burn.

Lamp glow gilded his swarthy skin, purple shadows carving deep valleys over the rugged terrain of his chest and shadowing the granite cliff of a jaw. As if viewing someone else, Olivia glanced down at herself, realising she wore a gauzy white gown as sheer as it was simple…and where was her underwear?

Her arms were crossed at the wrists, bound with silky cords and placed above her head on the pillow so that her breasts pouted up at him like an offering. Her legs sprawled across the bed, her ankles bound with the same silky cord and tied to the bedposts.

'Captain Jett Black at your service.' His reply was whisky-smooth arrogance and rich with innuendo. And didn't that name suit his looks and soul perfectly?

Those *jet-black* eyes traced an impertinent path over her face to her rapidly tightening nipples, her belly…lower, sensuous coils of heat drifting over her skin.

She writhed on the bed, rough sheets chafing ultra-sensitised flesh. 'But you're a pirate.'

'I'm your fantasy.'

'No!'

But her breathing quickened as he slid a callused hand between her trembling thighs and inched the hem of her gown up over her knees. Higher…

'I don't need a man in my life.'

'I'm here to prove you wrong. You'll surrender to me. What's more you'll do it willingly.'

Her head thrashed on the pillow. 'I'll never surrender.'

He bent his head and sucked a nipple through the sheer fabric, the moist decadent heat of his mouth making her arch her back and cry out.

She couldn't think. Not with his fingers sliding along her moist flesh, then plunging deep, drawing out slowly only to push inside once more, over and over, dazzling her with unspeakable delights, unimaginable pleasure.

'You want me,' he whispered, his breath harsh against her ear, his palm hot and hard and heaven as he ruched the fabric up over her concave belly, the dip of her waist, leaving her exposed to his lusty gaze. Vulnerable and on the edge of insanity.

'No…'

He shifted lower, his perfectly sculpted masculine body sliding over hers. Down. His stubble chafed on delicate skin, then soothed the sudden tenderness with lazy laps of his tongue. On the brink and helpless, she looked down her body and met his eyes and knew what he was going to do. He grinned then bent his head.

'Yes,' she moaned, throwing her head back and giving herself up to the glory. Surrendering gladly. 'Yes!'

'You're as needy as all the rest.' He slid off the end of the bed and stood, a triumphant smirk on his pirate lips. 'Maybe more.'

She blinked awake to find Jett watching her, a mug of something steaming in his hands. 'Just as I thought.'

She cringed beneath his scrutiny, her lower body throbbing with unsatisfied desire. *'What?'*

'I said you needed the rest.'

Her hands rushed to pull the light blanket she'd thrown over herself earlier up to her chin. 'No, I meant what are you *doing here*?' She prayed she hadn't moaned or called out or worse.

'Waiting for you to wake up.' He raised the mug. 'Thought you might need a cup of green tea. You've hardly slept a wink the entire trip.'

'I don't *need anything* from you.' She struggled to sit up, still holding the blanket close and glaring at him, hoping he'd take the hint and disappear. How could she have dreamed of *him* when it was her mother she'd come in here to be close to? To think about? And she'd hardly thought of her mum at all. Guilty heat rose up her neck.

'A grumpy riser.' His shoulders lifted and bunched, his thumbs rubbing the side of the mug. 'A sure sign you didn't get enough. Sleep,' he clarified, a hint of humour in his eyes.

'Don't you have something to do? A watch to be on?' A plank to walk?

'Free as a bird. Which reminds me, you missed the albatross we spotted off the starboard side about thirty minutes ago.'

'Thirty minutes ago?' She swung her legs over the side of the bunk.

'That's a sign of good luck, right?'

'I hope so.' A thought struck her as her feet hit the floor with a thud. 'Isn't your surname Davies?'

'It was my mother's name. Why?'

'Never mind. Thanks for the tea.' She indicated a cubby-hole beside the bunk preferring to avoid even the slightest possibility of skin contact lest she spontaneously combust in an inferno of lust. 'Here's fine.' *Now go away.*

He set it down. 'Brie says to tell you we'll have a fair wind the rest of the way and all is under control.'

'Tell Brie I'll be five minutes.'

The instant he'd gone, she blew out the breath she'd been holding and hugged her knees to her chest. She wished *she* were under control. Ever since she'd met this man her hold on life as she knew it seemed to be slipping away.

'Skipper?'

She whipped her head around to see him there again.

'Just so you know, I won't be participating in any after-race celebrations.'

'That's up to you. You've done more than enough for our cause, so thank you.' She picked up her tea, lifted it to her lips and studied him over the rim, telling herself she wasn't disappointed. 'Sick of our company already, huh?'

'I've got other plans.'

'But you and Brie—'

'Already arranged.'

'Oh. Great. Good.'

He started to turn then stopped, raised a finger as if some-thing had slipped his mind. 'Another thing. I won't be pur-suing our promised discussion. If you were expecting me to call,' he added.

'Fine.' She said it like an accusation. Her fingers tight-ened on the mug. 'Why not?' The fragile words spilled free before she could censor them, which only infuriated her further. She'd been so determined not to come across as that *needy* woman.

'You made it clear that's the way you want it. I respect that.' But he reached out, tucked a loose strand of her hair behind her ear and she caught a whiff of his soap on his hands. 'Breanna has my phone number if you change your mind.'

She watched him turn and leave. He'd done some thinking on board and decided Olivia's type didn't appeal to his sophisticated taste. Probably relieved she'd knocked his offer back.

A part of her wished he hadn't, another part earned her respect.

CHAPTER EIGHT

'JETT'S GONE INTO lockdown because he doesn't want any more media hassles,' Brie told Olivia as she packed her bag. She was flying to one of tropical northern Queensland's remote islands with some fellow beauty therapists later this afternoon. 'I think he's well and truly done his bit. Which means he could probably do with some company. Being on his own and all.'

Olivia and Brie had been staying in one of Hobart's luxury hotels near the waterfront, recuperating after the race and enjoying Tassie's Taste Festival. Despite their upgraded suite having three master bedrooms, Jett had conveniently found accommodation in the penthouse upstairs. Who else but the Jettsetter Chef would be able to source five-star penthouse accommodation in a fully booked city during the busiest week on Hobart's calendar?

The press had swooped and swarmed all over him when they'd docked. Olivia had been surprised and eternally grateful for his good humour towards the reporters—he'd been a genuine and enthusiastic spokesperson for the foundation, even agreeing to an appearance on the local TV morning show in the coming week.

So Brie had told her.

Because Olivia hadn't seen or heard from him since he'd walked away from *Chasing Dawn* at the marina.

'Liv, did you hear me?'

'Yes.' Olivia looked up from the novel she was trying to read. 'Company.' She'd never liked the taste of sour grapes but there was a whole bunch in her mouth right now. She knew Brie and Jett had caught up. She hadn't asked for details but he was obviously the reason for Brie's happy demeanour. 'What sort of *company* are we talking about?'

'Companionship. For starters anyway. You can move on for the main course if things go well.' Brie tossed a new orange bikini on top of her overstuffed bag. 'It's New Year's Eve tomorrow. And I know for a fact his evening's free. Like yours.'

'What if I've made plans and I just haven't told you?'

Brie looked her over, brows raised. 'Have you?'

Olivia ran a lazy finger over her e-reader's screen, waited for the next page to load. 'Maybe.' She continued staring at her reader.

'I know you, my friend, and there's not a chance. He's leaving on New Year's Day,' Brie continued. 'To work on his new book.'

'Inspirational spot, Cradle Mountain. I'm sure he'll enjoy it.'

Brie let out a long-suffering sigh and walked over to where Olivia was curled up on the couch and stuck her hands on her hips. 'It's New Year and you have the hots for each other.'

Olivia glanced up. 'So? Are you saying I should phone him up and ask for sex?'

Brie's grin was fast and wide. 'As long as you're careful. He's a casual sort of guy and I know you're not…'

'Experienced.' Olivia stretched lazily, waggled her fingers. 'Maybe it *is* time I tried something different. And if I want to play with fire I've got to expect to get a little singed along the way, right?' She dropped her hands and picked up her reader again. 'Having said that, nothing's going to happen.'

'Hey, I've seen you two look at each other and it's combustion central. So I'm saying yes, definitely try that new adventure, have some fun—you both deserve it.'

Combustion central? Not any more. She'd told him no. He'd accepted it. 'We admitted the attraction. Now we've moved on.'

'Yeah, right.' Brie patted Olivia's hand then rose and walked to her wheely bag. 'It's not too late to ask him down for a drink,' she said as she checked her purse. 'Or if you're feeling shy, you could meet in the lobby, go somewhere on the waterfront and enjoy the view. Oh, and for your convenience, I've put his phone number in your contacts list.'

'Me? Ask him?' Olivia's chin lifted. 'And I'm not shy.'

'I know you're not—usually. You're an equal rights ambassador and you demonstrated that to him very clearly, more than once.' She cocked her head to one side. 'Maybe he feels threatened.'

'Threatened? Jett?' Olivia laughed—a little hysterically—and stood too, hands in the pockets of her jeans as she walked to the door to see Brie off. 'Is this the same guy we're talking about?'

'He's my brother, obviously I don't see him the same way you do. Happy New Year,' Brie said against her cheek. 'Go out and have a good time.'

'Yep.'

Brie studied her a moment. 'You're really not even going to try, are you? I should have insisted you come with us instead of letting you opt out as you always do.' She pulled out her phone to check her messages, then opened the door. 'Phone coverage isn't reliable that far north. If anything urgent happens…'

'Nothing's going to happen. I'm going to open a bottle of

champagne and drink it in the spa then go downstairs and enjoy the street party. Have a great trip.'

New Year's Eve on Hobart's city streets was alive with people and action. Eyes disguised behind a pair of reflective sunglasses, Jett stepped out of the crowded hotel lobby and into a cab. Knowing trouble was in the same hotel alone and a few floors below him, he needed the distraction. He watched the casino's twinkling lights come into view.

Endless opportunities abounded in love and luck with plenty of attractive women on the prowl. If he chose, he could celebrate the stroke of midnight back in his room with a bottle of chilled champagne, and a willing body to slake another kind of thirst.

To his surprise and chagrin, the thought of spending the evening going at it with a faceless woman he'd never see again left him cold. Ten minutes after setting out, he was back in the hotel, scowling. What the hell? He was never indecisive.

If he wanted to rid himself of a case of inconvenient lust for a leggy redhead, there had to be another option.

A swim in the pool? A cold shower? Only one thing was going to rid him of the simmering heat in his veins—and it wasn't happening: she'd made it abundantly clear it wasn't happening. He watched revellers spilling out of the popular restaurants around Sullivan's Cove and knocked back a can of soda.

The muted TV screen was showing ten minutes to midnight. Swapping his handmade silk shirt for a soft worn jersey, he poured himself a large Scotch from the suite's minibar, drank it down. He was looking forward to a few hours of oblivion.

Olivia pressed her lips together and waited for Jett to answer the intercom to his penthouse apartment. She was wearing a stupid party hat and juggling a supermarket bag filled with New Year cheer and her nerves were stretched to breaking point.

Three hours ago she'd been eating a late dinner alone in the hotel room, listening to other people having fun, watching the celebrations from her balcony. Where would she be next New Year? Next New Year, she'd know—one way or another. She'd wanted to reach out, grab hold of life with both hands while she still could and join in.

Her focus had been so narrow, so sharply defined by the goals she'd set for herself. The race, the fundraising and memories of her mother had reminded her that time was a gift that couldn't be bought or bartered for and could be snatched away without warning.

And she'd made a decision. Changed her mind. Jett. Tonight. This was her chance to take time for herself before she knew for sure what her future held. The result would surely be positive. She'd have no choice then but to make those difficult decisions she'd put at the back of her mind for so long. Surgery. Lifestyle.

But not tonight. Not even next week.

She'd had the entrée with Jett, and Brie was right—she wanted the main course.

She shifted impatiently on the balls of her feet. What if he wasn't in? What if he was sharing a New Year's bonk with some other random woman he'd picked up? The way he'd done with *her* on Christmas Eve?

She heard a crackle through the speaker then, 'Olivia.' The disembodied voice didn't sound particularly pleased.

He had the advantage and she wished the video worked both ways so she could see his expression. So she'd know whether she was making an idiot of herself. She tapped her silly hat and smiled. 'You still recognise me, then.'

The pause lasted long enough to write Happy New Year with a blocked glitter pen. 'What's up?'

'Brie mentioned you were on your own tonight… And since I…' She trailed off, biting back the needy, desperate words on the tip of her tongue.

Dammit, she wasn't taking no for an answer. She wasn't *needy*—she was taking control. She rose up on tiptoes, closer to the intercom as if to draw him into her game. 'It's nine minutes to midnight. Let me in, I want to wish you Happy New Year.' She glanced at the bag in her arms. 'And I've got stuff.'

'Stuff.'

'Eight minutes thirty seconds and counting.'

The elevator doors to his penthouse slid open to her left.

Relieved, with dignity intact—for now at least—she stepped inside. And was tempted to back out again. The mirror on the back wall reflected a woman with wild red hair topped with a green foil cone hat on an odd tilt, eyes too wide for her face. Freckles and fine lines from years of sailing in the sun. Definitely not Jett's type—oh yeah, she'd looked him up on the Internet and seen his type.

She'd only hooked his attention the first time because it had been dim and she'd looked half decent in her new fire-engine-red cocktail dress. Tonight she was wearing an avocado-coloured ankle-length shift and gold sandals. Nothing too sexy and provocative in case he'd changed his mind about spending the night alone and had another woman up here.

Her fingers clenched around the bag. She'd die of embarrassment, she'd just die— 'Hi,' she said, breezing out as the door opened, *not* looking at him and heading straight for the fantastic view taking up one whole wall. The only light in the room came from outside and the muted TV screen.

'Wow, look at that. The penthouse view. Almost as pretty as Sydney Harbour.'

'You're a Taswegian, you're biased.' His voice, a mellow baritone, stroked up her spine and her eyes slid closed. His woodsy soap she'd become familiar with during the race teased her nostrils. His presence behind her filled her with a new kind of longing.

Turning, she set her bag of goodies on the smoked-glass dining table where his computer blinked and now she *did* look at the reason she was here.

Rumpled and casual in shorts that might have been white once upon a time and a soft-looking black T-shirt. The tight fit outlined hard-packed muscles and those powerful legs, which had caught her attention that first night, were tantalisingly bare from mid-thigh down. 'You're an Apple Islander too.'

With only a dim light in the corner, the dusky air was thick with tension. He furrowed a hand through tousled hair, obviously not for the first time tonight. 'I think you should go.'

She smiled and reached for her bag while butterflies swarmed in her belly. Stepped out of her sandals. 'That's silly, I just got here.'

Reaching into her bag, she placed the contents on the table one at a time. A bottle of her favourite sparkling white, a punnet of strawberries, a supermarket's pre-packed selection of cheeses. Grapes.

His reaction might have been bored, as if he was used to women bearing gifts, except for a telltale twitch at the corner of his mouth before he said, 'What's all this?'

'It's New Year...' she glanced at the countdown on the silent TV '...in four minutes and twenty seconds. And I want to celebrate.' Digging deeper, she snatched up one of those party favours that unrolled like a tongue and made a funny noise, and blew it at him.

No response.

'Party popper, then?' She snatched it from her bag of surprises and pulled. It sounded like a gunshot in the silence. 'Oh, for goodness' sakes.' Exasperated, she tossed the explosion of tiny streamers at him and moved to the TV, raised the volume so she could hear the party happening in front of the Opera House and Harbour Bridge. 'So…it's me.' She waited on tenterhooks, breath backing up in her throat.

'Yeah. And you're still trouble,' he said, finally, and maybe she saw a glint of humour in his eye before it vanished as quick as a blink.

She let out a relieved breath. 'Good. That's good. I think. Okay. It's New Year.'

'So it is.'

Slapping sweat-damp hands on her thighs, she glanced once at the screen where revellers were having fun at Circular Quay. 'Three minutes.' Nodding at the foil hat, she set to work uncorking the bottle of bubbly. 'I don't want to be the only one looking ridiculous.'

He shook his head. 'Ridiculous, never. You look gorgeous. Sexy and gorgeous and damn near irresistible.'

Her blood turned to syrup but she kept her tone light. 'Why thank you. Glasses?' As she ripped the foil she watched him walk to the bar and collect two tumblers rather than the crystal flutes. Fine. She wasn't going to quibble about details.

The cork popped and a cheery fizzing sound filled the room. 'Tassie's best.' She filled the glasses while he held them out, then set the bottle on the table. Their fingers barely touched as he handed her a glass but it was enough to send a *whoosh* through her skittering pulse. It hadn't done that since the last time Jett had touched her. She looked up into dark, unreadable eyes. 'Happy New Year, Jett Davies.'

'And you.'

They took a mouthful and she let the bubbles slide down her throat then licked the sweetness from her lips and said, 'If you won't, I will.' Grabbing the little foil cap, she reached up and set it on top of his head, secured the elastic beneath his chin with a little *ping* and a grin. 'Forty-five seconds till lip-lock time.' Her gaze dropped to his mouth and temptation ruled. 'Or we could start early.'

She didn't know who moved first but she was aware of two things: his lips were on hers…and she wasn't counting down those last seconds to midnight.

All she could do was focus on the guy she was kissing. Tasting of champagne and musky man and sweet, sweet temptation. Making her head spin. Driving her crazy and sending her to that place he'd shown her. That place she couldn't wait to revisit.

The instant their mouths touched, Jett couldn't resist. She was spontaneous and fun and her lips soft and warm and generous. Without thought he banded his arms around her and pulled her close, her body pliant and melting against his like brandy custard over plum pudding.

He heard the television's countdown click over to the New Year and lifted his head to look at the enchanting vision in front of him. The exploding fireworks outside showered colour over her face.

Stars shone in her eyes and her lips curved as she met his gaze. 'Happy New Year,' she said, softly. 'Again.'

He couldn't help but smile back as he let his hands roam lower, to the firm curve of her backside, and tucked her tighter to him, grinding his pelvis hard against her. 'Back at you.'

She groaned at the contact, her sweet breath fanning his

face. 'It's pretty good so far.' Grin widening, she cupped her hands around his jaw and pulled his face back to hers. He was more than happy to oblige, enjoying the way her fingers moved into his hair, against his scalp. Firm and flexible. Sure and strong. Competent. He closed his eyes and tried *not* to imagine how they'd feel manipulating other parts of his tight, tortured body.

He ran his hands lightly up her spine and she gave one of those little shivers of delight and leaned closer. Firm breasts pressed against his chest, hard nipples easily felt through the thin layers of fabric separating them. She was aroused. Ready. And so, so tempting.

Except Olivia wasn't the kind of good-time girl he enjoyed briefly before moving on. No matter how enthusiastic Olivia was to get on with it, no matter how willing he was to let her. She was also Breanna's best friend—definitely not to be messed with.

So this kiss was absolutely a one-off. A souvenir. Just for fun, for New Year.

Except it felt like…more.

Her unique flavour was as exotic as any taste sensation he could concoct, drawing him into some kind of maelstrom that made his head spin and his heart pound in a crazy way.

He told himself it was the Scotch he'd drunk, that he'd not eaten since breakfast, that he was still recovering from seasickness, but, like an addict, he couldn't seem to tear his lips away.

He wasn't aware how long they stood there locked together from neck to knees and mouth to mouth but finally they both had to come up for air.

It was the break he needed to pull himself out of the spell he seemed to be under. His breathing was unsteady and he struggled for cool, clear sanity. Cursing silently, he ripped off the party hat, tossed it to the floor. Gripping her upper arms, he looked into her eyes, determined to ignore the tempting invitation he saw there. 'This is not a good idea.' He spoke each word slowly and deliberately as much for himself as for her.

Olivia watched him through a fog of desire swamped with frustration. Because she knew it was mutual—his dark gaze and the hard, hot ridge of masculine flesh between them proved his words were a lie. She tossed her own hat away. 'Why?'

'Because if you stay, we're going to finish what we started a week ago. You're killing me here, skipper.'

Her spine tingled with the thrill that his admission brought. She wasn't going anywhere. She pushed at his chest. 'I changed my mind about being with you. And don't look so worried, it's just for fun. I know that.'

'Fun,' he echoed, his brows drawing together as if he didn't think her capable of such a notion.

'You're not a one-woman guy—you don't even trust people enough to make friends—so yes, fun. What else would it be?' Olivia picked up the supermarket bag still within reach on the table. Her hand trembled a bit as she drew out a smaller paper bag from the bottom.

His eyes darted to her package, back to hers. Heat smouldered in their depths, scarlet smudges flared high on his cheekbones. 'What trouble are you planning on getting us into now?'

'*I've* decided we need to finish whatever this is between us before we move on. And we're going to finish it.' She waved the paper bag in front of his face, opened it carefully. 'That's why I brought condoms.'

'Olivia…'

Letting the bag fall to the floor, she held up the packets. 'I didn't know what you prefer so I got three. Ridged, ultra lubricated and extra l—'

'Stop.' Placing a thumb against her mouth, he sealed off the rest of her sentence. 'Just stop.'

But Olivia refused to stop. She wanted him, and she was going to have him. She pried his thumb from her mouth and told him, 'We're just getting started.'

CHAPTER NINE

SHE'D NEVER PLAYED a seductress-in-the-bedroom game. Never wanted to, never even been tempted and certainly wasn't sure she knew how. But something deeper urged Olivia to try. *Tomorrow might be too late.*

And with Jett, it would be too late because this was their last night in Hobart. Tomorrow they'd go their separate ways. If they met up again—through Brie—it might be under very different personal circumstances.

She tucked the condom packets in the pocket of his shorts, then, since her hands were already in the vicinity, she took the opportunity to slide her fingers under his T-shirt. And up. She felt the hard muscles beneath his skin contract beneath her touch.

A strangled sound issued from his throat. She liked the sense of power his reaction gave her. That she could turn him on. She could get him to play.

'Your skin's so hot,' she murmured, rubbing her hands over two flat male nipples as she gained confidence, stepping into the role with apparent ease. 'Maybe you'd feel cooler if we just…take this…off.' Heart pounding, she waited, her eyes on his, and saw a battle waging within their dark depths.

'You'd better be sure about this,' he said. 'Because tomorrow I'm gone.'

'I know. And I'm sure.' Once started, her newly discovered inner seductress made it so easy to slip her hands onto his bare shoulders, lean in and convince him with her mouth, with her tongue. With a slide of her bare foot over his shin and up, agile toes finding purchase on the back of a hairy thigh.

He reared back, muttering something unintelligible, but his hands shot upwards and the T-shirt was gone, leaving a bronzed expanse of skin sprinkled with dark hair that arrowed down and disappeared beneath the waistband of his shorts.

Olivia dared her gaze to follow. Her mouth went dry, her legs turned to jelly and her core throbbed with desire and anticipation. He was even bigger than she remembered. Oh. Sweet. Heaven. Would all that fit? She couldn't wait to find out.

He reached for the straps of her dress but she shook him off. 'My turn tonight.'

He nodded, eyes heavy and smoking hot in the dimness. 'Help yourself.'

He appeared all casualness and acquiescence but Olivia could see the tension rippling across his abdomen. Perhaps he enjoyed having women perform sexual favours for him, or he was humouring her for the moment, because no way would he play the passive role unless it suited him. Even now, she knew he could turn this situation around and have her pinned beneath him before she could blink.

That made him dangerous. And exciting.

She reached out and touched him, a light stroke across his abdomen, a fingertip against his navel. 'Are you a brief or boxer man?' She slid both hands beneath his waistband. Her knuckles grazed firm, warm skin.

'Guess you're about to find out for yourself.' His voice sounded low, strained.

'Not here.' She prodded him so that he walked backwards

until his calves came up against a wide leather recliner chair, then nodded. 'Here's good.'

She reached into his pocket for condoms—she wasn't fussed which packet it was—and slapped them on the coffee table beside the chair. Then with a nerve she hadn't known she possessed until this minute, she shoved the shorts—and boxers too—over his hips and down. There was an awkward moment when he had to help her manipulate the fabric over his massive erection, but then he was stepping out of them and kicking them aside and he was naked and she was fully clothed and she felt amazing and powerful and sexy.

He cleared his throat. 'Do you want me to lie down?'

'Not yet.' Outside, the party lived on but the only sound in the room was their quickened breathing and her heart beating its way out of her chest. She shifted closer, felt his need, warm and tempting across the intimate space between them. Like a kid with a new discovery, she was compelled to touch, to explore. She'd never touched a man this way and curiosity and wonder filled her. Hot, silk-covered steel. Wrapping her hands around him, she looked up, watched his eyes darken as she acquainted herself with him. She experimented, squeezing gently and sliding her hand upwards. 'Wow.'

He shuddered, placed a firm grip on her shoulders. 'You keep doing that and it's going to be over in seconds.' His voice was gruff, his jaw tight.

She bit her bottom lip, and immediately let go. 'Sorry...'

A glimmer of what looked like humour lit his eyes. 'You're kidding, right?'

'I...it's just that you make me want to be adventurous and a little bit naughty.'

He grinned. 'Hell, skipper, you're already adventurous. And I'm all for a little bit of naughty.' He pulled her against him and toppled them both onto the butter-soft leather.

'Hey, it was my turn.' But she laughed, breathless, and

straddled him, arms straight, hands resting on his broad shoulders. His legs chafed against her inner thighs, his arousal nestled huge and hot against her panties.

He waggled his brows at her. 'You're on top, aren't you?'

She looked down at the seemingly innocuous smile with wicked fun smouldering in those dark eyes. 'Yeah...'

It was the oddest feeling being with this man with a play-boy reputation—the sort of man she usually had little time for. But she knew now that it was only a part of who he was, and right now he just made her feel special.

He tugged the zip at the back of her dress, his fingers grazing a shivery path down her spine along the way. It slid from her shoulders to hang, gaping and loose on his chest. His eyes didn't leave hers, glittering in the dimness as he flicked open her bra, pulling it away from her skin and exposing her tightening nipples to the cool air.

'You're amazing, you know that?' he told her while big palms smoothed the fabric up over her outer thighs, raising goose-bumps and heat and blood pressure.

She shifted, adjusting her knees so she was closer. 'This whole night's amazing.'

Jett agreed, his hands sweeping up the curves of her body as he divested her of her clothing. Then she was exposed to his gaze but for a pair of skimpy lace knickers and he took a moment to go slow, trailing his fingers over peaches and cream skin never touched by the sun. Pert pink nipples ripe for tasting. He filled his hands with her sensational breasts and listened to her breathing quicken and turn choppy, then raised his head and suckled her.

'Jett...'

Gasping, she threw back her head and Jett felt her nails digging crescent moons deep into his shoulders. He tipped back his head to see her better. Her lips were pressed together, her eyes closed.

'Right here with you,' he murmured.

She made a little sound at the back of her throat.

Ah…yeah. He wanted to hear those cute little noises she made when she came. He wanted to hear them *now*.

But more than that, he wanted *her*. Only her. All of her. He admired her control-freak nature, he'd found it a turn-on and he'd never want to break it, but tonight he wanted to bend that control. Just a little. To watch her fly apart and know he was responsible. He reached down between their bodies and with two swift tugs the last lacy barrier disappeared.

Her eyes went round with surprise, but only for a moment before her mouth kicked up at the corners. 'That was my best pair of knickers. I wore them especially for you.'

'And I appreciated them, believe me.' Without taking his gaze off her, he grabbed the condom packet, tore one open and sheathed himself. Something flickered at the edge of his consciousness, like sheet lightning on the ocean's horizon on a sultry summer night. Olivia wasn't like other women he slept with. And tomorrow— Nuh. He reached for her. She was here now, she wanted him, and for tonight she was his.

As his hands gripped her waist and lifted her hips she drew in a sharp breath and Olivia saw doubt cross his gaze. Still gripping his shoulders to support herself on arms that had started to tremble, she met his eyes. 'It's okay.'

He slowed, setting her down carefully on his belly. 'Please tell me you've done this before.'

Heat rushed to her cheeks. 'I have. But not often.' She bit her lips then said, 'I'm sorry.'

Dark eyes searched hers, brows lowered. 'What are you apologising for this time?'

'Because…I'm not very good.' Her most intimate parts on full view, she'd never felt more exposed. Except he wasn't looking at her intimate parts; his gaze was focused on her eyes.

'Who the hell told you that?'

'Jason… An ex-boyfriend. He said…'

'He was an idiot and he was wrong. And you're not getting away from me that easily.'

'Really?' Relief washed through her.

'Really.' A corner of his mouth lifted and he touched her cheek. 'We'll take it slow.' With an infinitely tender gaze, one she'd never thought Jett capable of, he drew her head down until their lips touched, ever so lightly. A butterfly's kiss that soothed and enticed.

And for a rare and precious moment she felt like that emerging butterfly—shiny and new, treasured even. She felt as if he were kissing her for the first time, his lips surprisingly gentle and so, so sweet, fingers tangling lightly in her hair and drawing it down so the tips caressed his shoulders. Creating a curtain so that all she could see when she lifted her lips and opened her eyes was the perfection of his face.

'Everything okay?' he murmured.

'I just want to look at you.' He stared at her and again she sensed his hesitation. 'Don't freak out,' she said tight-lipped. 'I have no interest in long term either, if that's what you're wondering.'

'Here isn't the right place for this.' Somehow he managed to push up, tucking her against him. She clung to his neck as he carried her across the entertainment area, down a short passage and into a luxury bedroom.

She got a glimpse of a massive bed piled with cushions and strewn with discarded clothes but then he tumbled her onto a cool cotton quilt and followed her down.

Stark white street lights shone through shuttered windows throwing silver bars across the bed as he stretched out, pulling her on top of him again, but slowly and close so that every exquisitely sensitive part of her slid along every hard and hot and masculine part of him.

Jett kept his hands casual and easy, his movements slow

and loose, but heat glimmered beneath skin, a banked fire—one spark and they'd both ignite. 'Just so you know, I want you too,' he murmured.

A purely female smile tugged at her lips. 'It's kind of obvious.' She straddled him again, one hand in the centre of his chest as she wriggled downwards. 'And while I'm on top I'm going to take full advantage.'

'I meant…' That swift silvery tug had snagged him mid-sternum. Caught him unawares. 'You're one of a kind.'

Her apricot fragrance surrounded him with warmth—and something more. It took a heartbeat or two to recognise it. Familiarity. And intimacy that went beyond the physical. He was unaccustomed to both. Solitary was his life. No hassles, no heartaches.

He'd be on the road out of town first thing tomorrow.

For now he concentrated on guiding himself to her entrance and arousing her with slow smooth strokes while she supported herself on her arms in such a way so that her breasts grazed his chest. The inexperienced seducing the player with the kind of sweet torture he almost wished could last for ever.

'We won't do anything until you're ready.'

Her laughter, surprisingly earthy, filled the quiet room. 'My one and only Secret Sinner-Santa. I've been ready for you since Christmas Eve.'

Unlike her robust amusement, beneath the cold white light filtering through the shutters her usually sun-kissed skin took on the fragile appearance of delicate porcelain, and he discovered *he* was the one trembling. Apparently his sexy skipper was as daring in the bedroom as she was on the ocean.

Fascinating, Olivia thought, how a man's body could be so different but fit so beautifully with hers. He'd set the mood to mellow, the pace to slow and for now she was happy to go with it.

Slow didn't mean less intense, oh no. For her tonight, the journey was as important as the destination. And since this was a one-off, she intended to make it last. All the way to Morningtown.

'Olivia…'

She'd noticed Jett only used her real name when something was serious. She looked down, met his eyes and saw something tender, almost vulnerable, beneath the raw and primitive. When she blinked it was gone.

'Jett…' she murmured back, instinctively lowering her mouth to his to soothe and assuage and distract. And seduce.

He gripped her jaw and let his lips slide over hers, back and forth. 'I'm glad you changed your mind.'

She nibbled the shell of his ear and whispered, 'So am I.'

'I love your breasts,' he murmured, his lips and tongue teasing the ruched tips.

Her breath caught. One day those breasts he so admired would betray her. She wondered vaguely how he'd feel about her if they were gone. How any man would feel about a woman who was only half a woman.

'Anything wrong?' He paused and his gaze flicked to hers, concerns and questions in their depths.

'Nothing,' she whispered, pushing bad thoughts away, pulling his head down to her breast again. 'Don't stop.' Her fingers tightened as she stroked his silky hair. 'Give me everything. *I want it all.*'

No lover could have been more caring and attentive and patient than Jett. The low rumble of his voice, the unhurried way he moved his hands over her. He knew just where to touch, to taste, how to make her body sing with nothing more than words.

Lovely lingering caresses, slow murmurs, exquisitely sensual. The drift of light over his face. Nerves melting away in the warmth of his gaze. Time to savour, to enjoy.

There was nothing but this moment, this place. This man. Her mind was filled with him, lazy limbs sliding against his, the scent of their mingled bodies rising up between them.

His muscles were taut, humming, and she knew what it was costing a hot-blooded, experienced man like Jett to go so slowly. A considerate lover, allowing her to set the pace, to take control.

There were no words exchanged as they explored one another. Just murmurs of delight at each new discovery. The way he shuddered when she licked inside his ear. The feel of corded muscle beneath firm skin. Contrasts and textures. She'd never thought a man's body would be so appealing to touch or feel so pleasurable against hers.

And when the unrelenting passion drove her to the point of madness, she lowered her body onto his heat and strength and, with a sigh of delight, she took him inside her. Their gazes fused and pleasure reigned. She arched and slowly began to move with him.

Finally, this time when she reached that glorious vortex, he was right there with her, sharing the flash and sizzle as they took flight over the edge together.

Neither of them moved for several minutes. Or it might have been hours. She might have slept but she was sure she hadn't. How could she sleep after the most amazing experience of her life? All she was sure of was that this guy lying beside her, his breathing slow and even and a hairy thigh resting heavy between her legs, was out for the count.

No pillow talk, then. And it wasn't what she and Jett were about anyway. One night was all it had ever been, all it would ever be; they both understood that. And she was relieved he was asleep because it would make it easier to slip away, redress and let herself out—*sans* panties.

No need for conversation. No awkward moments and face-to-face morning-after. She needed time alone to think about the night, to replay it in her mind—and store it in her heart.

Because in spite of all the warnings she'd given herself, she was falling for him. Falling for him in a bigger way than she'd ever dreamed of. Oh, he was a playboy and way too sure of himself, but the more time she spent with him, the more she discovered about him. And she liked what she was finding. Behind that devil-may-care attitude, he was the kind of guy who liked to have fun and respected others. He'd respected her decisions and let her make the first move. Respect was something Jason had never had. Certainly not for her anyway.

And if she wasn't careful, she could easily let herself be fooled into naïvely thinking Jett felt the same way she did. Just because they'd had great sex.

Except for her, the sex was only part of it. But it would be a fatal mistake to make more of this than what it was. A one-nighter. A fling. The knowledge that she'd know her future within weeks had given her the impetus to grab tonight and make some memories.

But no matter what future she was dealt, she didn't want a man and the complications that came with him. She had too many other commitments. Others were counting on her. So staying here snuggled up next to him was a *bad* idea. She shifted experimentally. If she could just extricate herself…

'Where do you think you're going?' a surprisingly wide-awake voice muttered next to her ear.

'Down to my room,' she whispered. 'Go back to sleep.'

'Like hell you are. And I wasn't asleep.'

'Oh.' She tried again to ease away but her leg remained trapped. 'I didn't bring anything with me.'

'You brought the important stuff.' A firm arm reached

around her waist and pulled her back until she was flush against him. He was hard and erect against her bottom and obviously ready to go again.

'Tell me about this idiot boyfriend,' he murmured against her ear.

'He doesn't exist any more. Not to me.'

'How old were you?'

'Eighteen.'

'No other boyfriends?'

'I went out with a few guys in high school, but they were mostly platonic, study buddies—that kind of thing. Nerds, you'd probably say. Then I met Jason, who wasn't a nerd by any stretch of the imagination. Our relationship was a bit like a cheap sky show. Bright sparks that fizzled fast.'

'That's all? Just a spark and fizzle?'

She remembered the way things had ended. 'So after the underwhelming experience, I decided I wasn't missing much. And I was studying—I didn't have time for guys. I should go…'

'Why?' His hand slid round and found a nipple to play with. 'Stay.'

And she couldn't think of a reason why she shouldn't. Didn't really want to because *she didn't want the night to end*. 'Since we're both awake…' She turned over so they were face to face and stared into his eyes and saw her desire reflected back. 'Want to play again?'

He grinned, teeth white, eyes laughing in the dimness. 'I'm ready if you are.'

She traced the curve of his lips with a fingertip and grinned back. 'I know.'

'My turn on top,' he said, and rolled her onto her back.

CHAPTER TEN

JETT WATCHED THE SKY turn grey and the first hints of dawn creep through the shutters. The sleeping form outlined beside him snuffled and shifted but remained asleep. A grin hooked the corner of his mouth. Who'd have thunk it? Olivia snored like a trooper.

He watched her face in the pearlescent light and was tempted to wake her with a kiss on those plump and pretty lips and have his way with her again. Something powerful and almost possessive snagged in his chest. He'd had beautiful women, experienced women with all the right moves, but none of them had seduced him the way Olivia had. She'd not only seduced his body, but also his mind, with her intelligence and humour and a stubborn determination to rival his own.

He gritted his teeth against such feelings. He'd sailed on her boat as she'd requested of him, suffered his bit for charity and was leaving this morning.

Just because they'd shared a bed, a few truths and something less substantial that he hadn't quite figured out yet, didn't mean he was going to change his plans. She knew he was leaving and she had her own career path mapped out. They both understood where the other was coming from.

He was up and showered and dressed before she woke. He ordered breakfast for two then checked his emails. He had the morning sorted. They'd share coffee and croissants before they parted ways. He'd offer any further assistance for her foundation should she need it, then his chauffeured ride would drop her home if she wanted before taking him on up to Cradle Mountain. He figured he'd enjoy the scenery along the way while he jumped on the Internet and got a head start on some foody ideas during the four-hour journey...

Except he'd got used to having her around over the past week. Her boundless energy and enthusiasm was contagious, giving a much-needed boost to his flagging motivation and lack of direction of late. The way her eyes flashed when she was angry or bewildered with him. When she smiled in his direction and made his heart pound a little bit harder.

Should he ask her to come with him? Just for a couple of days? Just until this spark lost its sparkle?

He scowled at his laptop screen. Him and his sister's best friend. Yeah, right. When the spark lost its sparkle it could all get *very* messy.

He was still scowling when the tousle-haired beauty walked into the room. Wearing last night's discarded silk shirt. The top two buttons were undone, leaving a generously exposed cleavage. Its hem barely covered enough thigh to be decent; her legs flashed honey-gold in the sun's early morning glow.

'Someone went clubbing last night,' she said, fiddling with the cuffs.

'I went to check out the casino earlier in the evening.'

'I've never been to a casino, but I've heard it's fun.'

'Never made it. Wasn't in the right mood.'

'Oh. Lucky for me.' She smiled, looking sexy and adorable, and his body throbbed to instant attention. He wanted to have her here, now, and to hell with breakfast and his plans. 'There's a hotel robe in the bathroom that might be warmer,' he suggested, tearing his gaze away and returning his focus to his PC.

'I'm not cold.' She'd moved in record time because an arm shot across his line of vision. 'See, no goose-bumps.'

He nodded, resumed tapping keys. 'Just finishing something here...' She smelled of warm, musky, satisfied woman and he couldn't help it—he filled his lungs with her scent.

'You're supposed to say it looks better on me than on you.'

He'd heard that cajoling feminine tone before, just not from Olivia. He spared a glance. Beaded nipples clearly outlined against the fine fabric. He knew they were the colour of coral and tasted like mulled wine. His eyes lingered longer than he'd intended. He could feel his blood pressure rise. And other parts. This wasn't going the way he'd planned. 'So it does. Keep it if you want.' He doubted he'd wear it again—he didn't keep mementos.

To his surprise, she agreed, 'No reminders,' then reached for last night's goody bag. 'We didn't get to eat the food I brought over.' From the corner of his eye he saw her pinch off a grape and hold it out to him. 'Hungry?'

He looked up and met pretty sea-blue eyes. Yes, he was, but not for food. 'I've ordered breakfast for...' he checked the time '...fifteen minutes.'

'So we have fifteen minutes.' Popping the grape in her mouth, she started unbuttoning the shirt in a brisk, businesslike fashion.

When he watched in disbelief, she shrugged, slipping another button free, her eyes twinkling like jewels. 'Once more for the road?'

He pushed back from the table, already pulling his shirt over his head, not bothering with buttons. 'You're trouble, you know that?'

'So you've said.' She pulled a foil packet out of the shirt

pocket before she let the garment slither off those elegant creamy shoulders and onto the floor. 'More than once. I—'

He'd grabbed her around the waist, swung her up, hoisted her onto the table and spread her thighs apart before either of them knew what he was about. A glass table arrangement rocked unsteadily behind her.

He paused for a second, stunned. Something that looked like panicked excitement streaked across her gaze.

'Don't stop.'

'Don't intend to.' He slid one finger inside her.

Her gasp fired his blood to fever pitch. Snatching the condom from her fingers, he fumbled as he rolled it on then dragged her buttocks to the edge of the table. Craving the clench of her hot wet heat around him. Craving that one last time, the way an addict craved his last fix before rehab.

She leaned back on her elbows, offering. Demanding. 'Yes! Hurry.'

His vision hazed, his body shuddered, and he heard himself swear once, violently, before he leaned over her, lowered his body to hers and plunged inside. The impact drove the air from both their lungs.

'Jett!'

It wasn't pain he heard in her breathless plea. It was the same urgency that beat through his own blood. His name on her lips, over and over, her hands barely clinging to his sweat-damp shoulders, hips arching to meet his thrusts.

No slow and gentle this morning, his control was in tatters, and, he knew by looking into her eyes, she didn't want it. She wanted fast, uninhibited abandon. That was what he gave her and what she gave in return.

Sheer mindless passion. Frantic mouths and muttered pleasure. Flesh met flesh, every harsh breath expelled matched the fierce pace they'd set.

She gave him everything without fear or hesitation, eager

for more, as if she'd never get enough, her whole body vibrant and alive, her face aglow.

As if she was trying to live an entire life in these few crazy moments.

He drove her up, higher, faster. The room around them blurred, lightning cracked and they flew together through the eye of the storm.

Olivia collapsed against the table, its glass surface cool against her damp back. Jett's body on hers was a still-unfamiliar and exciting weight, their sweat-slicked skin fused together in interesting places. She wondered if she'd find the strength to move before breakfast arrived.

He peeled himself off her, the sticky pull bringing a smile to her numb lips. He didn't speak when he lifted her off the table except to order her to 'Stay there,' and disappeared into the bathroom.

She picked the silk shirt up off the floor, brought it to her nose. His musky scent mingled with her own. *No reminders.*

She set it atop his packed bag, her mind still spinning, her legs still shaking. Who'd have thought sex could be like this? Not only the physical experience but the—she searched for a word—connection.

Had her life been different and if she hadn't applied her days and nights to the challenges of study and founding Snowflake with such dedication, maybe she'd have had more opportunities like this one.

But it would have been a waste. Because no one would ever do it for her like Jett.

No reminders? *Huh.* Maybe not tangible mementos but the memories were going to live on for a very long time. She was *so* going to pay for this one night.

Jett appeared, still bare-chested and holding the fluffy robe he'd mentioned. He didn't come close and slip it around her shoulders as she half expected and fully hoped, but held it out at arm's length. His eyes were dark and unreadable, giving her no clue how he felt. 'You okay?'

'Yes.' She took it from his hands. *It's over, Olivia. Pull yourself together and smile.*

It was a waste of a smile because she watched him shut his laptop, stow it in a briefcase beside his luggage. Not looking at her. All cool business. As if they hadn't just had wild animal sex on the table.

'Breakfast's late,' he muttered. As if he was in a hurry to get going and its tardy delivery was holding him up.

'Just as well, don't you think?'

She didn't know if he even heard. He seemed preoccupied. Almost on autopilot he reached down and swiped up the cotton shirt he'd whipped off earlier in his frenzy to have her and began undoing the buttons.

Desperation seized her. She wanted him to answer her, to notice her. To look at her the way he'd looked at her moments ago. 'Thanks for that,' she said, faking casual, glancing at the table still smeared with their skin prints.

No response.

'With everything so busy, who knows when I'll get lucky again.'

That got his attention.

What the...? Jett's gaze snapped to Olivia as she pulled the robe's tie firmly at her waist, swamping her in white terry towelling. He took a moment to process her words. Before he could draw breath, she beat him to it.

'Careful what you say, Jett, your sexist streak isn't going to impress me.'

He frowned, dumbfounded with the strange look in her eyes and her throwaway attitude. *Getting lucky.* He'd used the words himself more times than he could count. Some deep-down, primitive *possessive* part of him wanted to roar. He bunched the shirt in his fists before tossing it onto the sofa. 'Nothing to say.' Except, 'Just don't let anyone take advantage of you.'

Because he knew she was inexperienced and vulnerable and he couldn't stomach the idea of another Jason using her for all the wrong reasons.

'I've been practically celibate for twenty-six years—you don't think I know how to say no?' She pointed an accusing finger in his direction. 'Has it occurred to you that *you* took advantage on Christmas Eve? If Brie hadn't rung when she did… Think about it.'

'You'd have said yes.'

She rolled her eyes. 'Re-a-lly.'

'You wouldn't have been able to stop yourself.'

'Right,' she scoffed.

'Because we're good together, dammit. And you know it. You let me take advantage. You were *begging* me to take advantage.'

She shook her head. He watched her pace away and wanted to take her in his arms and hold her close and… And what? For God's sake. He drew in a slow, deep breath and somehow reined in his frustration.

'Okay, I admit it,' she said. 'You were different—*are* different. When I saw you I'd never felt that way before. Like I was shivery and melty at the same time. Like I was in a storm at sea with a broken mast.

'But none of that matters because I've no intention of having sex with you again, Jett. Next time we meet it'll be as friends. When Brie's there. Because one thing I sincerely hope is that this thing between us won't spoil what you and Brie have—family.'

Her absolute conviction in what she was saying riveted him to the spot. She infatuated him. That combination of strength and tenderness and understanding.

Breakfast interrupted anything he might have said and

while he signed for it and the staff set it up on a wrought-iron table in a corner overlooking the marina, Olivia grabbed her clothes and the handbag she'd left on the table and slipped from the room to shower.

Jett shrugged into his wrinkled shirt, poured coffee for them both and watched a few New Year stragglers down on the docks looking much the worse for wear while he waited for her.

He should be relieved. She wasn't some clingy female who demanded more than he wanted to give. He shook his head. Didn't mean he couldn't still ask her to accompany him to the mountains for a few days. He could talk her round. He could change her mind.

When Olivia didn't show after five minutes, he drank his coffee and broke open a croissant. He'd heard the shower switch off, but the women he knew spent an inordinate time in front of the mirror.

A few minutes later he heard her muffled voice through the closed bedroom door and got up and went to investigate. She sounded agitated but he wasn't about to eavesdrop on a private conversation. He tapped on the door. 'Everything okay in there?'

Instant silence, followed by a muffled 'I'll be there soon.'

Frowning, he returned to the table, poured himself another coffee, then dialled Room Service for a fresh pot.

She entered the room, dressed in last night's clothes, her bag slung over her shoulder, scrolling over the screen on her phone as she hurried to where she'd left her shoes and slipped them on. She didn't even glance his way. 'I can't stay for breakfast. I have to leave.'

He'd said the same often enough when *he'd* been the one rushing out after a night of casual sex. He raised his china cup towards her. 'Not even for coffee? I ordered another pot.'

She didn't answer; perhaps she hadn't heard him because she was busy digging around in her bag. 'Crap!'

He flicked her a look. 'Problem?'

She shook her head, still preoccupied with finding whatever she was searching for. 'Nothing for you to worry about.' She finally pulled out a set of keys, then put them back for no reason he could work out other than she was checking she had them. 'I hope you enjoy Freycinet Lodge.'

'Cradle Mountain. And I was thinking, if you—'

Eyes narrowed, he stepped closer and got his first good look since she'd come into the room. Her face was the colour of porridge. 'You said you were fine.'

She saw him looking at her trembling hands and clenched her fingers around her bag strap. 'I have to go.'

'Something's wrong.'

She waved him off and headed to the door. 'It's none of your concern.'

He slammed his mug down and walked towards her. 'I'm making it my concern.'

She kept her back towards him. 'I've got a cab waiting downstairs. I have to get home.'

Grabbing her arm, he swung her around. 'I'm not letting you out of here until you tell me.' Beneath his hand he could feel tremors running like quicksilver through muscle.

Her shoulders sagged, she closed her eyes briefly then stared up at him. They were dry and alarmingly devastated. 'My home's been broken into. The police tried to contact me last night and I didn't answer my mobile because I'd switched it off so they tried my room but I wasn't there because I was here. I've been making arrangements.'

He swore under his breath. 'Slow down. Take a breather.'

She thumped a fist against her thigh. 'Yeah? Your house hasn't just been burgled.'

He firmed his hold, said, 'What can I do?'

She shook her head. 'I'll contact you…some time.'

He didn't let go. 'What's the damage?'

'A security guy's meeting me there in forty-five minutes.'

'Did you have deadlocks?'

She glared at him. 'What do you think? And yes, the alarm was *on*.'

'Have you spoken with Breanna? I'll call her for you.'

'No, you will *not*. I don't want to spoil her holiday. And phone coverage is hit and miss up there. There's nothing she can do—'

'But I can.' Panicked eyes blinked at him. 'We can stand here wasting time or you can give in now, because I'm coming with you. End. Of. Discussion.'

CHAPTER ELEVEN

OLIVIA ACCEDED WITH a nod and Jett eased up a bit and released his hold. 'I've got a car waiting, I'll have it brought round.'

It was a simple matter to collect his gear and ride down the elevator, send her cab off, explain to his driver there'd been a change in plans and check them both out while she threw her stuff together. They were on their way in less than ten minutes.

He watched her stare straight ahead as they drove the short distance down the coast. She didn't even drink the take-away coffee he'd bought her while she'd been packing her things.

'I should've gone straight home after the race but I wanted to unwind in the city for New Year after all the work.'

'Why are you blaming yourself?'

'I keep thinking I must have missed something.'

'We'll know soon. Try to relax.'

She turned silent again but a short time later, her hand slammed against her throat. 'Turn here.'

He followed her gaze to a magnificent old home almost hidden by trees. They passed through tall iron gates and followed a long driveway to the house. Peeling garden gnomes and fairy statues played hide and seek amongst the foliage along the way.

A vast red-brick and cream lattice structure that might have come straight out of a luxury living magazine once upon a time came into view.

A guy in a car got out as they pulled up near the back entrance.

'Wait here,' Olivia told Jett firmly. 'I want to do this on my own.' She climbed out and the guy met her a few metres away. They walked to the back porch then disappeared inside.

Jett unloaded their bags, told the driver he'd be in contact, then looked about him as the car drove away. Fantastic views of the River Derwent, garden and natural bushland surrounded the property.

With Olivia still busy inside, Jett followed the scents of lavender and basil to a lovingly tended herb and vegetable garden. Organic, no doubt. Further on, he saw a pool, drained of water, the overhead glass structure grimy and cracked. A gazebo overgrown with weeds. The garden unkempt and parched. He'd have liked to have seen this place in its glory days.

With some physical effort and a sizeable injection of funds this place could be great again.

This place could be the retreat Olivia envisioned.

Right here. Her own home. Had she even thought of that? Excitement tingled along his nerve-endings. A new project, something different that he could really put his back into. Literally. He'd be doing something worthwhile. And at the end he could walk away with an honourable sense of achievement.

He heard the security guy's car leaving, and, following the sound, he retraced his steps through the bushland at the far edge of the property. As the house came into view he saw Olivia standing in the doorway surrounded by their luggage, hugging her upper arms, and scouring the grounds for him.

Such an unexpectedly domestic scene with the potted geraniums by her feet, her sun-stroked hair moving gently in the breeze, copper glinting amongst the red. She turned his way as if by instinct and their eyes met the way they had that first time.

And something huge swelled up inside his chest and rolled through him like one of those waves he'd experienced on *Chasing Dawn*, leaving an ache to settle uncomfortably in the hollow left behind.

He wanted to run the rest of the way, wrap his arms around her and tell her everything would be okay, but he knew she wouldn't welcome it. Not Ms Olivia Wishart, equal rights champion and feminist extraordinaire.

Olivia watched Jett's approach and she wanted to cry and be weak and female. She wanted to run to him and, just once, have someone be there for her. To have him wrap her up tightly and tell her everything would be okay. To feel safe.

But he wasn't that kind of a guy. Not Jett Davies, good-time guy and playboy.

And yet… For a moment there, she thought she'd seen… something in those deep chocolate eyes.

Probably the sun playing tricks. Blinking back those stupid female tears, she grabbed her bag and marched back inside as fast as its wheels would go. She made it to the kitchen before his hand on her shoulder stopped her.

'Whoa, slow down a minute. You'll give yourself a heart attack.'

His voice, low and steady and rational right when she needed it to be.

His aftershave reminded her that less than an hour ago they'd been lovers but he was here for her now as a support person. A friend.

His hand. Grounding her in reality.

Again she fought that urge to cling to someone strong and solid and trustworthy in a world where faceless people could take away or destroy your precious possessions and leave you feeling lost and empty and abused. She knew possessions counted for little but it didn't make it less painful.

'They knew what they were doing,' she said, turning to the window. Even the stunning coastline view failed to lift her. 'Professionals. They bypassed the security code then helped themselves. Not satisfied with that, they vandalised.' Violated her private stuff. She bit her lip, her stomach churning with so much *more* than anger. 'Who'd do that?'

'Scumbags, lowlifes. They're everywhere.'

'My bedroom.' Her lip trembled. 'They tipped out my drawers and…'

'We can fix it, skipper.'

His voice was so gentle she wanted to cry. Pride stopped her. 'Not all of it. My mother's heirloom jewellery. And I'll never be able to sleep in my room again.'

'Okay, maybe not all of it,' he agreed. 'Why don't you show me?' Still in that voice she'd barely heard from him until last night in his bed when she'd seen a side of him she'd not expected.

She led the way to her room, picked up the broken remains of an antique china ornament that had belonged to her grandmother. 'It's all so senseless.'

'Damn right.'

A chill shuddered through her. His arms came around her and this time she allowed herself to lean back and absorb a little of his strength.

'It'll be okay,' he said, combing gentle fingers through her hair. 'And you're not alone. I'm here.'

A comfort for now but so temporary. Maybe she could stay at Brie's for a while—she knew she'd be welcome—except she also knew she'd be intruding on her friend's busy social life, and late-night partying wasn't Olivia's thing. Meanwhile, 'I'll manage. They're not beating me.'

'Good girl,' he said, stepping away and pulling out his phone. 'You'll need help to clean up this mess. Do you know anyone?'

She shook her head. 'Don't worry about it. I'll do it myself.'

'Okay, then. I'll help.'

'No. I'll be fine. You should go.'

He frowned at her. 'Why do you feel you have to do this on your own? Is it because I'm a male? A chauvinistic jerk? You want to prove a point? What?'

'Cradle Mountain's waiting, remember?' Her only experiences with men had taught her that when the going got tough, the tough got going. All the way to Trinidad—or wherever it was her father had escaped to.

'You think I'd just walk away and leave you to it?' He took her hand in his big comforting one and led her down the hall and into the living room, pushed her gently into one of the overstuffed armchairs. He squatted down in front of her so that their gazes were level. Equals. 'Come on, skipper, talk to me.'

She understood now that she'd been basing her perception of men and their inability to stay and face the bad with the good on one man: her father. She'd not had many other male role models in her life to compare. Except Brie's father, who'd walked away from Jett's mother and his own son because it was all too complicated. Both had been selfish men who lacked responsibility and honour and common decency.

'I'm used to being independent,' she said. 'It's hard to be anything else.'

'We're the same in a lot of ways, you and me. We both value responsibility and achievement and independence.

Maybe we could try trusting each other more, leaning on each other a little, and see where it takes us?'

She nodded once. 'And just so you know, you're not a jerk.'

He laughed, a full belly laugh that rolled over her like velvet and relieved some of her tension, then kissed her full on the mouth. 'Don't ever change.'

'I don't intend to. I'm okay with who I am.'

'I'm okay with who you are too. I like that you can turn bad into good—Pink Snowflake's testimony to that. Let me stay for a bit and help you out here. Just temporary, until things are back to normal. It's New Year—hard to get tradespeople in when everyone's on holiday.'

His words sent warmth blooming across her cheeks and inside her chest. She was unaccustomed to acceptance and approval. Guys, even other girls, saw her as a nerdy, introspective individual with more qualifications than she knew what to do with. Jett didn't seem bothered. 'But what about Cradle Mountain?'

'It's not going anywhere.'

'I don't want to interfere with your writing.'

'To tell you the truth, I'm not in a hurry.'

She nodded. 'Thank you.'

'You're welcome.' He rose and straightened, rubbed his hands together. 'Let's get started.'

They worked the rest of the day, only stopping for a quick bite for lunch cobbled together from what she found in the pantry and freezer. They finished the meal with slices of the Christmas cake Brie had baked for Jett.

It was hard. Heartbreaking. But Jett's company and support went a long way to making it more bearable. Guys turned up to install a new security system. Late in the afternoon, Jett drove her car to the local shopping centre and bought ingredients for a creamy soup and pasta sauce and raspberry ripple ice cream. He added a DVD for later.

And a *food processor*.

'You might like to try it some time,' he suggested, setting it on her kitchen bench.

Where it would likely stay unopened in its box until hell froze over.

Jett asked about her house over fettuccini and a glass of red wine.

'Unfortunately, it's been let go,' she told him. 'I'm going to have to sell it and settle for sleeping on Brie's couch before we can even think of buying the land for our retreat and I know I'm going to have to settle for less than it's worth.'

He chewed for a few moments in silence, then said, 'This place means a lot to you.'

'It's home. The only one I've ever had.'

The look in his eyes told her he'd probably never called anywhere home but he could appreciate how it must feel.

'There are memories here. Happy, sad.' She took a mouthful of wine, nostalgia blurring her vision. 'I'd hang on to it if I could, but I have to be practical, not sentimental. The retreat's more important.'

He topped up their glasses. 'What are you looking for in a retreat?'

She blinked away old wishes. 'Something close to the city but not too close. With shrubbery. And a water view. Vacant blocks are hard to find. We're looking at those prefab kit homes that stack together, so it can grow as we do.'

'Have you ever thought of using this place?'

She chased the fettuccini around her plate with her fork. 'It's too small for what I have in mind and there's too much to do. We'd never be able to afford it. Have you *seen* the back yard? It's not been touched in years. The cost for that alone would be astronomical. We need to start modestly.'

He eyed her over his glass then set it down. 'I *have* seen the back yard. As a matter of fact I've had a second look. The potential's amazing. Think indoor heated pool and hot tub joined to the main house through a glass-covered walkway lined with luscious plants. You have all the basic ingredients, they just need to be used in a new way. You can create new memories to add to the old.'

She could imagine his idea, so tantalisingly real; she could almost feel the sunshine and water on her skin, could almost smell the tropical blooms. An all-weather paradise to lift flagging spirits.

For a wealthy chef with money to burn it might be a possibility, but for her it wasn't realistic. 'When I win the lottery.' She gave a half-laugh.

'You never know when your lucky numbers might come up.'

'Yeah, right, with the way my luck's going?' She deliberately switched topics. 'How about some ice cream and that DVD?' It was on the table and she flipped it over. '*Pretty Woman*? You got me a chick flick?'

He raised his glass. 'The title got me. There's one more thing.' He watched her over the rim. 'Where do the two of us go from here? Are we friends or lovers?'

Simple question, difficult answer. 'I know we're friends...' She met his full-on intensity with an intense gaze of her own. 'Everything's so complicated right now.'

He nodded, his expression unchanging. 'Friends, then.'

He'd agreed with her. No talking her into something she wasn't sure of. No trying to change her mind.

The way he'd not tried to change her mind on that last night aboard the yacht when she'd told him the same thing. He obviously respected the decisions she made.

She had to admire that.

* * *

Olivia woke next morning with a breathless gasp and yesterday's nightmare came crashing back. The last thing she remembered was the movie's opening credits. On the floor beside the sofa and his open laptop, Jett was surfacing too.

'Morning,' she murmured, staring into his dark, sleepy eyes. 'Sorry. I fell asleep.' Obviously. 'Why didn't you use one of the bedrooms?'

He blinked awake. 'Was awake till four working on a few ideas.' He stretched, looking gorgeously rumpled and sexy, darkly stubbled and bleary-eyed.

'Ideas? For your book?'

'Nope.' He leaned back against the sofa and watched her. 'We'll talk about it later.'

She was ultra-aware that yesterday morning's love-in was an unspoken conversation between them. She wanted, so badly, to slide down onto the floor and join him. Join *with* him. *Look away, Olivia.*

She pushed back the throw Jett must have covered her with and stood, still in yesterday's clothes and looking like something the cat had dragged in. 'I'll see what I can find for breakfast,' she said, and hurried to the kitchen.

Leaning on the open fridge door, she told herself she could come up with a cooked breakfast. She never bothered but Jett would want something.

And he was going to discover very quickly how limited her cooking skills were. She lived largely on a diet of healthy raw foods—often by necessity—but she could cook the basics. Very basic. Having a personal chef around twenty-four-seven for the next few days could prove a blessing. Or not.

'You go shower. I'll get breakfast,' Jett said, behind her, relieving her of the problem of how he wanted his eggs cooked and whether he was going to watch.

Maybe he'd already picked up on her lack of expertise.

Or he couldn't bear to look at her in her state of dishabille. Either way, she escaped without putting up much of a fight.

A short time later, feeling refreshed and towelling her damp hair, she followed the aromas of grilled bacon and coffee.

'Smells fantastic.'

When he saw her, he slid food onto two plates. 'Sit down and eat while I talk.'

She did as he told her. He didn't mean to come across so dictatorial. Since Jason, she'd never imagined feeling comfortable with a man who seemed to dominate everyone around him but Jett was different. Unlike Jason, she knew he'd at least listen. Also unlike Jason, with Jett she felt safe. And respected.

'I did some costing while you were asleep last night.' He set her plate in front of her, sat down opposite with his own. 'Ran a few ideas by an architect I know. With thought and planning we could turn this place into your retreat.'

'Jett...no.' She shook her head. 'I told you. An architect?' She didn't like that he was way ahead of her. 'Too expensive. You—'

'Hear me out. Just close your eyes and visualise. Please.'

'Okay, but this is *my* baby.'

'Goes without saying,' he reassured her. 'But it doesn't hurt to have another person's take on it.'

She closed her eyes.

'Improve and extend the kitchen garden so that in time, when the facility opens, it'll supply its own organic produce. Upgrade the pool facilities to include a relaxing fitness area and equipped gymnasium and join it to the main building. We knock down walls and extend the back of the house into—'

'Whoa.' She shook her head, her mind spinning. 'Even with the money we raised on *Chasing Dawn*, we'd only manage a fraction of that. We should rename her *Chasing Dreams.*'

He nodded. 'Why don't you? Sounds appropriate.'

'Because I'm going to sell her.' Her decision wasn't one she'd made lightly.

He frowned. 'Doesn't she hold special meaning for you and your mother?'

'She's done her job. I need the money for other things,' she said briskly, dropping her gaze to her plate.

'I've been looking for a new project,' he told her slowly. 'I'd like to work with you on this. You and my sister are in this together, which kind of gives me a foot in the door, wouldn't you say?'

'But what about your cookbook plans?' Your *life*?

'At the moment this is right where I want to be—working on something different. I'll still write but I'd like to be involved in this venture.'

She tempered the rising excitement; there was the complication of their relationship to consider, but she was thinking... Having him aboard had so many advantages. Brie could get to know her brother better. Jett would have his opportunity to look at something new. He'd bring a different perspective to the table.

She'd get to see more of him.

'I'll have to talk to Brie,' she said.

'That's all I ask. If you're both fine with it, do we have a deal?'

She agreed and they took their coffee outside so he could show her how some of his ideas might work around the property.

Jett watched her eyes light up at his suggestions. Her response further fired his excitement. But excitement of a different kind wasn't happening. *I've no intention of having sex with you again, Jett.*

He knew time and circumstances weren't favourable to revisit that particular conversation. More importantly, maybe she'd be willing to accept his support for now without the complication of sex getting in the way.

And he had a plan to make her smile again.

CHAPTER TWELVE

THAT EVENING, over the steaks he'd slapped on the grill while Olivia caught up on insurance claims and financial matters, Jett told her to keep the following day free.

'I can't just take the day off,' she told him in shock-horror and set down her cutlery with a sharp clink. 'You've seen this place.'

'Which is why I've arranged to fly my housekeeper over.'

Her brows rose into her hair. 'Fly her from Melbourne?'

'An hour's flying time away and she's excited about spending some time in Hobart. She's going to spend the day tidying up at your place then stay overnight with an old friend.'

'You've already asked her? Without speaking to me first?'

'I talked to her last night when I was making arrangements; you were asleep. I trust her. You can too.'

'I didn't think you trusted people.'

'I trust Emily Branson. She's a fifty-year-old church-going grandmother. Listen,' he continued when he saw a protest forming on her lips. 'Do *you* trust *me*?'

'Doesn't mean I go along with your plans like I don't have a will of my own. Or a brain. Okay, Emily can—'

'I've also made other plans for tomorrow.'

Watching him carefully, she nibbled on a piece of bacon. 'What kind of plans?'

'It's a surprise. But I can tell you a change of scenery and something new to think about will do you a world of good. You'll come back fresh and rejuvenated. Okay?'

She blinked several times, her eyes growing wide. 'Okay. But—'

'Pack an overnight bag—and a swimsuit—and be ready to leave at seven a.m.'

The early summer morning was clear when their small private aircraft landed at Tullamarine airport. Moments later Olivia and Jett were approaching Melbourne's CBD in a sleek red helicopter, skimming the Yarra River and landing on the helipad beside a pretty park opposite the biggest casino in the southern hemisphere.

Olivia watched the sleek skyscrapers as they travelled the short distance to their hotel within the casino complex. She'd been told to expect luxury and was enjoying every exhilarating minute, so excited she'd barely stopped to breathe. 'Where's your place? Do you live in the city?'

'See that building?' He pointed to a white tower spearing into the blue. 'Twenty-first floor. But we won't have time.'

'Oh.' Pity. His secluded world up in the sky might have given her further insight into Jett Davies but it wasn't going to happen today.

As they entered the sparkling lobby she wondered what arrangements he'd made regarding rooms but didn't have time to ask because a stylish woman in her mid-thirties wearing a trim white pant-suit with a multi-hued scarf was approaching with a smile on her glossed lips.

'Jett. Good morning.'

'Tyler.' He brushed a kiss over her cheek. 'Long time no see,' he said, then touched Olivia's shoulder briefly. 'I'd like you to meet Olivia.'

'Welcome to Melbourne, Olivia.' Her handshake was brisk and businesslike. 'Smooth flight over?'

'Thanks, Tyler, and yes, smooth as silk.'

'Jett told me it's a day of surprises, so if you're wondering what's next, say goodbye to him for now. I'm going to be your personal shopper for the next two and a half hours and we're going to have a *Pretty Woman* shopping spree in some of Melbourne's famous boutiques.'

She grinned. 'Sounds awesome.'

'Before you go,' Jett said, holding his hand out, palm up, 'your credit cards stay with me until tomorrow.'

'But—'

'Shopping time's ticking. The whole purse. Now.'

Knowing he meant it, that he wanted to do this for her no strings attached, Olivia met his eyes as she handed it over, mouthing, *'Thank you.'* She wanted to stop a moment and tell him how much she appreciated everything but Tyler was already moving off so she settled for a finger wave and a smile she couldn't have wiped away if she'd tried. 'Bye.'

She fell in love with Melbourne's quaint little arcades, Victorian architecture and exclusive boutiques. Tyler informed Olivia she was to purchase something sophisticated for the evening. Anything else she fancied was up to her.

They browsed designer wear. Metallic, silk, subtle, bold. Backless, one-sleeved, split thigh. 'What colour does he like?' Olivia wondered.

'He loves your hair. So earthy colours that bring out its beauty.' She pulled out an unusual metallic olive-green dress with a sheer bodice insert studded with tiny gold beads and held it up. 'Try this, see what you think.'

He'd told this woman he loved her hair? He'd never told *her* he loved her hair. She felt a warm glow inside her chest as she studied Tyler's choice. 'The colour's great, unusual, but the neckline's way too daring, even with the insert.'

'I guarantee you'll love it.'

'You know Jett personally,' she said, slipping it on. None of Olivia's business but she wondered if Jett and the striking blonde had been lovers.

'I took one of his cooking courses in France a few years ago when I was on vacation. I owned a little café here in Melbourne at the time and we stayed in touch. Oh, my.' She clasped her hands under her chin. 'That looks stunning on you. And it fits like a glove. Trust me, it's Jett's kind of dress.'

So she knew him *that* well? Olivia would never have chosen it but she had to agree, the gown looked amazing. And how long had it been since she'd spent anything on herself? Not that she was the one spending… The sunburst of beads flowed from the sheer bodice and down over one hip. And if the neckline practically plunged to her navel, so what? It had inbuilt support and this might be the last time she got to show off her cleavage.

She hadn't realised she needed this day until now. More, Jett had anticipated exactly what she wanted. Obviously Jett understood women. He knew what they liked, knew how to please them.

'I'll take it,' she decided.

Olivia managed to purchase some pretty underwear and a couple of outfits before time was up.

'Jett and I saw quite a bit of each other while I was in France,' Tyler said as the car drove them towards the hotel. She glanced Olivia's way, obviously reading her mind. 'I'd be curious too, if I was you.'

'No. No.' *I'm not curious.* 'We…he…' Olivia tripped over her own tongue. 'Jett and I aren't in a relationship.'

'There were some moments with Jett and me, but in the end we settled for friends.'

'And that's what we are. Just friends.'

'Olivia,' she said, shaking her head, a small smile on her lips. 'I've seen you two together for less than two minutes and I can tell you "just friends" is something you and he will never be.'

No time to protest because the car was already drawing up at the lobby. A porter collected her shopping bags, Tyler said goodbye and Jett climbed in.

Their chocoholic tour lasted over an hour, starting with a French morning tea and cake in a little café while they learned about chocolate making with a small group of other tourists.

Finally, wondering if she'd still fit into her new dress, Olivia had a chance to see her hotel room when she went upstairs to freshen up and find her swimsuit. The first things she'd noticed were the two queen beds but she didn't see Jett's bag. She reminded herself it was her choice to remain friends.

She stood a few moments alone, soaking in the floor-to-ceiling view of Melbourne and the casino and catching her breath. Her life seemed a world away. Her problems non-existent for now. This was a day in a million and she intended to make the most of it.

They spent the latter part of the afternoon in the fitness centre. Lazed in the infinity pool overlooking the city. They weren't alone—it was holiday season after all—but their interaction was companionable. Jett kept her focus on other topics—places they'd travelled, movies they'd seen, their tastes in music. Recognising him, a couple of women exchanged glances and watched with lust-envy as he rose from the pool, water sluicing off the hard planes of his body, his swimming trunks clinging to his powerful thighs.

Olivia knew how they felt and was relieved Jett had organised an aromatherapy massage for her. It helped iron out the kinks stress had brought on over the past couple of days.

But it didn't take her mind off Jett's near-naked body not far away. Nor did it stop her from imagining stripping off his swimmers and having her way with him on his lounger.

He was still stretched out on that lounger pecking away on his laptop when she returned. She drew in a deep breath, let it out slowly, indulging in the private fantasy.

Sensing her gaze, Jett dragged his eyes away from his screen to watch Olivia in her black swimsuit, hair piled on top of her head, her skin flushed rose and glistening with body oil.

He nearly groaned aloud. His whole body tightened, his blood turned to lava and flowed thickly through his veins.

'Feeling better?' He wished to hell he did. Today had been an exercise in self-control, keeping his hands to himself and refusing to think about the bottle of French champagne he'd put in the room's bar fridge for later tonight and whether or not he was going to get the opportunity to share it with her.

'I feel *fabulous*.' She stretched her arms up, drawing his gaze to the undersides of her Lycra-clad breasts, then she seemed to remember where she was and let them drop to her sides, pronto. 'I need a shower. What time's dinner?'

'Seven. You have the room to yourself. I'll meet you in the lobby at six-fifty.' He shifted uncomfortably. 'I suggest you go now before I decide to accompany you to that shower.'

She half smiled, half...*what*? before she turned, picked up her belongings and sauntered away.

Whatever it was he'd glimpsed in her eyes, he had a good feeling that his bottle of champagne was going to taste very sweet indeed.

A punctual woman.

Of course she was. Everything in Olivia Wishart's life was organised and shipshape. He stood near the lobby windows, his body in lockdown as Olivia walked towards him.

His throat went dry as his eyes feasted on the scrumptious vision. *Thank you, Tyler.*

The metallic sheen changed from shades of blanched asparagus to aubergine to sage depending on the down-lights. It flowed to mid-calf and caressed every curve. He thought vaguely that someone had forgotten to sew in a bodice then realised it was some sort of sheer lacy stuff studded with tiny beads. What fabric there was clasped her breasts, showing them off to glorious perfection right where he wanted to put *his* hands.

She looked like a goddess and he wanted to worship at her shiny stilettoed shoes, then work his way up.

She smiled, secure in her feminine knowledge that she was making an impact. 'Good evening.'

'I reckon it is.' He took her hand. 'And it's about to get a whole lot better. We'll walk—it's not far.'

The tables were set amongst trees lit with fairy lights, the early evening summer sun glinted off nearby buildings, turning the white linen cloths gold.

Over drinks and appetisers they talked about the day. As the evening wore on and the sky turned to purple conversation turned more personal.

And he found himself telling Olivia stuff about his life, about himself. General stuff. His years in foster homes, his time as a sous chef in Paris, but he'd never opened up so candidly to anyone before. Unlike other women she didn't prod or try to get him to talk about things that made him uncomfortable and yet she was interested in what he did share.

It was later than he'd intended when they finally finished their coffee. He reached across the table, touched her hand. 'I had plans to take you to the casino in that spectacular dress and make every man there jealous that you're with me.'

Her cheeks flushed and she smiled. 'Honestly, Jett, can I take a rain check on that? I'd just like to go on up to the room.' She turned her hand over beneath his and entwined their fingers.

Her eyes met his, darkening as desire and anticipation brought a flush to her cheeks. He watched the way her lips parted ever so slightly, giving him a tiny glimpse of pink tongue.

'We can do that.'

She hesitated then said, 'I didn't notice your bag there earlier.'

'It's there now.'

Her eyes darkened. 'I'm glad.'

He smiled. *So am I.*

In the elevator with another couple they stood millimetres apart, watching the numbers light up as they ascended.

The moment they were out of the lift, he gathered her in and touched his lips to hers. 'Are we on the same page here?' he murmured against her mouth.

'Yes.' She sounded breathless.

With his hand on her back, he steered her to their room, pushed open the door and pulled her inside. No need for lighting; the glow from the city bathed the room, giving her skin a pearlescent sheen. Eyes on his, she reached up behind her neck. 'I'm going to need some help getting this dress off.'

'I was hoping you'd say that.'

He loved the sexy sound of the zip sliding down her back, the warm sensation of her smooth skin against his palm, her little shiver of delight. He drew the dress down and she stepped out of it, leaving her in nothing but lacy black panties and stilettos.

Her breasts. Plump and full and tantalising. He moulded his hands around them, taking their weight, and blew out a slow breath. 'You're the sexiest woman alive.'

'You make me feel sexy.' She undid his tie, slid it off, dropped it on the floor. 'It's a good feeling.' Tracing a fingernail down his shirt, she stopped at his belt buckle. 'I've never felt sexy the way you make me feel sexy. From the first time we met on that little balcony you've made me feel desired and all woman.' She looked up at him. 'You were a master seducer then and you're a master seducer now and I'm afraid I've fallen under your spell.'

'You're wrong,' he told her, lost for a moment in the warm sea of her eyes. 'You're the spell-weaver.'

'This—*us*—like *this*…together…isn't meant to happen.'

No, he thought. It wasn't. He hadn't expected to feel the way she made him feel. Out of control one moment, invincible the next. Right now he was more out of control than superhero.

'Don't think about tomorrow,' he told her, as much to her as to himself. 'Or next week or the week after that.' He lifted her, carried her to the nearest bed and laid her down. 'Just think about tonight.' He slipped off her shoes, set them on the floor. 'Us. Now.'

'Great idea.' She smiled, her hands sliding beneath the pillow as she blinked up at him, looking deliciously naked and drowsy.

'Wait right there,' he told her.

'Not going anywhere,' he heard her murmur as he strode to the bar fridge.

In less than a minute he'd uncorked his bottle of vintage champagne, poured two glasses. He toed off his shoes, picked up their drinks, anticipation licking along his veins. 'Don't fall asleep on me…'

Too late. He trailed off at her side of the bed. Out cold. Soft snores she'd never willingly make—or acknowledge—if she were awake, he thought, a smile twitching at the corner of his mouth. She needed the rest. As he watched her face relax and the tensions of the past couple of days fade his disappointment that the evening wasn't going to end the way he wanted it melted away, overtaken by a tenderness he'd never experienced. He pulled the sheet over her utterly tranquil body then walked to the window and watched Melbourne's traffic below.

New and unfamiliar sensations were creeping under his guard almost without his knowledge—and definitely without his permission. He never let anyone close. What was it about Olivia? She wasn't like other liaisons he'd had. She was genuine, caring, not all about a good time. She put others before herself. Her brand of sexy was natural and almost naïve, no guile, no pretence.

Moving away from the view, he tossed back the contents of his glass, then stripped down to underwear and positioned himself as far as possible on the other side of the bed. Wasn't working. He could hear her breathing. Her musky feminine scent teased him. He pounded the pillows into submission and switched the TV on to mute.

Shopping TV. The last damn thing he needed.

'Come on, skipper. Time to wake up. Olivia.'

She heard her name, felt a hand on her shoulder as she stirred into consciousness. Jett. She groaned, covering her eyes from the glare with an arm. *What was that light?* 'What's the time?'

'Eleven o'clock.'

'That's a bloody lie.'

'I wish it was,' she heard him say. 'You've slept over twelve hours.'

'It's a relief to hear that,' she muttered. 'I thought for a moment we'd made mad passionate love and I'd forgotten.'

'If we'd made mad passionate love you wouldn't have forgotten.'

'No.' Holding the sheet in front of her, she pushed up and stared into those gold-flecked eyes and wanted to scream her frustration. 'I've never fallen asleep with anyone before and I've done it twice with you.'

His lips twisted. 'Great for a guy's self-esteem.'

'If you want to know, you make me feel safe. Last night was the first time I've felt truly relaxed since the break-in. No bad dreams, nothing but calm. So thank you.' And she was refreshed and ready to get on with the day…or anything else.

'I'm glad,' he said, kissing her brow. 'But the flight leaves in ninety minutes. I tried to delay it but the aircraft's schedule is chockers.' He gestured to a breakfast tray on the table by his laptop where he'd obviously been working. 'You've got time for a quick shower and there's something to eat.'

Then she noticed he was dressed for business. 'What's happening?'

'Seems my adventure on the high seas has attracted continuing interest in the media. I've been invited to appear on the *Taste Buds and Travel* show—a traveller's guide to eating around the world.'

'I know what it is,' she said, struggling not to be disappointed because she knew immediately he wasn't returning to Hobart with her.

'I told them I'll do it for double what they're offering me.' He grinned like a kid at Christmas. 'Timing, hey?'

Yeah, she thought. *Bad* timing. But why quibble about money? Didn't he have enough already? Frowning, she reached for her bag beside the bed and began pulling out clothes. She'd never thought him money-motivated. 'It's a great publicity opportunity.' Not that he needed it. Hadn't he been *avoiding* it?

'I've arranged to go in and discuss it later this afternoon, then I'll stay at the apartment for the night.'

'Sounds exciting.' She walked towards the bathroom, annoyed with him. Annoyed with *herself* for being annoyed with him. 'Don't forget to let me know how it goes.'

'You'll be the first to know. Olivia.'

His commanding tone had her stopping despite herself. She didn't turn around. 'Yes?' She heard the bite in her own voice.

'Snowflake's the *only* reason I'm considering it.'

She turned, looked at him, confused. 'Snowflake?'

'I'll get to promote it and my appearance fee will go straight to your retreat project along with any donations the show brings in. I've told them my terms and they've agreed.'

So generous. So unexpected. She'd misjudged him too quickly. 'Thank you. I don't know what to s—'

'I'll be back in Hobart tomorrow. If you're worried, I can get Emily to stay on with you.'

Her fingers tightened on her clothes. 'No, I'll be fine. Really.'

'If you're sure.' He poured coffee and held it out.

'Later,' she said, and hurried into the bathroom. Everything would have been perfect except that he wasn't asking her to stay another night with him.

CHAPTER THIRTEEN

OLIVIA SAT AT her kitchen table, mobile pressed to her ear, listening to Jett's deep voice telling her about the highlights of his day on *Taste Buds and Travel*.

'Sounds like fun,' she said, keeping her voice bright but feeling half-hearted. Her life sounded incredibly dull in comparison. So far, with the break-in and its repercussions she'd not done much of what she'd set out to achieve on her month's leave.

And she still hadn't heard from her specialist.

Jett's overnighter had morphed into its fourth day. The producers had wanted to do the show while public interest was high, which meant he'd put everything else on hold.

'We should have a fundraiser,' he said, switching topics.

She perked up. 'For Snowflake?'

'Of course for Snowflake, what else? I've got a few ideas if you're interested.'

She smiled. 'I'm interested.'

'We can discuss it when I get back tomorrow night.'

'You're done? You're coming ho—back?' Her fingers tightened on her phone. 'What time?'

'I'll be there around seven. I've got a dinner meeting with a publisher in an hour, so I have to go now but I'll see you tomorrow evening.'

Nerves did a crazy whirlpool in her tummy but her voice

was smooth sailing. 'See you then,' she said, and disconnected.

I love him. The words danced a drunken sailor's jig in her head and her feet followed, spinning across the kitchen floor till she bumped up against the kitchen table. She was giddy, head-over-heels in love.

But it was her forever secret because she could never let him know.

But she *could* let him know how grateful she was for all he'd done for her. Her gaze fell on the food processor he'd bought that was pushed to the far end of the table up against the wall, still lurking in its box, waiting for her.

A challenge. She stepped over, ripped the tape off the lid and glared at it. Not only a challenge, a distraction. She'd show him she appreciated all he'd been doing. That she appreciated *him*. That she could cook even if it was basic. She pulled out the shiny red machine. She'd find some simple recipes on the Internet.

The lamb casserole was in the oven, its delicious rosemary and garlic aroma filling the kitchen. The fruit salad was chopped and in the fridge. The ingredients for Tassie salmon mousse were ready to go. She'd had to dash to the shop to buy gelatine so she was behind schedule but that was fine. She had time—it was only five o'clock.

She added the ingredients to the new blender, covered it with the lid, switched it on. She wrinkled her nose—salmon sure smelled fishy. When the mixture was smooth, she untwisted the glass jug from its base. …Only the jug was supposed to be *lifted* off the base, not unscrewed like Brie's, she realised too late. A tsunami of salmon mixture flooded out of the bottom, over the new appliance, the bench, the floor. Down her T-shirt and jeans. By the time she'd switched it off at the wall before she electrocuted herself, it was impossible to screw it back on. The blender was ruined. Her hands stank.

Where was a cat when she needed one?

Eew! She was never going to eat salmon mousse again.

She was never going to cook for him again.

The sound of a car pulling up sent her rushing to the window. *Let it be the carpenter returning for his tools.* But no, Jett was unfolding his tall frame from the front passenger seat. Her heart went into overdrive.

Mr Jettsetter Chef himself.

No-o-o! This was not allowed to happen. She rinsed her salmon-stinky hands under the tap—couldn't do anything about the spatter on her T-shirt—then rushed to the door. And there he was, his stubble a tad more scruffy than usual, temptation and persuasion in his eyes.

'You're way early...' *I've missed you.* 'There's a bit of a mess...' *I've missed you more than I should have.*

The first thing Jett noticed as the door opened was the way his heart stumbled over itself at his first glimpse of red hair and blue-lagoon eyes. The second thing was the glop of something on her freckled cheek. The third was the fishy smell that wafted out with her.

'I got an earlier flight.' Because there'd been an inexplicable urgency to see her again. To watch her face light up in surprise—at least he'd hoped it would. But she looked more horrified than surprised. He reached out and flicked at the goop, sniffed.

'Oh, no.' Her cheeks turned a matching colour and she blinked at his thumb in disbelief. 'I was making salmon mousse.' She stared down at herself. 'I had an accident. Sort of.'

He licked the goop from his thumb and his gaze followed hers. 'I see. Sort of.' And it occurred to him—something that filled him with a warm, satisfied glow. 'Were you making dinner for me?'

'No big deal, is it?' She stepped back. Still her eyes didn't leave his. 'I'll go take a shower and change out of these stinky...' Her hands flapped about her. 'I'll just clean this kitchen up first... Your blender, I'm sorry...'

'Easy. It's okay. I'll get you another one.'

'Please don't.'

He laughed. He wanted to kiss her full on those passion-pink lips and drink her in, salmon smell and all. Hell, he wanted to help her out of those clothes and dive beneath that spray with her.

But the few days apart had changed the easy camaraderie they'd built between them in Melbourne and there was that awkwardness between them again. It was like starting over. 'Why don't you take that shower while I clean up here?'

'Right. Thanks. The casserole's—'

'Fine. I know.'

'Ah...yes, of course you do.' She turned and bolted.

He stared at the empty doorway. He'd never seen Olivia so flustered. It almost felt as if they were on a first date and she'd invited him for dinner but he'd turned up early. He glanced through the arch, saw the dining table covered in a lace cloth that hadn't been there before. Silverware. Miniature roses he recognised from the front garden. Five tall white candles in a bronze candelabra.

Dating. Now there was a word he hadn't associated with himself in for ever. And none of those 'dates' had ever been of the wholesome domestic home-grown variety.

Perhaps being apart wasn't so bad after all because coming back sure felt good.

Didn't mean anything, he assured himself. He was staying awhile longer and helping her out as they'd already talked about. He'd leave when things were moving along. As they'd already talked about.

A flicker of heat skimmed through his veins as he scooped up the blender, put it in the packaging it had come in to toss out later. What other surprises did she have planned for this evening? Filling the sink with soapy water, he sloshed the dishcloth over the benches.

He'd had women cook extravagant and sophisticated meals to impress, to please, to seduce him into their bed. And many had succeeded. Because he'd wanted to be impressed and seduced.

But Olivia didn't hang on his every word. In fact, she *argued* with him—long and hard. Her meal looked basic and she'd stuffed up with the salmon.

She was gorgeous, sexy, intelligent and brave.

Glad to have something useful to do while he waited, he wiped up the floor with kitchen paper towel, found a mop and bucket to finish the job.

With the kitchen restored, he set his bag in the bedroom she'd been using then sat on the edge of her bed and listened to the shower running in the en suite. He imagined her head tipped back as water splashed over her neck and darkened her hair to burgundy. Thought about that warm water sluicing over her breasts, rivulets flowing down her abdomen, collecting in her navel. And down...

The fragrance of her shower gel seeped out to flirt and lure. And before he knew it, he was tapping on the door. 'I'm going to open the door a fraction.' He yelled over the sound of the spray. 'I want you to listen to me. Okay?'

He heard nothing but water splashing on tiles and for a moment he thought she hadn't heard but then her muffled 'Okay.'

He cracked the door open and was greeted with a cloud of steam. 'Olivia.'

'When you use my name all serious like that I get worried. Is someth—?'

'Nothing's wrong. Do you trust me?'

Silence. He could hear his heart beating, the water splashing.

Finally a quiet 'Yes.'

He grinned to himself. 'I'm coming back in five minutes and I'm coming in. You can decide if you want to stay under the shower or get dressed—and if you choose the latter, *how* you dress is kind of key.'

A brief hesitation, then, 'All right.'

Olivia's pulse rate tripled and she gasped in large lungfuls of steam as the warm spray pelted her body. Her fingers curled on the gold-plated taps and the spray continued. She wasn't going anywhere.

She couldn't see him when he returned a few moments later but she saw the movement against the fogged glass.

'I'm back,' he informed her.

'So I see.' Or almost. From the looks of it, he was still wearing his jeans and black T-shirt but less than a dozen rapid heartbeats later all she could see was the nude colour of a tall male body.

She gripped the soap ledge for support. And waited.

'I need you to move so your head's not under the spray and close your eyes.'

She did as he requested and felt the draught ripple over wet skin as he opened the shower screen door. He didn't touch her but held something cold and smooth against her upper lip.

'You've brought *glass* into my shower?'

'Yes. What can you smell?'

'Alcohol. Are you planning to get me drunk?'

'A little tipsy, maybe. Alcohol,' he repeated. 'Details, please.'

A shiver of anticipation ran through her body. 'Spirits. Rum? And mint. So something cool, and possibly lethal.'

'Try it.' He tipped the glass against the seam of her mouth and she tasted a few drops on her tongue. 'What else?'

'Lime? Or lemon.'

'Good.'

She sipped again. 'It's nice. Sensual. Can I open my eyes now?'

'Not yet. Another sip. It's my Blue Mint Lagoon cocktail.'

'Ah, your specialty cocktail.' She did as he asked, taking tiny sips and letting the smooth ice-cold liquid slide down her throat. 'What else is in it?'

'I'll let you think about it. Meanwhile…' He removed the glass from her lips and she heard him set it on the vanity with a little *chink* on the marble. 'Eyes still shut, now.'

He nudged her mouth open with his thumb and slipped a cocktail-soaked strawberry between her lips. She chewed it slowly, enjoying the contrast in texture. 'Mmm, yum. Different.'

'Like you.'

She felt him move behind her into the shower stall. Its generous size accommodated two people and meant their bodies didn't touch, but she felt every single drop of water on her oversensitised skin. 'Place your palms flat on the tiles in front of you,' he told her. 'And be ready for a surprise.'

Tension built to a fever pitch, her whole body felt tight and strung out. Anticipation quivered through her. Then he stroked something cold and slippery over the back of her neck and she squealed with the sudden shock and the unexpected pleasure of hot and cold. 'Ice? What…?'

She trailed off because she was concentrating on the way the ice—in both his hands—felt, mingling with the hot spray as he stroked lower, all the way down her spine, slowing to massage a tight circle at the small of her back, then down the backs of her legs, lingering at sensitive areas behind her knees. And back up all the way to her nape.

She heard him crunch ice between his teeth then he was sucking on her shoulder, her ear lobe, her neck, with icy lips and tongue.

She thought she might melt like the ice and disappear down the drain in a mindless puddle but then he leaned close so that his body pressed against her back, a thigh between her legs to keep her in place.

His murmured 'Spread your legs for me' had her breath catching. The warm hardness of his body surrounded her while he continued to rub the slippery coldness over her nipples, making them impossibly tight and erect. Making her shiver and moan.

'Oh, my...' She squirmed back against him in delight then gasped, held her breath in awe as he pushed slowly inside her from behind. Filling her up with heat while he continued skating swirling patterns of ice over her skin. Hot and cold, slippery sensations. The squat fat candle she kept by the bath infusing the steam with an arousing and mellow scent of vanilla.

This was all about contrasts and new experiences and he'd planned it specifically for her pleasure. A quivering started low and deep in her belly and spiralled outward. The air moist and soft all around her, the torrent of water hot and stinging on her shoulders. His ice-chilled lips nuzzling her neck.

Her flesh yielding against his.

She'd always told herself she'd never give up control but it was indeed a delicious surrender.

'Lean back and hold on to the back of my neck,' he told her. Fierce, urgent, his lips moving over her shoulder. 'I want to feel you come.'

'Yes...' Flinging her arms tight around the back of his

neck, she shuddered as tremor after tremor rolled through her. She felt his own tremors, his breath harsh and fast as he climaxed inside her. And her body claimed him, her muscles clenched around him, pulling him deep inside her, touching her womb, her heart.

A short time later, as the setting summer sun painted the sky gold and crimson, they lay entwined on her bed, bodies still damp.

'It's past eight,' Olivia said lazily. 'Dinner's more than ready, if you're hungry.'

'I've got something we can enjoy first.'

'More?' She felt for him beneath the sheet. 'You really are magnificent.'

'Not quite that magnificent, for the moment at least.' Pushing up, he grinned, kissed her nose. 'Wait here.'

This time she didn't fall asleep while she waited. He returned with a drink-laden tray and a plate of strawberries. She felt like the cat who'd eaten more than her share of cream. 'More Blue Mint Lagoon cocktail?'

'I wanted you to appreciate it fully and leisurely so I made a couple of extras earlier.' He handed her one, took the other and they drank.

He swirled his glass slowly, looking at her. 'The first time I saw you it was your eyes that got my attention.'

'Not my breasts?'

'Nope—but they were a close second. I could feel those eyes on me as I came down those stairs.

'And then I saw them for the first time and they reminded me of this drink. Sea-green with that hint of cool blue lagoon and warm sandy shallows. I knew then I'd been captured.'

'By a mermaid.' She raised her glass at him again, drunk on happiness. 'Not a pirate.'

'Mermaids.' He took her glass and set it on the bedside table with his, then stretched alongside her. He cruised his fingers lightly down her belly, his gaze following his hand until they reached the top of her thighs. 'They don't have what you have.'

She grinned. 'You know, I had an erotic dream about a pirate during the race.'

He looked at her with interest. 'I hope you didn't surrender to his wicked charms.'

'Oh, but I did—Captain Jett Black, he was.'

'Ah, yes.'

Jett recalled finding her dishevelled and dispirited below decks on that last day of the race. He knew she'd been thinking about her mum because Breanna had told him. The skipper had made it clear she wanted nothing to do with him.

'You were most vehement you wanted me far, far away.'

'It was an erotic dream, Jett, of course I wanted you far, far away. How embarrassing.'

She blushed, and he grinned at her. 'You mean you were…?'

Her chin jerked upwards. 'You'll never know, Captain Black.' Then her feistiness turned mellow and she was nestling her head in his shoulder. 'Was my asking about your surname that day a problem for you?'

'No. It just brought it all back—remembering the day I met my father.'

She lifted her head to look at him, her brow creased in puzzlement. 'Brie never told me about that. She didn't even know you existed till your father died.'

'Breanna never knew. She was only a couple of months old. I was five and my mum had died a few months previously. Of a drug overdose.' He shrugged. 'Past history.'

'Jett.' She placed a warm hand on his chest, over his heart. Her gaze, so clear and honest and open. 'I think it's time you told me, don't you?'

He blew out a slow sigh, remembering the day as clear as if it had happened yesterday. 'It was Christmas Day and

I'd been taken from the foster home to meet him. A kid's dream come true. But then Breanna was there...'

She kissed the place where his messed-up heart beat strong against her cool lips, then rested her chin on his chest and waited.

'I was the unwanted result of an affair. And I resented Breanna for something she had no control over. So I made my foster families' lives hell. Pushed kids away because I didn't want to risk having them like me then turn against me because I couldn't stand the idea of being rejected again.'

'Brie doesn't know all this stuff,' Olivia said softly when he'd finished. 'She'll understand you better if you tell her.'

'I will. Soon.'

'She wants to help but doesn't know how.'

'When Breanna located me, it was a shock. Family and belonging and being close to people was new to me. Still is.'

'It destroyed her when her father came clean,' Olivia said. 'She'd lost her mother in a car accident a few years earlier. Everything she'd thought about her family was turned on its head. But she wants that connection with you. You're all she has.'

He tangled his fingers in Olivia's hair and stared into those emotion-filled eyes. 'She has you.'

'I'm not her family, Jett. She needs that family connection. And so do you.'

Her words struck deep. He wanted to tell her she was wrong but the words stuck in his throat. Because she wasn't wrong. Through her own actions, she'd demonstrated family love could be strong and committed and unconditional. And he could have that too; he just had to reach out and take it.

He continued stroking her hair. 'I'm sorry your mum passed away. You two obviously had loads in common and were very close.'

'In so many ways.' Her voice turned sadder than he'd ever

heard. Her eyes filled with clouds before she turned away to stare out at the night.

He sensed there was more she wasn't saying.

'What do you mean?' When she didn't respond, he was seized by a fierce need to know. He wanted to hold her close and demand she tell him. 'I just told you stuff I've never told anyone and you don't want to return the favour?'

'It's not about returning *favours*.' Irritation in her voice. 'Why is everything—?'

'What's your secret, Olivia?' He rolled her over so she was beneath him. Held her face between his hands so she had nowhere else to look but at him. 'Because I know you have one. I see it in your eyes. I hear it when you speak.'

Those eyes glittered with unshed tears. 'Make love to me, Jett.'

No words, just sighs and murmurs and whispers in the deepening twilight. They made love as if they hadn't had enough. As if they'd never get enough.

Make love to me, Jett. Her emotional plea echoed in the darkness for hours afterwards and it occurred to him as they lay in each other's arms that with Olivia, it wasn't just sex. It was deeper than pleasure. A closeness he'd never allowed himself to feel. It was a connection of more than mere body parts fitting together and it was unique, like her.

And *that* was the difference. He'd had sex with count-less women but he'd never made love with anyone before.

CHAPTER FOURTEEN

THE NEXT MORNING they *eventually* got around to discussing their fundraising event.

'We can't have it till Brie comes back,' Olivia said, tapping her pen on the table.

Jett tipped back on his chair, studying the note pad in front of him. 'So three weeks?'

'Yes. It'll give us time to set it up.'

'So which idea are we going with?' he asked. As if he didn't know her mind was already made up.

By the end of the following day their plans were taking shape. Jett had taken her suggestion for a glitzy overnight dinner cruise in Hobart in his stride. It was a fitting way to honour her mother—yachting was in their blood, after all. He'd been assured this luxury cruising yacht was nothing like *Chasing Dawn* and they'd be on the calmer waters of the Derwent River, rather than on the high seas. They were to spend the night aboard. How could he refuse?

And all thanks to a multimillionaire oil magnate from Sydney with whom Olivia had made contact on Christmas Eve. Joe McPherson had listened to her story. His first wife had died of cancer and he was happy to make the trip south before he and his new wife set sail for Hawaii. The date had been set.

She arranged an online auction within the yacht clubs,

with the top five bidders and their partners at the end of one week to be the successful candidates. 'I know that's not many but it's a quality night and these people are seriously loaded. They'll also spread the word.'

'Whatever you want, it's your call.'

'It's about networking,' she told Jett. 'They knew Mum so it follows that they want to help Snowflake and will bid high. We don't need a crowd, we just need classy.'

Jett would be in charge of the menu and catering and would oversee the kitchen—*ahem*—galley. He'd hit on a few chefs he'd worked with who were prepared to work the evening at no cost and in return Jett would pay for their flights and upmarket overnight hotel accommodation.

By the end of the week they had their successful bidders with twice the amount they'd hoped for promised. Jett took Olivia to one of Hobart's fine dining restaurants at a popular art hotel on the waterfront to celebrate.

When Olivia thought she heard her phone buzzing a couple of nights later, she ignored it, burrowing deeper beneath the sheets and snuggling into the warm body behind her. She was exhausted, sleep-deprived—in the best way—and then there was that delicious man lying buck naked against her back. Nothing and no one was going to tempt her to leave her bed until at least lunch time. Maybe not even then.

An indeterminate while later she woke to the sound of her back door opening and footsteps crossing the kitchen tiles.

She shot upright, dragging the sheet to her chin, just in time to see Brie poke her head in her bedroom door. 'Hi ya, sleepy-head. Oops…' Her friend's eyes rounded in surprise and she looked away from the dark head on the pillow beside her. 'Sorry,' she whispered, backing up. 'I'll just disappear—'

Swinging her legs off the bed, Olivia glanced at Jett, oblivious to the world. 'The kitchen. Coffee. Go.'

'Sorry, Liv, I used my key when I couldn't get hold of you at the airport,' she said when they were both in the kitchen. 'I got a bit worried. But I can see everything's fine.' She lowered her voice. 'Who is that and where do I get one?'

Olivia couldn't help the smile that almost burst from her lips. 'You don't recognise him?'

'I only saw a broad outline and a nice firm slab of bronzed back and dark hair and—' Her eyes widened again. 'You've stolen my brother?'

'Not stolen. Borrowed.'

'You and Jett.' Her hands snuck up to her face to smother a grin. 'I thought he was going to Cradle Mountain?'

'He liked the view here better.'

'I want to hear everything. Or maybe not; he is my brother after all.'

'After coffee.' Olivia laughed. Hard to imagine they'd been lovers for a couple of weeks already. 'I'm starved—we didn't get around to dinner last night. It's become a bit of a habit I have to admit, which is a shame since his talents extend to the kitchen… But this one's my handiwork.' Olivia pointed at the slow cooker. 'Help yourself.'

'You *cooked*? *You*? For a *chef*? And not just any chef—'

'He bought me a cooker the other day. What else could I do? I won't tell you what happened with the salmon mousse when I tried to use the new food processor.'

'Ooh,' Brie murmured delightedly. 'You naughty girl.' She walked to the coffee machine and switched it on.

'No. No, it was nothing like that.' But Olivia's cheeks burned and she climbed onto a stool at the breakfast bar. 'Stay for lunch?'

They caught up on news over coffee. New Year's Eve, the break-in, Brie's holiday, the fundraiser plans. The renovations and retreat. By the time they paused for breath they were prepping salad for lunch.

'Hey.' The Voice. Deep, husky, morning-after voice.

They turned as one. 'Jett. Hi.' Brie set down the cucumber she was slicing and crossed the room to peck his cheek. 'This is a nice surprise.'

'What is?' he asked, feigning innocence as he touched his lips to her brow while his eyes twinkled mischief at Olivia over his sister's head.

Brie punched his arm. 'You, you idiot. And don't you look relaxed? I like seeing Livvie pink-cheeked and happy too.'

While they all caught up, Olivia made a salad dressing and thought how it could be—the three of them bound by friendship, love and family. But he wasn't called the Jett-setter Chef for nothing. He was always off on some new culinary adventure on the other side of the world. He was helping out now but give him a couple of months in Tasmania to write his books and he'd be gone again.

She was darn well going to make the most of him while he was here.

Over the next couple of weeks, funds for the dinner cruise and late donations from the race rolled in. When Brie didn't have clients, she came by to help with writing up job and person specs for the new staff they'd need and to chat over a wine or share a professionally cooked meal with them.

In addition to Brie's beauty therapy skills and Olivia's business and natural therapy qualifications, they needed a fitness instructor, a grounds-person, a therapeutic chef with an enthusiasm for organics and raw food nutrition. A qualified accountant on the books. Building contractors. More.

Jett enjoyed the freedom of working his own hours. Getting down and dirty in the garden. He experimented with recipes in Olivia's kitchen and gave her some lessons in the basics. Meanwhile he took inspiration from Tasmania's pure air and magnificent surroundings.

Every night he took a different kind of inspiration from the special woman he shared a bed with. Neither tried to define what they had or how long it might last. He pushed it to the back of his mind.

In the middle of the night when those thoughts and questions refused to stay away, he wrote. Within the week he'd finished a draft of a book that took his writing in a new direction. Its working title was *The Bare Ingredients: For Lovers of Food*. The Blue-Mint-Lagoon-cocktail-in-the-shower recipe featured front and centre. He was also working on other themes that Olivia had helped him come up with over hot chocolate when neither of them could sleep. She loved his idea of *Hot Tarts and Sexy Sauces* while the profits from her more demure suggestion of *Sugar and Spice and All Things Nice* would go into Snowflake's account.

They'd tried out some of his new sexy food ideas in the kitchen; he couldn't wait to try out more sensual food ideas—in the bedroom.

After the charity dinner cruise.

Before he left town.

He reminded himself he loved his unpredictable jet-setting life. New cities, new sights, new people. Freedom. No one to be accountable to. No reason to stick around.

Until now.

He frowned. *Now* his solo writing retreat and jet-loving lifestyle didn't excite him nearly as much as it had. Because now maybe he did have a reason to stay awhile—longer, even. He needed to be sure Olivia felt the same way.

She wasn't only his lover and confidante and friend. By her own words and actions, Olivia had taught him compassion and empathy. More, she'd made him reflect on his life and some of his decisions. She'd turned a cynical, commitment-phobic, self-centred guy into a better man.

A man who might even take a risk and consider something more…permanent.

He wanted to be with her, simple as that. Which meant putting his travel plans on hold indefinitely. For the first time in his life he wanted to build something that lasted.

And for the first time in his life if it didn't work out, it mattered.

Olivia snuck in a quick tour of *A King's Ransom* before their guests were due to board. The experienced crew remained aboard to sail the magnificent yacht, which dwarfed the marina with its sleek white lines, but the owner and his wife were staying ashore, enjoying a night at one of Hobart's top hotels.

Which left the captain's quarters—a stunning suite of several rooms—free for the two highest-bidding couples. She and Jett, Brie and her partner for the evening were bunking in the crew quarters, leaving the three staterooms for the remaining couples.

She checked her reflection on her way through one of the staterooms. Since she'd not had time to buy a new dress, Jett had organised Tyler to send her something a couple of days ago. A figure-hugging silver-grey halter neck with a thigh-high split. A flattering counterfoil for her sea-green eyes and auburn hair.

'Perfect.'

She glanced up at the familiar voice; her eyes flicked to Jett, who'd snuck up behind her. She'd never seen him in his chef's whites and her female hormones sighed. Her gaze gobbled him up as it drifted lower to admire a pair of black-and-white cargo pants. 'And you look sexy enough to eat.'

He moved in behind her, lowered his chin to the sensitive spot between neck and shoulder. 'Later,' he promised, a sinful glint in his eye.

She laughed. 'We're sharing space with two others tonight.'

'There's always tomorrow night.'

That glint changed from lightly teasing to something darker, deeper. It made her heart skip a beat then falter, and her humour faded. Maybe it was a trick of the light because he knew, like her, that there wouldn't always be a tomorrow night. Didn't he?

They'd not talked about the future; it was a tacit understanding that he'd move on, she'd stay in Tasmania. And that was how she wanted it. People were counting on her. Her career was mapped out for her. Her life—whatever happened—was here.

'I've been thinking about that chef's position for the retreat,' he murmured, his warm breath whispering over her shoulder.

Dread chilled her blood. No way could she allow Jett to see her deal with the imminent decisions she'd have to confront. To endure his pitying look if she chose a double mastectomy. He was making it impossible to ignore what she was trying so desperately to forget.

She flicked him a too-bright smile in the mirror. 'I wouldn't wait if I was you. It'll be months before the retreat's up and running. Your plan's always been to move on.' She switched topics, fingering the gown's fabric. Silky, smooth, sleek. 'Tyler's amazing. This is beautiful.'

'Not as beautiful as the woman it was made for.' His hands moved to her waist, down over her hips then they slid slowly up, cupping her breasts, his gaze following his movements in the mirror.

She smiled back, searching his eyes, hoping, *hoping* to

see the return of that flirty glint she'd seen a moment ago. Reminding her that they were just temporary.

'Your retreat may be a reality sooner than you think,' he said, then suddenly he was sliding a fine-spun rose-gold chain around her neck. Suspended from the chain was a small filigree snowflake the size of a fingernail sparkling with tiny pink stones.

Diamonds? Lord, she hoped not, but what else sparkled so brilliantly? Her heart skipped another beat as trembling fingers reached up to touch. 'Jett, I—'

'Good luck tonight,' he whispered, and was suddenly gone. As if he'd been about to say more but had changed his mind.

She stood a moment, staring at the gift in the mirror, unsure what to make of his words and the gesture. They'd been lovers such a short time. They'd made no secret of not wanting reminders so why had he given her something so expensive? So personal? So *memorable*?

He knew how upset she'd been about her stolen jewellery. That must be his reason. His words and actions tonight confused her.

'You okay, Livvie?' Brie asked from the doorway.

'Of course. I'm fine. Why wouldn't I be?' She pasted on a smile and admired Brie's backless midnight-blue dress. 'You look sensational. What's your date's name again?'

'So do you, and it's Theo. Liv…' She came right in and sat on the bed. 'You and Jett…it's getting serious between you two.'

'No.' Olivia fingered the necklace, avoided looking at her friend. 'It's just a fun ride and we're both enjoying it.'

'Can't you at least talk with Jett—?'

'No.' Shaking her head, she glared at Brie in the mirror. 'Promise me you won't either.'

Brie sighed. 'Okay, Liv. For now.'

'I want to live my life like everyone else. The way you do. Enjoy a fun no-strings romance with a nice guy. Until it's time to say goodbye.' Grabbing Brie's hand, she tugged her towards the door. 'It's going to be a fabulous night. You work one end of the room, I'll work the other.'

Olivia forced herself to cast doubts and questions aside and get on with the task of entertaining. The yacht was soon swamped with voices, movement and colour as the glitterati arrived, dripping in jewels and high-end fashion. The evocative sounds of flute and violin drifted from the classical music duo on deck. Expensive perfume mingled with the aroma of canapés being prepared in the galley. Wait staff circulated with drinks.

The water reflected a sliver of golden moon in a violet sky and they were about to set sail on a floating palace. But Olivia didn't have time to enjoy the view, ensuring guests were comfortable on the awesome outside entertainment area strewn with candles in coloured glass pots.

'And the big question on every woman's lips is will the Jettsetter Chef be making an appearance?'

'After dinner,' Olivia told a female reporter, almost wishing she hadn't invited the media to attend the guests' arrival and to interview her. 'But you won't be here then.' She smiled sweetly because she knew the woman would be disappointed, and slid a glass of sparkling water from a passing waiter's tray. 'But Pink Snowflake—'

'There he is!' The woman swivelled on her heel, sidestepped Olivia and made a beeline towards him, her heels clicking over polished wood.

Olivia turned, surprised to see his unexpected appearance, and their gazes clashed across the deck. Without thought, her hand reached up to touch the chain at her neck. He noticed her small movement, and a slow smile spread over his face. Then the reporter blocked her view and Olivia turned away, her mind whirling, only to be confronted with another journalist who'd obviously witnessed the intimate exchange.

She studied Olivia's face, her eyes alive with speculation. 'And will we be seeing more of the pair of you out and about?' Her ID showed she was from the women's magazine that was donating a hefty sum for an interview.

'Whatever do you mean?' Olivia said. 'We're not here to speculate on gossip. We're here to talk about the Pink Snowflake Foundation—that's the important message for tonight...'

At last the media left and the magnificent cruise yacht sailed out of the marina, the lights of the CBD and the casino glittering from the shore.

The main course was a choice of liquorice-braised leg of lamb with Jerusalem artichoke and caramelised onion purée or roasted pork shoulder with swede, pickled rhubarb purée, sage and apple dressing, all served at a massive oak dining table.

Olivia found herself sitting opposite James Harrison, owner of a string of successful Sydney nightclubs. Mid-forties, attractive. A playboy edge about that smile even with his partner, Sue, right alongside. Sue paid him no attention, more interested in talking to Sandra Hemsworth to her right.

'I hope you'll drop by the club when you're in Sydney.' He twinkled those playboy blue eyes at her and slid a business card across the table. 'Contact me and I'll make sure I'm there.'

Not *we*, she noted. 'Um...I don't know when I'll get to Sydney, James, with so much going on at the moment.'

'Jim.'

'Jim.' She glanced at Sue, who'd turned and was watching them with a smile on her lips.

'I'm his sister,' she said. 'In case you were wondering.'

'Oh.' Olivia laughed, but suddenly a new kind of tension gripped her. Because James—Jim—was definitely interested. And Olivia definitely was not. She snatched up her wine glass. 'So does being in business with family members work for you…?'

For the remainder of the meal she managed to keep the conversation focused on their nightclubs and her charity. And yachting of course. She slipped *Chasing Dawn* into the conversation in the hope that James or Sue or anyone in on the conversation might know of an interested buyer. Someone who'd love the little yacht the way she did.

A selection of desserts and coffee was served in the entertainment area where the only formalities for the evening took place. Jett and his assistant chefs made an appearance so the guests could acknowledge their efforts.

He and his mates accepted the applause with good cheer. Olivia made a short speech thanking everyone for their amazing support and wishing them a pleasant evening. Finally, Brie spoke about Snowflake on Olivia's behalf.

When it was over with guests free to choose whatever they wanted to do until breakfast, Olivia escaped to a dark corner of the deck alone. She hugged her arms in the coolish briny air. Jett's work for the night was done. He'd be looking for her any minute and she wished she knew what she was going to say.

How was she going to respond if he mentioned the chef's position again? Because then she'd have to put him—

'It's a pretty night.'

She glanced at the masculine voice beside her and wished herself elsewhere. But she lifted her voice, smiled to match. 'James.'

'Jim.'

'Jim. Yes, it is.'

'So…you're serious about selling *Chasing Dawn*?'

She turned to him, found him not as attractive as she'd first thought. But then she'd never find another man as attractive as Jett. 'She's a seventy-year-old wooden-hulled boat. I need someone who'll love her like I do, scars and all.'

'Whatever your asking price, I'll double it.'

She hesitated. Silly to be sentimental over a pile of old wood. She could do so much more good with cold hard cash. And she'd still have the misty, water-coloured memories of her and her mum exploring the bays and inlets around Tassie.

But why did a man like James Harrison, a previous winner of the Australian Bluewater Classic with his ginormous maxi yacht, want an itty-bitty scrap of a boat like *Chasing Dawn*?

Jett caught sight of Olivia on the deck and was about to head over when he realised someone was going to beat him to it. The same guy who'd been eying her off when Jett and his fellow chefs had joined the guests for coffee. And a feeling he'd never known had gripped him hard, held him so tightly he'd barely been able to breathe.

It was still there, like an iron fist clamped around his gut. *Jealousy.* His chef's jacket was suddenly strangling him and he flicked open the top button. He could hear their conversation on the still evening air. Not only was the man eying his woman off, he wanted her boat.

She was still considering selling *Chasing Dawn*? *No way.* She loved that boat too much. Jett was by her side in a few quick strides. 'Mate, you're too late.'

'What?' Olivia's hand flew to her chest, her eyes widened in fright. 'Jett, where did you spring from? And what do you mean?'

'Sorry, babe, didn't mean to scare you.' He stuck out his hand to the guy. 'Jett Davies.'

'Jim.' The man shook Jett's hand. 'Nice meal tonight, Jett.'

Nice. Right. Spectacular, more like. Jett's lip curled but he managed to transform it into a rough resemblance of a grin. 'Yeah, as I was saying—sorry, Jim, she's promised it to me.' He tugged her to his side. 'Right, skipper?'

Jim frowned, looked to her for confirmation then frowned again, his gaze flicking between the two of them. 'Is that right, Olivia?'

She slipped out of Jett's hold and stepped away from both of them, hands raised in front of her breasts in a defensive gesture. 'I…um. I'm still deciding.'

And Jett had a bad feeling it wasn't only the boat she was talking about. The first trickle of real unease rose up his throat. 'Olivia, I—'

Her eyes widened, then turned hard and uncompromising. 'If you'll both excuse me…' She turned on one stilettoed heel and walked away, leaving the two of them standing on the deck throwing metaphoric daggers at each other.

Dammit. He shrugged at Jim. 'That's Olivia for you. She's been under stress to get this night happening,' he explained. 'I'll make sure she rests when we get home tomorrow.' He saw he'd got his message across and walked away whistling.

But he knew he'd stepped over a line with Olivia. She demanded her independence and he'd not respected her decision to sell her boat if that was what she chose to do.

He needed to fix his wrong. But how? He knew from experience she took that kind of behaviour very much to heart.

CHAPTER FIFTEEN

OLIVIA DIDN'T FIND it hard to avoid Jett for the rest of the evening because he seemed to be staying well away. She didn't see him on the deck again when she walked there with a few guests to watch the yacht pass beneath the Tasman Bridge. Nor in the entertainment area when nightcaps were served. But it played on her nerves until they were stretched to breaking point as they tied up at the marina for the night. At last the final couple said goodnight and headed to bed and she breathed a sigh of relief.

He was waiting for her in the crew's quarters, lying on a bunk, hands behind his head. The moment he caught sight of her, he tensed and pushed up, dominating the cramped space with his size. 'You all right?'

No. 'What were you thinking overriding me that way? I do not need you or anyone else telling me what to do. It's my life, my choices.' She didn't want to know his reasons. For any of it. 'I don't want an argument, I—'

'Which is why I'm leaving.' He reached for his bag, hefted it over his shoulder.

'Leaving?' Olivia's stomach dropped like a stone. 'I just meant—'

'It's okay, skipper.' He smiled but it wasn't the brash, confident Jett she knew and respected.

And loved.

'I know you don't want a scene,' he continued as he side-stepped past her in the narrow space between bunks on his way out. 'And this isn't the time or place.' He dropped a feather-soft kiss on her brow. 'The evening was a well-deserved success for Pink Snowflake. Congratulations.'

She wanted to put her arms around his neck and tell him she hadn't meant to jump all over him like that the moment she'd seen him, like some nag. She wanted to say sorry and ask him to stay but she knew he was right, there was too much unresolved tension between them, and nothing could be resolved here tonight within earshot of others. 'I couldn't have done it without you,' she said to his back.

He turned at the doorway and smiled that tired kind of smile again. 'Sure you could.'

She barely slept. The night seemed interminable. She blamed the narrow bunk but she missed the feel of Jett's warm body beside hers. His last words echoed in her head with the far-away look in his eyes. *Sure you could.*

What had he meant by that? Was it a genuine belief in her abilities or was it her cue to go it alone? The truth was she didn't *want* to do it alone. Not any more. She'd miss his confidence and his culinary skills, the way he made her laugh and forget her problems. She'd miss their robust discussions.

She'd miss *him*.

The more she thought about the evening, the more she knew he was letting her down gently. He was leaving. The necklace was a parting gift. His talk about the chef's position and the retreat being a reality sooner than she thought… he meant the foundation was growing quicker than they'd expected, that was all. That he wouldn't be needed; it was time to move on.

And she was ready. Her heart was breaking but she was

prepared. She didn't want to do it alone, but she could. She would.

It was almost a relief to get up and check that everything had been cleared away to her satisfaction and check that the informal breakfast had been set out before the catering crew had left.

She'd arranged to meet the owner and his wife, Joe and Tessa McPherson, for coffee at nine a.m. in the hotel, so she wasn't expecting them to board while she was still breakfasting with the guests at seven-thirty.

'Joe, Tessa. Good morning to you.' She rose to meet the well-dressed couple. 'Did I get the times wrong?'

'No.' Joe beamed at her, his ruddy complexion glowing. 'Tess and I wanted to make sure to catch you before you all left. We have a little something for you.' He drew a piece of paper from the inside pocket of his navy jacket. 'We believe in the Pink Snowflake Foundation and what you're doing. You blew me away with your enthusiasm on Christmas Eve—Tess'll tell you I kept her awake half the night talking about it. I love a good cause.'

Olivia smiled. 'So do I. Sorry, Tessa, if I was the reason for you not getting a good night's sleep.'

'No problem.' Tessa smiled back, her carefully styled blonde hair glinting in the morning sun that slanted through the windows.

Joe exchanged a fond glance with his younger wife. 'She and I had a talk,' he went on. 'We loved the philosophy behind the name—individuals together making a difference. We'd like to be a part of your retreat. And we'd like to see it built in the next six months rather than the next fifty years, so we're giving you a head start.' He handed Olivia a cheque made out to the Pink Snowflake Foundation.

Enthusiastic applause followed and then Brie was hugging her and looking over her shoulder. 'Wow.'

'Oh, my.' Olivia stared at the six-figure amount for a long moment as a numb feeling of disbelief and excitement and gratitude crept up her body. 'I don't know how to thank you.' She paused, suddenly knowing the very best way. 'Yes, I do. We'll name it the McPherson Retreat.'

Sweat poured down his back, into his eyes. Jett yanked off his T-shirt, tossed it across a stunted bush and jammed the spade into the hard-packed earth again. Again. He wanted the distraction of heat, the heavy load, the hard work.

'Jett…'

He looked up, slightly dazed in the heat, realising he'd heard his name more than once. Olivia was watching him— had been for some time by the look in her eyes. Her apricot-cucumber fragrance rose to greet him as she held out a glass.

'Here, drink.'

'Thanks.' He swallowed it down in a few greedy gulps. 'How long have you been back?' He picked up the spade again.

'Long enough to see that you're going to do serious damage if you don't slow down.' All calmness, she took the spade from his hands, tossed it down. 'No more. You worked all yesterday, then last night. It's hot out here and heatstroke's not funny.'

'Last night was worth it, right?' With nothing in his hands, he struggled to channel his energy—he was a volcano about to erupt. 'You were sensational.'

'It was worth it, but it wasn't only me. The menu was amazing. You and your staff were fantastic. And you haven't heard the good news. The McPhersons donated enough money to build the extension. We'll have it up in months.'

'That *is* good news. But I let you down. I shouldn't have left you to do breakfast on your own.' He ran a grime-smeared hand through his hair, annoyed at her calm demeanour. He wanted her angry. He wanted fire; he wanted that edge, that connection, not this calm woman with no bite.

'Not a problem. Everything was already there, we only had to—'

'What were you thinking?' he shouted, switching to what was *really* pissing him off. '*Chasing Dawn*'s not for sale.'

Her eyes widened in surprise and her voice rose. 'Says who? *You?*'

Better. 'Yeah. Me. Not to him.'

'Jim? Why not?'

'I didn't like the cut of his jacket. Hell, I didn't like the man's name, the man's aftershave, the man's— He was coming on to you—didn't you realise that?'

'And what if he was?' she demanded, white-lipped now, eyes spitting fire. 'I wasn't reciprocating—or didn't you notice? But you and me—we're temporary. We've always known that. Sooner or later you're leaving.'

'Hang on—'

She waved him away. 'You said I could do it on my own.'

He frowned. '*What?* When?'

'Last night. When you left me standing there with your parting gift around my neck. I said I couldn't have done it without you and you said—'

Sure you could...

She'd misinterpreted his words. Frustration zigged up his spine and he scratched the back of his neck.

'Olivia…sweetheart… That's not what I meant.' He saw confusion cloud her eyes and took a step forward, hands raised. 'I meant you are the most capable woman I've ever met—not that I wanted you to go it alone. If I didn't make it clear enough, I'm sorry.'

She shook her head once, and seemed to shrink in on herself, as if she didn't want to hear.

'And *parting gift*?' Unease was crawling over his skin

like ants. 'It was a thank-you-I-think-you're-pretty-damn-special gift. You didn't pick up on that?'

'I…don't know… A man's never given me anything so… intimate or expensive.'

'And you're the first woman I've ever bought jewellery for,' he told her as he approached, partially reassured by her sudden stillness. 'The *only* woman I'll *ever* buy jewellery for.'

'Jett. I think you should…'

When he reached her, he gripped her fine-boned shoulders and poured his heart and soul into the bottomless well of her gaze. 'You made me look further than skin deep. I love how you make me laugh. I love how we argue and make up. How you turn good into bad. How you make me accountable for the words that come out of my mouth.'

His grip tightened because for the first time in his life he was laying everything he had on the line and she wasn't responding—at least not the way he'd hoped. 'I've been a drifter all my life. You're the only woman who's ever made me want to stick around. To take a risk on us. I want to stay here with you and be a part of your dream.

'I'm applying for the chef's position, even if it's two years down the track, because I'll still be here in twenty years, working alongside you to make that dream reality.' He brushed the damp hair back from her brow, struggling not to panic.

'If it's still not clear, I'll put it in a few simple words. Commitment. For ever. Family. I want to see you in a rocking chair nursing our first child at your breast. I want to see you in that same rocking chair when we celebrate our sixtieth wedding anniversary surrounded by grandch—'

'And if I don't have those breasts you so admire, *what then*?' The words spilled from Olivia's tongue before she could censor them. Pain at the injustice of it all lanced through her heart. *Why her?* Why was fate denying her what she wanted most?

His brow creased. 'What do you mean?'

'Kids? Marriage?' Her eyes stung with tears she *refused* to allow. 'What's wrong with what we have now?'

The power of those turbulent dark eyes was a physical force. 'It's not enough now. I want more. I found a sister, then I found her best friend and I've decided family's a pretty good deal.'

'No.' She shook her head, her heart breaking. 'I have my life planned out and it doesn't include family. Jett Davies, Jettsetter Chef extraordinaire, globe-trotter and the brother of my best friend, Brie's your family and she loves you.'

'I know who I am,' he snapped, 'and I know who you are. *You're the woman I love.*'

Love. The word reverberated in the air between them and their incredulous gazes clashed. As if Jett was as surprised—and devastated—as she.

There was a cruel fist squeezing her heart, crushing it to dust. She shook her head. 'No. That's not what we agreed on.'

His fingers tightened on her arms and he pulled her up, so her feet dangled off the ground, so all she could see was him. Desperation. Despair. Anguish. 'So tell me to go away. Tell me you don't want me in your life.'

'It's not that simple.'

'Yes, Olivia. It is.' He loosened his hold so suddenly that she stumbled backwards. She saw the tormented twist of his mouth, the desolation in his eyes and knew she'd hurt him the way he'd been hurt so many times in his past.

'Please, Jett, it was never my intention to hurt you. You have to believe that.'

'I'll be out of your way in thirty minutes,' he said, defeat reducing his voice to not much more than a harsh under-tone. 'Until then, I'd appreciate it if you stay out of mine.'

He turned away. He was doing as he'd said. Walking out of her life. For ever.

'Wait.' *One more look.* Her hand fisted against her breast-bone. He stopped but didn't turn around. 'I need to tell you something before you leave.'

A bare nod was his only response. She couldn't see his expression but his posture was so tense she wondered that he didn't snap in two. 'Thank you. For everything.'

There must have been something in the way she spoke because he swung back to her. Dark eyes probed hers for a long moment. 'Are you ill? Is that it?'

A glimmer of a smile touched her lips that he'd got it so right. 'Not that I know of.' Yet.

His shoulders relaxed marginally, but his expression re-mained grim, his jaw rigid. 'Anything else?'

She shook her head. *Except that I love you and maybe you'll understand why I made this choice one day.*

He shook his head and resumed walking.

Olivia kept out of his way. She sat on the balcony, star-ing dry-eyed but sightless in the direction of the Derwent River until she heard Jett's rental car leave. Then she got busy. She stripped her bed, changed towels. *No reminders.*

When Brie's happy tune jingled on her phone an hour later, she switched it off and buried it at the bottom of her handbag and kept working.

She'd call Brie tomorrow. Explain. Make her understand. Then she'd take out *Chasing Dawn* and maybe spend the night on the water under the stars, the way she and her mum used to do. As she'd done the night after she'd died.

Her ruthless frenzy didn't abate until mid-afternoon. Until she found his favourite jumper tucked down the edge of the sofa amongst the cushions. The pain knocked the breath from her lungs and she sank to the floor, remembering how the soft cashmere had felt when he'd held her against his chest only a couple of chilly evenings ago. She buried her nose in its folds and the floodgates opened.

Jett parked his rental halfway up Olivia's driveway, cut the engine. From here he could see her car, so he knew she was still inside. And if she had any ideas about leaving she'd have to detour around him. Make that *try* to detour around him because neither of them were going anywhere until she told him the whole story.

He'd gone to the one person he could turn to. Breanna had hugged him then ordered him to sit down and share the pot of rosehip tea she'd just made. And while he drank, she'd talked.

'I promised not to tell,' she said, 'but have you wondered why Livvie's so driven? Why everything's got to be done yesterday? How she can study, work, run a charity and plan a retreat?

'Why she'd push you away when her eyes tell you something entirely different?'

And in his mind's eye he saw her New Year's Day when they'd made love on the dining table in the hotel. Radiating such a vibrant energy it was *as if she was trying to live an entire life in those few crazy moments.*

He had his answer.

And the bottom plunged out of his world. 'She's dying.'

'No.'

Breanna smiled but her eyes were different and he knew he had part of it right. 'Then I don't get it. Her mother, her family history…'

'Go back. Make her talk to you.'

* * *

Olivia didn't hear him come in, didn't see him until he sat down on the floor beside her and a half-empty box of tissues. 'Olivia.'

His voice—calm seas. But she got a glimpse of dark, stormy ocean in his eyes before she looked down at her hands twisting in his jumper. 'How did you get in?'

'Breanna gave me her key.'

She swiped at her wet cheeks. 'She told you. She promised—'

'She didn't tell me,' he said quietly. 'She gave me her key so *you* could tell me.'

She closed her eyes. 'Why have you come back?'

'Some treasures are worth sticking around for—so are some troubles. And sometimes they're one and the same.'

'Not this trouble.'

'Let me make my own decisions about the kind of trouble I want to get involved in. And it *is* my concern, whether you like it or not. Because I love you. I'll always love you. Whatever happens.'

Tears filled her eyes and spilled over in her heart. 'You shouldn't.'

He shifted closer, so that their shoulders touched. 'Just answer me this. Do you love me back?'

She could no longer deny her heart. 'I do. I love you.' She sighed, drained to the bottom of her soul. 'But it doesn't matter.'

'You're wrong. It matters. Look at me.' Tucking a finger beneath her chin, he turned her towards him so she could see the truth in his eyes. He brushed her hair off her face and said, 'It matters more than my next breath. You've trusted me before—do you still trust me?'

'Yes…but this is dif—'

He pressed a finger to her lips. 'No buts. I promise I'll

still be here in the morning. And next week. Next year. For however long you love me.'

'I'll always love you, Jett. But I don't know how long that "always" might be.' She turned away. 'I'm not a long term kind of girl.'

'You're *my* kind of girl. Who knows how long any of us have? We could be swept away in a flood tomorrow. Talk to me, sweetheart.'

'I'm waiting on some test results.'

'And…?'

'And…the women in my family all carried the same gene mutation. The test will show whether I do too.' She bit her lip. 'I'm scared.'

'It's okay to be scared.' He wrapped his arms around her, enfolding her in a comforting blanket of warmth and security. 'I'm scared too. But we're going to deal with it together. You're tough, resilient, formidable even. We'll get through this even though you tried to spare me and make a difference to others facing the same illness. Which also makes you the most unselfish person I've ever met.'

She shook her head. 'Not so unselfish. I've crammed my life with work and fundraising as a distraction as much as anything else.'

'You could have distracted yourself in plenty of other, more self-satisfying ways.'

'I did. That's why I messed around with you.'

'A very good decision.'

His arms tightened and she leaned against his chest and said, 'When I knew I was falling for you…' she took a stuttering breath '…I tried to keep it casual. I pushed you away because maybe you'd meet someone who wanted long term, with…kids and everything.'

'Who are you to make that decision for me? I deserve to make that choice myself. I thought we agreed on making our own choices a while ago.'

'I guess I didn't see it clearly in this instance.'

'What are the chances of a positive result?' he murmured into her hair.

'High.'

He kissed the side of her face. 'Better to know the worst now than to have it nagging at the back of our minds. Whichever way it goes, we can make plans. Together.'

'But what about kids? Family?'

'Without you? Not a chance.'

He was risking his own happiness, his shot at a family. He'd stay with her for however long or short that might be. Relief and happiness were washing over her like waves. 'I didn't realise how much I needed you until you walked away.'

'No one's ever needed me before. Do you know how that feels?'

'Wonderful. Special. Amazing. Because now I know you need me too. I was wrong to deny you that chance.'

'So get it into your head, I'm with you all the way. But I'm confident it's going to be good news.'

'Good news. But if it's not, there are important decisions to make, like whether to have surgery or—'

'Not now.' He stopped her with a finger to her lips.

'If you'd gone…'

'I wasn't going anywhere without answers. I don't give up that easily. But when I realised what was going on I didn't know the best way to get through to you. Lucky I have Breanna.'

She wrapped her fingers around his and squeezed. 'Lucky. Families are the best.'

* * *

'Satellite number two, right on time, skipper.' Jett pointed to the night sky a couple of weeks later. They'd taken *Chasing Dawn* out for a short sail while the weather was calm, and were lying side by side on the deck and watching the stars. Only their fingers touched and for Jett it was the most spiritual feeling he'd ever known. The two of them alone beneath the wonders of the universe.

'Well spotted.' His stargazer, satellite-spotter sailor lover tapped the back of his hand with a fingernail.

'I read up on how to interpret the test results,' he said, still tracking the satellite's slow steady arc across the sky. 'If your results are negative for a known family mutation, your risk of developing cancer is no greater than mine. It's called a true negative.' He turned his head to look at her. 'But I guess you already know that.'

'Yes.' She turned her head on the wooden deck and looked back at him, her eyes reflecting the star sparkle. 'We just have to wait.'

'There's something I don't want to wait for,' he said, and raised himself up on one elbow. She looked so beautiful lying there, bathed in starlight, his pink snowflake charm winking at her throat. 'This is as good a place as any to ask you to marry me.'

Her eyes went round and wide. 'Marry you? But don't you want to wait until—?'

'Not another word.' His eyes narrowed.

'I only meant until the moon rises.' She cast her gaze to the growing shimmery glow on the eastern horizon, then smiled back at him. 'In ten minutes, give or take.'

'Okay.' He relaxed again and rolled towards her. 'I guess I can find something to do for ten minutes. Give or take.'

'Are you planning on getting *nautical* with me, Chef Davies?' she said, reaching for his belt.

'With a dash of piratical flavour,' he promised.

'Marriage…' Olivia tried out the word a short time later, feeling incredibly lazy and loose and loved, as they watched the first sliver of moon rise over the rugged coastline.

'Commitment. Now. No matter what happens we're in this together. And to prove it…'

He slid a ring onto the third finger of her left hand. A snowflake mounted on a rose-gold band to match the one around her neck. 'Oh, my. Pink diamonds. Again.' She grinned at him and caressed it with her other hand. 'It's perfect. Absolutely perfect. And it matches my necklace.'

'I doubt it's practical for everyday use but when I had the other one made, I decided I wanted this too.'

Laughing, she threw her arms around his neck. 'I love impractical. And I love you… Hang on—' Pulling back, she watched his expression while she replayed his words in her head. 'You had it made *when* exactly?'

He didn't reply but his trade-mark cocky grin spread over his face.

She grinned back. 'I do love a confident man.'

EPILOGUE

'BRIE'S LATE. I don't know why we didn't pick her up on the way.' Olivia tapped her fingers on the snowy cloth in one of Hobart's premier restaurants. Which drew her attention to her engagement ring glittering like a million dollars. She couldn't keep the grin from her lips. She'd spent a lot of time gazing at her left hand over the past couple of weeks, reminding herself that no matter what the future held, she'd not be alone.

That if the going got tough, Jett wasn't going anywhere.

Even though it made no difference to their plans, she and Jett had kept their upcoming nuptials a secret until Olivia had her test results in her hot little hand. Today's negative result meant she was no more at risk of cancer than anyone else in the community. And she couldn't wait to tell her best friend and future sister-in-law.

'Relax.' Jett poured chilled champagne into two glasses. 'Breanna's not famous for her time-keeping skills. She was meeting someone first.' His lips twitched. 'She texted me they were having car problems.'

'Oh? *Oh*...' Olivia nodded. That said it all.

She spotted Brie making her way between the tables a couple of glasses of wine and an entrée later.

'What are we celebrating?' Brie wasted no time asking

as she sat down and took the glass Jett held out to her. 'We did the engagement, so it has to be something else.'

'Two things, actually.' Olivia clasped her hands together in front of her mouth, unable to contain her joy a second more. 'I got my test results today. And it's negative.'

'Oh, Livvie!' Brie jumped up and came around the table to hug her. 'I'm so, so happy for you. For both of you.' She moved on to Jett and hugged him too. Finally, she leaned back, her gaze flitting between the pair of them. 'You said two things.'

Jett looked at Olivia and all the love and promises and future shone in his eyes. 'We're getting married in a week.'

'A week?' Brie squealed. 'My brother the fast worker.'

Olivia laughed. 'We want to be a family. And, my wonderful sister-in-law-to-be, that includes you. The ceremony's going to be on *Chasing Dawn* at sunset on Sunday and we want you and a friend to be our witnesses.'

'So romantic.' Brie nodded, a playful smile around her mouth. 'Count me in. Oh, wait up.' She whipped out her phone and began snapping photos. 'I want memories for that album of yours, starting now.'

Olivia met Jett's persuasive chocolate eyes and, as always, felt herself surrendering to his wicked sense of fun, to his easy friendship. To his love. And she knew they'd make a long and happy lifetime of memories. 'I think it's time we posed for a kissy photo to put on the front cover.'

Jett smiled and leaned down, stroking a strand of hair behind her ear and cradling her chin in his cupped palm. 'I reckon it is.'

* * * * *

MISTLETOE KISS WITH THE MILLIONAIRE

DONNA ALWARD

To Boo and Romeo,
who never fail to let me know when it's dinnertime,
and give the best head-butts and purr-rubs.

CHAPTER ONE

SOPHIE WALTHAM LOOKED at the couples turning on the
dance floor and pursed her lips. A Pemberton social function hadn't been on her "must attend" list in her diary, but
her parents had decided to go to Prague for a week to celebrate their anniversary and had insisted Sophie represent
the family at the event. She tapped her toe impatiently,
wondering how long she had to stay before she could po-
litely leave. It was an engagement party for Bella Pemberton and Viscount Downham. So why was she expected to
"represent" as if this were a business function?

The dress she'd chosen had been a mistake. Her go-to
little black dress was fitting a bit too snugly these days,
and she wasn't comfortable in it or in the stilettos on her
feet. Her dark hair was down around her shoulders, and a
Waltham original piece graced her neck—a narrow, glim-
mering necklace of pearls and diamonds that she'd designed herself. She'd deliberately chosen it instead of an
Aurora Gems piece. If she wanted to build her name as a
designer, she should be wearing her own creations.

What had begun as Waltham Fine Jewelry nearly a cen-
tury ago was now simply "Waltham," the name alone syn-
onymous with quality on Bond Street. It was also one of
the exclusive distributors of Aurora Gems, the jewelry
line for the Aurora, Inc. dynasty. Which was why she was

standing here, on the sidelines of the party, sipping club soda and lime and wishing she were home with her feet up, reading. She was tired. And her feet hurt.

She sighed and went back to the bar to refresh her drink. Just as she picked it up, a smooth voice sounded behind her that eased some of the tension in her shoulders.

"Well hello, stranger."

There was still a hint of French accent in Christophe Germain's voice, despite being brought up at Chatsworth Manor, the family home of the Earl of Chatsworth. She smiled and turned, happy to see his smile, his curly dark hair, and his right eyebrow. For as long as she could remember, he'd been able to lift that eyebrow just a tad when teasing, giving him a roguish air.

Christophe Germain was secretly her favorite member of the Pemberton family. He was also newly in charge of Aurora's jewelry division. Despite that important fact, she hadn't seen him for several months.

It was lovely to see that, unlike her, he hadn't changed.

"Christophe!" She leaned forward, and they bussed cheeks. "I'm so glad you're here."

"You are? How delightful." He looked her up and down and grinned. "You look like Holly Golightly."

"Thank you... I think?" Her hairstyle certainly wasn't the short, gamine look of Audrey Hepburn in *Breakfast at Tiffany's*, but she supposed the dress fit the bill and the necklace, too.

"It's a compliment. You are elegant, as always."

She knew some women would find the compliment boring and colorless, but not her. Understated, classic elegance was her preferred style; avant-garde wasn't. She saved the creativity for her gemstones and precious metals.

They moved away from the bar so as to not interrupt the flow of thirsty guests. "I've been meaning to pay Waltham a visit," he continued. "The last few months have been so busy, though. Maybe I can set up a time in the next few weeks. Before the holidays, for sure."

"My father would love that. And so would I." Though she'd never admit it, she'd always had a bit of a crush on Christophe. Oh, she'd never acted on it—she appreciated their friendship too much. Besides, if he knew, he'd tease her mercilessly about it. "He and Mum are on their anniversary trip this week. Thirty-three years."

He lifted his glass in a salute. "Now that's something to celebrate."

It certainly was, especially after her mother's illness a few years ago. Time was no longer something they took for granted. She looked at Christophe. Her mum had survived, but he'd recently lost the man who'd been a father to him most of his life.

She put her hand on his arm. "How are you doing, since Cedric's passing?"

The Pemberton family had been left grief-stricken and reeling since Cedric's death. Sophie had attended the funeral but hadn't had the opportunity to really chat with Christophe since.

"I'm all right. Tante Aurora is a strong woman. I still miss him and his advice, though. And the last few months have been a bit crazy on the family front."

"I heard about William's marriage, and Charlotte's, too." She'd offered congratulations to both of Christophe's cousins earlier. Charlotte looked ready to pop, expecting her first child with her husband within a few weeks. Seeing her glowing and happy had made Sophie's heart soften with wistful wishing. It wasn't often she let down her guard, let emotion override her determination. But seeing a very pregnant Charlotte had made her realize that by the time January rolled around, none of her dresses would be fitting anymore. She had already made her decision about her baby, but no one seemed interested in hearing it.

"Yes," Christophe said, "and now Bella and Burke. Very happy for them, of course. As long as the marriage bug doesn't bite me, I'll be fine." He winked at her, and she laughed. It was no secret that Christophe was a die-hard bachelor.

"Come, now. You're one of France's most eligible, aren't you?"

"That does not mean I have any desire to settle down." His voice held a touch of humor, and he offered her a bland look. "There's been more than enough drama at Chez Pemberton for a decade." He winked at her. "I suppose it does keep the days from being monotonous, though. Or, you know. Makes me look up from my desk now and again." He pretended to adjust his tie. "Put on a tux now and again."

"What about the woman you were dating last… What was her name? Elizabeth or something?"

Christophe lifted his eyebrow. "My, you've been paying close attention. Lizzy, yes. That ended a while ago." He sighed. "Suddenly she was all about marriage and babies."

Sophie watched him closely. "And you're not that guy?"

He shook his head. "I'm very much not that guy. Besides, I'm too busy for a social life right now. Company functions are about it."

She linked her arm through his and they walked to a nearby table. "Has the workload been daunting? With Aurora semi retiring?"

"A bit. I still run the jewelry section, but I've taken over some of Bella's cosmetics division, as well." He laughed and shrugged, his shoulders rising and falling in his perfectly tailored tuxedo. "Me, in cosmetics. There's been a learning curve."

She laughed, too, and the night suddenly seemed

brighter. She had known Christophe for several years, and she'd never been as intimidated by him as she had been by his cousins. She knew that he'd gone to live with the Pembertons when he was nine and had been brought up as one of the children with the same advantages and love. And yet she knew, too, that he still felt the difference. He was Aurora's nephew, but Aurora had also come from humble beginnings. Stephen, William, Charlotte, Bella…they were all Cedric's natural children, born into English aristocracy. Stephen was the new Earl of Chatsworth.

Once she'd heard Christophe refer to himself as "the bastard cousin," and she'd told him firmly that he was never to refer to himself as that again. As she looked him over, she remained convinced that there was absolutely nothing wrong with Christophe Germain. Nothing at all.

"Your necklace is lovely. And not one of ours, I don't think."

She took a sip of her drink and met his gaze. "I've been doing some designing. This is one of mine. Though one of the simpler ones." The small double strand of pearls was joined together by a glittering diamond clasp in the shape of a honeybee.

"I like this." He reached out with a finger and touched the clasp. A shiver skittered over her skin. She hoped he didn't notice the reaction. The last thing she needed was for him to clue in that she was attracted to him in any way. That would remain her little secret. Besides, he'd just admitted he wasn't into marriage and babies, and Sophie was a package deal now. That would be enough to send him running for the hills. No, he need never know of her crush.

"I—I've been using some elements of nature in my latest designs," she admitted, trying to regain the slip in her composure. "Flowers, leaves, fruit, bees."

"Fertility," he mused, and she choked on her sip of club

soda and began to cough. She wasn't showing yet. It was too early. There was no way for him to know she was pregnant. But had she been, subconsciously, bringing those elements into her work because of what was happening in her personal life? It was an interesting observation, and something she wanted to think about more later, when she considered what direction she wanted to take her new designs. As a gemologist, she oversaw Waltham's inventory. Each stone had to be of the highest quality to meet Waltham standards. She was good at that, but what she really wanted was to create her own original pieces.

He patted her back gently. "You all right?" he asked, that silly eyebrow puckered now in concern.

"Oh, yes. Of course." She cleared her throat. "Sorry about that."

"Don't be silly."

The song changed and he smiled at her. "Come on. Let's dance. You've been standing on the sidelines for the better part of an hour."

He'd noticed. What did that mean?

He held out his hand and she took it. How could she refuse? Besides, they'd danced together lots of times before. This was no different. He led her to the floor and brought her into the circle of his arms, moving smoothly, leading her effortlessly.

For a poor boy from a little French village, he had moves. In some ways, he was Pemberton through and through. His hand was strong and sure as it clasped hers, and he smelled delicious…hints of bergamot and sandalwood, perhaps. Whatever it was, she liked it.

His light chatter put her more at ease, and by the time the song was half over, she'd relaxed substantially, even laughing at some of his anecdotes about the family's mishaps over the past few months. He managed to take some of their hardships—the media storm after Stephen was left at the altar, the sabotage of the Aurora line at New York Fashion Week—and make them into colorful stories. His face had softened as he told her about his Aunt Aurora's heart troubles and how wonderful Burke had been. In addition to being Viscount Downham, Burke was a highly regarded cardiologist. And now he was marrying Bella, who, Christophe said, was so deserving of a happy ending.

What struck Sophie was the obvious affection he had for his family. She only had her brother, and as she'd been off to boarding school when he'd still been very young, they hadn't really grown up together. It made her the smallest bit lonely, hearing Christophe talk about his cousins in such a way. She thought about the tiny bundle of cells growing within her belly. She didn't want him or her to grow up as an only child. Which made her decision of last week even more…well, not confusing, really. But she could understand why some would think she was making a big mistake.

When the dance was over, Christophe led her to a table and held out a chair. She sank into it thankfully; the shoes were killing her feet and she was ready for bed. The baby was the size of a strawberry. How it could make her so exhausted was unbelievable. She stifled a yawn, then blushed as Christophe's keen gaze held on her face.

"It looks like someone is putting in extra hours at work." He frowned, then raised that quizzical eyebrow again. "Either that or there is someone keeping you up all hours of the night. Is there someone new in your life, Sophie?"

His teasing was going to be the end of her. "Wouldn't you like to know," she responded, offering a smile. One of the waitstaff stopped by and offered champagne. Christophe took a glass and she asked for iced water, hoping he wouldn't notice and ask why. Worse, however, was when the circulating waitress approached with her tray of hors d'oeuvres. Sophie took one look at the salmon and trout tartare with pressed caviar and felt her stomach do a slow, sickening roll.

No raw fish. No soft cheese. The first she could do without; the second was more of a hardship. She adored cheese. Now she felt Christophe's eyes on her again, so she smiled and chose an onion tartlet. She hadn't had dinner yet, and right now just wanted to go home to her flat and make a cheese toastie.

Her water arrived. She smiled at Christophe and nibbled on the tartlet, while he smiled back and bit into smoked salmon on some sort of brioche.

The fishy smell hit her nostrils and she tried valiantly to swallow the tartlet. The onion, however, caught in her throat and she hastily reached for her water. Christophe had put down the rest of his brioche and was watching her curiously now. "Sophie, are you all right? Is there something wrong? You don't seem yourself tonight."

Because I'm not, she thought, but kept the words inside. Instead, she jumped from her chair and headed for the closest powder room. The onion had been a mistake, and the salmon smell had only made it worse. She couldn't think about Christophe's alarmed expression right now. She had only one thing on her mind—get to the bathroom before she embarrassed herself.

Christophe stood as Sophie rose from her chair, but he wasn't even all the way upright when she dashed away, making a beeline for the ladies' room. She definitely wasn't okay. Hopefully it wasn't food poisoning. The family would be appalled if such a thing happened at one of their events, and so would the hotel. Not that he particularly cared about that—about appearances. He was more worried that his friend had suddenly run off, ill. If she were truly sick, she should go home. Be in bed and sleep off whatever it was.

Christophe abandoned his champagne and the tiny plate of food and followed her, waiting just inside the ballroom where he could see the door to the bathroom. Several people passed by and said hello; he greeted them cordially but never lost sight of the door. When Sophie finally appeared, her face pale and eyes looking bruised, he grew even more concerned. He stepped forward, noting the surprise in her eyes when she looked up and saw him there.

"You...you're waiting for me." She bit down on her lip, and her eyes slid away from his. Something was very off with her, and the more time went by, the more concerned he became. He'd known Sophie for probably seven, eight years. The relationship between her family's company and Aurora went back a very long way. And in all that time, he'd never seen her act so strangely. She was always warm, upfront, and easygoing in a way that was intimate.

"You're not feeling well. I wanted to make sure you were okay and offer you a way home if you want to go."

"It's still so early." But there was a tinge of relief in her tone, too, that belied her words.

"You saw Burke and Bella, didn't you? You don't need to stay longer if you're worried about any sort of obligation. Everyone will understand."

"I doubt it," she muttered, low enough he barely caught the words. What on earth did that mean?

"Soph?"

She finally met his gaze and let out a sigh. "I'm sorry, Christophe. I know I must seem all over the place. To be honest, I'm not feeling well, and I think I'll grab a taxi and head home."

"Let me drive you."

She glanced up in surprise. "You have a car here?"

Christophe was generally based in Paris, and he didn't keep a flat here in London. But this trip was a little longer in nature, and the cars at the manor house sat idle too often. "I'm using one of the family's cars," he explained. "I hate being driven everywhere. This gives me more freedom."

"And London traffic. Brave man." She smiled slightly.

"So, what do you say? I think we could both sneak off and no one would even notice. I'll give you a lift home and make sure you're okay, and then I can have a little of my own downtime. It works for me, too."

She looked as if she might refuse, so he added, "I love my cousin, but to be honest, all this romance lately has got to be a bit much. You'd be saving me."

Her shadowed eyes lightened, and she laughed a little. "All right, then. I think I left my clutch at the table, though."

They walked back into the ballroom, Christophe following just slightly behind her, and the smile on his face faded. Sophie wasn't herself, and there was no denying the grayish pallor of her skin when she'd come out of the bathroom. He hoped it wasn't anything more serious than a twenty-four-hour virus.

In no time at all they were on their way. Sophie gave him directions to her flat in Chelsea, and he navigated the streets easily. London was truly a second home, even if he didn't have a property here. He generally stayed at his Paris flat, or at the manor house when he was in England; the commute to the city wasn't horribly long, and the manor house was the only home he really remembered. Sophie was quiet in the seat next to him, her pale face illuminated by the lights from the dash. Christophe glanced over at her several times before speaking.

"Are you sure you're all right?"

She nodded. "I'm fine, really. My stomach is just a little off."

He stopped at a traffic light and spared a longer look at her profile. "If you're sure…"

"It was the fish. The smell didn't agree with me tonight, that's all. And I'm tired, so I think it's just a case of needing some rest. I'm sure I'll be fine tomorrow."

Something about her words didn't sit quite right. And yet they made perfect sense, so it wasn't like he could press the issue. His concern wasn't allayed, however, and he caught himself frowning several times before they arrived at her flat.

"I'll see you in," he said, parking the car in a surprisingly free spot in front of her building.

"Christophe, you don't have to do that. I'm fine." She smiled at him then, her eyes soft. "I appreciate the concern and the lift home. I truly do."

"Then indulge me. Let me make sure you're all right and settled. That's what friends do, after all."

"You're not going to let this go, are you?"

He grinned and unbuckled his seat belt. "See? You do know me. Come on. Let's go in."

The night was soft and quiet as Sophie let them into her flat and flicked on a light. He'd never been inside; the last time they'd hung out together she'd been living elsewhere with a flatmate, and before that she'd been at her family's home when she wasn't away at school. He liked the look of this place. It reflected her personality more than the previous apartment, which had been comprised of a varied assortment of furniture belonging to both her and her flatmate, a scuffed hardwood floor, and some sort of chintz curtains on the windows.

This place was decorated with intention and looked like

a bit of country home inside an eight-hundred-square-foot space. The small foyer opened up into the living room. There was a fireplace surrounded by a white scrolled mantel, a Turkish rug on the floor, and a comfortable-looking sofa flanked by two chairs. A television was above the mantel, attached to the wall. Graceful tables flanked the sofa, and a glass-topped coffee table sat on the rug, a novel on its otherwise flawless top.

"This is different from your last place," he remarked.

"I finished school and started working full time. It made a difference."

It was an expensive flat for someone on a regular salary. But the Walthams had money. It only made sense that some of that had found its way to their only daughter.

She shrugged out of her coat and hung it in a small closet. "Do you want to come in?" she asked. "I can offer you coffee or tea. Sorry I don't have anything stronger."

"I had a glass of champagne and I'm driving. But I'll take tea."

"Do you mind if I change first?"

"Of course not." Though he had to admit, it wasn't a hardship seeing her in a little black dress. He and Sophie were friends, but that didn't mean he was blind. She was ridiculously beautiful.

"Make yourself at home," she suggested, and disappeared down a small hall into what was presumably her bedroom.

Christophe ambled into the living room and stopped to glance at a few photos that were framed and around the room. There was one of her family, all four of them smiling with the Waltham garden in the background. The other, which sat on an end table, was a black-and-white photo of Sophie and her brother, Mark, making silly faces. He smiled at that one. For all Sophie's quiet elegance, she had a goofy side that he admired. Putting it on display in a framed photo told him she didn't take herself too seriously, either, and wasn't afraid to show that side now and again.

Which made her awkwardness this evening very out of character.

A meow sounded and Christophe looked down to see a long-haired tabby padding over the rug. "Well, hello," he said softly, kneeling and holding out a hand. "What's your name?"

The cat came forward, purred, and rubbed along the side of Christophe's hand.

"That's Harry," Sophie said, and Christophe looked up to find her changed into a pair of black leggings and a long gray sweater.

"You look much more comfortable," he said, then lowered his gaze to the cat again. "This is a very handsome kitty." He scratched beneath the cat's chin, earning more purrs and rubs.

"Oh, that's his favorite scratchy spot. You've earned a friend for life, now. And you're going to have cat hair all over your tuxedo."

He chuckled. "That's what the cleaners are for." He stood again and put his hands in his pockets. "Your color is better. I'm glad. I was worried."

She smiled and turned away, going to the kitchen. "Oh, you don't have to worry about me," she called. "I'm fine."

He wasn't completely reassured. Something was still off. She'd meet his gaze but not hold it for too long, as if she didn't want him looking too closely. He watched as she filled the kettle and set it on the burner to boil, then went to a cupboard and opened it. "What would you like? I have a decent selection of herbals, and some decaf black tea." She looked over at him expectantly. Harry twined himself around her legs, and she took a moment to croon at him and dig a few treats out of a cupboard.

His brows puckered. Okay, something was definitely wrong. She'd been drinking club soda tonight and didn't have any alcohol in the house. Now her teas were all herbal and decaf? Was she on some sort of health kick or something? Because the Sophie he knew loved champagne and would mainline coffee if she could. She never started her day without it. And she was too young to worry about it keeping her up at night.

He looked at the package of peppermint tea in her hand and then met her gaze. "You'd better tell me what's going on, Soph."

Her eyes clouded with indecision for a moment, and, if he guessed correctly, a bit of panic. Then her lips set, as if she'd come to some sort of decision.

"I might as well tell you, since I won't be able to hide it forever. I'm pregnant, Christophe."

CHAPTER TWO

THE KETTLE BEGAN to whistle behind her as she heard the words leave her mouth. She hadn't intended to say anything this soon, and certainly not to Christophe. They were friends but not overly intimate. They saw each other a few times a year, hung out now and again like they had tonight, at industry functions, that sort of thing. She hadn't even told her brother about the baby yet. And by the staggered look on Christophe's face, she wished she could take back the words. What had she been thinking, confiding such a thing?

Instead, she turned, removed the kettle from the burner, and poured the boiling water into mugs. Without asking, she dropped a bag into his, knowing that he'd drink the tea anyway after a bombshell like that.

There was a quiet *thunk* as she put the kettle back on the stove and turned to face him again.

"That explains a lot," he said weakly, and his gaze dropped to her belly and then back up to her face. He blushed when he realized what he'd done. "Sorry," he offered.

"Nothing to see there yet. I'm not quite through my first trimester. So yeah, it explains the dash to the ladies' tonight and why I didn't eat." She fought through her embarrassment. "Do you want milk in your tea?"

"No, thank you," he replied, and she dipped the bags out of the mugs with a spoon and put them on a saucer before handing him his cup.

"Let's go sit," she said quietly. "And I'll explain."

She led him into the living room and took a seat on the sofa, cradling the warm mug in her hands. The soothing scent of peppermint wafted up, and she took a cautious sip. Peppermint tea seemed to be the one thing that settled her stomach these days.

He sat next to her, but not too close, holding his steaming mug but not paying it any attention at all. "You're how far along?"

"Eleven weeks or so. Hopefully the morning sickness, or all-day sickness, rather, will ease up soon."

Silence fell between them for a moment, and then Christophe asked the question she'd been waiting for. "And the father?"

"Eric."

She didn't have to say more. She'd dated Eric for nearly two years, and occasionally the stockbroker attended events with her. Eric Walsh was practically perfect, as her mother continually reminded her.

"So are congratulations in order? I mean, how do you feel about it? How does Eric feel? Does this mean you two will finally be getting married?"

She took a sip of tea to buy herself some time. He'd fired out four questions and none of them were easy to answer. She'd already gone through all of this—with Eric, with her parents.

Sophie was quiet for so long that Christophe reached out and took her hand, a sheepish grin on his face and that eyebrow doing its quirky thing again. "Sorry, was that too much?"

"A little," she admitted.

"Then maybe I should just say, what are your plans?" He sat back against the cushions.

She put the tea on a coaster on the coffee table, pleased that he'd kept his fingers linked with hers. It was…reassuring. Kept her grounded, which was a nice feeling since she almost always felt her life was spinning out of control. "Well, that's a good question, really. I mean, I'm sort of happy about it? Clearly it wasn't planned, and it's taken me a good bit to wrap my head around the idea, but I like children, and wanted them someday, so this is really just moving up the timeline." She smiled, hoping it was convincing. Truthfully, she was still getting used to the idea. At times she was awed and amazed and even excited. That euphoria was generally offset by panic and worry. She knew nothing about being a parent.

"And Eric?"

"We broke up in September."

"Befo—?"

"Yes, before I knew about the baby." She met his gaze with her own. "We're still broken up, Christophe."

His lips firmed into a line and his throat bobbed as he swallowed, but to his credit, he didn't say anything.

"You're silent. It must be killing you." She offered a small smile, and to her relief, he smiled back.

"Not killing me. It's just…"

"I know." She squeezed his fingers. She was one of the few who truly knew Christophe's history. Despite them not being super close, he'd confessed it one evening years ago when he'd come 'round to her flat for pasta and wine and they'd had a little too much to drink. They'd played "two truths and a lie," but his had been easy to spot; he couldn't conceal the pain in his voice even though it was clear he'd tried. The truth of Christophe's life was that his father had abandoned him and his mother when Christophe was a toddler, and when he was nine, his mother had sent him off to live with his aunt, the great Aurora Germain Pemberton. He'd gone from living in poverty in a small French town with few opportunities to being part of an incredibly rich and powerful family.

"So you're not going to marry him."

She shook her head. "I'm twenty-nine and financially independent. I can do this on my own, you know."

His jaw tightened. "Of course you can. Still, I can't believe he didn't ask you. What kind of man doesn't take responsibility for his own kid?"

Her heart gave a heavy thump as she stared into his face. She knew his wounds ran deep. A small child didn't get over being abandoned. Because she understood his history, the next part was even harder to say.

"Christophe, look at me." When he did, his dark eyes stormy, she felt the contact right to her core. He was a paradox right now, with his rigid posture expressing his outrage but his eyes vulnerable and hurt. She wanted to soothe the furrows off his brow, bring back his smile. She took the mug from his hands and placed it beside hers on the table, then turned and took both his hands in hers. "You are a good friend, Christophe. You always have been, even though we go months between seeing each other. I have always felt comfortable with you, and protected. But you can't get protective now because you need to realize that this is my choice. I'm the one who broke up with Eric, and I did it before I knew I was pregnant. He did ask me to marry him, and I refused. Carrying his baby doesn't miraculously change my feelings for him. I don't want to spend the rest of my life with him. And I certainly don't want to put the pressure of a marriage's success or failure on a tiny, innocent baby."

He sighed. "But—"

"No buts," she said firmly. "Listen, I know how hard a subject this is for you. I know you have a lot of lingering feelings and that's okay, but it's not okay to judge me because of that, all right?"

His eyes finally cleared. "Sophie, I would never judge you."

"Wouldn't you?" She could practically hear him judging her right now, even though she knew he didn't want to.

He sat back. "Not intentionally." He sighed again. "You're right, though. I'm sorry. Being abandoned by my father, and even my mother, has left a mark. I can hardly be unbiased in this situation."

"I know that. I just…" She trailed off, picked up her tea and took a drink to hide the sudden rush of emotion. "My parents think I'm crazy. Eric is being persistent. No one seems to want to listen to what I have to say."

"I'm listening," he said softly.

She looked up at him, and the moment seemed to pause in time. Sophie had eyes in her head; it was easy for her to admit that he was astoundingly good-looking. But more than that, he had *depth*. He felt things. Cared about things. Even the small chip on his shoulder was understandable. His greatest quality was his loyalty. She knew without a doubt that she would only have to ask for his help and he would be there. To ask for his support and it would be granted. Friends like that were as rare as a Burma ruby. Tears formed in the corners of her eyes. Of course she'd trusted him with the news. Even if Christophe didn't agree, he'd offer his support regardless. It had nothing to do with her secret crush. She'd invited him in tonight and told him the news because she'd known he'd be on her side.

"Hey," he said, leaning forward. "Don't cry. It's all right."

"I know it is. It's everyone else who thinks I'm making the biggest mistake of my life."

He nodded. "Are you? Are you sure you don't want to be with him? I know how stubborn you can be, Soph. And how you resist being told what to do." He smiled a little, the curve of his lips making her smile despite herself.

"I'm sure," she said, starting to feel better. "I don't love him, not the way I should. I loved him out of habit and not passion. Out of complacency and not joy. We'd been together long enough that it made sense to start looking at our future. When I did, I knew I couldn't marry him. My feelings haven't changed just because I'm pregnant. If anything, I'm more sure now. I…" She hesitated before voicing her biggest objection. "Honestly, I can't imagine us raising children together. He works so much and frankly, we don't have a lot in common. I can't picture us being a team when it comes to bringing up kids. Or sticking together during thick and thin."

Christophe nodded. "I can understand that. I still…well, you know me. I still believe a child needs two parents."

"It's funny," she mused gently. "I had two parents and I'm positive I can do this myself. You didn't and you're sure it takes two. And somehow, I think the answer is in between somewhere. I will say, Eric agrees with you. He wants to marry me and make things 'legitimate.' The problem is that legitimate is a concept on a birth certificate. It wouldn't extend to the marriage, you see?"

"It would be easier if you loved him."

"You're telling me!"

She said it so emphatically that they both ended up laughing a little.

Sophie sighed. "I know he'll support his child. And Christophe, just because I'm positive this is the right thing, doesn't mean I don't have guilt about it. Misgivings. Nothing about this is perfect." She put her hand on her still-flat tummy. "And none of this is my baby's fault. Talk about innocent and caught in the middle."

Christophe tried to make sense of the thoughts swirling through his head. Of all the things he'd expected tonight, hearing that Sophie was having a baby was so far off the mark it didn't even register. And yet here he was, in her cozy little Chelsea flat, drinking horrible tea and getting all the sordid details.

Well, not all the details. Thankfully she'd left out any account of conception. He'd met Eric before and he'd seemed like a nice enough guy, but the last thing Christophe wanted to think about was Eric and Sophie in bed.

He shouldn't be thinking about her in that way at all, considering she was his friend. Especially since she was carrying another man's child.

She was right about one thing, though. The baby was innocent in all this.

He tamped down all his personal feelings—she'd been right on that score—and simply asked, "What do you need from me right now?"

"You've given it," she said softly, her eyes shining in the lamplight. "You listened. You didn't say I was being stupid and foolish. And you haven't given me a laundry list of Eric's attributes to try to convince me to change my mind."

"Your parents?" he guessed.

"And Eric, as well. But Christophe, all those things don't matter if the love…if that certain something just isn't there. You know. Your Aunt Aurora had it with your Uncle Cedric. And your cousins… Look at Bella and Burke. You can tell they think the sun rises and sets in each other. They're so devoted." She sniffed. "Am I wrong to want that for myself?"

"No," he replied, touched. She wasn't wrong about Tante Aurora and Oncle Cedric. Perhaps that was part of his resentment. They'd taken him in but as a result he'd seen what a real, committed love looked like. It was something he'd never witnessed before. Certainly not from his parents. "No, you're not wrong. I want that for you, too. I just don't want you to throw this away if it might be it."

"It's not," she answered, her voice definitive. "I just look at my mum and dad and know Eric and I will never have what they do. When Mum was ill, Dad's devotion was so beautiful. I can't settle for less than the example they've set."

Christophe merely squeezed her hand in understanding.

A gurgling sound interrupted the moment, and they both looked down at her stomach. She laughed a little, a blush tinging her cheeks an adorable pink. "I really should have eaten, I guess," she mused.

"We could order something in."

"Honestly? I've been dying for a cheese toastie."

He laughed. *Dieu*, she could be so adorable. Earlier she'd been in a killer dress and stilettos wearing thousands of pounds worth of gems, but what she really wanted was the simplest comfort food.

"Then a toastie you shall have. And I will make it."

"Oh! You don't have to. I can—"

"Shh." He lifted a finger and put it against her lips. "Let me look after you. This is a simple thing. I promise I won't set off any fire alarms, and it will be delightfully edible."

Her blush deepened and he removed his finger, suddenly disconcerted by the innocent-meaning touch. It had felt... intimate. And that was a new sensation where Sophie was concerned.

He covered by getting up from the sofa and going to

the kitchen, where he could think without being so near to her. As he took a copper pan off a hook and found bread, cheese and butter, he took deep breaths. He could understand why Eric was determined to marry her, and not just because of the baby. After having a woman like Sophie, who would willingly let her get away?

CHAPTER THREE

SOPHIE PUT DOWN her loupe and the engagement ring she'd been studying and stretched on her stool, arching her back to ease the constant ache that plagued her lately. The stones in the ring were of impeccable quality; the cushion cut center stone was ideal, and she rated the clarity at a VVS1. It was a new addition to the Aurora line, and she should be excited about it, but engagement rings just weren't doing it for her lately. For obvious and not so obvious reasons.

She'd been working on a different design lately, one that she thought had great potential. The stones had to be perfect for the colors to work exactly right. Clear, bright aquamarines, deep sapphires, golden citrines, and sparkling diamonds set in waves of color reminiscent of Van Gogh's *Starry Night*. The more she looked at the design, the more she considered an entire line inspired by works of art. She pictured perhaps Monet's *Bouquet of Sunflowers* or *Artist's Garden*, Degas's *Dancers in Pink*. She reached for her sketchbook again and started sketching out ideas.

Working at Waltham was a wonderful job, and she was happy she'd followed in the family footsteps and become a gemologist. But she didn't want to sit at a desk and appraise all day. She wanted to create. Anytime she brought it up, her parents brushed it off. It was fully expected that she'd simply take over Waltham when they retired. Many looked at Sophie and saw a life full of opportunity. She saw a box, hemming her in with expectations.

And it wasn't that she was against taking over, necessarily. It was that she wanted more. She wanted to be able to explore her career a bit first before settling in a permanent spot of her choosing.

Her pencil paused over the paper. Maybe that was it. Maybe that was the way to frame the discussion…taking time to spread her wings within the industry, to learn outside of Waltham. She stretched her back again and sighed. Well, whatever that plan was, it would have to wait a while. In six months, her world was going to shift substantially. She'd have a child to consider.

She continued sketching. The movement of the pencil tip on the paper was soothing, focusing her mind on the shapes in front of her rather than her troubles.

Eric had called again last night. He'd pointed out the life she'd be giving up, as if money were an enticement. When she'd replied that she had plenty of money of her own, he'd gotten angry and hung up.

The shape on the page became reminiscent of a ballerina's skirt and Sophie worked away, fashioning it into a pendant. Oh, she liked this one. Pink sapphire would do nicely, with diamond accents and set in warm rose gold.

She was deep into the sketch when her mobile buzzed, the vibration on the table making her jump in surprise and dread…was it Eric again? A quick look at the screen showed Christophe's ID, and she smiled as she picked it up. Right now, Christophe was the calm in the middle of a storm.

"Hello, you," she said into the phone, correcting her posture once again.

"Hi yourself. Busy?"

"Doing some designing. Why?" She tapped the pencil on the pad as she cradled the phone to her ear.

"I'm in town for another few days. I wondered if you'd like to catch some dinner tonight. No raw fish. Promise."

"I thought you'd gone back to Paris after the party."

"Well, there's been a development. Charlotte had her baby girl on Monday. Everyone stayed at the manor to be able to visit. Even the staff is aflutter."

"The first grandchild. Aurora must be in heaven."

"She is. And has already started sending Will and Gabi pointed looks. Anyway, I wasn't going to be the jerk who abandoned the family, even if I'm not quite as excited as Bella and Gabi. I've been holding down the fort with Will and Burke and Stephen."

"Sounds delightful."

"It's not. They're horrible company. Definitely not good-looking and boring conversationalists. You'd be saving me. Truly."

She laughed, utterly charmed. "How can I refuse?" The day suddenly looked much brighter. Definitely better than going home to a silent flat and scrounging for something appetizing.

"What do you fancy? I mean, other than bread and cheese."

"Pasta. I would love a plate of pasta and warm bread and salad. If that works for you."

"I know just the place. Pick you up at yours or from work?"

She checked the clock. How had it got to be four o'clock already? "I think from work. I'm not ready to leave yet, and by the time I go home and change… Is it too much trouble to come here?"

"Of course not. What time's good for you?"

"Six?"

"Perfect. See you then, Soph."

He hung up and Sophie put the phone down. How was it that her day went from blah to brilliant in a few moments, all because the charming and sexy Christophe Germain asked her out for dinner? Surely it wasn't just the company. It was the prospect of carbs and Bolognese, certainly. She was hungry. Lunch had been crackers, hummus, some veg, and fruit. Tasty, but not overly substantial.

No matter, there wasn't time to think about it too much. She still had a number of pieces to assess before she could leave for the day, and she'd faffed about with her sketching instead of sticking to her job.

At quarter to six she finally shut down her computer and locked everything away for the night before going into the bathroom and touching up her hair and makeup. Just because they were friends didn't mean she shouldn't put in a little effort. The fall day was cool, so she'd paired narrow trousers with heels and a collared blouse, and then a cashmere shawl as a wrap against the chill. With her hair up and a refresh of her mascara, her skin glowed and her eyes shone as she stared into the mirror.

This was not a date. It was Christophe and pasta. Nothing more. No reason to be excited or flushed.

He arrived precisely at six, just as she was walking out of Waltham's and onto the dark street. He rounded the hood to open her door and met her on the curb, stopping to buss her cheek with his lips. "You look better," he said warmly, stepping back. "Roses in your cheeks this time."

She was certain the roses took on a pinker hue at his words and hoped he didn't notice. He wore jeans and a bulky cream sweater that made him look both cuddly and incredible masculine, and the little bit of neatly trimmed facial hair was downright sexy. It occurred to her that for the first time she could remember, neither of them were dating anyone…

This was ridiculous. She shouldn't be thinking this way about Christophe. Particularly since she was pregnant and the idea of dating was now very, very different. There was no such thing as casual dating when a child was involved, was there? Even if that child wasn't yet born. "I'm feeling much better, thank you. And I'm hungry." She grinned at him, and he grinned back, and the old comfort between them returned.

He shut the door behind her and then got in the driver's seat. "Where are we going?" she asked.

"An old favorite of mine in Pimlico. Glad you're hungry. You won't be when you leave." He glanced over and grinned, then turned his attention back to the traffic. She marveled at how he weaved in and out with no anxiety whatsoever. She relaxed back against the seat, enjoying that for the second time in a week she was out with Christophe after months of not seeing him at all.

When they reached the restaurant, the street was packed so they parked a few blocks away and walked. A raw chill had descended with the darkness, and Sophie guessed that they were in for a bitter fall rain sooner rather than later. At the restaurant, Christophe opened the door for her and then chafed his hands as she passed by him. Once they were inside, though, all thoughts of the weather disappeared as the most gorgeous smells touched her nose. Tomato, garlic, the starchy scent of pasta and bread. Christophe came up behind her and put his hand lightly on her waist as a hostess approached. "Table for two?" she asked, and at Christophe's nod, she led them to a secluded corner.

It was every Italian cliché in one spot: the candle in the Chianti bottle, the checkered tablecloths, the music that could barely be heard above the happy chatter of the patrons. They'd been seated only a few moments when their server arrived to take drink orders.

"Still water for me, please," Sophie said.

"I'll have the same," Christophe ordered.

"Just because I'm not drinking doesn't mean you can't," she said once the server was gone. "It's okay. Truly."

"I'm driving again, remember?"

She laughed. "Oh, right. I'm so used to not having a car that it's usually not a consideration."

"Besides, it wouldn't be fair for me to enjoy a nice robust red while you're stuck with water."

"Ouch. You know how to hit a girl where it hurts."

He laughed. "Does it help if I remind you it's not forever?"

"No." She was gratified when he laughed at her flat response.

They looked at their menus. "I still want the spag bol," she said, closing it again. "I can't help it. I've been thinking about it ever since you called."

"Interesting. You've been thinking about pasta, and I've been thinking about you." His dark eyes held hers across the candlelit table and she bit down on her lip. Was he…flirting? Of course not. Why would he? They were friends, and she was pregnant with someone else's kid. But it felt nice anyway to be the center of his attention. Nothing would ever happen between them, but she could still enjoy the attention, couldn't she? Was that so very wrong?

"I highly doubt that," she returned, placing the menu on the table. "But I appreciate the compliment anyway."

He took a few moments to stare at her, and she was just getting to the uncomfortable stage when he spoke again. "I have been thinking of you, you know. About what's going on with you. About what you said the other night."

"Not you, too," she said with a groan. "You're not going to try to get me to change my mind about Eric, are you?"

As if on cue, her mobile rang. She fished it out of her purse and her stomach sank at the number on the ID. She rejected the call and put the phone down, but a few seconds later it rang again. Christophe raised his damnable eyebrow and she sighed. "Give me a sec," she muttered.

Eric's voice came on the line as she put the phone to her ear. "Sophie. I need to see you. We need to talk about this."

"Hello to you, too," she said, frustrated and embarrassed that this was happening in front of Christophe.

"I mean it, Soph. You can't keep avoiding me. I'm the baby's father."

"Yes, you are. And as I told you, I'll keep you updated on everything that's happening. You don't need to call me every day."

"I wouldn't have to if you'd quit this ridiculous… I don't know what to call it. Marry me. I can provide for both of you."

She closed her eyes against the repetitive argument. "I don't need you to provide for me. I can provide for myself. This isn't the 1950s, Eric."

"That's not what I meant."

But it kind of was, and they both knew it.

"Can we discuss this later, please?"

"Where are you, anyway?"

"I'm having dinner."

"With a man?"

He sounded so appalled she wanted to smash her phone on the table. She took a deep breath instead. "Eric, I'm going to say this just once more. You are the father of this baby and I wouldn't dream of keeping you from him or her. But I'm not going to marry you. I don't love you, Eric, not the way someone should if they're going to get married. A baby won't change that. So please, please, stop. This is bordering on harassment."

She felt Christophe's intense gaze on her and fought back the urge to cry. She refused to be the stereotypical emotional pregnant woman. Instead, she hung up the call and turned her phone off.

"Sorry," she said quietly.

"You have nothing to be sorry for." He reached across the table and took her hand. "Are you all right?"

She nodded. "A little anxious. His calls always do that to me."

"He calls a lot?"

She nodded again. "He doesn't like to take no for an answer. Oh," she continued, as Christophe's expression grew alarmed, "he'd never harm me. But he thinks he can convince me that marrying him is for the best. I'm sure he thinks he can wear me down. Have me come around to his way of seeing things."

"Ha. You're far too independent for that."

His simple words sent a warmth through her chest. Their server returned and Christophe ordered for them, choosing family-style servings of the Bolognese and salad. When the server departed, Christophe rubbed his thumb over the top of her hand. "I'll confess that I've been having trouble with this myself," he said. "I understand completely what you said to me the other night. I think you're right. And there's still a part of me that wonders if your little boy or girl will wonder why Dad isn't around. If they'll wonder if it was something they did."

Her heart melted a little. Christophe was still that little boy sometimes, unwanted and an afterthought. "I'll make sure that doesn't happen," she assured him. "And Eric plans to be involved. He's taking this responsibility seriously." *Too seriously*, she thought, but didn't say it out loud. "Honestly, I wish he'd just accept what I'm saying so we can work out what parenting is going to look like. I don't want to have him as an adversary. His constant pressure isn't helping."

"Maybe he really still loves you."

She shook her head. "But that's not enough, don't you see? He would have us marry for the sake of our child, but what about us? What about me? Don't I deserve to be happy, too?"

His face softened. "Of course, you do. I'm sorry, Sophie. I've been pushing where I shouldn't be. You get enough of that from Eric."

"And my parents."

"Then I promise I'll back off on the Eric thing. You're the best judge of your own happiness."

His willingness and openness took a weight off her shoulders. Their salad arrived, and Sophie dived at it both as a distraction and because she was so hungry her stomach was starting to get queasy again. She served them both helpings of the greens and then swirled a little olive oil and balsamic vinegar over top. The first bite was crisp and flavorful—a perfect choice.

When they'd eaten for a few moments, she asked, "Have you seen your new little cousin?"

"I have. Her name is Imogene and she's red and wrinkly."

Sophie nearly choked on a leaf of rocket. "You don't mean that!"

"Well, she was at first. She's not as red now. And her nose is like a little button." He smiled and touched the tip of his nose. "Hey, I have zero experience with babies and children. But I do have pictures."

He pulled out his phone and brought up his photos. "Here. There are three or four there."

She took the phone and stared down at the little sleeping face. Heavens, she was an angel, all long lashes and pouty lips and a fuzzy little cap of dark hair. Her heart did a big thump. In a few months she'd have her own little baby. She was so not prepared! And yet she was excited, too. There were other pictures of Charlotte with her sister, Bella, and sister-in-law, Gabi, and for the first time in a long time, Sophie wished she had a sister or two to share this with.

"She's gorgeous. Please send Charlotte my congratulations."

"You should call her yourself. She'd be delighted to hear from you."

Sophie wasn't so sure, as she wasn't as familiar with the other members of the Pemberton family. But it was a nice thought just the same.

"I have six months before this happens to me, and a lot to figure out by then." She frowned and handed him the phone back. "Life is going to change so much. Every now and again that sinks in and I get a tad stressed about it."

"I'm sorry it's not been easier for you. I mean, it's a big deal. It would be a big deal even if the two of you were still together, you know? Is there anything I can do to help?"

She smiled and picked up her fork again. "You're doing it. You're a lovely distraction, you know."

"Ouch. A distraction?"

"In the best possible way, darling." It was impossible not to smile back at him when he was so obviously teasing her. "You entertain. You're easy to look at and you feed me. And you don't ask me for answers I'm not ready to give. You're the perfect date, actually." Well, not quite perfect. There was still a missing ingredient, but she knew better than to look for it in Christophe.

"You're forgiven. And by the by, I have an idea. Do you know what you need?" Christophe pointed his fork at her, a slice of avocado stuck on the tines. "You need to get away for a bit. Take a few days off, have some time to escape and think and unwind. Give yourself some real self-care, as Bella would say."

She laughed. "You're forgetting my parents are on vacation. I can't leave Waltham without a captain at the helm."

"When are they back?"

"Saturday."

He speared some more salad and shrugged. "So next week, then. When *was* your last vacation, anyway?"

He had her there. She'd thrown herself into work after breaking up with Eric and had been so determined her pregnancy wouldn't affect her job that she hadn't missed a single minute. Even if some of those minutes had been spent in the employee bathroom.

"May," she admitted.

"I've got it." He sat back in his chair, a satisfied smile on his face. "It's perfect. You can come back to Paris with me. I'll be working, so you can have the days all to yourself. You can do whatever you like. You can visit Aurora, too, if you want, and I can show you next season's designs. But only if you want to. How can you say no to Paris?"

"And I'd be staying…with you." They were friends. There shouldn't be any sort of undertones. She'd always managed to keep her attraction to him tamped down. So why did the idea suddenly seem so intimate? Why was she looking at Christophe and appreciating all his attributes with new eyes? Pregnancy hormones? She'd heard of such a thing but hadn't believed it…until now. Christophe wasn't just charming and handsome. He was desirable. She resisted the urge to hide her face in her hands. He must never find out the thought had even crossed her mind.

"My flat's more than big enough. There's an extra room and a big kitchen and you'd have your own bathroom. You'd hardly have to see me if you didn't want to." He winked at her. "But I can be rather charming company."

She laughed then. He'd made her laugh more in their two evenings together than she had in weeks, and it felt good. Normal. She almost said *What will people say*? But that went against everything she believed in...mostly, minding your own business. She didn't have to explain herself. Especially not to staying with a trusted friend for a few days to decide exactly what steps to take next. Nothing would happen because whatever attraction there was, it was completely one-sided. And as long as Christophe never knew, it would be fine.

Besides, she did love Paris.

"I'd have to make sure my cat sitter is available to look after Harry."

Their pasta arrived then, and the conversation halted as they placed servings in bowls. It smelled absolutely heavenly, and she twirled some pasta around her fork and popped it into her mouth...delicious.

"I told you this place was good," he said, twirling his pasta expertly and taking a bite. "Mmm."

Spaghetti was a messy dish, and not one she'd generally order if this were a date. There was too much potential to get sauce on her face or have a piece of pasta take on a will of its own. Yet with Christophe she didn't mind. It was the strangest thing. One moment she was noticing all sorts of things about him and then next, she was the most comfortable she'd been in weeks. She picked up her napkin and wiped her chin.

That she was actually considering going to Paris told her that she'd been going full tilt for too long and needed some downtime. Work was one thing, but the breakup had been hard to begin with. The pregnancy complicated that a hundred times over. Emotionally she was worn out. Physically she was exhausted.

"You're serious about your offer? To stay with you for a few days?"

He nodded. "Of course. There's more than enough room. What are friends for?"

Friends indeed. As they continued their meal, Sophie wondered how everything could possibly work out the way she wanted…peacefully. Maybe she'd come to some conclusions when she had a chance to remove herself from the situation a bit. And if she got a chance to get an early look at the new Aurora Gems line, all the better.

Christophe wasn't sure what had prompted him to suggest Sophie get away to Paris, and now the idea of having her in his flat sent a strange sort of hollow feeling to his belly. Had he been wrong to offer?

He hadn't liked seeing the strain on her face as she'd taken her ex's call. He'd met Eric and thought he was a decent guy, but clearly he wasn't handling this situation well. Christophe also appreciated Sophie's assertion that she would never try to keep the child away from their father. It seemed that Eric's problem wasn't about being a dad, it was about letting Sophie go. Whether it was love or pride, it didn't matter. Harassing her wasn't okay.

He also knew Sophie would be justifiably angry if he approached Eric on his own. That left giving her space and time to sort some things out and get some rest.

"Dessert?" he asked, when their pasta bowls had been removed.

"I couldn't possibly. I haven't eaten that much since my morning sickness began." She smiled at him, and he noticed the edge of her top lip was slightly orange from the sauce. He lifted his napkin and wiped the smudge away while her cheeks pinkened.

"Good. I'm glad." He took out a card to pay the bill and

then sat back in his chair. "I was planning to go home on Sunday, and back in the office on Monday. We could travel together if you like."

"This all feels quite spontaneous," she said, and she frowned, a tiny wrinkle forming between her brows. "I'm not sure..."

"It's up to you. If it makes you feel better, you can make it a working trip with a light schedule." He smiled at her, knowing she was more likely to agree if he appealed to her practical side. "Waltham distributes our Gems line. You'd get a firsthand look at the new designs. Give some feedback, even."

Her eyes sparkled at him. "You mean have input into Aurora's jewels? That's a big deal, Christophe."

"Unofficially, of course. Unless you're looking for a job. Are you?"

Was that temptation he saw on her face? She looked as if the word "yes" was sitting on the tip of her tongue, and that surprised him. Waltham was the family business and she'd always seemed happy there.

"I'm not, but this is certainly a wonderful opportunity."

"You must take it easy, though. Get rest. Relax. It would be good for you and the baby, too."

"I thought you didn't know much about babies," she pointed out, picking up her water glass and taking a sip. There was a teasing glint in her eye. That hadn't changed. They still loved teasing each other. Not quite flirting, not quite not. His gaze dropped to her lips and he wondered what it might be like to kiss her.

The idea had his blood running hot and he tamped the response down. If she knew what had just passed through his brain, she certainly wouldn't agree to stay at his flat. He couldn't think of Sophie that way. It was just *wrong*.

Besides, he wouldn't endanger their friendship by messing it up with sex.

"I don't need to know a lot to know that taking care of yourself is good for both of you."

She nodded. "You're not wrong." After a moment or two, she nodded again. "All right. Let me run this past my parents first, as they'll be returning in a few days and will have to take up my slack while I'm gone. And like I mentioned, I have to make sure Harry's sitter is available."

"That's all fine. You can just text me to let me know either way, and I'll send you the travel arrangements. We're flying out of Gatwick."

"We?"

He grinned. "Why, Bella and Burke, of course. They're returning, as well. Stephen and Will already went back this morning."

"So your whole family will know."

"They don't need to know anything," he assured her. "Just that I've invited you to have a look at the new line. They know we're friends, Soph. You don't need to tell anyone about the baby if you don't want to. That's entirely your call. I won't say a word."

The server brought back his credit card and as he was tucking it back into his wallet, Sophie spoke again. "Why are you doing all this, Christophe?"

He pondered for a moment, and then thought back to his own childhood, and his mother, and even Charlotte and Jacob's new baby. "Because you need a friend. Because maybe if someone had been kind to my mother, she might not have been forced into a marriage with a man who abandoned her anyway." The truth hit him square in the chest, opening old wounds, but somehow eradicating the infection within. "My parents married because she got pregnant, and it ended in disaster. She married him because she didn't have options and he still left her without a penny. You do have options. And you deserve to be happy, Sophie. You deserve that so much."

He swallowed against a lump in his throat. For all of his charmed life, at least since he'd been nine, there'd always been the knowledge that he wasn't a true Pemberton. He was the poor relation. He worked hard to earn his place in the family ranks, and of course everyone had always been good to him. His cousins loved him and he loved them. But that small difference held on stubbornly, like a splinter under the skin that tweezers just couldn't reach. As if somehow his acceptance and worth was tied into his value at Aurora, Inc.

He had so many conflicting feelings about his upbringing that he wasn't sure what to think. A child deserved two parents who loved each other. But love couldn't be forced, so what was the alternative?

The answer was suddenly clear. Two parents who were, if not in love, at least committed to being parents.

No matter what happened, Sophie was going to be tied to Eric forever. He hadn't actually considered that before. They were broken up, but their relationship had simply changed. The last thing he wanted to do was get in the way of that.

Which meant his earlier thought of kissing Sophie could never be realized.

He helped her put on her wrap, swallowing tightly when his fingers brushed her shoulders. They walked quietly back to the car, a light drizzle hurrying their steps. "You were right about the rain," he said, trying to shift any conversation back to safe, uncharged topics.

"It's not bad yet," she said, and then, fifty yards from the car, the drizzle changed to icy droplets that clung to his hair and the wool of his sweater.

"You were saying?" he asked, and then they dashed for the car, Sophie's heels clicking on the pavement in a rapid staccato. He hit the locks on the key fob, and they flung open the doors and hurried to get in, shutting the doors again and laughing.

"I tempted fate with that one," she admitted, brushing some damp strands of hair off her face.

If she only knew. Looking at her now, beneath the light of the streetlamp and with rain droplets clinging to her face and hair, Christophe made a startling discovery.

Sophie had been right in front of him all along. And it was his bad luck that he'd waited until now to notice. Or perhaps it was for the best, because the last thing he wanted was to hurt her. Which he surely would if they were to get involved.

Sophie Waltham wanted what he could never give her: love and commitment.

CHAPTER FOUR

SOPHIE WAS AT her parents' house in Kensington when they arrived back from their trip, happy and tired. She was full of anxiety about the visit, as she didn't want a repeat of past conversations of late. Most of which concerned the baby and Eric and basically pigeonholing her into a marriage she didn't want. Wasn't it enough she was taking over the family business? Shouldn't she have some choices left?

The sharpness of the thought took her by surprise, and she let out a breath before moving forward to give her mum a hug. She loved Waltham. She did. She was only feeling cornered just now, that was all. Like nothing in her life was within her control.

"Hello, darling. How are you feeling?"

Sophie smiled. "I have my moments, but everything's okay. How was your trip?"

Her father came in with the cases and stopped to give her a kiss, then kept on toward the bedroom. "It was just lovely," her mother said. "Prague is so gorgeous. We had a marvelous time."

"I'm so glad."

"And how about you?"

"Well, I want to talk to you and Dad about that. How about I put on some tea?"

"I'd love a good cup. I shall need to put in an order from the market. There's nothing in the house."

"Oh, but there is. I picked up a few essentials on my way. We can have tea and biscuits at least, and I grabbed an entrée for you to heat up for you and Dad tonight, as well."

"You're so thoughtful." The praise was punctuated by a loving squeeze on her wrist. "And how is Eric?"

Sophie rolled her eyes and took a full breath. "I wouldn't know, since we're still not together."

"Sophie."

She put the kettle on and got out the package of biscuits. "No, Mum. And to be honest, he's putting a lot of stress on me right now, so I'd rather not talk about him."

Her mother pursed her lips, but thankfully said nothing more about Eric.

"Do you know who I did run into, though? Christophe. He was at the engagement party. It was very nice to catch up after so long."

The mention of Christophe Germain was a deliberate plant in order to get her mum off her back. Christophe was gorgeous, rich, and part of the Pemberton family. He wasn't an aristocrat, but he was related, and heaven knew he checked all the right boxes where her family was concerned. More than that, the Walthams had always liked him. Easy to see why. He was incredibly likable.

"How is he? So sad about Cedric, but lovely that the family seems to be getting settled. This is the third engagement this year."

"The wedding isn't until spring, or so Bella said. I'm sure it'll be a grand affair."

"You're due in the spring," her mum said. Because of course, every topic of conversation should somehow make its way back to her pregnancy.

Sophie prepared the teapot and before long they took a

tray to the living room. Her dad had reappeared, changed into casual trousers and a fresh button-down, and she poured him a cup of tea. "Here you go, Dad. Fresh cup, one sugar, no milk."

"You're a blossom."

She laughed, then continued pouring. "Actually, I came to talk to you both about something. I know you're just back, but how would you feel about me going to Paris for a few days this coming week?"

Her dad hesitated with the cup halfway to his mouth. "Paris? What's in Paris?"

Christophe, she thought, but pushed the thought away. "I've been invited to have a look at Aurora Gems' new line for next year and offer some feedback." She figured it was far better to take the first approach from a business angle. "It puts me out of the office just as you're back, but everything is caught up on the schedule and the shop is managing just fine. I'll be back before we reset the store-front for the holidays."

Her mother reached for a biscuit. "I suppose Christophe invited you?"

"He did. He's running the division now. All the children have director positions, actually. I have expertise that he doesn't. We've been friends a long time, Mum. And truthfully… You know I love Waltham, but I'd like to get out in the industry a little more before the company becomes my responsibility. Knowledge can never hurt, and this is almost like acting as a consultant. It's an incredible opportunity."

"It's a grand idea," her dad said, taking a hearty sip, then smacking his lips as the tea was still piping hot. "I'm sure we can manage just fine for the week." He looked at her closely. "After all, we're going to have to manage when you have the baby, aren't we?"

Her mother was far less enthusiastic. "Shouldn't you be more worried about making plans for the future?"

Meaning, patching things up with Eric. Her mother was nothing if not consistent.

"I am planning for the future. The future of Waltham. Besides, it's not a grueling schedule while I'm there. Getting away from London and having a little time to think might give me the clarity I need."

Boom.

"It might not be a bad idea," her mother admitted. "When do you leave?"

"I'd fly over tomorrow with Christophe, Bella, and Viscount Downham." When it came to her mother, it never hurt to throw in a title.

"It's short notice. But I suppose it will be fine. What about Harry?"

"I have my service taking care of him for the week. I'll be back by Friday." They were getting into a busy season, with the holidays right around the corner, and it wasn't unheard-of for the Walthams to spend time behind the counter during a busy retail season. "I know it's a hectic time of year. I won't stay away long."

She took a sip of tea, telling herself the tiny bit of caffeine in a single cup wasn't going to do any harm and was worth it for family harmony.

"And you're feeling all right?"

"I'm fine, Mum. Truly. But I should get back so I can pack for tomorrow. If you need me, I'll have my mobile on."

"Oh, that's good. I'll be sure to check in—"

"No, you won't," interrupted her father, who aimed a stern look at his wife. "We agreed to give Sophie space. She can figure this out on her own."

Sophie's lips dropped open in surprise as she stared at her dad. She honestly hadn't expected the support as he'd also put in his two cents about reconciling with Eric. It seemed now, though, he was backing off, and it took a substantial weight off her shoulders.

"I truly can," she assured them. "I just need some time and space to do that. I appreciate you giving it to me."

Her mother didn't look pleased but said nothing more. As Sophie said her goodbyes and headed home to pack, she realized she was more than ready to leave London, and all its pressures, behind for a few days.

Christophe waited impatiently for Sophie to arrive. Bella and Burke were already here, and their departure was supposed to be in twenty minutes. He checked his phone again—no call, no text. He hoped she hadn't changed her mind.

A few moments later he looked up to see her rushing down the corridor. "I'm so sorry," she called, her heels clicking on the floor. "There was an accident and traffic got backed up. I planned to be here thirty minutes ago!"

She reached him, slightly out of breath, pulling her suitcase behind her. Her cheeks were pink from the jog and her normally tidy hair was coming out of its anchor, some sort of bun on the back of her head. But she was smiling, as if she were truly happy to see him.

"Better late than never," he said, leaning over to kiss her cheek. "I see you've come prepared." He sent a pointed look at her rather large suitcase.

"Clothes for casual, different clothes for visiting the offices, and one nice dress in case something formal crops up. I am indeed prepared for anything."

He got the sense she always was. Prepared, that is. Sophie always seemed to have herself together. It made her current predicament all the more unusual.

"The pilot is ready for us to board," Burke called over. "Hello, Sophie."

"Burke. It's good to see you again."

"I'm delighted you're joining us."

Bella waved and gave her a big smile. "Me, too! It's been too long."

They all boarded the jet and got settled, and before long they were in the air for the short flight to Paris. Christophe had made sure there was a ready stock of beverages on board so she could have her choice, including peppermint tea. She chose orange juice, though, while the rest of them drank strong coffee and nibbled on biscotti.

"So you're joining us for work and pleasure, I hear," Bella said, looking between Christophe and Sophie.

"It looks that way. I'm dying to get my hands on the Aurora jewels."

Burke burst out laughing and Sophie blushed, while Christophe grinned and reached for another chocolate-dipped biscotti.

"You guys and your dirty minds," Bella chided, but chuckled. "Sorry, Sophie."

Sophie was laughing too, her face half covered with a hand. "I walked right into it. Anyway, when Christophe asked if I'd like to see the new line, I couldn't resist. I haven't left London for months. It'll be good for me."

They chatted a while longer about the business, but the flight got a little bumpy and the pilot asked them to put their seat belts on. Christophe looked over at Sophie and realized she'd turned that gray color again. He leaned over and whispered, "Are you okay?"

"I think so," she replied. "I don't usually get air sick…"

He reached into a compartment and took out a bag. "Here, just in case."

"I don't want to…in front of…"

"I know. It's just for insurance. Hopefully we'll be through it soon."

He kept an eye on her for the next ten minutes, saw her close her eyes a few times and swallow convulsively. Sympathy welled inside him. He hadn't really talked to Charlotte about her pregnancy and didn't think she'd been particularly unwell. But this was different somehow. Charlotte had Jacob. Sophie had…well, Sophie was well-loved, but it wasn't the same as having a partner there to share it with.

The turbulence finally cleared, and then it seemed no time at all and they were preparing for their approach. When they landed, Christophe shouldered his single bag and then reached for Sophie's suitcase.

"I can manage that," she said.

"But why would you, if you don't have to?" He gave her a shrug, and she pursed her lips but didn't respond. He didn't mind pulling her case along and would have felt like a heel, walking along with his small carry-on and leaving her to tug her full bag. "I've got a car waiting to take us to the flat. We'll be there in no time." He gave her elbow a nudge. "Hopefully you won't get car sick."

He was teasing but she sent him a wry grin. "I put the bag in my purse just in case."

She was so practical. He kind of loved that about her. The drive to his flat on Avenue de Wagram was a half hour, give or take. Traffic was light since it was Sunday, and as they zipped along, Sophie told him about her conversation with her parents. "It's strange," she said, "but when I said I was taking a few days away I got the sense they were hesitant. As soon as I used the word 'consultant,' though, they brightened right up."

"Maybe they're just used to you being a bit of a workaholic," he suggested. "You've dedicated a lot of your time to your studies and then to the company. When do you ever spontaneously take time off with no reason?"

She seemed to ponder his words. "You think I'm a work-aholic?"

"I think you're driven. And organized. And because of it, taking time with no purpose seems strange to you, and therefore probably to them, too."

"That's very insightful."

"I live in a family of driven women. It's not such a stretch to recognize it." He lifted a shoulder. "Maybe breaking up with Eric was the first nonpractical thing you've done in a while. Having a baby complicates it, though." He frowned. "You're going to be tied to him forever."

"I know." She sighed deeply, and the sad sound reached in and touched his heart. He hated seeing her so distressed. He was sure he was right about the work thing, though. While he admired her work ethic, the all-work-and-no-play thing couldn't be sustained forever. Perhaps she was starting to realize that.

He recalled the comment she'd made about Eric working all the time. One thing he knew for sure: Sophie would put her all into motherhood the same way she put it into everything she did.

"Sorry. I didn't mean to bring you down. How do you feel about ordering something in? I will cook for you this week, though. I'm actually very good in the kitchen." He really wanted to treat her; let her relax and be cared for.

"I'm game for whatever," she answered. "Except sea-food. It's killing me, too. Normally I love it."

"Noted. And...we're here."

The car pulled up outside his building and he sent Sophie a smile. For the next five days, they were roommates.

Sophie tried to calm the nerves in her stomach as she exited the car and Christophe retrieved her bag. He was right about one thing. She didn't do spontaneous things. Her life was planned and orderly, though perhaps not quite as rigid as he'd made it sound. Still, agreeing to stay with him at his flat for the better part of a week and leaving work behind was definitely more adventurous than normal.

Four and a half days. With Christophe. In his flat.

She hadn't had a roommate for a few years now and it showed, she realized, as she followed him to the lift that would take them to the fifth floor. Without someone else to balance her out, she'd become a creature of habit, only accountable to herself and her cat, who also liked to be fed on time and was very vocal if his schedule wasn't adhered to. The elevator hummed as it ascended, and she tried to quell the butterflies that had taken up residence in her belly. This would be fine. Christophe was wonderful and he wasn't interested in her *that* way. And why would he be? Being pregnant with another man's child had to be a pretty big turnoff. This really couldn't be any safer.

And why was she thinking this way, as if she wanted him to be? Maybe she needed to get out of her own head a bit.

"Here we are," he said as the lift door opened.

The wheels on her suitcase echoed in the hall as she followed him down the corridor to his door. He opened the door and stepped inside, pulling her case in and making room for her to enter. "Welcome to your home away from home," he said warmly. "Consider whatever I have yours for the duration."

"This is lovely." Indeed it was. The small foyer led to an open concept room with large windows facing the street, letting in tons of natural light and giving the entire space an airy appearance. His furniture was simple yet comfortable looking, with oak floors and golden draperies dropping in columns at the side of each window. To the left was the kitchen area, with all sorts of natural wood and gleaming appliances, including a double wall oven. Above the breakfast bar was a rack that held at least a dozen wine-glasses. She glanced over to the working area and said, "Does that door open onto a terrace?"

"It is. I grow my own herbs out there."

"You…grow your own herbs?"

"I told you I liked to cook, and herbs are actually quite easy. In the colder months, I bring them in, see?" He gestured to a large, sculpted iron stand holding several plant pots.

She'd known Christophe for years but had not known this about him. She realized suddenly that she'd never visited him at any of his homes over the years other than the manor house, and she'd only been there a time or two. A person's home was key to their personality, and she realized this space reflected Christophe perfectly: warm, bright and without the need for affectation. She loved it.

"Come with me. I'll show you to the guest room."

He led her down the hall to where the bedrooms were. Presumably his room was on the left, and hers on the right. Her window was smaller, at the end of the room, but it still provided lots of natural light. Tawny beige curtains hung to the floor, and the bed was plush with an upholstered headboard and a duvet the color of the sand she remembered from the beach in Cornwall, where her parents had taken them in summers long ago. Simpler, easier days filled with the ocean and ice cream.

"This is perfect," she said, turning around to look at Christophe. "It's so relaxing and serene."

"I hope you'll be comfortable." He smiled at her and stood her suitcase just inside the door. "Over here is your bathroom."

He opened a door and she stepped into her own bath. Beige tiles and white fixtures kept up the light, airy feeling of the bedroom, and there were fluffy towels sitting on a table, waiting for her. A huge tub promised long, relaxing soaks, and there was also an oversize, glassed-in shower. The potential for relaxation was huge.

"I feel so pampered," she finally replied, facing him. "This is gorgeous. Your whole place is."

"Thanks. It's the first place that has been all mine, so I'm glad you like it."

"You chose everything?" She hadn't really considered him the decorating type, but maybe he truly did have a keen eye.

"Oh, no." He laughed. "I had help. I had a decorator help me pick the pieces. I had a strong hand in it, though. I knew what I wanted, and she knew how to make it happen."

Sophie loved every square inch of it so far. It was completely different from her flat in Chelsea and nearly twice the size, but it was absolutely perfect for Christophe and for the space.

"Why don't you get settled? Come out when you're ready, and we can decide on dinner. You're going to love the view from the terrace, too. Paris at night is too good to miss."

"Thank you, I will." She wanted to unpack and perhaps take off her heels.

He left her then, and she let out a breath. Christophe was going to be the perfect host, she could tell. Charming, polite, accommodating…perfect. So why did she feel uneasy? Was it simply because she was doing something a bit out of character, or was there something more to it? Like a six foot one with curly hair something?

CHAPTER FIVE

WHEN HER CLOTHES were hung in the closet and tucked away in the dresser, Sophie changed out of her dress and heels and put on leggings and an Irish wool sweater—perfect for relaxing in. She'd brought a book with her, too, as she didn't expect Christophe to entertain her every moment. But he did want to have dinner tonight, and as she'd unpacked the sun had slipped below the horizon, shadowing the city skyline. She supposed now was as good a time as any to venture out.

She opened the door and went to the living room, which glowed from the light of a pair of lamps. "Hello again," she said.

"Hi, yourself." Christophe was in the kitchen, pouring something into glasses. "Cocktail?"

"Um…" She couldn't imagine he would have forgotten she was alcohol-free, but it certainly looked like he was using a shaker.

He came around the corner with a pair of glasses. One had a slice of lemon, the other, orange. He handed her the one with the orange. "Don't worry," he said, treating her to that warm smile again. "Yours is a variation. I looked up how to make it without alcohol and I had all the ingredients, so…"

She looked into the drink. "What is it?"

"A French 75. Mine's the gin and champagne version. Yours is tonic and bitters and lemon juice. A little sugar." He was watching her hopefully. "Try it."

She tried a sip and found it to be tart and refreshing. "Oh, that's nice."

"And it won't put you on your ass."

She burst out laughing, nearly spilling the drink. "Fair enough. Thank you."

"I thought about dinner and there's a restaurant I like a few streets over that will deliver. If I promise no seafood, do you trust my selections?"

She blinked, unsure how to answer. This whole trip was out of her comfort zone, but she wasn't sure how much control she was willing to relinquish. It was only a menu selection, but it was still one more decision, however small, out of her hands. Still, perhaps she needed to learn to be more flexible and trusting.

"I promise that if you don't like it, I'll make you whatever you want."

She laughed. "How about if I pick dessert?"

"That sounds like a fair compromise to me. I trust you." He handed her his phone, with the dessert menu up already. She scanned the offerings—so much deliciousness—and chose the lemon tart, a particular favorite.

"Hmm. Lemon. I had you pegged as a crème caramel kind of girl."

"Anything lemon. I love it." She held up her drink. "Which is why this is particularly tasty. Thank you."

"You're welcome."

He placed the order and while he was on the phone, Sophie went to her room and took her sketch pad out of the dresser. If she wanted to set the tone for the visit as platonic and businesslike, it made sense to talk shop. No one had seen her drawings yet, but she trusted Christophe to be honest and fair. Besides, he was the head of Aurora's jewelry division. It made sense to get his input before casting a wider net. Hopefully they were good, and she wasn't about to embarrass herself.

"What have you got there?" he asked, crossing an ankle over his knee.

"The stuff I've been working on. You said you liked my pearl and diamond piece, but I've got a lot of ideas in here that I'd like to run by you. Not just if they're aesthetically pleasing, but if they're even marketable."

"Exciting. I love that you've been designing a little."

"Just a few pieces as samples and for myself. If these have any potential, I'd like to look at doing my own collection or something."

"Someone is spreading their wings," he mused, his tone approving. "Let's have a look."

Her heart stuttered as she handed over the sketchbook. It took a lot of trust to let him see what she'd been up to for the past few months. He opened it and gave each drawing a solid perusal before flipping to the next page. "I like this a lot," he said, lifting the book to show a sketch of a slim gold bracelet with a bumblebee held in place by two honeycomb-shaped pieces. "It's simple and youthful. What do you think for the gems? Onyx and yellow diamond?"

"I was thinking more a yellow tourmaline for a deeper color."

He nodded thoughtfully, turning the page.

"These next few pages are a different concept. I got looking at classic paintings and how to translate those into—"

"Smaller works of art," he finished for her. "I get it. This is gorgeous. Tourmaline again?"

"Citrine. With diamond, sapphire, aquamarine."

He kept looking, pursing his lips occasionally, nodding as well. She held her breath, waiting for his verdict.

"You've been busy," he said, closing the book and handing it back to her.

Her heart sank. That was it? "It hasn't felt like being busy at all. It's been more like a treat to myself." She was determined not to let him see her disappointment. "A chance to be creative. It's no big deal."

Christophe patted the cushion beside him. "Sit down. You're all tensed up. Did you think I wouldn't like them? I do. Very much. You should show them to François, our head designer."

She sank onto the sofa. "Wait. I thought you didn't like them."

He laughed. "Of course I like them. You're talented and inventive, with a great sense of color and balance." He turned a little sideways and looked into her eyes. "It's not like you to be insecure."

His insight was startling and accurate. "Maybe because it's different, and it's…creative. I'm not so sure of my abilities in this area."

He flipped open the pad to the page where she'd pasted a small pic of Monet's *The Artist's Garden* and pointed at the sketch below. "Your use of color here, and shape. It's perfect for an open neckline and yet not too deep."

"I envisioned it as a Princess style, as the stones and settings are substantial. It'd be heavy."

"Exactly. And amethyst is perfect here, with peridot and emerald above and chocolate diamonds below. So unusual and yet it absolutely works." He tapped at the picture. "I'm not a designer, but my instinct is the balance at the bottom might be off a bit. I love the concept, though." Then he flipped to the pink sapphire in the shape of the ballerina gown. "This is lovely, too. I can see it repeated in earrings with a marquise cut diamond above. What do you think?"

She could see it clearly. More than that, Christophe was showing genuine interest in something that meant a lot to her but that she'd kept to herself for fear of looking foolish. She doubted he'd understand how grateful she was, so she nodded and merely said, "Yes, I agree. I hadn't thought of the diamond above, but shaped right it absolutely mimics the dancer's body. I like it."

Then he turned back a few more pages to the Van Gogh. "This," he said, "is perfect as it is. The ring and the necklace."

"I'm partial to that one, too," she replied. "Thank you, Christophe. I was so afraid to show them to you, but I don't want my ideas to sit in a drawer, either."

He patted her hand. "I'm thrilled you trusted me with them."

"I trust you with a lot," she admitted, and their gazes clung for a few charged moments. She must trust him, for she was here, wasn't she? He was the only one outside her parents to know about the baby. Truthfully, she was putting a lot of faith in him, and it frightened her.

His phone rang with a call from the lobby, and he grinned at her. "Food's here. I hope you're hungry."

The interruption banished her thoughts, and within a few minutes they were seated at his dining table. Christophe had lit candles and got them each sparkling water to drink, then plated the food from the restaurant and served it to her with a flourish. "Madame," he said, putting the plate before her.

Her mouth watered just looking at it. A delicious pinwheel of rolled pork Florentine, plus a puffy and perfect cheese and herb souffle and *haricots verts amandine*. "Christophe, this looks amazing."

* * *

The food was superb, and so was the company. Over the course of the dinner they chatted and laughed, and Sophie got caught up on all the Pemberton family happenings of the past year. It was hard to believe how much had happened since she'd sat in the chapel at Chatsworth Manor for Stephen's wedding that wasn't. Despite the coverage in the tabloids, several details had been kept quiet. She realized, as they chatted, that as much as she trusted Christophe, he trusted her, too. Otherwise, he wouldn't be so open about his family and the intimate details.

She liked that. It made her feel as if they were equals, something that had often been missing in her past relationship.

After he removed the plates, he returned with the lemon tart. At the first bite, she closed her eyes and simply savored the tart smoothness of it, the buttery, flaky crust. "Oh, my God. This is perfection."

When she opened her eyes, he was smiling at her, his dark gaze warm and amused, but with an edge of something more. She quickly dotted her lips with her napkin and hoped she wasn't blushing.

Now she'd created atmosphere, all because she'd groaned over her dessert. She started another conversation, hoping to dispel the moment, but the way he'd looked at her sat in the pit of her stomach, a delicious, scary sort of something that she didn't want to feel when it came to Christophe. She needed a friend right now. She didn't need her crush getting in the way this week. Or him getting any ideas. One of them was bad enough.

She insisted on helping him clean up, so they went into his kitchen and she rinsed plates while he put them in the dishwasher. She was just handing him the flatware when her mobile rang.

She took it out of her pocket, looked at the display and ignored it, shoving it back into her pocket again.

"Eric?"

"Right on cue."

Christophe took the cutlery and put it in the rack. "He really doesn't know when to give up, does he?" Christophe's eyes took on that stormy look again, which she was learning was his "protective" look.

"No, he doesn't. I think he's sure he'll wear me down. If anything, it's just making me resent him more. I wish he could just accept that I won't marry him so we can move on and sort out what co-parenting is going to look like."

Her phone vibrated in her pocket, announcing she'd received a voice mail.

Christophe paused his tidying up and leaned back against a counter. "I can make myself scarce if you want to listen to that."

"No, it's fine. You might as well hear. Unless it makes you uncomfortable, in which case I'll go into my room."

"Not uncomfortable, exactly. I just don't like seeing you distressed. I want to help."

"Why?"

He tilted his head a little as he looked at her. "Because I've known you a long time, and we're friends, and I really don't like to see anyone bullied."

"I'm not sure I'd call it bullying. It's more desperation on his part, and a lack of understanding about what I really want."

"And what do you want?"

She met his gaze. "Love. I won't marry for anything less. My child will see a happy marriage with two people who love each other and are totally devoted to each other, or they won't see a marriage at all."

She took out the phone again and hit the buttons to play the voice mail.

"Sophie, it's Eric. You need to start taking my calls. This is ridiculous. I stopped by your work today and your father said you'd gone away for a few days? And you didn't think to tell me? Sophie, come on. It's time to stop being foolish. You know marrying me is for the best. I know you don't want our child being born a bastard. Call me, please."

The message ended and Sophie lifted her gaze to Christophe's. His mouth was hanging open and his eyebrows—both of them—were raised. And not in a teasing fashion.

"If you're looking for romance, you're not going to find it there," he said. "Wow."

"Our relationship was always comfortable. Not a great passion, if you know what I mean."

One eyebrow came down, the other stayed up, and she started to laugh. "Well, okay. I mean, passionate enough I got pregnant. But you know what I'm saying."

"I do."

"I don't like that he's pestering my father." She put the phone on the countertop and then twisted her fingers together. "I have to do something, but I don't know what. Nothing I say makes him give up. I've tried over and over to tell him that I want him to be a part of the baby's life, I just don't want to marry him, and it's like he doesn't hear me at all."

"Maybe he regrets losing you. Even so, I can't believe he said what he did about his kid being a bastard. Who does that?"

Her heart melted a little. Who, indeed? Christophe knew more than anyone how horrible that must feel as a child. "If you're going to tell me he's right, I'm going to stop you right there," she warned.

"I'm not going to tell you anything of the sort. But you can't marry him."

"I can't?" She looked up in surprise.

"No," he said firmly. "Because you're going to marry me."

CHAPTER SIX

"You've got to be joking," Sophie said, stepping away. "Didn't you hear what I just said? That I would only marry for love or not at all?"

Christophe nodded, his posture still relaxed and in control. She, on the other hand, wasn't sure if she wanted to run or cry, but every muscle in her body had tensed. She'd expected a lot of things from Christophe, but this wasn't one of them. Marry him? It was impossible. He was suggesting the exact same solution as Eric, just substituting himself as the groom. How did that solve anything?

"I did," he answered, "and I agree with you."

"Christophe," she said slowly, not wanting to be cruel in any way, "we are not in love." She would admit to herself that she was attracted to him, but that wasn't love. She was smart enough to discern one from the other.

A smile spread across his face. "Well, I know that, and you know that, but no one else knows that."

"I'm confused."

"I'm suggesting we get engaged for appearances. Think about it. It'll get your parents off your back, and Eric won't have any choice but to accept your refusal if you're engaged to someone else. With that out of the way, your conversations can focus on the baby and how you want to share custody. Meanwhile, I have a date for the Aurora,

Inc. holiday party." He winked at her, as if he had it all figured out.

"Wait. I need to sit down for a moment."

"Of course. Do you mind if I have a glass of something?"

"Not at all." She went into the living room, leaving him in the kitchen, and sank onto the plush sofa. He was proposing a fake engagement. It was the craziest, most outlandish idea, so why was she even hearing him out?

Engaged. To Christophe Germain.

For the flash of a moment, she had an image of what it might be like if they were actually together. There'd be laughter for sure, and lots of wonderful conversation. But passion? Would there be that?

Then she remembered how he'd looked at her at the restaurant last week, his dark eyes smoldering across the table, and her stomach tumbled. Yes, she decided, there would be passion between them.

This was ludicrous.

He came in with a glass of what looked to be cognac and put it on the coffee table as he sat down next to her. "You all right?"

"I'm still trying to wrap my head around what you just said," she admitted. "You want us to pretend to be engaged."

"Yes. For appearances only. Just to buy you some time to deal with everything you need to deal with."

Sophie bit down on her lip. "You realize this sounds like some archaic way of offering me your protection, right?"

He chuckled. "Are you saying I have a knight in shining armor complex?"

"If the shoe fits, Germain."

He was quiet for a moment, then his eyebrows dropped and his lips sobered. "Perhaps I do. It just disturbs me to see you upset every time he calls. Like I said, if you and I are engaged, he'll have to stop proposing."

She couldn't believe she was considering it. "We'd be lying to everyone."

"Yes, we would. So it's okay if you say no. I'm throwing it out there as an option to solve your current problem." He put his hands over hers. "Sophie, I hope you know you can trust me."

She did know that. "It's the only reason I haven't said no yet. I trust you to keep your word. I've never known you not to."

She was transported back several years to that night of too much wine and shared confidences. They'd been young and foolish, and she in particular had overindulged. She'd awakened the next morning snug in her bed, still in her clothes but tucked under the covers, a glass of water and a bottle of paracetamol on the nightstand. She didn't remember going to bed. After, her roommate had told her the story of how she'd draped herself over Christophe, clearly flirting, and when she'd passed out, he'd carried her into bed and taken care of her. He could have left her sprawled in the living room, but he didn't. He'd made sure she was safe and comfortable before sleeping in a cramped chair. He hadn't even slept on top of her covers. That night was the beginning of Sophie really developing feelings for him. He was the most gentlemanly man she knew.

Her phone buzzed again, still on the kitchen counter, but she heard the notification and tensed. If pretending to be with Christophe would get Eric off her back, then maybe she should just do it.

"What if it doesn't work?"

"Then we call it off, no harm, no foul."

"And how long would we pretend?"

"As long as you need. As I told you in London, I have

no desire to join my cousins in their pursuit of matrimony. You won't be cramping my style at all. In fact, you'd conveniently give me a plus-one to events. You'd be my cover and I'd be yours." He sounded completely happy with the idea.

"I see." But she didn't, not really. She still couldn't quite understand what was in it for him. It didn't make sense. She'd seen him with Lizzy. He'd looked contented and happy. Maybe their breakup had affected him more than he wanted to let on.

"Why don't you take your time to think about it this week? You can still get some relaxation in and come to the office. I meant what I said about the designs and about looking at our new spring additions. If you say no, you go back to London and that's that. If you think the ruse will help your situation, consider me your accomplice and we can announce our engagement on Friday."

"I'd like to take the time to think about it," she said, and the fact that she wasn't outright refusing took her by surprise.

"That sounds perfectly reasonable."

But there wasn't anything reasonable about it at all. So why was she seriously considering it? Was she that desperate?

Christophe wasn't quite sure what had prompted him to propose, even if it was just a fake engagement. Marriage wasn't a game and even if it were, he was determined not to play. His few memories of seeing his parents' relationship disintegrate was enough for him. Being left behind, with no support from his father, had made their lives a hardship. Maybe his aunt and uncle had had an idyllic union, but he knew many more who didn't. As much as he thought a child deserved two parents, he knew that without love, a marriage wouldn't survive.

He'd made his position on marital bliss crystal clear to Lizzie, or at least he'd thought he had. She'd seen it differently.

He sat on the sofa now, absently flipping through Sophie's sketchbook again. She'd gone to have a relaxing bath. He knew his proposal was a silly idea, and yet if it meant her ex would back off...

He hesitated on the Van Gogh drawings again. It was far and away his favorite of the designs, and he wanted to get François's opinion. This week was going to be an interesting one for him, both on the personal and professional front. Depending on how things went, he'd consider making Sophie an offer for the designs. After months of playing it safe, Bella was after him to expand and do something new with the division. He tapped the cover of the pad and pursed his lips. Sophie could be just the person to help him do that. She wanted her own collection. What if Aurora could give her the opportunity?

When she came out to the living room again, she was dressed in soft sleep pants and a T-shirt, her hair wet against her shoulders. "Better?" he asked.

"A little. My mind is still spinning, though." She sat beside him again and tucked her legs so she was sitting cross-legged on the cushion. "I have a few more concerns that popped up while I was soaking."

He tried not to think of her in the tub surrounded by scented bubbles and reminded himself that she was his friend. If she knew what direction his thoughts had just taken, she'd not only say no to the engagement, but she'd be on the first flight back to London. Still, the image remained...her long legs, sleek with water, the bubbles hovering just below her breasts as the steam curled into the air...

"…and I'm sure they won't appreciate being lied to. Are you listening?"

"Hmm? Sorry. Who won't appreciate it?"

"Your family."

"Don't worry about them. Stephen and Gabi were all set to have a fake marriage, remember? We're not even planning to go through with it. We'd just be pretending to be engaged."

"And then I thought of the tabloids. The Pembertons do find themselves in the gossip rags quite often at the moment. Any engagement will surely make it there, and it has the potential to get ugly, especially if they find out about my pregnancy. What if Eric talks to them?"

He thought for a moment, then remembered all the damage control they'd done after Stephen's failed wedding and how they'd mostly controlled the story by selectively feeding tidbits to the press. "They'll tell the story we give them," he answered. "And the one we show them. Eric won't say anything."

"How can you be sure?"

"Because he won't risk custody of the baby. It's in his best interest to stay quiet."

She nodded. "This is a lot."

"I know. Take your time, and no pressure. Like I said, take the week to think about it. In the meantime, I truly, truly want you to relax and enjoy yourself. How about a movie? There's got to be something streaming that's good."

So in the end, they spent the evening with tea and a flick, and when Sophie started to get tired, he got her a throw blanket and she drooped against his shoulder.

It was entirely too domestic. Too…settled. And yet it was perfect. And that was what scared him the most. Not fake engagements or the paparazzi or her persistent ex. But this warm bubble of contentment stirring inside.

He couldn't embrace it. Because the last thing he would ever do was let himself get hurt the way his mother had had her heart broken.

Sophie woke to bright sunlight streaming through her window. The flat was silent except for the rustle of her sheets as she rolled over and checked her phone charging beside the bed. It was almost nine! She sat straight up and pushed her hair off her face, and then a smile blossomed. When was the last time she'd actually slept in? She couldn't remember. Even on weekends, she tended to be up no later than seven. Frequent trips to the bathroom meant that she woke early and then didn't really get back to sleep. But today…she'd slept a remarkable ten hours.

Maybe this Paris trip really did have some merit.

She threw off the covers and got out of bed, and once she'd gone to the bathroom and then brushed her teeth, she headed for the kitchen. Christophe was nowhere to be found, obviously gone to work already. There was a note on the table scrawled in his handwriting.

Soph,
Have gone to work and should be back around six.
Help yourself to what's in the fridge—I know, I know,
I need to go to the market.
Have a great day.
PS I left a key for you on the table in the foyer.

The fridge revealed sparse contents for breakfast, probably because Christophe had been away for a week. She found some yogurt that was still good and some apples and oranges, which made for a healthy start to her day along with her vitamins. She made a tea and then ventured out onto the terrace for a moment. He was right; the view was spectacular, and she imagined how fragrant it would be in the summer with all of his herbs growing.

When she was done and had tidied her dishes, she texted him and let him know she'd pick up some things today and that she'd cook for them tonight.

Which meant peeking in his cupboards and making a shopping list.

Her purpose set, she brushed out her hair and braided it, then changed into another pair of leggings with a tunic-style blouse over top. Even though she wasn't showing yet, her waist was thickening, and her usual tailored clothes were uncomfortable. Pairing the outfit with boots and a soft scarf made the look a bit smarter, and she left her face bare save for the rich moisturizer she used. It was freeing to know that she was on her own today to do whatever she liked, with no responsibility to anyone. Perhaps before the market she'd go for a walk in the Jardin des Tuileries, only a short distance away. Whenever she visited the city, she rarely had time for leisurely strolls. In the southwest part of the garden was the Musée de l'Orangerie. Considering her recent interest in Monet, visiting the museum could be an additional sort of inspiration. She tucked her sketch-book and pencils into her handbag just in case, feeling absolutely decadent in her day's schedule.

The late morning air was cool but surprisingly mild for November, and the light jacket she wore over her tunic kept out the cold. She took a moment to get her bearings and then started her walk. The journey took her along the Rue du Faubourg St-Honoré, past the Canadian embassy, and then down the Avenue de Marigny, past the president's palace. The time of year meant fewer tourists about, and she took her time, soaking in the precious sunshine until she reached the Jardin des Champs-Elysées and the opportunity to leave the traffic behind.

The tree-lined paths offered a respite from the rush of cars, and burbling fountains partially masked the sounds of traffic rushing along the broad Champs-Elysées. Sophie let out a breath and felt the tension of the last three months melt away. Why had she waited so long to get away? Her troubles seemed smaller somehow, just by stepping back from them for a moment. She rolled her shoulders and slowed her steps; there was no one rushing her to get from one place to the next today.

The *jardin* bled into La Place de la Concorde and its stunning Luxor Obelisk. Intrigued, Sophie took a moment to retrieve her sketch pad from her bag and did some rudimentary sketches, then snapped a few photos on her phone. Not all of her inspiration had to come from paintings. The Egyptian monument was also a stunning work of art. She could do a lot with the shape of it, envisioning a gold and platinum pendant.

The Jardin des Tuileries was beautiful even in the off-season, and she spent a good hour walking through, the crowd a little thicker now the closer she got to the Louvre. She'd perhaps make another visit to the iconic museum another day; it had been a few years since she'd indulged in a trip. Instead, she made her way to the Musée de l'Orangerie and the paintings waiting for her there, and she spent two hours studying and sketching, letting her creative side out to play.

When her stomach growled, she left the museum and stopped for a quick ham and cheese baguette at a café in the gardens, and then started her walk back to Christophe's, looking for a good market along the way to purchase what she needed for dinner.

It wasn't until she was halfway to his flat that she realized she hadn't spent her morning agonizing over decisions that needed to be made or stressing over her situation. Nor had she felt ill, which hopefully meant her morning sickness was abating. She was so relieved to know there was still life outside of the bubble she'd unconsciously put herself in. And she had Christophe to thank for that. He'd been the one who'd seen she needed to get away, and he'd been so right.

Was he right in his proposition, too? Could she fake an engagement with him?

She thought of her mother's constant pressure. Sure, her dad had silenced her mum the other day, but it wouldn't last. Mum and Dad were old school; they, too, thought that marriage was the natural step. It amazed her that they couldn't see how she wanted a marriage like theirs—built on love. And Eric, too. She suspected what Christophe had said was true. If they got engaged, Eric wouldn't speak to the tabloids because he was concerned about their child's future. Something inside her softened. Even though he was driving her crazy, at least he was taking the responsibility of fatherhood seriously. If she said yes to Christophe's idea, maybe he was right: she and Eric could start a dialogue about how to navigate their relationship as parents and not partners. It was worth a shot.

Still, she had a few more days to decide, and she was going to take them. She'd needed today desperately; a few more days of no pressure and no decisions might actually deliver the clarity she was actually missing.

The market shopping took a quick thirty minutes and then she was back at the apartment, long before dinner needed to be started. Sophie picked up her book, curled up on the sofa with the throw she'd used last night, and within ten minutes had fallen asleep, the fresh air and day's exertions catching up with her.

CHAPTER SEVEN

THE NEXT MORNING, Christophe entered the kitchen to discover Sophie already there, cooking eggs and pouring coffee from his French press. "Good morning," she said brightly, and he blinked.

Never had he been in the position of having a woman in his kitchen making breakfast. Not even if she'd spent the night, which was rare. Having a woman in his space… there was nowhere to go.

He reminded himself that Sophie wasn't any woman, and their relationship wasn't like that, so he could just dismiss the panic that seemed to have settled in his chest and the sudden domestic image before him.

"You didn't need to do this," he said, stepping into the kitchen. "You're my guest, and you made dinner last night, too."

The Moroccan stew had been delicious, and he'd mopped up the juices with fresh bread from the *boulangerie*. They'd chatted about their respective days, and she'd told him she'd totally indulged and had a nap. The conversation had stayed light, and Eric hadn't called, though he had sent a text message. Christophe had to give the guy top marks for effort and persistence.

"I was awake at six, and not queasy. I'm taking advantage of it. Yesterday I slept until nine and then had a nap! I never do that. I feel wonderful."

She looked wonderful, too. Today she'd put on an off-white sweater dress with a wide brown belt at her waist and beige knee-high suede boots. Her hair curled around her shoulders, the thick waves inviting. If they weren't friends...

But they were. And he wouldn't play with her. Not ever. There were lines a man didn't cross. Any woman he dated knew the deal. He was not in anything for the long-term.

"So you're coming into work with me today?"

"If you're okay with that, I'd like to. I've never actually had a tour of Aurora HQ, you know. But only if you have time."

"I'll make time. Bring your sketch pad. I'll see if François has time to see you today, too."

Her eyes lit up. "Really? I'd love that. I added more ideas yesterday, though they're very rudimentary."

"This excites you. I like it."

"Know what else excites me? Scrambled eggs." She took the pan off the burner and spooned them onto two plates. "I don't know how you like your eggs, so I made them the way I eat them right now. Scrambled and fluffy, not creamy. I can't do soft eggs at the moment, especially yolks." She shuddered.

He laughed at the face she made. "As long as they're not raw, I'm fine," he replied. She'd also put a bowl of mixed berries on the table, and his coffee was strong and hot, just the way he liked. He wouldn't read anything more into this or let his own neuroses bring down the mood. She was his friend and she'd made breakfast. That was all.

After breakfast they took a taxi to the Aurora offices, a few blocks closer to the Seine than Sophie had walked yesterday. This area was home to the big names: Dior, Valentino, Vuitton, Saab. That Aurora could hold its own was a testament to his aunt's savvy and determination. It was also a lot of pressure. He was a boy from the outskirts of Orléans. What on earth was he doing managing a whole division of this company?

His aunt had sat him down a few years ago and had given him a stern talking-to. "Don't forget," she had said, her gaze steady. "We come from the same place. Never use it as an excuse. Use it as an asset."

Sophie carried a hobo bag the same color as her belt, and together they walked through the glass doors into the black-and-white lobby, a testament to the signature Aurora colors.

"*Bonjour*, Monsieur Germain," said the receptionist.

"*Bonjour*. I'm signing in a guest for today, Giselle. Could you give her a pass, please? All access."

"*Bien sûr,*" she replied. She retrieved a swipe card from a drawer and prepared it. "*Bonjour, madame. Voici votre carte-clé.*"

"*Merci,*" Sophie replied, and then to Christophe's surprise, proceeded to have a brief conversation with Giselle in flawless French.

"Well done," he said moments later as they walked to the elevators. "I didn't know you were so fluent."

"I'm a bit rusty. But I can manage."

"Come on. Let's give you a tour. I don't have any meetings until ten thirty."

For an hour, Sophie toured Aurora HQ, her head swiveling back and forth as she met tons of people, and she caught a glimpse into the well-oiled machine that was Aurora, Inc. By the time they reached the top floor and executive offices, her head was swimming. Everything about it screamed elegance and luxury, from the white-veined marble floors to the stylized black "Aurora" logo prevalent in each section. Glass and chrome kept the atmosphere modern and professional, and everyone offered a friendly *"bonjour"* or "good morning" to Christophe as he passed. Often she saw people smiling and laughing—this looked like a happy workplace.

He showed her his office, a moderate-sized room with a stunning view of the Seine. "This is gorgeous," she said, going to stand by the window. "How do you get any work done with that view?"

He grinned. "It's a good thing I have it. The work is pretty intense, and sometimes I need to look up and see the weather or just the outdoors, and remember this office isn't my whole world."

"Ah yes. The rich and privileged."

"I am, and I know it. But it doesn't mean I don't work hard. With jewelry and cosmetics, I feel like I'm having to spend a third of my time researching and getting up to speed."

"You just need to surround yourself with knowledge-able people you trust," she said, trailing her fingers over a glass-topped table. The office was incredibly neat, even neater than his flat. She looked up at him, a smile teasing the corners of her mouth. "Christophe Germain, I just realized that you're a neat freak."

He lifted his eyebrow. "You're not the only one with control issues, apparently."

She laughed. "I'm surprised. You're so chill most of the time."

He joined her by the window. "Yes, but I find it easier to concentrate and stay 'chill' if my environment is tidy." He hesitated for a moment, then added quietly, "The house where I lived before, it wasn't very neat. My mother worked long hours just to keep the rent paid. She was too tired to worry about our place that much. I suppose I associate mess with insecurity."

"And if everything is tidy and organized, then everything is all right."

"It probably sounds silly."

"I think that some experiences shape us, especially when we're young and process it differently than an adult. But thank you for sharing that with me."

"You trust me," he said, "I trust you."

This trusting each other thing was nothing new, but there was an added element now, since his unusual proposal, and she fought back the sense that she was getting in too deep. She was just about to reply when Bella poked her head in the door. "Meeting in the boardroom in ten," she said brightly. "And hello again, Sophie. Christophe, I didn't know it was bring your friend to work day."

He turned around and aimed a million-dollar smile at his cousin. "That's because you have no friends."

"Ouch!" She laughed and threw Sophie a wink. "I love teasing Christophe the most, you know. He knows how to give it back."

"I do have a better sense of humor than Stephen," he mused.

"Did I hear my name?"

Stephen Pemberton, Earl of Chatsworth, halted in the hallway and joined Bella at the door. "Oh, hello," he said when he saw Sophie.

Christophe stepped in. "Sophie, you remember my cousin, Stephen, don't you?"

Yes, the new earl. Her tongue tangled in her mouth as she scrambled to come up with the appropriate address. Should she actually call him my lord? It sounded so antiquated! But he was actually an earl...

Stephen stepped inside, a tall, formidable kind of man with dark hair and eyes, and a face that didn't have the easy humor of Christophe's. "Sophie, it's nice to see you again. Call me Stephen," he said, as if sensing her quandary.

She let out a relieved breath. "Lovely to see you, as well. Christophe was giving me the tour this morning."

"Are you in Paris for long?"

Christophe stepped in smoothly. "I invited Sophie to look at the new spring selections. I was just going to take her to meet François before joining you in the boardroom."

Stephen snapped his fingers and smiled. "That's right. Sorry, it slipped my mind. You're the gemologist."

"I am. Waltham is thrilled to be one of your distributors."

"Sophie's got a fabulous eye. She's going to be here for the week, offering some thoughts and taking a little time for relaxation."

Speculative looks were exchanged between Bella and Stephen, then Stephen looked at his watch. "Better get going. I'll see you in there, Christophe. Sophie," he added, giving a nod and disappearing.

"Me, too," Bella said. "Will's probably already there. The department heads are joining us at eleven, so we need to get a move on."

Christophe took his cue, and when Bella left, he turned and squeezed Sophie's hand. "I'm sorry. I let time get away with me. I'll run you to François's office, and then I'll have to dash. You'll be all right?"

"I'm sure he'll take excellent care of me. And if he's occupied, I have my sketchbook. Never fear."

"We should be done by one. I'll text you and we'll grab some lunch?"

"That sounds lovely."

He led her out of the office and down one floor. The

area was quiet, and he swiped his card for access into the department. All of Aurora's gems weren't on-site, but there was enough inventory that security measures were tight. The appearance here was far more utilitarian and less showy, scrupulously clean and neat. François's office was in the middle, and it was like a dream. Gone was the sterile environment outside the door and inside was a mishmash of equipment. A laptop with a much larger monitor, a workbench with an array of equipment, a drafting table, and books. Lots and lots of books. On the wall were photos of some of Aurora's finest pieces, including a stunning sapphire teardrop necklace surrounded by diamonds that Sophie remembered from maybe three years ago. It had been a one-of-a-kind bespoke piece for a member of the royal family.

Behind the desk sat a small man, squinting at something on the desk and then up at the monitor, as if his eyes couldn't adjust fast enough.

"François, this is Sophie, the gemologist I told you about."

François jumped, then pressed a hand to his chest. "*Mon Dieu*, Christophe, you scared me to death."

"Sorry. I'm late for a board meeting. I wish I could stay for a longer introduction."

"Do not worry." He smiled up at Sophie. "We are big kids, eh? We can handle it."

She was already charmed. When he stood, she realized he was a good two inches shorter than she was, and his head was three-quarters bald. He reminded her of a little chipmunk, with a wrinkled shirt and yet a precisely knotted tie.

"I'll text when I'm done," he said to Sophie. "Okay?"

"Big kids. I'm good. Go to your meeting."

He flashed her a smile and then disappeared.

François clapped his hands. "Perfect. Christophe says you're to have a look at the spring catalog. Let me get you a copy of what we're planning to send out."

"That would be lovely. And your office… I love it."

"The chaos drives Christophe mad, but it's my space, not his." François looked up at her with a sparkle in his eye. "I had my reservations when *madame* put him in charge of the division, but he's a good kid. He knows he knows nothing, and is not afraid to learn or ask questions."

He rummaged around in the mess and then took out a mock-up of the catalog. "Ah, here you go." He looked at her keenly. "You're a gemologist at Waltham. You, you know something. Your reputation precedes you."

She got the feeling it was high praise. "Thank you so much. Where would you like me to go? I don't want to be in your way or distract you from your work."

"Not at all." He gestured toward the drafting table. "It's not the most comfortable spot, but you're welcome to it."

"Are you joking? I spend most of my day on a twenty-year-old stool hunched over a microscope. This is lovely."

He laughed then. They both knew the ins and outs of the job and embraced them. As his eyes twinkled at her again, she got the feeling she'd just met a kindred spirit.

While she knew François didn't construct the pieces here in this space, she also knew that he was the final word in each design and oversaw the process. Every stone had to meet his standards, and each setting must be perfect. Design was nothing without craftmanship. She settled on the chair and opened the catalog.

She spent a long time poring over each page, from the ever-popular engagement rings to pendants, earrings, bracelets. There was a high jewelry section with gorgeous diamond collars, but there was something missing.

It was all completely on brand. Timeless, elegant, flawless. But also lacking an energy and inventiveness. How could she say so to the man who was the chief designer?

"You look displeased, *mademoiselle*."

"Oh? No, not at all. It's just…"

François had slipped on a pair of reading glasses. He now took them off and put them on his desk. "*Oui?* Do not be afraid of me. I can take the bad news." He put his hand over his heart, as if she were wounding him, and she smiled. She liked him very much.

"Each design is stunning. Classic, elegant. Everything Aurora stands for."

He tilted his head a little. "But?"

She sighed. "But it's…" She tried to search for the gentlest word. "Oh, François, never mind."

He got up from his desk, grabbed a stool, placed it beside her, and sat. "Christophe brought you here for your feedback. He wouldn't do that unless he trusted you. So tell me. Be honest."

"All right. I'm sorry, François, but it's…boring. I can't see anything that really sets it apart from the previous year."

Her cheeks heated and she waited for him to express his disapproval. Instead, a broad smile overtook his face.

"*Merci!* Thank you! That was what I've been trying to say for months!"

Sophie was startled and turned to look at him. He seemed almost joyful. "You have?"

"*Oui*. The last eighteen months have been very hard. First with the earl passing, and then all the executive changes, and then Aurora's semi-retirement. *Mon Dieu*, it has been enough to drive me…" He made a swirly motion around his ear and she laughed. "I tried to do something different with these designs last summer, but Christophe just kept saying to 'keep it on brand, keep the ship steady.' He was afraid and with everyone else adjusting…" He suddenly stopped talking and his cheeks colored. "Oh. I have said too much. I admire Christophe very much, but he's new and lacks confidence. That is all."

"He should have trusted you, though. You're a wonderful designer. We carry the Aurora Gems line. I know." She pointed at the photo of the sapphire necklace. "That is a gorgeous, gorgeous piece."

"Thank you."

She sighed. "There's nothing wrong with these pieces, but they're not going to cause a stir or be accused of being innovative. You've used the tried-and-true gems—ruby, sapphire, emerald, with a few yellow diamonds thrown in. But there are so many other colors and combinations. Citrine. Tanzanite. Pink sapphire." Her brain was racing again. "Asymmetrical settings, too. Something really unique. I'd love to see your other designs sometime."

"I'd like that very much." He patted her hand. "Christophe mentioned yesterday that you've started designing, as well. You're serious about it?"

She nodded. "I think I am. It feeds a part of me that assessing and selling just doesn't. We got on the subject because I wore one of my designs to Bella's engagement party."

"Do you have a picture of it?"

She nodded. "Of course." She grabbed her phone and logged into the cloud, retrieving the picture of the necklace on a black velvet stand. François took the phone from her hand and examined the photo, then used his fingers to enlarge it. "The clasp is lovely. A bee?"

"I've been fascinated with nature."

"It adds a bit of whimsy to a very classic pearl choker."

"That was my intent."

He gave her back the phone. "I'd like to see your designs, Sophie. Perhaps tomorrow you can come back, and we can meet in the afternoon?"

"You'd really like to see them?"

"Of course. When someone accuses me of being boring, I'm curious as to what they find exciting." He winked at her. "I have high expectations, you know."

Nerves centered low in her belly, but they were the best kind. "I'd like that very much. I'll warn you though, some sketches I've just done in the last week so they're rudimentary."

"I can see past that, as you can imagine."

Her phone buzzed and she looked down. "Oh. The meeting is over."

"Just on time, then. I shall go mend my wounded pride and you shall go to lunch. And tomorrow we will meet and be creative, *oui*?"

"Oui," she answered. "Thank you, François."

"No, thank you," he responded. "I think you're just what was needed around here."

CHAPTER EIGHT

CHRISTOPHE TOOK A few moments to clear his head before collecting Sophie from François's department. The meeting had taken a toll. Department managers had attended as well, and it was clear that Aurora's retirement, Charlotte's maternity leave, and the general inexperience of the rest of the Pemberton siblings in their new roles was taking a toll. Will was back and in charge of fashion, and he had a good staff, but with Charlotte out they'd had to hire an outside PR consultant and assistant, and they were still getting up to speed. Stephen was head of acquisitions and now operating as COO, while Bella had left cosmetics behind to move into the vacated CEO position. She left some of those duties to Christophe in addition to his workload, and delegated others to their former head of fragrance, Phillipe Leroux. But Phillipe's background was in chemistry, not business, and he was going through his own learning curve making the leap to management. It was enough to give Christophe a headache.

But when he stopped by the elevators and found Sophie waiting for him, the stress melted away. "You're beaming," he said, unable to hold back a smile.

"I had a lovely morning with François. He is incredibly charming and wonderful."

"How charming? Should I be worried?"

She laughed. "Maybe. He has opinions. You should listen to them. But not today. François and I are going to look at my designs tomorrow, and then I'll fill you in."

"You two are in...what's the term? Cahoots?"

She laughed. "Yes, we are."

"And your thoughts on the spring line?"

"Tomorrow," she said, dimples popping in her cheeks. "Right now, I'm starving. Let's lunch. When we come back, I can find a corner where I can sketch until you finish. Unless you'd rather I went back to the flat."

"You are more than welcome to find any nook or cranny that captures your fancy." He took her hand and pressed the button for the elevator.

He took her to a restaurant with cozy alcoves, where they wouldn't be rushed, and the noise would be minimal. He knew the menu here and what normally would have been a typical hour for a meal ended up spread out over nearly two. Still, he didn't feel the need to hurry to get back. It was too lovely watching Sophie chatter, talking with her hands. He'd never seen her this animated.

"You," he said, gesturing with one of his *frites*, "are lighting up the room. You're very excited."

"I truly am." They'd started the meal with onion soup and now she was picking at her entrée of duck breast, which smelled heavenly and had him regretting his choice of roast chicken. "This was something I was tinkering with, but suddenly it matters so much." Her smile faded. "Which I don't think is going to be good news for my mum and dad."

"You're still poised to take over Waltham."

"I am."

He shrugged. "Sophie, you can own a business and still hire someone to manage it."

"I know that's not what they have in mind."

He held back the response that had immediately come to the tip of his tongue. What did it matter what they envisioned after they were gone, and it was Sophie's? She couldn't tailor her life to their expectations forever. But he expected that if he said so it would seem like piling on, so instead he thought about her brother. "What about Mark?" Her brother was younger and just finishing his MBA from Brookes at Oxford. "What are his plans after he graduates?"

"Not Waltham, I don't think."

"Hmm. Well…" Christophe thought for a moment about the merits and burdens of carrying on a family business. Was there something he'd rather be doing right now? He didn't think so. He'd done his studies in business as well and had worked various jobs within Aurora over the years, as they all had. It had always been assumed that they would all take their place one day, even Christophe. He loved the business. The past year had been tough, but the only thing he'd change would be having Cedric back with them once again.

"Anyway, how was your meeting? You were looking a little stressy when I met you." She changed the topic smoothly.

"Intense. We covered a lot of ground. Many of us are new to our roles, so we've really got to rely on each other as a team. That includes the family, of course, but also the management we've put in place." He went on to talk about Phillipe and how much he liked him. "I think we're going to get along just fine."

It was long past time they went back to the office. The afternoon had taken on a raw chill and he held Sophie's wrap for her, his fingers brushing her shoulders as he tucked it around her. She stilled beneath his casual touch, and his stomach tumbled. Was she as aware of him as he was of her? The soft scent of her perfume wrapped around him, disturbed by the movement of her clothing and hair. Awareness was one thing. Acting on it was another. Besides, if she took him up on his offer, he'd have to get used to being this close to her. Casual touches would be more frequent, at least in public. They'd have to appear as a couple.

He was probably crazy to even suggest such a plan, in hindsight, but when he thought of how upset Sophie got when dealing with Eric, and how innocent her baby was, he knew it was the right thing. He'd support her no matter what. This little awareness that kept cropping up was just an annoyance. Nothing to really worry about.

"Ready?" Sophie asked, peering up at him. "You look like you're a thousand miles away."

"Just thinking." He smiled down at her. "Sorry."

"It's all right. Occupational hazard." She led the way back outside. The overcast sky pressed down on them, making the November afternoon seem bleak and drab. "Oh, it's so gloomy today. The sun's completely disappeared."

"Christmas lights will be out soon, though," Christophe said, and he cheered a bit. He really did enjoy the festive season. "Have you been in Paris at the holidays? There are lights everywhere. The entire length of the Champs-Elysées is lit, and of course the storefronts, and all sorts of other areas. It's magical. Chases any gloom away, guaranteed."

"I haven't been at Christmas. But can it rival London?"

"If you're here this year you can compare."

She got strangely quiet, and he expected she was thinking the same thing he was. Would she be? Here? If she said yes to his fake proposal, perhaps. And then he could show her the Aurora storefront dressed for the holidays, as well as the other luxury shops along the Avenue Montaigne. He imagined holding hands with her as they strolled along… it didn't bother him as much as it should.

Which meant he'd have to remind himself to keep her at arm's length. It would be far too easy to get caught up in things and forget this was a temporary solution to help a friend.

"You feeling all right?" he asked, when she continued to be quiet.

"Oh…oh, yes." She shook her head slightly and offered a small smile. "Sorry. Got into my own head there for a moment." The heels of her boots echoed on the sidewalk as they headed back to the office. "I'm feeling quite well, actually. I think you were right. I did need this week away. I mean, I'm still tired most of the time, but I haven't been sick since Sunday morning."

He wasn't sure she realized that her hand had drifted down to cover her tummy.

"I guess my book was right. Once you start moving into the second trimester, the sickness often eases."

"Your book?"

She nodded. "Of course. Did you think women are born with some internal knowledge bank that we can just search when we're pregnant?"

He laughed. "Okay, fair enough."

"I mean, certainly I knew how it happened, and what happens at the end, but all the in between stuff…there's a lot."

"That's what Charlotte said, too. Maybe you two could chat. I'm sure she'd help."

Sophie's face softened. "Actually, I might like that. I don't know anyone with small children just now. My life's revolved around my job and other social occasions that are more scheduled than, I don't know, spending time with friends. Present company excepted…"

"And I'm hardly a good source of information on having babies," he added, chuckling. They reached the Aurora doors and he stopped, taking her hands. "But I am your friend. I hope you always remember that."

A puzzled look blanked her face. "Why wouldn't I?"

Christophe held the door open and they entered the building. He got the sneaky suspicion that he was the one who needed reminding, not her.

Sophie had chosen a little alcove next to the on-site café with a large window and a comfortable chair, but after an hour of sketching she'd nodded off. When she woke, she found the afternoon had disappeared, the sky was dark gray, and her pencil had dropped onto the floor.

She reached down to retrieve it and let out a sigh. She supposed her nap was the result of a morning of excitement and then a full stomach after their delicious lunch. But she had wanted to work on her designs a lot more before tomorrow. Tonight she would, after she and Christophe went home.

She stopped herself. Not home. His flat. She had to remember that and not get too used to having him around. It had been so easy, being with him the last few days. Comfortable in a way she'd never experienced before. She'd almost say brotherly, but that would be a lie. There were times when he looked at her that she would swear there was fantastic chemistry simmering beneath the surface. And today, when he'd helped her with her wrap, the light touch of his fingers had sent a frisson of longing down her body. She'd wanted him to touch her. Thankfully they'd kept clear heads and had gone back to chatting as they returned to the Aurora building.

But before she'd fallen asleep, she'd imagined what it might be like if he kissed her. Her *tendre* for him wasn't going away. If anything, being with him more, getting to know him even better, put her more in danger of liking him far too much. If the objective of a fake engagement was to get Eric to see reason, then she had to be aware that the result also had to be that she was able to walk away unhurt. The only way to ensure that was to pretend that this crush didn't exist.

She packed up her things and made her way to his office, prepared to wait for him to finish for the day. Instead of Christophe at his desk, however, she popped in the door and discovered Aurora herself.

"Oh!" she exclaimed, before she could think better of it.

Aurora looked up, reading glasses perched on her nose.

"Aurora! I mean, Lady Pemberton." Her cheeks flared as she wanted to swallow her tongue. "Oh, bother."

Aurora slid off her glasses and offered a small, elegant smile. "Aurora is fine, Ms. Waltham."

Aurora knew who she was. While she was still absorbing that fact, Aurora stood and held out a hand. "I don't know if we've ever been properly introduced."

Sophie reminded herself to be calm and graceful. She stepped forward and took the hand offered. "It's lovely to finally meet. Officially." She smiled at the older woman and hoped she didn't sound as awkward as she felt.

"You're looking for Christophe. He's just down the hall and let me use his desk for an hour or so. I can show you where he is, if you like."

"I don't mind waiting. I don't want to interrupt his meeting." Her cheeks remained stubbornly hot. "I'm visiting this week, you see, and we were going to go back to his flat together."

Aurora's sharp eyes assessed her coolly. "Yes, I've

heard." She stepped back and leaned her hips against the desk, crossing one ankle over the other in a relaxed yet commanding pose. There was no question who owned the room.

Sophie found Aurora incredibly intimidating. Not because she was domineering in any way. Simply because she was so successful and so...composed. Always. A woman in complete control. It made her incredibly resilient and a formidable negotiator. "I didn't realize you were in Paris," she said, clutching the strap of her bag.

"I wasn't, until this afternoon. Bella rang me after the meeting and asked if I'd mind spending a few days helping her with some transitional things. Since my schedule these days is flexible, I was happy to help." She smiled then, a truly warm smile. "Besides, I missed Paris."

"It's beautiful, isn't it? I haven't been in so long, and yesterday I spent the whole day walking and taking in art and visiting a market...ordinary things, but then, nothing is ordinary in Paris, is it?"

Aurora shook her head. "No, it's not. Come, let's sit and wait for Christophe. Would you like a glass of wine? Tea, perhaps?"

"Tea would be lovely," she admitted. When she was at work at home, she almost always had a cup on the go. She missed it. Even if she was now drinking herbals more often than not.

They sat in the more comfortable chairs in the corner, and Sophie put down her bag and told herself to relax. Aurora was a big presence, but she didn't have to be frightening. "Congratulations on your first grandchild, by the way. Christophe showed me pictures. She's gorgeous."

"She is, isn't she? You know, for all the success of the company, I do miss the days when my babies were small."

It was hard to imagine Aurora as the mother of small

children. Her bob-length blond hair—colored, of course— was always perfectly coiffed, her clothing impeccable.

The tea arrived and Aurora thanked the assistant and then took on the job of pouring. "The most fun was Cedric playing tag with them in the garden. They would run and run and run and then when he got caught, he'd freeze in the most ridiculous postures." She smiled in remembrance. "There were always dirty faces and hands in those days, but I wouldn't trade them for anything."

"It must have been hard trying to balance motherhood with building the company."

"Oh, it was. Cedric was such a support, both with the children and financially, too. My name might be the company, but it is every bit as much his as mine."

"I'm so sorry," Sophie whispered.

"Thank you, dear." Aurora picked up her tea. "We had a wonderful life. I couldn't ask for anything more." She laughed. "Well, except more grandchildren. With Will married and Bella on her way to the altar, perhaps I won't have to wait too long."

Sophie hid behind her teacup. If she and Christophe went through with their ruse, they'd be deceiving Aurora as well as everyone else. They would have to be very convincing, because Aurora was sharp.

"Christophe tells me you've been doing some designing." Aurora changed the subject. "I'd love to see your ideas."

Sophie paused. It was a great compliment and opportunity, but she wasn't as comfortable showing Aurora as she was Christophe, who was a friend, or even François, who she knew understood her sketches were concept only and not a formal design. She put her cup back on the saucer and tried a nervous smile. "I'm very flattered, of course, but I'm not sure my concepts are ready for your eyes, Lady…

er… Aurora. They're only sketches at the moment, and really need refining. In fact, I'm meeting with François tomorrow. They may not even be any good. But I know he'll tell me the truth."

"You don't think I will?"

Oh, heavens. "Of course, ma'am… I'd just rather go through the proper channels. If there's anything in my concepts that is worthy of exploring, I look forward to a much better presentation to Christophe, and Bella, and you, of course…"

"Because I'm no longer the CEO."

"That hardly matters. You're Aurora, ma'am."

"If I insisted?"

Sophie rather thought she was being tested, and while she wasn't overly confident about her designs, she was no fool. "I'm afraid I'd have to decline at this time. Not until they are ready."

Aurora smiled then, and her eyes warmed. "I like you, Sophie Waltham."

"Thank goodness, ma'am."

They shared a laugh while Aurora reminded her, "No ma'am-ing me. You call me Aurora as everyone else does."

By the time Christophe returned to his office, Aurora had moved her chair closer to Sophie and was showing her pictures of baby Imogene. While delighted at the way the meeting had turned out, Sophie couldn't help but wonder what Aurora would say if she knew Sophie was pregnant. And she was sure Aurora's opinion would change if they announced their engagement and then news of the baby. A tension headache started across her forehead and she smiled faintly as Christophe strode back into his office, his curls mussed from presumably running his fingers through it. He looked tired, she realized.

"Maman," he said, and Sophie realized that despite

being Aurora's nephew, he'd just addressed her as his mother. It was a telling detail about their relationship. "Are you showing off the baby pictures again?"

"Naturally." She stood and took a few steps and kissed Christophe's cheek. "Thank you for the use of your office. Everything all right?"

"Yes, I think so." He smiled. "You've met Sophie."

"Indeed. She refused to show me her drawings."

Christophe turned startled eyes to Sophie, and Aurora laughed, a rusty chuckle that Sophie was starting to enjoy. "That is her prerogative. She is a smart woman, Christophe."

"Don't I know it."

Aurora looked from Christophe to Sophie and back again, putting two and two together. Neither of them spoke to disabuse her of the thoughts running through her head.

"Well, I'm spending the night at Bella's, so I'd better get on. And you look tired, darling. You should go home. Tomorrow is another day."

"I am. We are," he amended. "Heading home. Will we see you tomorrow?"

"I'm going to stay until the end of the week. Charlotte begged me to give her some peace and as I was telling Ms. Waltham, I've missed Paris."

"Then we should have dinner before you return. Perhaps all of us together?"

Sophie could see where this was going, and it felt as if she were on a runaway train. A family dinner, where they could possibly make an announcement? She wasn't sure she could go through with this, even with pressure from Eric. It was a foolish idea. No one would believe them anyway.

"I have a better idea," Aurora said. "Let's all head to the château on Friday afternoon. We can have dinner there, and a little family time. I'll run it past the others." She looked at Sophie. "You're invited of course, Sophie. If it fits your schedule?"

Christophe sent her such a pleading look over his aunt's shoulder that she smiled and nodded. "I just need to make a call to my pet service," she said. "And extend my stay by a day or so. Thank you so much for including me."

And thank goodness she'd packed the cocktail dress in case of a more formal occasion. A family dinner at the famed château in Provence?

As her mother would say, out of the frying pan and into the fire. She just hoped she could take the heat.

CHAPTER NINE

By the time Thursday arrived, Christophe still hadn't spoken to Sophie again about the engagement. Tuesday night she'd disappeared to bed early with a headache, and he'd been tired, as well. Then she'd spent all afternoon Wednesday with François, the two of them with their heads together, and he found he was jealous. Not of the two of them, but knowing they were, as he'd put it the other day, in "cahoots." Nor had she heard from Eric in that time. Perhaps the engagement wasn't going to be necessary after all.

He shouldn't feel disappointed, not even a little bit. If he wanted to spend time with Sophie, to be closer friends, all he had to do was keep in touch and make an effort.

And yet when he returned home on Thursday, and saw her standing out on his terrace, he couldn't imagine her not being here in his flat. She added something to his life that he hadn't realized was missing. When this was over, he was going to miss her.

"Soph? I'm home." The kitchen light was off and he could see her form silhouetted in the darkness, looking out over Paris at night. She had the throw from the sofa wrapped around her and looked small and vulnerable. Without thinking about it, he stepped out onto the concrete terrace and put his arms around her, tucking her close in a back-to-chest hug. She looked as if she needed it.

But when he heard her sniff, he let go and turned her around by the shoulders. "What is it? What's wrong?" A look at her tearstained face sent alarm skittering through his veins. "Is it the baby?"

She shook her head quickly. "No, the baby is fine and so am I. It's just…" She sighed, turned away and put her elbows on the terrace railing. "How do you get through to someone who sincerely just keeps hoping they'll get a different answer?"

Ah. The fear slid out of his veins and understanding took hold. So the two days of respite from her baby's father had ended. "He called?"

She nodded. "And I answered. I thought maybe the last time I'd got through to him. Instead he…" She sniffled again. "I know he's frustrated and he won't let go, and that's not okay. But he also has good intentions, even if he's not handling it in the best way. He told me that he's been looking at country properties, where a child could have room to run and play, outside the city. That he's researched schools and health care and he just wants us to be a family. That all that's missing is me saying yes. Christophe, I feel like I'm destroying his dreams. Am I just being selfish?"

"Do you love him?"

She turned back and met his gaze. He watched her steadily, waiting for an honest answer. Somehow her answer was very, very important. Like something was hanging in the balance and would slip to one side if she answered no, and to another if she answered yes.

"Not anymore," she answered truthfully. "But I think he loves me. And that makes me feel horrible."

"You're not responsible for someone else's feelings," Christophe said, lifting his hand to wipe away one of her tears. He hated seeing her cry. Was pretty sure she wasn't the crying type. But tonight she seemed…forlorn. Worn out. As if all the ebullience and effervescence of the last few days had disappeared, like a glass of flat champagne.

"I know that, in my head. It's just hard. It's easier when I think he only cares about the baby, but I'm not sure that's true. I was the one who broke up with him, you see. I was the one whose feelings changed. They are what they are, but I still feel awful if I've truly hurt him."

"I don't know what to say."

"There's nothing to say. I'm torn between being gentle with him and ripping off the bandage. I don't want to give him false hope."

"The man has been, for lack of a better word, harassing you and not taking no for an answer." He felt duty bound to remind her of that fact. "A broken heart doesn't excuse his methods."

She sighed. "I know." Then she sniffled again. "Could you just hug me again? That felt awfully nice."

What could he say to that? He opened his arms and welcomed her—blanket and all—into his embrace. She sighed and rested her head on his shoulder. "Thank you. For all that you've done this past week. For putting up with my back and forth."

"You've met my cousins, right? Drama comes with the family. This is nothing."

She chuckled against him, her breasts lifting and falling against his chest. She felt good. Too good. If it were anyone else, he'd tip up her face and kiss her. But this was Sophie. It was a line they dare not cross. Especially because he found himself wanting to so very badly. She needed him to be strong and steady. Not muddy the waters with his own desires.

"Better?" he asked, rubbing his hand over her back.

"Much." She pulled back and looked up at him. "And I think I have my answer. If you're still up for it, I'll say yes. Perhaps the kindest thing to do right now is to let Eric think I've actually moved on, so he can, too. No more false hope. Rip off the bandage."

His throat closed over as his gut tightened. He couldn't rescind his offer now, and besides, he didn't really want to. It was a short-term, temporary thing that would help out a friend. More than that, there was her baby to think of and the ultimate goal: a safe, secure home filled with love. It was all he'd ever wanted for himself as a child. He knew what it was like to be a kid and feel like a burden. To have his mother look at him and see failure. If he could help Sophie provide that for her baby in some way, it would be worth everything.

"Let's hold off and tell the family tomorrow night, at the château."

She pushed away, taking a few steps back. "That will make it a big family thing, though. I'm...wow. I'm not sure."

"But it also means only having to tell people once, because we'll all be together."

"There is that."

"And it'll give me time to get you a ring tomorrow."

She bit down on her lip. "I didn't think about that. It's not necessary, really..."

"It will be expected. It's no big deal, Soph." But it was. He knew it and he knew she felt the same.

"Are you sure this is the right thing?"

"No." He could tell his response surprised her. "I've thought about it all week, to be honest. But I keep coming back to how he just won't let you go." Her eyes held his in the darkness of the terrace. "I wouldn't either, if you were mine."

"Christophe..."

Was that longing in her voice? Doubtful.

"The thing is, this is the soft tactic. The other option is getting lawyers involved, and I don't think you want to do that."

She shook her head. "I really don't. I don't want this to be combative in any way."

"This gives you time to have him come around." He put his hand on her shoulder. "You're not alone in this. As antiquated as it sounds, having the Germain-Pemberton name behind you gives you some protection and influence."

She smiled faintly. "Ah, yes. Using your powers for good."

"Something like that." He smiled back. "There is a third alternative, I suppose."

"Which is?"

"I go back to London and meet with him to make him see sense."

Her eyes widened. "You wouldn't."

"Only because you'd hate it."

"All that would be missing would be pistols at dawn. No, that's not what I want."

He laughed at her quip and she visibly relaxed. He pulled her into a hug again. "It's going to be okay. Promise. Come on, let's order some dinner and relax in front of the TV or something."

"I'd like that."

"Good. We can worry about tomorrow when the time comes."

He led her back inside where it was warm and suggested she choose their last meal in his flat. For now, anyway. She was about to become his fiancée. Who knew how much more time they would spend together here before the deception was over?

Sophie found herself on the Aurora, Inc. company jet for the second time in a week, this time transporting most of the family from Paris to Avignon. Christophe had explained that they would be picked up in two separate limousines in Avignon, and then make the drive to the château from there.

She'd lived a privileged life, but this sort of thing was a definite novelty. She'd brought her suitcase—she planned to head home tomorrow afternoon now—and found herself joining the jovial atmosphere of the family in private, rather than the slightly more formal Pembertons in the social sphere.

There were eight of them all together: Gabi and Will, Bella and Burke, Stephen and Aurora, and Christophe and Sophie. Charlotte was still resting and adjusting to motherhood back in Richmond, but once they were in the air Aurora set up a video call so they could all say hello and see Imogene, who was definitely looking less pink and wrinkled and more plump and adorable. Sophie stared at her tiny nose and nearly translucent eyelids, and Charlotte's tired but blissful expression. In a few months this would be her, holding her precious baby in her arms. Her heart melted a bit, and she surreptitiously touched her tummy. Her baby was in there. Growing, developing, becoming a little person. She'd been so caught up in her body's changes and the situation that she hadn't had much time to really think about how miraculous it all was. And how scared but excited she was, too.

She looked over and caught Christophe watching her, a tender smile on his face. For the first time, she let her hopes have their freedom. She wished this was different. Wished that he were the father and that this wasn't all for show. He was so kind, so funny, so supportive. And the way he'd hugged her last night… She'd felt safe, comforted. It had reminded her of those tough times her parents had shared when Mum had been going through chemo, and how she'd often come across her father offering a supportive embrace.

There'd been something else, too.

For a moment last night, she'd thought he'd been about to kiss her, and in that moment, she would have let him. But she couldn't let those thoughts in. They were friends. And he'd made it very clear that marriage and a family life weren't for him.

Any thoughts of Christophe had to be put aside, no matter how much she might want them to come true.

Once they landed in Avignon, Sophie and Christophe shared a limo with Gabi and Will. The pair had been married since the summer, and still snuggled up in the buttery-soft leather seats like newlyweds. The conversation between the two couples was light and fun, and it was Will who finally brought up the subject of Sophie's designs.

"I heard you spent time with François yesterday. Christophe has been raving about your designs all week."

She blushed and turned to look at Christophe, who bore an innocent expression. "Oh, he has, has he? Well, everything is preliminary. There might be a few pieces worth pursuing."

Christophe shrugged. "To hear François tell it, you have definite opinions that he agrees with." He lifted his eyebrow at her. "Like how you agreed with his assessment of the spring line."

"He told you that?" She wanted to sink through the seat. "Oh, I…uh…"

"Go ahead," he urged. "Tell me what you told him." His smile widened. "I mean, you don't usually have trouble telling me what you think."

She lifted her chin. "It's a very careful choice. And it lacks innovation."

"See? That wasn't so hard." He patted her knee while Gabi and Will laughed.

"Says you. Well, I guess if I'm honest at least you can't fire me."

"Maybe you should work for us," suggested Will.

Sophie sat back, taken by surprise. Work for Aurora, Inc.? It would be a dream job, for sure, but leave Waltham behind? She just didn't see how that was possible.

They changed the topic back to the current Aurora Gems line, debating the strengths and weaknesses, until they arrived at the château.

Sophie had never been, and when the driver opened the door and she stepped out, it was like stepping into another world. The château was three stories of glorious stone, white and elegant with windows that winked at her from the setting sun. It was slightly warmer than Paris, too, without the raw edge to the cold that they'd experienced the last few days. Sophie breathed in the air and let it out again. She was here, at the family château, and tonight she and Christophe were going to announce their sham engagement.

A lot had happened in the past few months, but this was as surreal as it got.

"Come in! There's lots of time to get settled before dinner. Drinks in the library in an hour?" called Aurora, her step lively as she made her way to the front door.

"She's not as terrifying today as she was on Tuesday," Sophie whispered, and Christophe chuckled.

"She likes having her family around. And to be honest, semiretirement suits her. After her heart difficulties this past summer, we're all glad to see her slow down a little bit."

Once inside, Sophie was shown to a spacious bedroom with walls the color of the lavender that grew in the nearby fields. White moldings and ornate trim contrasted with the purple hue, and the rich, silk spread was a paler shade of mauve. Pillows covered in embroidered silk dotted the bed, and a vase of fresh flowers added contrast and a delightful scent to the air. "This is absolutely stunning," she breathed.

Christophe rolled her suitcase inside. "I'm glad you like it. There's a bathroom right in there." He pointed to the right. "I'm down the hall a few doors."

She was glad he was close by. This was far grander than she'd been prepared for, and as the minutes ticked by, she felt more and more like an interloper. "Are you sure this is okay?" she whispered. "Your family is going to think I'm… I don't know. A gold digger."

"They'll think no such thing. Besides, Sophie, you have money of your own. You don't need me for that."

She smiled. "You're right. I don't have a château, but I do have a rather nice Chelsea flat."

He let go of her suitcase handle and quietly closed her door. "So, before we go down for drinks, I think we need to make this official."

Her heart pounded so heavily she could hear it in her ears, but she tried to remain nonchalant. "Oh?"

He nodded, and the easy look slid off his face as he reached into his pocket. "Sophie Waltham, will you marry me?"

He didn't mean it. She knew he didn't, that it was all for appearances, so why did that single sentence from his lips send her brain and heart into utter confusion?

"Honestly, Christophe, you don't need to propo—"

The word was cut off when Christophe took the black velvet box with the stylized *A* on its lid from his pocket. Oh, goodness, he had a ring. An Aurora ring. This felt too real. And at the same time, like the world's biggest farce.

He opened the lid and she gasped.

"It's a little unconventional," he said softly. "Like us. I thought that when this is over you might just resize it and, well, there's a matching necklace and earrings. No sense in putting it in a drawer and never wearing it again, you know?"

His practicality popped the bubble of what had become a surreal moment, and she pushed away the wave of sentimentality that had washed over her. "It's gorgeous, Christophe." Indeed it was. Apparently he'd listened to her comments about predictability and uninspired designs, because this one was unlike anything she'd ever seen. Diamonds and rubies set in platinum, different cuts and an asymmetrical design. An offset troidia-cut diamond touched points with a princess cut, while two baguette-cut rubies flanked each side and another baguette diamond sat parallel on the band. The gems glittered and sparkled in the light as he took it out of the box.

"I don't remember seeing this in the collection," she murmured, holding out her hand, trying to keep her fingers from shaking.

"It wasn't," he replied, sliding the ring over her knuckle. "François designed it, and it was one of the ones I held back last spring when I was determined to play it safe."

Oh, that last phrase had the potential to mean so much more, but they had to remember that this was just for appearances.

"Remind me again why we're doing this?" she asked.

"For your baby. For your happiness. A little ruse to reset everything to just the way you want it." He smiled at her, the cheeky grin she'd come to love. Suddenly she wanted more, though. She wanted to slip past the facade, the wall he erected to keep people from getting too close. She'd been attracted to him for years. She could definitely categorize her feelings as a crush. But this was more. There was a wounded soul behind the flippant comments and charming smile, and she wanted to know that part of him, too. Not just because of a drunken game of two truths and a lie, but because he chose to let her in.

"And what's in it for you?" She resisted the urge to wiggle her finger and set the stones sparkling again.

He lifted her hand and kissed it. "I can't go back and help the boy I was. But maybe I can help another child." His dark eyes dimmed with sadness. "And maybe that child's mother, too, so she's not as unhappy as mine was."

"You felt your abandonment very deeply," she murmured, her hand tingling from his lips and her heart aching for his confession, not only for himself but for his mum. What a gentle soul was beneath all the charm. Perhaps he would let her in after all...

"I saw what can happen when two people who don't love each other try it for the sake of the child. One parent left me. The other loved me in her way, I suppose, but I was a reminder of what her life had become. She resented me. She never thought twice about me going to Cedric and Aurora's. It would kill me to see the lovely light go out of your eyes the way it went out of hers."

"Oh, Christophe." Tears had gathered in the corners of her eyes. "You felt so unlovable and unwanted. I can't understand that, not when you're—" She stopped, afraid of saying too much.

"When I'm what?" he asked softly. There was barely any space between them now, even though they had the entire room to themselves. Sophie's pulse hammered heavily in reaction to his nearness.

"When you're so wonderful," she whispered. "I don't know what I did to deserve your loyalty, but I'm very grateful for it. This goes above and beyond the bounds of friendship."

He leaned forward and kissed her forehead. "Soph, you shouldn't marry him if you don't love him. If this can help the two of you have a productive discussion about what is best for the baby, then putting a ring on your finger and hanging out with you for a while is easy." He smiled again, a bit wistfully, she thought. "You're actually kind of nice to have around."

She jostled his arm, needing to break the intimate spell. "You know I have to go back to London."

"I know. But all you have to do is call, and I can be there in a couple of hours on the train." His face lit up. "And you can come for Christmas at the manor house. You should see it when it's decorated for the holidays." He squeezed her fingers. "Do say you'll come."

A yearning swept over her as she pictured it. Of course there'd be a giant tree, and garlands on the railings. Perhaps a dusting of snow if they were lucky, walks through the village and mincemeat tarts and mulled wine…cider for her this year, she supposed. Already she felt as if this might be going too far, and they hadn't even told his family yet. What would happen then? "I'll think about it," she promised. Heck, she was already thinking about it.

Christophe checked his watch. "Are you ready? It's nearly time for drinks."

"Do I dress for dinner now?"

"A bit later. Drinks are more casual."

She took a breath and let it out. "Well, it's now or never."

They were almost to the door when she reached out and tugged on his hand. "Christophe, wait."

When he turned, she lifted up on tiptoe and gave him a hug. "You're an amazing friend," she whispered, knowing it was true, wishing it was more than that. Wishing, though it went against every instinct, that this wasn't fake. That their feelings were deep and true and sure.

But that wasn't Christophe. He'd made it clear back in London that he was not in the market for marriage or a family. He might want to help a friend, but this wasn't a life he wanted for himself.

And for better or worse, Sophie was now a package deal.

CHAPTER TEN

DRINKS WERE HELD in the library, and Sophie tried not to goggle at the sight of the floor-to-ceiling bookshelves along two walls and the paintings above a fireplace that had logs burning briskly, throwing off a delightful heat. Even though they were close to the Mediterranean, temperatures here were only a few degrees higher than Paris, and the warmth was welcome as she and Christophe made their way to a table with assorted decanters and bottles.

"Anything for you?" he asked, his voice low, and she took a wobbly breath.

"Not at the moment. Everything is…alcoholic."

"I can arrange for something."

"Not yet."

He grabbed a cut crystal decanter and poured some amber liquid into a highball glass. "Let me know," he answered, then lifted the glass for a sip. His jaw was tighter now than it had been upstairs, and she wished she could soothe the tension away with her fingers. Instead, she clasped hers, hiding her ring beneath her right hand.

Aurora was already in the library, wineglass in hand, and she came over to give Christophe a kiss on the cheek. "I'm so glad you both could join us for the weekend. It's wonderful to have the family together. Well, not quite the whole family, but that can't be helped."

"Charlotte will be sticking her nose in in no time," Christophe said, smiling at his aunt. "She does need to be in the middle of everything."

"As opposed to Bella, who bides her time," Aurora agreed, nodding toward the door where Bella and Burke were just now coming through, their faces happy and flushed, and Bella's hair not quite perfect. Christophe nudged Sophie's arm and cocked his eyebrow. She wanted to laugh but just barely held it in. It was easy to see that while Christophe had been proposing, Bella and Burke had indulged in a late afternoon pre-drinks interlude.

"Oh, my," Aurora murmured, dropping her gaze to her glass and sipping. Sophie couldn't help it; she let out a tiny snicker at Aurora's dry tone and was delighted when the other woman's lips tipped up in a discreet but amused smile.

"We're just missing Stephen now," Aurora said, as Will and Gabi entered the room and helped themselves to drinks. She looked at Sophie. "My dear, did Christophe not get you a drink? What would you like?"

"Oh, um, I just wasn't sure so…" She hated how she sounded ambiguous and unsure. Thankfully Stephen entered then, and Christophe reached down and took her fingers.

"Actually, Sophie and I wanted to talk to everyone for a moment once Stephen gets his drink."

Aurora's head snapped up, and her sharp gaze landed on Sophie. "Oh?" she asked, but Sophie couldn't tell if it was a good "oh" or a bad one. Nerves skittered up from her stomach and down her limbs. What was his family going to think? Would they be able to pull this off and make them believe it was genuine?

"Patience, Maman," Christophe said softly. "All is well. I promise."

It was another five minutes before the family was settled on the sofas and chairs surrounding the fire. Sophie
took a chair and crossed her legs, wondering if she should
have changed out of her trousers into a dress or something
a bit more remarkable. Christophe perched himself on the
arm of the chair, clearly pairing himself with her, and she
was buoyed by his presence.

She could do this. She could pretend to be in love with
Christophe. It wasn't that hard, after all. Or even much of
a stretch. Her feelings for him grew by the day.

The chatter had started to focus on the business, and it
was no time at all before Bella spoke up, addressing Sophie. "Christophe says you spent time with François, and
that you showed him some designs. I'm very intrigued,
Sophie."

Ah. Comfortable territory; her field of expertise. "François is utterly lovely and generous. He liked some of my
designs and told me the truth, that some others were not
worth exploring. He knows the business as well as anyone I've ever met."

"What are your plans, then?" Stephen asked. "Are you
looking to bring Waltham under the Aurora umbrella?"

She stared at him. Such a thought hadn't even crossed
her mind, and she certainly wouldn't speak of it without
having broached the topic to her parents. But Stephen was
in charge of acquisitions, so it was interesting to note that
this was on his radar. "That's very premature," she said
honestly. "I've just started exploring designing and find I
enjoy it immensely. Where that takes me in the future is
still very much undecided."

Christophe put his hand on her shoulder. "But speaking
of the future," he said, his voice confident, "Sophie and
I do have an announcement to make." There was a beat

of silence as all eyes fell upon them, and then he said, "I asked Sophie to marry me, and she said yes."

The moment of silence drew out as shock rippled through the room, and then as one the family seemed to collect itself and react with the appropriate well wishes and decorum. "Congratulations!" exclaimed Will, who put his arm around Gabi and squeezed. "I can tell you firsthand that marriage is wonderful, cousin."

"Congratulations," echoed Gabi, her eyes soft and loving. They were like a dart into Sophie's soul. Gabi and Will's love was so true, and here she and Christophe were in this sham of an engagement.

She reminded herself that this was not the Pemberton family's first experience with a sham engagement though, and it helped a little. Precious little, but still.

"Darling." Aurora got up and went to Christophe and kissed his cheek. "This is wonderful news. And Sophie." She rose and Aurora pulled her into a polite but still warm hug. "Welcome to our big and crazy family."

"Thank you," she whispered, her eyes pricking. She didn't deserve this. She didn't deserve any of it.

"Come on, then," said Bella. "Let's see the ring." She looked at Christophe with an accusatory glare. "You did propose with a ring, didn't you?"

Christophe laughed, looking far more at ease than she felt. "Of course I did."

Sophie held out her hand. "Oh…" Bella said, rising from the Louis XIV settee and coming forward. She took Sophie's hand and lifted it so that the light reflected off the brilliant stones. "I haven't seen that one before."

"It's one of a kind," Christophe said, beaming. "François helped me choose just the right one." He looked over at Sophie, his face perfectly adoring. "Nothing ordinary for my extraordinary fiancée."

God, he was such a good actor. She almost believed him…and she knew the truth! She could practically hear the internal *aww*s coming from his family.

"Christophe really knows me," she said shyly. "He did a wonderful job picking the ring. It's beautiful and yet unusual…just like our relationship." She laughed a little, knowing she had actually managed to tell the truth somehow in all this farcical sentimentality.

"When's the big day?" Stephen asked. He was the only one not to rise from his seat for a better look, but if what Christophe said was true, Stephen wasn't a big fan of matrimony at the moment, either. He'd had one engagement broken off and Gabi had left him at the altar. Even though that had all turned out for the best, Sophie could understand him not being the most excited person in the room.

"Um, we haven't really discussed it. It, uh…"

Christophe pulled her in close to his side and leaned over to whisper in her ear. "We might as well tell them. It's going to come out anyway."

She swallowed against a massive lump in her throat, a rush of cold panic racing through her veins. She nodded briefly, gathering herself together. *In for a penny, in for a pound*, she thought, and with all the courage she possessed, she lifted her chin and faced his family.

"We're not sure," she said clearly, "because I'm having a baby."

Bella gaped. Aurora sat down. Gabi and Will stared at each other, and Stephen kept his steady gaze on the two of them, rubbing an index finger across his lips as if deep in thought. That unsettled her the most. Stephen didn't even look surprised. How could that be, when she was?

Burke, bless him, recovered first. "Well. This family never does anything halfway, does it? How are you feeling? When's the happy event?"

Sophie sat down again, and Christophe resumed his perch on the arm of the chair, but he kept his arm around her shoulders, a firm show of support. "I'm due in the spring," she said quietly. "And I'm feeling much better, now that the sickness seems to have eased."

"I was sickest with my first," Aurora said. "I'm glad you're over the worst of it. It's so very unpleasant."

She was trying, Sophie realized, and she smiled at Aurora in gratitude. "It wasn't fun. But you should know…"

Christophe's fingers pressed into her shoulder. "The baby isn't mine. Sophie and the father had already split up when she found out she was pregnant."

"Dammit, Christophe, it's just bombshell after bombshell," Bella groused. "I think I might need another drink."

"Sorry," Sophie said, her voice small. It was a lot for them to take in. There was asking for support and then there was just…whatever strange thing this was.

"Don't be sorry." Christophe's voice was firm as his gaze touched hers. "It does nothing to change how we feel about each other."

Again with the wordsmithing. He'd managed to imply love without actually saying the word. *Well done*, she thought, her admiration for his quick thinking and fortitude growing.

"Of course it doesn't," Gabi added staunchly. "If I've learned anything over the past year, it's that love plus this family equals complicated. It also equals worth it. You've got our support." She nudged Will, who added his agreement with a nod, as if he didn't dare contradict his wife.

"And ours," Bella said, sounding slightly less convinced but holding Burke's hand just the same.

"Absolument." Aurora let a smile touch her lips although Sophie thought perhaps her eyes weren't as warm

as before. "This family sticks together, and now you're one of us, Sophie."

She appreciated the solidarity, but how much support would she have when they found out the truth?

Christophe clapped his hands, hoping to maximize the felicitations and make the scene joyful in order to avoid more questions. In hindsight, he and Sophie should have laid out a game plan. Still, it could have gone worse. Much worse. Thank heavens for Gabi.

"I think we should have a toast," he suggested, keeping his tone light and jovial. "Champagne?"

Aurora rose and smiled again, and he recognized it as a forced expression. She patted his arm and said, "I'll arrange it and be right back."

While they were waiting, Gabi and Bella offered their congratulations and surrounded Sophie to look at the ring and ask all sorts of questions about their courtship and her pregnancy. Thankfully, he heard her say that while it seemed sudden, they'd been friends for a very long time. What touched him especially was when she said, "In the past weeks he really has shown me he's the very best of men."

God, he hoped he was. Was this even the right thing? He wasn't sure. It was a crazy idea that made some sense, but certainly it wasn't the only solution to her problem. So why had he stepped in? Why had he taken the extraordinary step of suggesting an engagement, when the very word had sent him running in the past?

The question gave him a great deal of discomfort, so he ignored it and instead kissed her temple before turning back to his glass of Scotch and draining it in one gulp.

"So, fatherhood." Stephen's dry voice came from beside him and he turned around. Of all the family, Stephen would be the toughest to fool. Probably because he was the least trusting of all of them.

"Seems like," Christophe answered, clapping his hand on Stephen's arm and smiling widely.

"Are you sure about this?" Stephen's dark brows pulled together, but at least he kept his voice low so Sophie wouldn't hear. "Someone else's baby? And it's been such a short time."

Christophe met his eldest cousin's astute gaze. "We've been friends for a very long time, Stephen. I can't imagine anything better than marrying a friend, can you?"

He said it to appease Stephen, but when the words came out he realized that they were true. If he ever did marry—not that an actual wedding was in his plans—he would want it to be with someone he was friends with. Who he could be himself with. Who saw beyond the Pemberton and Aurora, Inc. façade.

"I thought I was going to marry a friend. Then she married my brother."

"Perhaps it has to be both," Christophe suggested. "A friend but also a…a lover." He stuttered over that last bit. His fingers were still twined with Sophie's even though they were facing opposite directions. And for a flash of a moment, he thought about being her lover and his blood ran hot.

No, no, no. This was not part of the plan. That sort of thinking had to be nipped in the bud.

"Perhaps," Stephen acknowledged, but he didn't sound convinced. Christophe was saved, though, by Aurora returning with a chilled bottle and a maid following behind with a tray of crystal flutes.

There was a general bustling around as glasses were filled and handed to everyone, even Sophie. Christophe noticed she took the glass with a wobbly smile and shrugged.

As head of the family, it was up to Aurora to give the toast. She took a breath and then lifted her glass as they all gathered in the center of the room, the fire crackling behind them.

"To my son, Christophe, and to Sophie, his bride-to-be. May your lives be filled with blessings and your hearts with love."

Christophe's throat tightened as her words hit home. Not her nephew, not someone she loved as a son, but *her son*. No qualifiers. He called her Maman, but in his head she was always *ma tante*, not *ma mère*. He did love her. But there would always be one other woman who held that place, whose love he craved more than anything. How stupid was that, when he hadn't even seen the woman in five years?

"To Christophe and Sophie," Stephen said, lifting his glass, and the other couples echoed the words.

Everyone touched glasses and drank. Christophe noticed that Sophie touched the rim to her lips and tasted the fizzy champagne, and then lowered it again, taking part in the toast but abstaining from consuming any alcohol. He drained his glass and then took hers from her hand and put both on a nearby table.

"Well, aren't you going to kiss your fiancée?" asked Stephen.

Christophe looked into Sophie's eyes and saw confusion beneath the dark depths, but also acceptance. If they were going to convince everyone this was genuine, they had to get used to touching each other. It was one kiss, and it could be a chaste one, really. They were in front of others, and it didn't need to be a big display. Just believable.

Christophe channeled all of his charm and let a slow smile lift his lips as he gazed into her eyes. It wasn't hard to act attracted to her; she was utterly gorgeous, and he cared about her deeply. Indeed, in another time or place this might have been the natural progression of things. "That sounds like a wonderful idea," he murmured, just loud enough for everyone to hear. Then he lifted his hand and cupped her neck in his palm before dipping his head and touching his mouth to hers.

He hadn't been prepared, though, for the contact to rocket through his body. He hadn't expected her to be so responsive, either. As their lips met, hers parted slightly, softly touching his with shyness and uncertainty but definitely with participation. Sophie, who had never been shy in her life from what he knew of her. Her breath came out on a small sigh and the muscles in her neck were tense, but a quick check showed her eyes were closed, the dark lashes lying innocently on her cheeks. He moved his mouth over hers, taking a few precious moments to taste the supple flavors of her before drawing away, but not before the contact shook him to the soles of his feet. It was the smallest of kisses, without any dark promise of the night that lay ahead, and yet he was completely and utterly undone by it.

Sophie. His Sophie.

Where had she been his whole life?

Sophie ran her tongue over her lip to make the taste of him last a little bit longer. Her heart was knocking about in her chest as if she'd just run a marathon, and she was sure there were stars in her eyes. What in the world was wrong with her? It was a celebratory engagement kiss in front of his family. So why had her whole world just tilted?

He was smiling down at her, a private smile that did nothing to quell the conflicting feelings racing through her mind. She had to get ahold of herself. Keep up the pretense, act as if kissing him was the most natural thing in the world. She had to push away the need to kiss him again. Forget the other desires running through her body right now, and her heart, too. This had been such a bad idea. There was absolutely no way she was going to come out of this unscathed.

"Aw, you two are so sweet." Gabi's voice reached Sophie's ears and she reluctantly turned away from Christophe's magnetic gaze.

"What can I say?" She laughed lightly and waved her hand, the jewels in her ring sparkling in the light. "It's been a whirlwind time, really."

"But when you know, you know," Christophe added, and Sophie thought maybe he was laying it on a little thick. He couldn't mean such a thing. For the millionth time, she reminded herself that Christophe didn't do love or commitment. He'd said it himself—his last relationship had ended because he'd been unable to commit.

Sophie's glass was replaced with one of sparkling water, but she noticed that Christophe picked up her champagne and drained it, too. That made three drinks in the thirty minutes they'd been in the library. Perhaps this was more difficult for him than he let on, and for some reason it felt as if someone had let the air out of her happy balloon. This wasn't real. Why did she have to keep reminding herself of that?

The cocktail hour wound down and Christophe reappeared at her side, ready to escort her back to her room as everyone went to change for dinner. "Shall we?" he asked, his voice low, and it shivered along her nerve endings.

He dropped her at her room, with promises to come back in twenty minutes to collect her again, lest she get lost in the hallways of the château. Once inside her room, Sophie turned on a soft lamp and sat down on the edge of the bed.

The ring sparkled in the light and she held her hand

aloft, studying the gems and the way it looked on her hand. It was unlike anything she'd seen before, but it suited her, too. Funny how Christophe had been able to see that when no one in her life seemed to get who she really was. It was as if the people who cared about her put her in their own private box of expectations, but with Christophe, she could just be Sophie—her own version of herself.

After a few minutes, she got up and went to her suitcase to take out the cocktail dress she'd brought along. Tonight she would eat dinner with the Pembertons. Tomorrow she would have to go back to London to face the music—and Eric.

The Pembertons might be the first test, but seeing Eric was going to be the hardest one.

CHAPTER ELEVEN

DINNER WAS ABSOLUTELY divine and in a number of courses that boggled Sophie's mind. First a small salad of cucumber and apple in crème fraiche, then a fish course of seared scallops, a main course of guinea fowl and steamed vegetables, followed by a cheese course. Sophie avoided the soft and blue cheese varieties, but it was no problem, as she was already stuffed. The cook at the château was clearly very talented. She hadn't had such a meal in a very long time, and that included the fine dining at exclusive restaurants she'd experienced while dating Eric and during the past week with Christophe.

"This was amazing," she said, after touching her napkin to her lips. "The guinea fowl was perfect."

"It's not often so many of us are together," Bella said, sipping on the last of her glass of white wine. "And tonight we had a real reason to celebrate."

"Hear, hear," said Will.

"Thank you all. For the lovely welcome and the support."

Stephen studied the rim of his glass, then met her gaze. "What you need to understand, Sophie, is that once you're one of us, we all come with the package. That means you're not alone. You have the Pembertons behind you."

Her lips fell open in shock at the unexpected support.

"Thank you, Stephen." Christophe acknowledged his cousin with a nod.

The jovial mood had sobered quite a bit, and it was Aurora who finally voiced the question that Sophie had been waiting for. "And the father…is he in the picture?"

"Yes," she answered, determined to keep her voice clear and strong. "He intends to be a father to the baby, and for that I am thankful. He's…he's a good man. He's just not the right man for me, that's all." She looked around the table. "But I do hope you'll understand if I leave tomorrow to go back to London. I'd like to tell him and my parents the news before there's a chance of it leaking." She looked at Christophe. "And I think it's only right I do it in person."

"Of course, *ma chère*," he said, picking up her hand and kissing her fingers.

The gathering broke up after that, and Sophie was more than ready for bed. Dinner had gone on until well after nine, and it had been a long and emotional day. Keeping up pretenses was exhausting work. She wasn't prepared for one last edict from Aurora, however, as she and Christophe were leaving the dining room.

"Christophe, while I appreciate you putting Sophie in a guest room for appearances, now that everything is official, you don't have to have separate rooms."

Oh, Lord. Sophie was sure her ears were flushed bright pink as the two of them stopped and stared at his ever-calm aunt. She laughed, that rusty laugh that Sophie had admired earlier but now…now it made her feel incredibly awkward. "Good heavens, you two. You've been staying at the flat all week anyway. It's not exactly been a secret." She gave a wink. "Besides, I knew it was like this when I first saw you together. It's in the way you look at each other. It reminds me of me and Cedric."

The teasing expression softened into one of sentimentality. "Your lives together will sometimes be complicated," she offered, "but if you face it together, as each other's best friend, and with commitment, you'll be just fine. Good night, darlings."

Christophe took Sophie's hand and they escaped to the stairs and the upper floor to the bedrooms. It wasn't until they got to the empty hallway that he let go of her hand, halted, and let his head drop.

"Are you all right?" she asked, immediately putting her hand on his arm in concern. "I'm so sorry about that last bit. I knew pretending would be hard, but—"

"Shh," he commanded, and they turned their heads together toward the sound of Will and Gabi coming up the stairs, talking and laughing. Christophe took her arm and spun her toward her bedroom door, turned the knob, and hurried them both inside.

"Sorry," she whispered.

Gabi's and Will's voices sounded outside their door; there was a little giggle and Will's deeper response, and meanwhile Sophie was pressed against Christophe's front while he had his shoulder against her door. It was utterly dark in the room; not even the lamp was on. They were cocooned in blackness, and all Sophie could hear now was the sound of their breathing, rising and falling quickly.

And still she did not step away.

"Soph," he murmured. "This…dammit."

He kissed her then, and it was as different from the kiss downstairs as day was from night. This was dark, seductive, passionate. It ignited something deep in her core, and her brain simply stopped working as she wound her arms around his neck and kissed him back fully.

Nearly a decade she'd known Christophe, nearly a decade she'd wondered and occasionally fantasized. And yet she hadn't ever realized he had this dark, intense passion about him. Having it focused completely on her was a glorious revelation. He shifted his weight and she found herself pressed against the door, sandwiched between the heavy wood and the hardness of his body. And it was hard, she realized, as his lips slid from hers and skittered over her neck. A gasp erupted from her throat, calling his mouth back to hers.

A welcome heaviness centered in her pelvis, and she knew that either they had to stop or he was going to have to take her to bed. Her body cried out for the latter, but common sense had to prevail at some point.

This was a fake engagement. Christophe didn't want marriage or a family. This could go nowhere.

"Christophe." How she managed both syllables of his name was a miracle, because his mouth was a wicked, wicked thing as he kissed the tender spot just below her ear. "We have to stop. We can't do this."

It might have had more effect if she hadn't pressed her breast into his palm. She wanted him so badly. Wanted the heat and passion of him, so different from—

The comparison that popped into her brain had the desired cooling effect. She put her hand on his wrist and moved it off her breast, then slid out from between him and the door. Her breath was coming heavily, and her lips felt deliciously swollen, but they really did have to stop. It wasn't fair to her or especially to him to start making comparisons. Exploring whatever this was would only complicate things. And potentially harm their friendship, which was far too important to jeopardize.

"I… I'm sorry." Christophe ran a hand through his rumpled curls. She could just make out his features in the moonlight coming through the window now that her eyes had adjusted to the dark. "I don't know… I mean…"

"I know. There's our friendship to consider."

"Yes," he agreed emphatically, taking a step toward her. "I don't want to mess anything up. And yet…" She saw him swallow, and there was still this tense energy radiating from him, as she was certain must be from her, as well. They were turned on…by each other.

"I know. I didn't expect it. Didn't… Please, don't be too sorry. We just can't let it go any further."

"Which is a damned shame," he replied, and the desire in his voice nearly had her reconsidering. Her whole body was crying out for him, craving satisfaction. Over the past two weeks she'd noticed things about him, certainly. She'd been able to explain them away. But this… there was no denying that in addition to being wonderful friends, there was amazing chemistry between them. She'd always wondered. Now she knew. It was almost impossible to walk away from, even knowing it would blow up in her face in the end.

"A damned shame," she echoed.

"I'll be right back."

He disappeared into her bathroom and she heard water running. Then he returned with a glass of water in his hand and a little moisture clinging to his hair. "In lieu of a cold shower," he explained. "So I can attempt to have working brain cells when we talk about this."

"I agree." She passed by him and headed to the bathroom, as well. At the sound of his muffled laugh, she pointed out, "You're not the only one who needs cooling off."

The cold water didn't really work, however. When she returned to the bedroom, he was still standing there, in his trousers and shirt and tie, looking devastatingly sexy and rumpled. Need pulsed through her. Pretense was gone. For the past week, they'd carefully avoided too much touching, hadn't crossed a line. Now it had been crossed and she'd had a taste of him. Was it wrong that she now wanted it all?

"Sophie, if you don't want this to happen, you have to stop looking at me like that."

She bit down on her lip while a war raged within her. Once again, she reminded herself that the engagement was fake. That Christophe couldn't give her what she truly needed: love, security, a life together. A partner to see her through the rough times, because there would definitely be hardships. The only thing he could give her was this moment, right now. Was it enough? She didn't know. She wasn't sure of any of her decisions over the past few months. And yet a singular thought persisted…if she walked away tonight, that would be it. She would never know. And she would always regret it.

They'd already crossed a line. There was no more pretending that attraction, chemistry didn't exist. Three minutes against her bedroom door had told her exactly what she needed to know.

"This," she said softly, taking a step toward him. "What do you mean by this?"

"I mean…" The words were taut, bound tight by the restraint he seemed desperate to maintain. "I didn't mean for this to happen. And then we kissed downstairs…"

"And we had to stop pretending?" She took another step closer, her heart thundering.

"You're my friend. This is wrong. I shouldn't think of you this way."

"Think of me how?" she asked.

"You need to stop asking me questions."

A small smile touched her lips. The closer she got to him, the more certain she became. She was about to leave her past life behind. No more twenty-something young professional. She was going to be a mother, with new responsibilities. One night. One night with Christophe to hold on to. She'd had a thing for him for so long, and here he was in front of her. Could she really pass up what was likely to be her only chance?

"Then let me answer," she said softly. She was now only inches away from him, and she saw a muscle flex in his jaw. She reached up and loosened his tie, sliding the end out of the knot. "I've been thinking of you this way for the past four days. I've thought of you this way long before this, but I didn't want to let it get in the way of our friendship. But the moment you pressed me against that door and said my name, well, that ship sailed, *mon ami*. This engagement might be fake, but my need for you isn't. I want you, Christophe." She let the tie fall to the floor.

He let out a breath, as if she'd just ripped the rug out from beneath him. "You. Need me."

"Touch me again and find out," she said, daring.

"I can't make promises," he said, the words strangled. She busied her fingers with the buttons on his shirt now, slowly releasing each one from the buttonhole.

"I know that. I'm not asking for any. I'm not asking for a thing besides tonight, in this bed, with me." She pressed her lips to his chest, just below the hollow at the base of his neck. "Tell me you won't always wonder if we don't."

He made a sound in his throat that rumbled beneath her lips.

"Tell me you don't want me, and you can go to your room and I'll stay here and that will be it. That's all it takes, Christophe. Just say the words. *I don't want you, Sophie.* Say it."

She looked up into his hot, dark gaze. Every nerve ending in her body was begging for stimulation and release. *Touch me*, she silently begged. *Love me.*

"I can't say it, because it would be a lie. I want you so much I'm dying with it. Sophie…" He curled his hand around the nape of her neck. "I want you so much right now it scares me."

Victory.

"One night. The only promise I want is that tomorrow we'll still be friends."

"Always," he said. "That's an easy one."

She wasn't so sure, but he was stripping out of his shirt and she moved her fingers to the zipper of her dress. It caught and he turned her around by the shoulders, working at the zip in the dark, sliding the dress off her shoulders while the hot skin of his chest grazed her back.

This had escalated so quickly. Her crush had been one thing. This explosive desire was another. Downstairs she'd kept her response to his kiss sweet and shy, playing a part. Now, though, now she wanted so much more. All it had taken to make that fire come to life was the way he'd responded to her moments before. As if he couldn't help himself, couldn't get enough of her.

She needed him, but being needed in return was the biggest turn on she could imagine.

"Sophie," he whispered, his breath warm on her neck. "Kiss me, Sophie."

He didn't have to ask twice. She turned around, dressed now in only her bra and panties, and slid her arms over his shoulders. Their mouths met, this time without the uncertainty of the first time and the frantic passion of the second, but with mutual acknowledgment and desire. His lips were demanding and she answered the call, then slid her hands down his hard chest to his belt buckle. Hands working quickly, she undid the button and zip on his pants while he flicked open the clasp on her bra. She shimmied it down her arms and let it drop on the floor, then hooked her thumbs in her panties and skimmed them down her legs.

"You are so unexpected," he said, reaching for her.

"I'm surprising myself," she admitted, and was glad that in the midst of the scramble to disrobe they'd found a way back to their easy banter.

But Christophe had his own surprises. He swept her up into his arms and crossed the room to the bed, then with one hand, flipped the covers down to the bottom and laid her on the silken sheets. He joined her there, lying beside her, braced on an elbow so they could kiss and touch and explore. There was a moment when his palm covered her belly and wishes filled her heart, but then his hand slipped lower and she let the wishes flutter away on her sighs.

And when the touches grew desperate, she reached for him. "Don't make me wait," she whispered.

There was a moment where they paused, as if realizing that birth control was not a concern, and then he was there, joined to her, and the world stopped turning.

Sophie arched her neck and said his name.

If this was one night only, he was making it one she'd never forget.

Christophe woke with the sun in his eyes. He squinted, then realized the walls were purple. A glance to his side showed Sophie, still asleep on her belly, her hair spread out in a cascade of chocolate silk.

They were both gloriously naked.

God. He should never have slept here. Images of the previous night raced through his brain, causing both arousal and panic in his blood. What had they done? At the time it had seemed the most natural thing in the world. Kissing her the first time had been the mistake. He should have left her at the door and that was it.

And yet…it was hard to regret something so amazing.

She'd been so confident. So sure of herself. Had he ever met anyone who knew their own mind more than she did? When Sophie went after something, she just did it. No second-guessing. She made decisions and moved forward. He admired that about her. And he couldn't complain. Making love with her had been spectacular.

There'd been a moment, just beforehand, when his fingers had trailed over her belly. He'd remembered then that a life grew within her, just beneath his palm, and he'd been awed and humbled at her trust in him. She wasn't showing, but he'd noticed the small, firm bubble where her child grew. It had unlocked something in him that was so uncomfortable he'd nearly stopped and walked away.

Instead, he'd done what he always did: pushed the thought aside and ignored it. He was rather good at that.

Which meant this morning he'd have to compartmentalize the feelings crowding his chest, strangling him. Tenderness. Protectiveness. Need. He had to get up now, get out of this bed, because if she rolled over and touched him, he wasn't sure he'd have the strength to turn her away.

One night. That was what she'd asked for and that was what he'd given. Friendship. Her one condition.

It was going to be hell, but he would give her what she asked for. Because if nothing else, Christophe kept his word.

He slid out from beneath the covers and gathered his clothes on the way to the bathroom. When he returned, fully dressed, she had rolled over in bed, the sheets gathered beneath her armpits, her eyes sleepy. "Good morning," he said softly.

"Indeed," she replied, but he noticed her eyes were more guarded than usual. Interesting. Maybe he wasn't the only one who could compartmentalize.

"I thought I might go back to my own room and shower. I don't have any of my things here."

"Sure." She sat up a bit. "Christophe, are we okay?"

"Of course we are." He took a chance and went to her, perching on the side of the bed, though not too close. She was naked and tempting and this was not the plan—even if they'd thrown out the playbook on the first night.

"Okay. I just wanted to be sure. I don't think we should act as if it never happened."

He chuckled. "I don't think that's possible, *ma chère*. It was pretty amazing."

"It just can't be repeated."

"That's right."

"For obvious reasons."

"Exactly."

She nodded at him. "I know that." She reached for his hand. "I would never ask you to compromise your own needs. I know you don't want marriage and children. I'm not looking for you to change. It's the one thing I truly love about our relationship. We each get to be exactly who we are."

Then why did he feel so let down? Why did he feel as if the man he was was somehow wanting?

"Last night was unexpected," he acknowledged. "But I will keep my promises, Soph. One night only, friendship firmly intact."

She lifted her hand to his cheek, the ring he'd given her sparkling on her finger. "You are the best of men," she murmured, meeting his gaze. "I said it to your sister last night and I meant it. I trust you, Christophe. You have honor and honesty."

He kissed her forehead, but that was all he dared, and with a smile of farewell he got up and left her bedroom. Once alone and in his own shower though, the hot spray sluicing down his body, he put a hand along the tiles and hung his head.

He didn't have honor or honesty. An honorable man would have done the right thing and turned down her invitation. And an honest man would have admitted that one night with her would never be enough.

CHAPTER TWELVE

SOPHIE SPENT THE morning feeling entirely off balance. On one hand, the effect of good sex left her body relaxed and still humming with pleasure. On the other, navigating a new normal with Christophe, while under the watchful eyes of his family, took some mental and emotional finesse.

Thankfully, breakfast was a casual affair with people eating at different times and picking and choosing something light. Pastries, Greek yogurt and fruit fit the bill for her, as well as tea instead of the bottomless coffee service. She'd dressed in a long skirt and boots, as well as a sweater and belt, as she wanted to be comfortable on the flight back to London. Her flight left at noon, and it was nearly an hour to the airport at Aix-en-Provence, which had a daily direct flight to London. She'd be home early afternoon, leaving France and Christophe behind, but his ring still on her finger.

Christophe was always there, making sure she wasn't alone, being supportive and kind. It seemed to her that he had an easier time of regaining his equilibrium than she did, but she let it steady her. Before long, she was putting her suitcase in the limousine. She'd said goodbyes to most of the family, and thanked Aurora for her hospitality, and now there was just Gabi and Bella, who had followed her outside, and Christophe—the hardest of all to say goodbye to.

She'd turned down his offer to go with her to the airport. Instead, he'd return to Paris with the rest of the family that evening, on the company jet out of Avignon.

"I'm sorry you couldn't stay longer," said Bella, giving Sophie's elbow a squeeze. "But we'll see you soon, I'm sure. Either in Paris, or for sure at the château for the holidays. It's only five weeks away."

Five weeks. Christophe had asked her to join him...perhaps their relationship would be back to somewhat normal by then.

Gabi nodded. "I had my first Christmas there last year. You'll love it." She smiled her soft, sweet smile and said, "One of the best things about becoming a Pemberton is that I keep gaining sisters. I quite like it, really."

Sophie struggled to keep smiling. Oh, they were going to hate her when the engagement suddenly ended, weren't they? This had to have been the most foolish idea on the planet.

"Get going, so I can say goodbye to my fiancée, and so she doesn't miss her flight," Christophe chided, shooing them away.

With a last wave the two departed. Christophe turned back to face her, and her pulse jumped. It was good she was leaving. They needed some space to deal with what happened. To put it in perspective.

"Will you call me tonight? Let me know how things are? I'll be worried about you."

"Of course. Or at the very least, I'll text, okay? Depending on how I feel."

"I wish I could be there with you. Not because you can't handle it. Just because I feel like I'm leaving you alone for the hardest part."

She met his gaze and squared her shoulders. "This is my life, my parents, my ex, Christophe. It's not up to you to make things better." She softened her voice. "But knowing you're supporting me helps. I know you're there. I know you have my back."

"All right. And if things get to be too much, in any way, you call. I can be there in a few hours. Or you can come to me." He held out his hand. "You gave this back to me yesterday, but I want you to keep it."

He dropped the key to his flat into her palm, still warm from his skin.

"Christophe, I don't know what to say."

"Last night changes nothing," he said. "One night only, friendship intact, remember?"

"I remember. Thank you."

He leaned forward and kissed her forehead for the second time that morning. She was starting to hate that, actually. A gesture that implied intimacy but was guarded. Still, she said nothing, gave him a smile, and slid into the limo.

"Goodbye, Christophe. I'll be in touch later."

"Safe travels," he said, and shut the door.

The tires of the limo crunched over the drive, and she turned for one last look at the château. She'd hoped Christophe would be standing there still, but when she looked, he'd disappeared back inside.

She let out a breath and sat back against the plush seat. Then she took out her phone and started making plans for the day. A message to her pet service that she would be home this afternoon. One to her parents that she would like to have breakfast with them in the morning, and finally, a third to Eric, asking if they could talk later today, at his place. His because she wanted to be able to leave if things didn't go well.

Security was not overwhelmed midday on a Sunday, and it took very little time before she was at her gate, ready to board. Every minute took her farther and farther away

from Christophe and the past week. Boarding was called
and she made her way to her seat, then took her sketch
pad and colored pencils out of her bag once they'd taken
off. Working on her designs would surely ease some of the
anxiety settling in her gut.

She picked a blue pencil and stared at her hand. She
hadn't got used to the ring, and it stayed there as a reminder
of the previous evening. Now instead of a family dinner
stuck in her mind, she had Christophe's kisses, the feel of
his hands on her body on replay.

They'd agreed to one night. He'd seemed completely
fine with that this morning. She wasn't, though. She finally
could admit it to herself now that there were several miles
and twenty-odd thousand feet between them. It wasn't fair
to compare; she knew that. But being with Christophe…it
had been different from anything she'd ever experienced.
And if she ever admitted that he was the best sex she'd
ever had, she could just imagine how he'd laugh at her.

She smiled despite herself. Here she was in the biggest
mess she'd ever been in, and he didn't even need to be
present to make her laugh.

She wanted to go back to Paris. Back to his flat. Back
to Aurora, to François, to all of it. The entire week had
been perfect. Life altering. It had made her question everything she thought she knew.

Once she'd landed and collected her bag, she took a cab
to her flat and asked the cabbie to wait. Eric had messaged
back that he was home all afternoon and would be available. There was no sense putting it off. She took a moment
to give Harry a quick cuddle and a promise she'd return
soon, and then she went back to the cab and gave the cabbie instructions to Eric's executive flat in Canary Wharf.

He greeted her at the door with a wide smile. "Darling!
I'm so glad you messaged. Come in. I've made tea."

She stepped inside and he removed her wrap, but she kept her gloves on, not wanting him to see her ring just yet. Maybe she should have taken it off, but it would add weight to what she was about to tell him, and she could use all the help she could get. He looked good, she realized. Not a strand of his dark blond hair was out of place, and even on a Sunday he was perfectly groomed. Clean-shaven, neat trousers, collared shirt under a sweater.

She thought of Christophe coming out of his room for his morning coffee, dressed in sweatpants and a rumpled T-shirt. She knew which she preferred.

He hung her coat in the closet. "Thank you, Eric."

"Did you have lunch?" he called as he headed toward the kitchen. She closed her eyes. It would be so much easier if he were less likable. She reminded herself that he'd said his share of hurtful things over the past two and a half months, and that he'd been pressuring her unfairly. She had to keep perspective here.

"I'm fine, thank you." She followed him into the kitchen area. "Tea is lovely, though."

He poured from a pot—no bag in a cup for him—and hit the button on his espresso machine, making himself a coffee. "When did you arrive back in town?" he asked.

"About an hour ago."

"I see."

She knew he didn't, but that was fine. She took the cup from him and had a sip, just to keep her hands busy while he waited for his coffee.

"I was in Paris. At Aurora, doing some…consulting."

His eyebrows went up. "Wow. Nice gig for you." His beverage finished and he took the cup from the machine, then waved her into the living room overlooking the river.

She'd spent many hours in this room, and now he would buy her a place in the country if she wanted it. Somewhere to raise their baby. She almost wished she could say yes; it would be so much more uncomplicated, but it would be a lie. When she looked at him now, she had no hard feelings or regrets about the time they'd spent together, but it was over. If she'd had any doubts, last night would have laid them to rest. She could never accept anything less than…love.

Her throat tightened, and she was afraid she might burst into tears. It was love, then, this feeling that filled her heart to bursting, that made her anxious and sad and thrilled all at the same time. To find it in a good friend was even more shocking. And knowing she could never have it was devastating.

"Are you all right? Is it the tea? What do you need?" He reached for her hands.

She brushed his hands away. "No, I'm fine. So is the tea. Please, Eric, sit down. I came here to tell you something and I don't want to put it off."

His easy, friendly expression turned wary, and he sat on the sofa across from the chair that she chose. Nerves tightened her muscles as she stiffly tugged on her gloves, first taking off the right, then the left, before laying the soft leather in her lap.

Then she put her left hand over her right, looked him in the eye and made herself say the words. "Eric, I came here to tell you that I'm engaged to marry Christophe Germain."

Eric jumped to his feet and stared down at her. "I beg your pardon? Who the hell is Christophe Germain?" He frowned, a deep furrow appearing between his eyebrows. "I know I've heard that name. Who is he? And engaged? We've only been split up a few months! Does he know about the baby?"

"Sit down, Eric, and stop shouting, or I'll get up and walk out. I would rather stay and talk."

He sat, but looked remarkably unhappy about it.

"Christophe is the cousin of the Earl of Chatsworth and one of the heirs to the Aurora fortune. I've known him for years." The engagement might be false, but that much at least was true.

"Years. Of course. He's the French one, right?"

"Obviously." She resisted the urge to roll her eyes. "You met him once or twice, I think. And he was at Stephen's wedding." Eric had gone as her plus-one.

"Ah yes, the wedding that never was." He didn't bother hiding his disdain. "But engaged. When did this happen?"

She swallowed and forced herself to remain calm and still and tell as much truth as possible. "Well, he asked me on Monday, and I answered him on Thursday night, and we told his family last night. I flew back this afternoon because I wanted you to hear it from me in person, and Mum and Dad, too."

He sat back on the sofa, still scowling. "This is ridiculous. For two months I've been asking you to marry me. Offering you an amazing life, and you...you never once thought to tell me you were seeing someone else?"

Ah, now it was becoming sticky. She looked him in the eye and considered her words. "I wanted us to discuss our future as parents. I already told you I wouldn't marry you. I shouldn't have to qualify that with whether or not I'm seeing someone else." She didn't bother to gentle her words. "This is between you and me, Eric. I truly don't want this to be acrimonious. I want us to figure this out together. But we can't do that if you won't accept that marriage is not in our future. I'm marrying someone else."

He got up again and paced to the window, then turned back again, his hands on his hips. "You told me that you could never marry unless it was for love. You're telling me that you love him? That you are undeniably, forevermore, head over heels and every other cliché in love with him?"

She wouldn't cry. Even though his words were meant as an accusation, they effectively echoed everything going on within her right now. It didn't matter what boundaries they set or what Christophe was or wasn't capable of. Feelings were feelings, and she had a lot of them. But her lip wobbled just a little as she nodded. "Yes, that's exactly what I'm telling you." She lifted her hand and wiped away the one small tear that had escaped.

When she did, he noticed the ring, and his face fell. "You really are engaged."

She nodded.

"You accepted his ring."

"I did." She fiddled with the diamonds and rubies, nerves still jumping about.

"Dammit, Sophie."

Silence fell in the flat, a resentful, awkward silence that had her shifting on the chair. She would give anything to be back on Christophe's sofa right now, watching a movie with a throw blanket over her and a bowl of popcorn between them. But that wouldn't happen again. At least it was improbable. She focused instead on the baby, and the future she would provide for them, and how this moment was going to lay the groundwork for that.

It would be enough.

"You really won't marry me."

She shook her head. "I'm sorry. You deserve someone who loves you better than I can. Someone who can make you happy. That wouldn't be me, Eric. But we can work together to make sure our baby is loved. I meant what I said. I want you to be a part of their life, to be a father. Let go of this fantasy of the life you had laid out for us and try to picture a new one. We can make it work."

He turned back to the window again, his posture stiff. "You broke my heart, you know."

Her eyes stung. She knew it wasn't just words. "I'm sorry for that. Truly. I don't know what else to say."

"There isn't anything to say."

Her tea was cold now and she left it on the table; it had only been a prop anyway. "We can talk about arrangements another time," she suggested softly. "There's almost six months before the baby is born. We have time."

"I don't want to have to fight you for custody," he said, turning to face her once more.

"Me, either. I would like for us to come up with our own workable solution. But I'm also happy to get that in writing. I think it would make us feel better."

"When did we get to be strangers?" he asked, pain in his voice.

"I don't know," she answered, but she knew deep down they'd always been strangers of a sort. There'd always been a barrier between them; their relationship had been comfortable but merely adequate. Routine. But she'd hurt him enough. She would never say so and hurt him further.

"I should go," she said then, standing. "I do have a scan in a few weeks, and if you'd like to go, I can send you the appointment information."

"I'd like that," he answered stiffly.

It wasn't great, but it was a start. And Christophe had been right. Being engaged to him was a big signal that marriage was off the table. Now they could focus on their child's future. The plan had worked.

But there'd been a cost she hadn't anticipated. As she slipped on her coat and said goodbye, she felt pity for Eric, looking adrift and alone in the doorway of his flat. After all, she now knew exactly what it was like to love someone who could never love you back.

CHAPTER THIRTEEN

THE NEXT WEEK passed in a blur. Sophie hadn't been up
to talking to Christophe the first night, so she'd merely
sent a text and said she'd keep him updated, but she was
fine. The conversation with her parents had also been
tense. They were far more skeptical of her relationship
with Christophe, as if they sensed something wasn't quite
right. It wasn't until Sophie had tearfully brought up her
mother's illness that her mum came around. "The way
you and Dad came together, the strength and love you
showed even though we were all afraid we were going
to lose you…"

"Oh, darling."

"It's true. It's your fault for setting such a perfect example," she accused through a watery smile. "Mum, how
can I settle for anything less?"

Her mother had then shifted her focus from wanting
Sophie to marry Eric to fretting over how they'd manage
co-parenting. Then there were the professional questions
to which she had no answer. What were her plans where
Waltham was concerned? Where would they live? How
could they have a marriage based in two different coun-
tries? It had given her a whopping headache, and she'd
spent the entire Sunday on her sofa watching *Pride and
Prejudice*, eating ice cream, and feeling like she could re-

late to Lizzy very closely when it came to Mrs. Bennett's poor nerves.

Monday she was back at work but distracted. Every time she moved her hand, the ring glittered, reminding her not only of their bargain but of that night. The proposal, the kiss…making love. She missed most of Wednesday afternoon because of an obstetrician appointment. She texted Eric with the date and location of her sonogram. And Charlotte phoned, asking if she'd like to meet for tea the following week, as she was going to be nearby doing some early Christmas shopping.

By Friday, word of her engagement had leaked, and she started getting messages from acquaintances who'd seen the news on the internet.

She went home Friday night utterly exhausted. And she hadn't had the time or the energy to even work on any designs this week. By seven p.m., she'd turned off her phone and was debating either taking a soak in the tub or putting on some music and reading. Anything to relax.

When there was a knock on her door, she let out a massive sigh and tiptoed to the entry, where she could peek through the peephole and see who could possibly be on her doorstep. When she saw Christophe's face, her relief was so great she nearly wilted.

Instead, she opened the door. "I wasn't expecting you."

"I tried calling." He held up his phone. "Then I got worried." His normal teasing expression was uncharacteristically serious. "Is it okay that I'm here?"

"Yes. God, yes." And she surprised them both by bursting into tears.

"Whoa, hey. What's wrong?" He stepped inside and shut the door, then pulled her into his arms. "Whatever it is, it'll be okay."

"I'm so sorry," she said, her voice a half-wail. "I don't know why I'm crying. It was just such a week."

He chuckled and tucked her head under his chin. He was so strong and reassuring. She hadn't truly realized how much she missed his steadying presence until he was here again, holding her. That he wasn't really hers made the moment bittersweet, but she stayed where she was, needing the solace in the moment.

"You were so quiet all week I couldn't stop worrying, but I didn't want to blow up your phone. Today, though, I couldn't wait. When your phone kept going to voice mail, I knew something had to be up. It's not me, is it?"

For the first time, he sounded insecure, and she sniffed back her tears and looked up at him. "No, it's not you. Not really. I didn't mean to ghost you."

"We're supposed to be engaged," he reminded her.

"I know. I just didn't know what to say and so I turtled. It's been a lot. And now it's online…"

"Come on, let's get out of your doorway and you can tell me about it."

He hung up his coat and followed her into the living room. She'd left last night's mug and plate on the coffee table, and her favorite blanket was in a heap on the end of the sofa. Her purse was thrown in a corner, and she'd left her laundry in a basket on the hall floor. What on earth had come over her this past week? The mess was totally unlike her, and she rushed around, trying to pick up.

"Hey, stop. You don't need to tidy." He grabbed her hand and she looked up. His eyes were troubled.

She let out a long, slow breath. She really was wound rather tightly. "I wasn't prepared for this week, that's all. Talking to Eric, then my parents, and then work was crazy with me coming back after a week away and then resetting the storefront for the holidays. I had a doctor appointment, and the news came out and it's just...too much."

He led her to a chair, gently pushed her into it, then went behind her and started to rub her shoulders.

"Oh, God." His fingers were strong and sure and felt so good. "I really am wound up."

"Yes, you are. Your shoulders are a mass of knots. Do me a favor and drop your chin a little."

She obeyed; his fingers worked their magic, easing so much of the tension she was carrying in her upper back and neck. "I'm sorry I didn't answer your calls today," she murmured. They'd agreed they were in this together, but she'd kept him out of the loop most of the week. She knew why. Because after spending the night together everything had changed, and she hadn't wanted to deal with that. Because she'd realized she loved him. What she was realizing now, though, was that she needed him. She needed his friendship, and she'd just have to find a way to deal with her deepening feelings.

"We all get overwhelmed sometimes." His thumbs dug into her muscles and she began to unwind. A sigh escaped her lips.

"So what has you so tense? Is it work? Or is it Eric and your parents?" He hesitated. "Is it me?"

"All of the above?" she said, but gave a small laugh. "I think it's a bit of everything. I guess we never really prepared for what would happen, you know? What we would tell people. Eric was hard, but he took my words at face value, thank goodness. Ripping off the plaster was the right call. I think he's ready to accept that the two of us aren't going to happen. But my mum and dad...they were harder to fool. And they started pressuring me about the business, and I didn't have any answers."

He let go of her shoulders and came around the chair,

squatting in front of her and putting his hands on her knees. "Pressuring you how?"

"Like what this means for me taking over Waltham. Where we're going to live. Did we really think this through?" She lifted an eyebrow. "News flash—we thought we did, but we really didn't."

A grin crawled up his cheek. "No, I guess we didn't. What did you tell them?"

"That we hadn't decided any of those things yet, but that it would all fall into place."

"Nice."

"Except my mum knows me. She knows I always have everything planned, so she didn't really buy it."

The smile on his face grew. "She's right. You do always have a plan."

"Well, maybe this time I don't want to." She sounded so petulant that she couldn't help but laugh. "Oh, my. How much did I just sound like a four-year-old?"

"You had a hard week because nothing was in your control." He offered that wise bit of insight without the smile. She was glad, too, because it meant he wasn't teasing her about her need for control but accepting it as part of who she was. Because he understood her.

But he didn't love her.

Ugh.

"You're right. I hate it that you're right, but you are."

He patted her knee and stood. "I'll try harder to be wrong sometimes. But for now, you need to relax. How were you going to spend your evening?"

"I was debating between the tub and a book. Exciting, right?"

"Why don't you run a bath? Have you eaten yet? I haven't. I can order something in for us."

That sounded perfect. "I'm not fussy. You know the drill for me. No seafood or soft cheese but otherwise I'm good."

"Then we have a plan."

Because he understood how important it was for her to have a plan. To have some sort of control over the situation. She'd been sitting here twenty minutes ago in an emotional mess, and suddenly he appeared just when she needed him most. Like a true and valued friend.

As she went to the bathroom and started filling the tub, she wondered if that could ever really be enough.

Christophe did a quick search and ordered ramen to be delivered. He was starving; he'd eaten a dry sandwich on the train while working on his laptop. He'd also checked into a hotel, since he didn't want to presume to stay at her flat and he really didn't want to show up at her doorstep with an overnight bag.

The truth was, he didn't need to be in London this weekend. He was only here because he'd sensed something was wrong. They'd come up with this plan, and then he'd left her to execute it all on her own. In hindsight, he should have come with her a week ago. Sure, it was best she spoke to Eric alone, but he could have been here for moral support after, and with her family, too.

He'd been a coward when all was said and done. The night they'd spent together had scared him to death, so he'd let her face things by herself. And she'd become overwhelmed.

That wasn't being a good friend or showing support.

There was a strange chirping sound followed by a meow, and suddenly Harry was up on the sofa beside him, head-butting his arm. "Well hello, Harry," he said, adjusting his posture so he could pat the cat. "Look at you. You're so fluffy."

Another plaintive meow and Harry was on his lap. The cat kneaded his paws a few times and then, calm as you please, curled up in a ball and started purring. Christophe tried not to laugh. He'd never really been a cat person. Cedric had always kept a few dogs at the manor house, though there hadn't been any there for several years. But never any cats. It was beyond strange that Sophie's pet had taken to him so suddenly, but here he was, stroking Harry's head while the cat's purrs vibrated against his stomach.

"Oh, heavens. Harry, what are you doing?"

Christophe turned his head. Sophie was standing at the juncture of the hallway and living room, bundled up in a plush pink robe with her hair wet and her skin flushed from the hot water. She was so beautiful. So lovely. Christophe imagined he could undo that tie at her waist to reveal the soft skin beneath in about two seconds. The scent of her bath salts reached him, and he imagined what that skin would taste like. Lavender? Rose? His groin tightened, and he hoped to God the cat didn't decide to start kneading again.

"He made himself comfortable," Christophe answered, hoping his voice didn't sound as strangled as he felt. "Feel better?"

"Much."

"I ordered us some ramen. It should be here soon."

"That sounds absolutely perfect."

When she came back to the sofa, he noticed the ring on her finger. "I see you're still wearing it."

"Well, we are still engaged. At least to the world." Then she smiled as if sharing a secret. "And to be honest, I like it."

"I'm glad."

When the meal arrived, he moved Harry off his lap and went to the door, and once they'd eaten, he also tidied up the empty containers and put everything in the bin. He was just rinsing off his hands when Sophie came up beside him. "Thank you for that. There's not even any mess to clean up."

"It was my pleasure. Honestly, it's a breeze to make sure you're fed and pick up a few things. It's the other ways you need me that I'm unsure of."

"How do you mean?"

He didn't particularly want to have this conversation, but figured they had to. "We never really talked about what happened last weekend, other than agree it couldn't happen again. But it's not quite that simple, is it?"

She bit down on her lip and her gaze slid away. "No, I suppose it's not."

He put a finger beneath her chin and lifted it up. "It changes things when friends see each other naked."

Her lips twitched. "I shouldn't find that funny, but..."

"I know. The thing is, Sophie, we were really good at it. I don't think either of us expected what happened or the force of it, either. And on Saturday morning, your departure made it easy for us both to retreat."

She nodded. "It did. Part of why I didn't call you all week was because I didn't want to rely on you too much. And I thought you probably regretted what happened."

"Not in the way you think."

Now his pulse was hammering, from anxiety more than anything. He made it a practice not to be too vulnerable with people. He tried to be kind, charming, easygoing, so no one could find fault. So people would want him to be around. It was wearing sometimes, but he'd been doing it for so long now it was simply who he was. But Sophie... she pushed so many buttons. She made him open up when he'd rather remain a closed book. And God help him, there was a part of him that wanted to reach for that robe and have a repeat of last Friday just so he wouldn't have to talk about himself.

But something Cedric had said to him years ago had stuck in his brain. Cedric had sat him down to talk to him about girls, responsibility, and consent. "Grown up people have to have grown up conversations," he'd said. "And if you're old enough to take a woman to bed, you're a grown up. Be sure you act like one."

He certainly wasn't the fifteen-year-old youth he'd been during that lecture, but the lesson had stuck.

"What do you mean?"

"Let's sit. I think we need to talk."

He led her by the hand back to the living room and they sat next to each other. Her hair was nearly dry and curling around her shoulders, and her skin… He'd heard someone tell Charlotte once that pregnant women had a glow, and he realized how true that was. He lifted a hand and touched her cheek, a soft, tender touch that made his heart clench. She deserved so much better than him. Someday someone was going to come along who could give her all the things she wanted. The thought caused a pain in the center of his chest.

"I do not regret last weekend," he said softly. "It was amazing. You were…" He let the thought hang. "There's only one thing I regret, Soph. And it's why I asked you to promise we could stay friends. I can't offer you what you want. You want love and a family and I… I decided a long time ago that marriage wasn't going to be for me."

"I know that. You said from the beginning that you're not the marrying type."

"You talked about false hope. The last thing I want to do is give you the wrong idea."

"And what would the wrong idea be?" She leaned forward a little, looking up into his eyes.

"That I might change my mind and decide I'm the marrying kind."

Her gaze clung to his, and she nodded slightly, a tiny movement of her head that acknowledged his words. "Christophe, tonight you understood my need for control. That's because you know who I am. I like to think I know who you are, too. I know you're not interested in marriage. And the last thing I'd ever do is try to convince you to change your mind."

Of course not. Because she didn't love him, either. Which was fine. It was exactly what he expected and wanted. It was better to know than to hold on to a little bit of hope that someone might care enough to fight for him. To come back for him.

There were no disappointments that way.

She cupped his face in her hand. "One of the best things about our friendship is that we understand and accept each other just as we are. I never want that to change."

"Me, either."

"I'm sorry I shut you out this week. You were right. I was hiding."

"I was, too, so let's not worry about it. Instead, why don't you tell me how I can support you this weekend?"

"You're staying?"

He grinned. "Have laptop, will travel. If I need to do something, I can. But otherwise, I was going to be spending the weekend at my flat." He shrugged. "I don't even have a Harry to keep me company."

As he heard his name, the cat came around the corner and gave a sad meow.

"It's his bedtime," she said, laughing a bit. "He's very particular about things like that. So now he's telling me it's time to go to bed so he can get up on the covers, too."

Lucky cat.

"And you're tired. I should go."

"You could stay," she suggested. "On...on the sofa."

She couldn't know how difficult that would be. Knowing she was so close, knowing how she looked in sleep, wanting to pull her close against his body. Part of what had shaken him so much last weekend was that he couldn't remember the last time he'd slept as well as he had holding her in his arms.

"We'll see."

The cat meowed again, this time a bit more insistently, and even Christophe laughed. "It really is bedtime."

"I kind of want to chat a bit more, though." She paused, and then said, "If I promise nothing will happen, you could lie on the bed and we could talk for a while."

She really, really didn't know.

"You don't think Harry will be put out that I'm taking up some of his space?"

"I don't know. He's never had to before."

Christophe considered. It was playing with fire, going into her room, lying on her bed, whispering in the dark. But if he could do that, maybe he could actually make it through the next time, and the time after that, and eventually he wouldn't want her so much.

"Come on, then. I'll tuck you in."

He waited while she brushed her teeth and changed into pajamas, and then after she'd crawled into bed, he lay on the top. With another chirp Harry jumped up, stared at Christophe for a solid minute, and then settled down by Sophie's feet on a folded-up blanket. "His bed," she whispered. "Or His Lordship's throne. However you look at it."

"He's a good companion."

"The best."

Their voices were low. Christophe rested his head on an elbow while she rolled to her side and cushioned her head on her hands. "So," he said, trying to keep the mood light, "what should we talk about?"

It wasn't as difficult as he might have imagined. She told him about her visit to Eric, and about her parents' pointed questions, and how she'd felt seeing her name paired with his online. "We kind of expected that to happen eventually," he said. "Don't worry about it. I'm not Stephen or Bella or even Will. I'm the nobody in the family. Trust me, we'll get a mention online and probably on page ten of some gossip rag and that'll be it."

"Don't say you're nobody. You are. You are Christophe Germain. You heard Aurora last weekend. She called you her son. She loves you like her own. You are smart and successful and run an entire division of a multinational billion-dollar company. Don't ever let me hear you say you're nobody again."

His heart swelled. No one ever came to his defense like that. "My head knows that. But it's different. Different when other people call you stupid and in the way. Then you feel like you don't matter. It sticks with you, even when logically you know it shouldn't."

"You matter to me," she whispered, and he thought again that she would be easy to love...if he let himself.

"Thank you for that," he replied.

"Your mum said that to you, didn't she?"

That and so much more, but Sophie didn't need to know all about that. "Mum was single and trying to provide for us both...and incredibly unhappy." That was something else he could rationalize, but it still didn't take away the sting of hearing that she'd wished he'd never been born. "That's why I want to help you, Soph. I know you're going to be a wonderful mother. But it's hard on your own."

"I would never say those things to my child. Or even think them."

His eyes stung, and he hoped she couldn't tell her words had made him well up. "I know that. You're stronger than she was. When Tante Aurora came and offered to take me away, I think I had my backpack ready before she'd finished her sentence."

But it had still been difficult. He'd left because he'd known he wasn't wanted. He'd heard his mother and aunt arguing, too. "My mother was drinking too much," he murmured, and Sophie reached out and took his hand in the dark. "Aurora got angry with her and said if she put her mind to it she could make something of herself. And my mother yelled back that she wasn't going to whore herself like Aurora had."

"Oh, Christophe."

"My aunt and uncle had a deep, strong love. My mother was wrong about them. She's stayed bitter and resentful."

"How long has it been since you saw her?"

"Five years."

Five years, and she lived barely an hour away from him if she was still in Orléans. Sophie's hand felt good on his, and she rubbed her thumb over his knuckles in a soothing gesture.

He cleared his throat. "Anyway, I made sure I put my mind to it. I figured if my own mother could send me away without a thought, why would Aurora and her husband keep me? So I studied hard and did what I was told and learned that being charming got me a long way."

"Aurora would never send you back."

"I know that now. Nine-year-old me did not."

"That's fair."

"Anyway, that's a lot about me. How did we get on this topic, anyway?"

"You said you were a nobody, and I disagreed."

He smiled. "My champion." He twined his fingers with

hers now and changed the subject. "So, back to what we were talking about before. What can I do this weekend to be supportive?"

"I don't have much planned. I have tea tomorrow afternoon with your sister, actually. She invited me earlier this week."

"Lots of baby talk. Count me out."

She giggled and he smiled in response to the sound, so much nicer than her tears when she'd first opened the door.

"I was going to do some Christmas shopping. That probably bores you."

"Not at all. I can carry your bags."

"You're ridiculous."

"Probably." They were bantering again, and it was far more comfortable than revealing details of his past, which he hadn't intended to do but somehow had been persuaded by her gentle questions. "How about we take your parents for brunch on Sunday? My treat. Give me a chance to win them over."

"You don't think they'll see through it? I mean, us?"

He thought for a moment, but remembered the past weekend. "We completely fooled my family, didn't we?"

She nodded. "Yes, we did. Somehow."

"Because we're friends. Because we do actually care about each other, even if we aren't in love."

She was quiet for a moment, a moment during which he wondered if that was actually the truth or if he was lying to himself. And wondered if it even mattered, since the end result was going to be the same.

"We do care about each other," she whispered. "Okay. I'll message them in the morning."

"Feel better now?" he asked, noticing her eyelids were starting to droop.

"Yeah," she answered, and she blinked. It took a long time for her lashes to come back up again.

He should get up right now, put on his coat and go back to the hotel. He'd just wait until she was asleep and then he'd sneak away.

Just as soon as she was asleep.

CHAPTER FOURTEEN

WHEN SOPHIE OPENED her eyes, she found herself staring at Christophe's face.

There was a hint of stubble on his jaw and chin, and his hair was pressed to one side, the curls sticking up. He was still in his jeans and shirt, and Harry, the traitor, was curled up right against Christophe's chest, his ears just below Christophe's collar.

He'd fallen asleep on her bed, and he was cuddling her cat.

She held in the sigh that was building in her chest. Seeing Christophe on her doorstep had been the answer to a prayer she'd never made. All the stress and anxiety of the week melted away when he put his arms around her. She'd relaxed, and then she'd felt a new energy. He made her come alive. And she'd wanted him, so much. It was only the fear of messing things up even more that had kept her from touching him. Instead, she'd run a warm bath, put in scented salts, and touched herself.

It had relieved some tension, but not for long. Eating ramen, talking, listening about his childhood...just when she thought she could maybe not love him, he had to make himself vulnerable and trusting like that. Burying her feelings had to be her only option, because right now he was her lifeline. The one person who knew everything, who kept her secrets, who supported while asking nothing in return.

He would never accept her love or return it. So she'd just have to hold on to it for safekeeping until she didn't need it anymore.

His lashes flickered and she put a smile on her lips as he woke. "Good morning, sleepyhead," she murmured.

He shifted, then seemed to realize he was curled around the cat. "Harry. Thanks for keeping me warm, buddy."

"If you were cold you should have..." She let the thought trail off as she searched for a different phrase. "Should have got a blanket."

"Naw. But I do need a shower and a change of clothes. Everything's back at the hotel."

"Right."

"You can come with me. We can do that shopping you wanted before your tea this afternoon. What time are you meeting?"

"At three, at Fortnum & Mason."

"Brilliant. There's a bookshop nearby, and I can hide there while you talk about baby things. How do you feel about walking?"

"I suppose it's fine if it's not raining."

"Let's spend a day like tourists." His smile widened. "If you were new to London, where would you go?"

She scowled. "I am not going to Harrods."

He laughed. "Point taken. Selfridges? It's an easy walk to Fortnum's from there, and it has everything."

He really was ridiculous, but it was one of the things she really liked about him. "Hmm, shall we take one of those bus tours around the city, as well?"

He tapped his lip. "We could. It's hop on hop off, and would save you walking."

She swatted at his arm, which sent Harry scurrying. "Stop it. I'll say yes to Selfridges but no to guided tours."

He sighed. "Fine."

Harry let out a pitiful howl.

"Breakfast time?" Christophe asked.

"Indeed." She stretched and crawled out of bed. "Give me thirty minutes to get cute. You can make tea if you like."

He scowled and she picked up a pillow and threw it at him. "Decaf tea or nothing," she said. And then she left the bedroom to feed Harry.

She took the full thirty minutes to get dressed and style her hair, which was floofy on one side from sleeping on it while it was still damp. If they were walking, she'd need to wear comfortable footwear, so the suede boots came out again. She tried a pair of skinny jeans with them and after three minutes gave up trying to fasten them. But before she grabbed a pair of leggings she stopped in front of the mirror and placed her hands on her growing belly.

"Hello, in there," she whispered, and a smile bloomed on her face. It was the first time she'd actually talked to the little one growing inside her, and her heart expanded. "I'm going to be your mum. And look at you. You're right here." She looked at the just-noticeable bump. "We're going to be fine, us two," she promised.

"Did you say something?" Christophe's voice came through the door, and she scurried away from the mirror.

"Just talking to myself!" she called back, feeling slightly foolish but with a new sentimentality where her baby was concerned. Somehow things had changed. The baby had gone from being a concept to something suddenly very tangible and real.

The lovely feeling carried through the morning. After

her decaf tea, they walked back to Christophe's hotel where she took the time to message her parents about brunch and they set a time and location. When he returned to the lobby in pressed clothes and a fresh shave, she had to stop herself from staring. He was so…everything. *It's enough he's on your side*, she reminded herself. It was hard, though. Even her very discriminating cat loved him! And Harry hardly ever liked anyone.

She liked, too, that he didn't put on airs or flash his money around. His first demand of the morning was to find coffee, so they sat in a café while he drank his dark roast and she ordered orange juice. They got bacon butties and ate them on a bench in the sunshine, folding the waxed paper around the bread to avoid any sauce drips. After that they headed to Oxford Street.

"I'd like to get something for Charlotte and the baby," Sophie said, squinting up at him. The day was uncharacteristically bright, and Sophie noticed that many of the holiday decorations were out now, brightening the shops. It put her in a holiday mood for the first time. "Can we go to the baby section?"

"Of course we can. The day is yours. I'm just here to carry your bags, remember?"

She wiggled her eyebrows. "You might regret saying that. When I'm in the mood to shop, it can be dangerous."

He replied with an eyebrow quirk of his own. "I'm part of Aurora and have two cousins who are champs at it. I have experience. Bring it on."

The warning was timely, as she found an adorable set of soft shoes and then a package of bamboo swaddles and a stuffed rabbit that was the softest thing she'd ever touched. At the bookstore she added a copy of *Jemima Puddleduck* to the gift, as well as a new paperback for herself and a travel book for Iceland, which was her parents' next trip, planned for the summer, and would be part of their Christmas gift. Noise-canceling headphones were purchased for her brother and went into another bag.

"You weren't kidding." Christophe looped the handles of the yellow bag on his fingers. "Who else is on your list?"

"Well, you, I suppose."

"You don't have to get me anything."

He said it so sharply her feet stopped moving and she stared at him. "I…what?"

"I just mean, I know we're keeping up appearances. But it's not necessary."

His refusal hurt her feelings, and she wasn't sure why. Maybe it had something to do with the fact that he seemed perfectly fine doing stuff for her but was hesitant to let her reciprocate. "Maybe I want to get you something."

"Well, I can hardly stop you." He smiled a little, as if making up for his previous sharpness. Maybe he wasn't that into Christmas. Either way, she wasn't going to press the issue and mar the day they had together.

Holiday music played in the background as they entered the Christmas area, chock-full of decorations and trees and everything one could possibly need to celebrate the day. Getting even more into the spirit, Sophie oohed and ahhed over beautiful table linens and chose a deep red damask tablecloth with a pattern of holly and berries, white napkins, and a set of napkin rings in silver with green holly leaves and red berries in crystal. "I've always wanted something this pretty," she said, holding the items close. "So I can set a real holiday table."

Christophe was even getting in the spirit a little, looking at Christmas ornaments. "Look at these," he said, and lifted up a small box. "They're pretty."

Indeed they were. Iridescent baubles were cradled inside, soft and pearly, and Sophie had a sudden urge to put up her Christmas tree. She usually didn't until the week before Christmas, but it was December already, and why not? "Let's get them," she said, adding them to her stack of holiday kitsch. They explored the section some more, and when they came upon a Paddington Bear ornament, Sophie stopped and got all broody again.

"You should get an ornament for the baby," Christophe suggested. He picked up the ornament and dangled it from his finger. "Look, he's in his little blue coat and red hat."

It was adorable. Sophie looked up at him. "I haven't done any shopping for the baby yet. It's been so surreal and confusing that I haven't thought about a nursery or anything." She realized she was in a one-bedroom flat. That wouldn't do, would it? For someone who always had a plan, she'd dropped the ball on this.

"So you start with a single ornament and go from there." His smile was understanding. "No wonder you're exhausted, Soph. This has got to have thrown you off so much. But you only have to figure out one thing at a time."

Which was true. But it didn't help that her feelings were all over the place. His support helped ground her, but realizing the depth of her feelings? Took all that progress and tossed it out the window.

"You're right. Starting with this Paddington bauble." She looked at her watch. "Are you ready for tea? We should probably head there soon."

"I'm ready if you are."

She paid for her purchases and just as he'd promised, Christophe carried the bags as they made the journey to Fortnum's. Charlotte was already there, and he kissed her cheek in greeting before putting down the bags. She held baby Imogene, and as Sophie took off her jacket, Charlotte pressed the baby into Christophe's arms.

When Sophie turned around, her heart exploded. Men

with babies was one thing, but Christophe holding a baby, while she was carrying her own precious little one, did something to her that she couldn't ignore. Imogene stared up at him with wide eyes and he looked so natural holding her there. Sophie imagined him holding her baby and felt a longing so sharp and deep it made her catch her breath. Why, why couldn't he see that they could be right for each other?

If she even suggested such a thing, he'd be gone in a flash. Christophe handed the baby back to Charlotte. "I'll be back in an hour or so," he murmured. "Enjoy yourself."

"I will," she replied, her insides fluttering as he pressed a kiss to her cheek.

Charlotte looked over at Sophie with a satisfied smile. "I never thought I'd see Christophe lose his mind over a woman, but here we are. I'm really happy for you two, Sophie."

Sophie didn't correct her, but the kindly meant words were another knife to her heart. Because maybe Christophe had lost his mind, but he'd never give her his heart.

Christophe spent the better part of an hour at a bookshop, and then returned to pick up Sophie from her tea with Charlotte. He was thankful he hadn't been expected to stay. Of course he hadn't been able to say no to Charlotte when she'd put Imogene into his arms, and to be honest, it hadn't been that bad. Imogene was a cute little thing, and she'd just stared at him with something that looked like wonder. No crying, no messy diapers…but he'd also been relieved to hand her back. Babies terrified him. Not only because he had no idea what to do with them, but because fatherhood scared the hell out of him. It didn't help that Sophie was too adorable today. For the first time, he'd heard her speak not of the pregnancy but actually of the

baby. Her face when he'd held up the Paddington ornament had been beautiful. If he wasn't careful, he'd end up
caring for her too much.

Sophie and Charlotte were still inside, the remnants of
a pot of tea, sandwiches, and cakes littering the table. "It
looks like you had a marvelous time."

"We did." Sophie held Imogene now, and she was glowing. Did she realize how great a mother she was going to
be? His stomach clenched at the thought, and he turned
his attention to the plate of sandwiches. "Is that Corona-
tion Chicken?" He plucked it from the plate and popped it
in his mouth. "Yum."

"I really should get back," Charlotte said wistfully.
"This has been lovely. I needed to get out. But she's been
so good she's bound to be cranky soon."

"She's an angel," Sophie said, tucking the blanket
around Imogene. "I almost don't want to give her up."

"Do you want to borrow her for the evening?"

Sophie laughed. "Maybe not tonight, but… I wouldn't
mind babysitting sometime. It would give me some practice."

"Be careful what you agree to. I'm liable to take you
up on it."

"Please do," Sophie said. "And thank you for tea, Charlotte. It really was lovely."

"You're family now," Charlotte said simply.

The whole exchange made Christophe vastly uncomfortable. His family was accepting their engagement so
easily. What were they going to say when they called if
off? They all loved Sophie. They would blame Christophe
for sure.

Charlotte packed up all of her baby things—there was
a lot, he noticed—and left. "I suppose we should get back,

too," Sophie said. "With all the bags, would you mind if we got a cab instead of walking all the way back?"

"That's a great idea. I'll go hail one while you get ready."

It took a few minutes and when she joined him on the pavement, her face was far more relaxed than it had been last night. "Today was good for you," he observed.

"It was. And do you know, I wasn't even tempted to go into work, even though we were so close."

"Hmm. Are you perhaps achieving…balance?"

"I'd better learn at some point." She touched her stomach. "Or this little one is going to make me learn."

He lifted his own bag with his bookstore purchases. "Actually, I got you something while you were at tea."

"You did?"

He nodded. A black cab pulled up and he opened the door. "Climb in and I'll give it to you."

They got inside and he gave the address, then handed her the bag.

"Christophe, what did you do?"

He smiled at her, loving what a simple gift did to her face. "You said you hadn't done any planning, so I thought you could use some ideas." Inside the bag were three baby magazines, all with features on creating the perfect nursery. He'd got her a book, too, something about chicken soup and expectant mothers, that the lady at the shop had suggested. Sophie held it in her hands and then looked up at him, her eyes shining.

He didn't deserve the way she looked at him. And he wished he could look at her with the same unreserved affection. But it wasn't who he was. She said he was lovable, but he knew differently. And it wasn't just that. It was that he didn't know how to love in return, as if there were a switch somewhere but it had never been wired in.

"They're okay?"

"They're perfect. And so thoughtful. Thank you, Christophe."

"It was my pleasure."

They were almost to her flat when she said, "Stay for dinner? I'll actually cook tonight."

He shouldn't. He should go back to the hotel, work a bit, meet her tomorrow for the brunch thing. Instead, he found himself replying, "That sounds great."

He didn't know how to say no to her. And yet he was going to have to learn, because the longer they carried on like this, the more potential there was that he'd hurt her. That was the last thing in the world he wanted to do.

CHAPTER FIFTEEN

SOPHIE SET THE TABLE with her new linens, still slightly wrinkled from the packaging but she didn't care. Her white dishes looked lovely against the rich color of the tablecloth, and the napkin rings were a festive touch. She'd put a small beef roast in the oven and surrounded it with little potatoes, carrots, and parsnips. A hint of bay leaf and rosemary scented the air, and the day with its Christmas atmosphere put Sophie in a holiday mood. As the meal cooked, she disappeared into a closet and came out with a long box.

"What is that?" Christophe asked.

"My Christmas tree," she said proudly. "Today really got me in the spirit. Will you help me put it up?"

He stared at her. "You want me…to put up a Christmas tree."

She nodded. "I know it's not as nice as a real one, but it's the perfect size for my flat." She tapped the box. "It's actually flat on one side, so it takes up less space."

He got up from the sofa and went to her. "That," he said, "is a travesty. It's bad enough that you don't have a real tree."

"Um…" She waved her hand around the space. "It's not like I have a lot of room. Not compared to Chatsworth Manor."

He pointed a finger at her. "There you will definitely

see a real tree. I think the one last year was around twelve feet."

"Twelve!"

He laughed. "All right. I'll help you set up your little tree. It shouldn't take long."

She moved a few items of furniture around to make room, and then while he was taking it out of the box, she found a Christmas mix on her phone and ran it through a wireless speaker. Christophe lifted his eyebrows as Bing Crosby came on, but said nothing, which made her smile. Maybe he was acting Grinchy, but she got the feeling he was secretly enjoying himself.

By the time the tree was up and she'd fluffed out the branches, the timer on the oven dinged and it was time to eat. "We can decorate after dinner," she said, arranging the vegetables on a platter and letting the meat rest before carving it. "You must be starving. I had tea, but all you had was a tiny sandwich."

"I could eat," he said, and they sat down at her festive table.

This was something new for her, she realized. Last year, she'd put up her tree alone, and she hadn't really done any other decorating. Eric had never been one for carols, either, so cozy meals for two with Nat King Cole in the background simply never happened. Christophe spent most of the meal telling her about the holidays in the Pemberton family, and she sat back and enjoyed the stories of when they were kids and how different Christmas was now.

"And a new generation will make things different again," she mused, putting down her fork. The beef was tender and vegetables flavorful, but she was stuffed. "Charlotte's baby, and I'm guessing there'll be more to follow. Aurora is going to love that."

"Nan Aurora. Has a special ring to it, doesn't it?"

"She's more of a *grand-mère*, I think," Sophie said, smiling.

"You might be right."

But neither of them mentioned that Sophie's child wouldn't be part of that circle. She certainly wasn't going to bring it up and mar the lovely vibe of the evening.

Christophe helped with the cleanup and then they plugged in the tree, the white lights gleaming in the darkened room. "What's next?" he asked.

"Ribbon," she said. She went back into the storage closet and took out a box of decorations. When she held up the first roll of wired mesh ribbon, Christophe put his hands up.

"I think that's going to be your job. I have no idea what to do with that."

She laughed. "Then just hold the end so it doesn't roll everywhere. If Harry gets his claws into it, we'll never get it back."

He held the end while she wound the strands around, anchoring each loop with a twist of the wire around a branch. The gold mesh reflected the glimmer of the white lights, casting a romantic glow in the room.

"How do you do that?" he asked.

"You like it?"

"It looks lovely."

"Good. Because that box over there has the rest of my decorations. It's your turn to help."

Together they put the baubles on until each empty space was filled with something sparkly and shiny.

Sophie looked over at Christophe and her heart swelled. The lights gave off a glow that highlighted his face, and the soft smile on his lips made her feel so secure and happy. They could be happy, couldn't they? If she could just show him that he was lovable...that he was deserving of love and happiness. It seemed impossible that he didn't already know so, but he'd also had a very different childhood from hers. She tried to think of how she'd feel if she were rejected by her own parents, the two people in the world who were supposed to love her no matter what. She understood that such a thing would leave an indelible mark.

But even indelible marks could heal. Scars would remain, but only as reminders of bad times. The bad times themselves didn't last forever.

The song on her playlist changed to one she hadn't heard in a very long time, and as Tony Bennett's crooning voice started to sing about what he wanted for Christmas, Christophe turned his head, discovering she was looking at him and not the tree. Something hummed between them, something good, and she held out her hand. "Dance?" she said simply, but her heart seemed to freeze for a moment as she waited for his answer.

He took her hand and they moved toward each other until she was in his embrace, his feet moving in small steps in her tiny living room as they swayed to the music. To say anything would break the spell, so Sophie kept all of her words inside and let her body tell the story as she shifted slightly closer and rested her head in the hollow of his shoulder. His chest rose and fell as he let out a breath, and then he turned his head slightly so that his chin grazed her head, a subtle acceptance of their closeness. This moment was beautiful in its perfection and in its imperfection. Their relationship was complicated. Their engagement was a lie. But these feelings were undeniably real, and she didn't want to hide them anymore.

She shifted her head, just a little, nudging his chin with her temple, lifting her face a tiny bit closer to his as butterflies winged their way through her stomach. Their breaths mingled as their faces drew closer, tempting, hesitant, wanting. When she couldn't wait any longer, she rose up on tiptoe and brushed her lips along the corner of his mouth.

He turned his head the last bit and met her kiss, softly, sweetly, sending a line of joy straight to her heart.

The song ended but still they remained, kissing in the middle of her living room. He lifted his hands and cupped her face like a precious chalice, sipping from her lips and making her throb with need. She slid her hands over the hard wall of his chest, wanting to feel the warm skin beneath her fingertips, but needing him to take the lead. He needed to come to her willingly, completely.

"Soph," he murmured, but she put her finger over his lips as her gaze met his. There was fire there, the same flame that had burned for her back at the château. Desire. Passion. If that was what he needed, then she would give it to him. She would give him that and so much more.

But he shook his head, nudging her finger away. "We said one time." His voice was rough, and it slid over her nerve endings. Did he have any clue at all how sexy he was when he left his carefree self behind and let his intense side take over?

"Once didn't cure me of wanting you," she answered. "Once wasn't enough."

His stormy eyes searched hers, and then he reached for the buttons on his shirt. A thrill zipped up her spine as she pulled off her sweater. She reached behind her for the clasp of her bra, and when it let go, she realized how much fuller her breasts had gotten over the past month. With a low growl of acquiescence, Christophe came forward and cupped one in his hand as he kissed her again and again and again.

I love you. She tried to show him the words as she knew he'd reject them if she said them out loud. Instead, she put all of her attention into worshipping his body with hers. They made love there, on her living room floor, their skin golden by the light of the fire and the tree, and Sophie hid the tear that slid out of the corner of her eye at the sheer wonder and beauty of it.

Tomorrow she would tell him. But for tonight, she'd do everything to show him that friendship would never be enough. She'd show him that he was everything.

Christophe straightened his tie and tried to get his head on straight. Sophie was sitting on the end of the bed in his hotel room, looking beautiful and remarkably calm. Considering her parents had been skeptical of the whole engagement, he thought she'd be more nervous.

But the exertions of the night before might have served to relax her. And there had been exertions. Unlike last weekend at the château, once truly hadn't been enough. She was looking rather well-rested, considering they hadn't had much sleep.

He was in this far too deep, but it wasn't the time to go into it. He had another two hours of pretense to keep up before he could let down his guard. It didn't help that she was watching him tie his tie.

"Okay?" he asked, dropping his hands and letting her inspect it.

"Perfect." She placed her hands flat against his chest. "You look dashing, as always. Even your curls are on their best behavior today."

Which was miraculous, as he'd showered at her place… with her in the shower with him. If it were anyone else, he'd chalk it up to a pretty damned good weekend. But this was Sophie. He couldn't be flippant about it.

He checked his watch. "We should be going. Our reservation is at eleven."

He'd picked Aurora's favorite spot for brunch, thinking it might also appeal to Sophie's parents. He'd never done a "meet the parents" event before, and this was even more pressure as there was a fake engagement to uphold. And yet pretending wasn't the most difficult thing. The hardest thing was reminding himself that it was all a ruse. Especially after last night.

It was glorious and terrifying, how consumed he was with her.

Mr. and Mrs. Waltham were already there when they arrived at exactly five minutes before the hour. "My parents are sticklers for punctuality," Sophie whispered, as they were guided to the table. "Five minutes early means we're off to a good start."

Great.

Mr. Waltham stood as they approached. "Hello, blossom," he said, a warm smile on his face. "Christophe. It's good to see you again."

"And you, sir," Christophe replied, shaking his hand. He smiled at Sophie's mother. "Mrs. Waltham, you're looking lovely today."

"Yes, well," she answered, and it set Christophe back on his heels a bit. Sophie was frowning, too. It seemed he had his work cut out for himself.

So he held Sophie's chair for her and then took his seat, reaching under the table to take her hand for reassurance.

Sophie took up the challenge, and after greeting her parents ordered champagne. "Champagne for three, please, and may I have something nonalcoholic? I'll leave it to you to come up with something special."

"I have just the thing," the server assured her. "I'll be back with your drinks momentarily and take your orders."

"Wow," Christophe remarked. "You're leaving your drink to chance. This is big progress."

She smiled up at him. "I try," she said. "I'm learning that sometimes unexpected things happen and they can be really great. I'm trying to go with the flow more."

Mr. Waltham coughed and covered his mouth to hide a laugh. Even Mrs. Waltham's tight lips had relaxed a little at Sophie's pronouncement.

"Sophie, you have never been a go with the flow person," Mrs. Waltham remarked. "But I can't deny, it looks good on you. You're feeling better, aren't you?"

A delightful blush tinted her cheeks. "Um…yes. I suppose I have been feeling rather well lately."

Her foot touched his under the table.

She was playing footsies with him. Unbelievable.

Their drinks arrived and once they'd ordered, Mr. Waltham offered a toast. "To Sophie and Christophe. And to unexpected blessings. Congratulations, you two."

It was spectacularly generous, considering that until just over a week ago her parents had wanted her to marry Eric. But they loved her. Approval or not, she would always have their support.

"Thank you," Christophe said, and they all touched rims before drinking. Sophie's glass held a pinky-red liquid with some sort of bubbles in it. "Good?" he asked.

She nodded. "I think it's the raspberry and pear juice, with something it in for sparkle. It's just right."

"Have you set a date yet?" This was from Mrs. Waltham, and Christophe let Sophie field the question.

"Not yet, Mum. We're not in a big rush."

"But with the baby coming…"

"I was thinking we'd wait until after he or she is born." Sophie took another sip of her drink. "My clothes are already starting to not fit. Trying to fit a dress and constantly needing alterations would be a nightmare."

There was a silent beat of disapproval.

"Mum," Sophie said, "we've only been engaged a week. There are a lot of things to sort out. We have time, though. Let's just enjoy brunch and celebrate. It's a chance for you to get to know Christophe a little better. Besides, wedding plans would just bore the two of them," she said with a nod toward Christophe and her father.

That drew a reluctant smile from her mother. "You're right, Sophie. I just want to see you settled and happy."

Sophie laughed. "You mean you want to know I have my ducks in a row. I did inherit my organizational skills from you, you know."

Despite herself, Mrs. Waltham laughed. "Fair, darling. Fair." Her attention turned to Christophe. "My daughter does like to have things just so."

"Don't I know it. It's one of her most endearing qualities."

Mrs. Waltham flapped at hand at him as if to say "go on," and Sophie nudged his arm. Charm points: one.

Their starters arrived then: Porthilly oysters and caviar, and fruit with lemon verbena for Sophie. Christophe watched her carefully, and she turned her nose a little at the oysters but gave him a small smile. "It's a lot better," she whispered, leaning close to his shoulder.

After the oysters came a full English breakfast complete with black pudding for Mr. Waltham, eggs Benedict for both Mrs. Waltham and Christophe, and French toast with blueberry compote for Sophie. "No eggs, darling?" Mrs. Waltham asked. She looked at Christophe. "Sophie loves eggs Benny."

"I believe soft yolks are a firm no at the moment," Christophe stated, picking up his knife and fork. "But that looks delicious, Soph."

"Christophe has taken very good care of me," Sophie said, looking at him adoringly. "He always makes sure I eat and take downtime. We had a lovely day yesterday. We did some holiday shopping and then I had tea with Charlotte, his cousin."

"Ah yes. She just had a baby, didn't she?"

"Indeed," Christophe said. "And she is just as beautiful as her mother."

"I got to hold her yesterday, Mum. She's the sweetest thing."

The conversation seemed to loosen after that, and by the time brunch was done, Christophe felt he'd done his duty playing the doting fiancé. There was a bit of unease since the fiancé bit wasn't true, but he'd been honest in everything else. He did care for her, so very much. He wanted her to be happy. It just couldn't be with him. And yet the thought of her sharing that sweet smile with anyone else…of sharing her body and passion with someone else…it tore at his insides.

"Will you be around for Christmas, Christophe?" They were getting up from the table and getting ready to depart when Mrs. Waltham asked the question.

"The family has invited Sophie to join us at the manor house for Christmas. I'm happy to extend the invitation to you both, if you'd like to join us." He knew Aurora wouldn't mind two more, and the house was more than big enough.

"Oh, my… Christmas at Chatsworth Manor. We'll definitely consider it, won't we Sam?"

They parted ways outside the restaurant, and Christophe looked down at Sophie. "I think that went well, don't you?"

"You totally got my mum with the invitation to the manor. She's not above being seduced by spending Christmas with the Earl of Chatsworth and family at the country estate."

He rolled his eyes. "That doesn't impress you, though."

"As long as you're there." The words were said lightly, but there was something about them that sent alarms ringing. He lifted his arm, hailing a taxi.

"When do you have to go back to Paris?" she asked.

"This afternoon. I have meetings with Phillipe in the morning."

"Could we talk before you go?"

"I can drop you at home first. Anything important?" She didn't meet his eyes, which sent another ripple of unease through him.

"A little."

A cab pulled up, and they said nothing else as they climbed in. But Christophe felt the walls closing in around him. Last night had been too good. This morning too easy. Whatever was coming wasn't going to be as pleasant. It occurred to him that during the entire weekend she hadn't mentioned Eric, either. But if she'd already achieved her objective, why would she have made a point of perpetuating the lie of their engagement?

CHAPTER SIXTEEN

SOPHIE FELT AS IF her heart was sitting at the base of her throat. She was so nervous about the conversation to come but determined to see it through. Today had shown her all she needed to know; Christophe was perfect for her. She loved him, and if he could trust her with that, they could have a future together.

The cab dropped them off at her flat, and they were both unusually quiet as she unlocked the door and led the way inside. There was no sense procrastinating by offering him a drink or something to eat; they'd just had brunch. She took off her coat and draped it over a chair, then twisted her hands in front of her. She had never had such difficulty saying three simple words before, and it occurred to her that it was because never before had they been this true. There was also the chance that he would hand them back to her, and the thought of him turning away was crushing.

"Are you all right? Is it something about the brunch?" He came up behind her and put his hand on her shoulder.

She placed her hand over the top of his and gathered strength. "No, it's not about the brunch. You were perfect." She took a deep breath, corralling all of her courage as she turned to face him. "You *are* perfect, Christophe."

His face changed. Oh, he still looked pleasant enough, but she knew him well enough now to know when he was erecting walls. "Don't do that," she whispered. "Don't shut me out."

"Sophie…"

"No. I need to say some things and you really need to hear them. You need to believe them."

He shook his head and stood back, and she realized that he suddenly looked very much like a scared boy.

Love scared him. It scared the crap out of him. And maybe she should wait, but what would be the right time? Just like she'd needed to rip off the bandage with Eric, she felt like she needed to put one on Christophe so he could start to heal. "Don't be afraid of it," she said softly. "This thing between us…last night…we both know it's not always like that. I was there. I know you felt it, too. It's not just chemistry, Christophe. It's love."

"We're friends, Sophie." He said it firmly, as if reminding himself as much as her.

"That's what makes it so much better, don't you think? That we trust each other? That we take care of each other? I know this scares you, Christophe, but I can't pretend not to feel something when I do. I love you. I know because this is so different from anything I've ever felt for anyone before." Her voice shook, but she forced herself to keep on. "A few years ago, my mum had leukemia. We weren't sure she was going to make it. But my dad…the way he loved her, the way he could still make her smile, the way they loved each other through all of that…it showed me what real love looks like. And Friday night when I opened the door and saw you there, I knew. You were here when I needed you, even though I didn't even call."

He turned away, his posture stiff, rejecting her words. Her heart took the hit, but she wasn't ready to give up. "I know you feel you're unlovable, but nothing could be further from the truth. Your parents abandoned you. How could you not feel that way? And you said that you always felt as if your aunt's and uncle's affections were contingent on good grades and hard work, but you know that's not true now. They would have loved you anyway. Aurora does love you. She thinks of you as a son."

"You don't understand." He turned back to her, his jaw tight, his eyes dark with hurt and strain. "Until you've had someone say out loud that they wish you'd never been born, you don't understand. Don't you think I know I was deserving of love? That's not what scares me, Sophie."

"Then tell me what does."

He ran his hand through his curls, leaving them rumpled and agitated. "It's believing that someone does, and then having them leave. I don't trust anyone to stay, you see. Not even you."

She fell quiet, any argument she'd formulated in her brain rendered silent.

"A parent's love is supposed to be unconditional. If I can't trust a mother to stay, a father to stay, how can I trust anyone else?" His lips thinned as his voice strengthened. "Eric loved you, and you left him."

The jab hit its mark and she gasped. "That's not fair."

He softened slightly. "I'm not accusing you. If you don't love him anymore, you don't. But it does go to my point that nothing is guaranteed. And it's not a risk I'm willing to take. Not knowing how much it hurts."

"So all of this—the last few weeks—means nothing to you?" She swept out her hand, knowing she was losing the battle to reach him and desperate to regain ground. "We trusted each other with things we haven't shared with anyone else. We became lovers. We were vulnerable with each other, and now that's it?"

"This isn't what we agreed," he said calmly, "and I can't

offer you more than that. It was why we laid ground rules to begin with."

"Ground rules that have already been broken!"

"Yes, you're right. We said one night only. But last night…"

"Last night you weren't such a stickler for the rules."

This time he was the one who was silent.

"I don't want it to be this way," she said, her voice breaking. "We also said always friends, but I can't just be friends with you, Christophe. I love you. And that means all of you. Not as just a friend."

"Are you saying you want this engagement to be real?"

The implications swirled around them. The ring on her finger. Marriage. Christophe as a partner and father. Yes, she thought she wanted those things. And it was clear by the tone of his voice, by the accusation behind it, that he did not. She should have known better. He'd already told her this had ended his previous relationship. Why had she thought she'd be any different?

"I love you," she whispered. "But if you don't love me, then this conversation has no point."

"I'm sorry, Sophie. You have no idea how sorry. I wish I'd never come up with this stupid idea."

And that cut most of all, because it meant regretting everything that had happened between them, and she would never do that. She'd cherish it, not regret it.

She moved to take the ring off her finger, but his voice cut into the silence. "Keep it. I won't say anything for a while and if we break off the engagement now, you'll have to deal with Eric again."

"I don't care. I can deal with him. I didn't need a ring when I told him the truth anyway."

"You told him the engagement was fake?"

"No. I told him that I was in love. He had no argument

against that." She lifted her chin. "I love you. A ring isn't going to change that." She wrested it off her finger and held it out.

"Keep it. It was always meant to be yours, even after the engagement was over. And it'll keep you from having to answer questions right away." He turned away, refusing to take the ring from her. Her hand trembled as she dropped it down to her side. She'd thought she'd be able to get him to see he didn't have to be afraid, but he didn't love her. Cared for her, yes. She believed that, at least. But he didn't love her. Maybe he wasn't capable of it.

He looked back at her. "I'm sorry. You have no idea how much. This wasn't how it was supposed to happen."

"We were fools to think it wouldn't," she said. "To think we could pretend like this and there not be consequences. I know what mine are now."

"I can't lie to you and give you what you want. You said from the beginning that you would only marry for true love. It would be unfair of me to let you believe in something that doesn't exist."

She hadn't thought he could wound her further, but that did it.

"Just go," she whispered.

"I'm sorry," he said, one last time.

And then he walked out her door.

Christophe kept the door shut to his office and focused on the spreadsheet in front of him. For four days he'd buried himself in work, trying to forget the hurt look in Sophie's eyes on Sunday afternoon. It was no use. He'd hurt her and he'd lied to her. Not about everything. He didn't believe in love, or at least didn't believe in it lasting. But he did feel it, and he felt it for her. She'd been a friend for years, but in the space of three weeks she'd become his lover and his everything. And that scared him to death. She was the control freak, but she was willing to relinquish that for something unknown and risky. He, on the other hand, was supposed to be so easygoing, but he was the one who was terrified of his out-of-control feelings.

It was better to stop the charade now, when they could both still recover and move on. And maybe someday they'd be friends again.

The last three weeks, well, they felt like a runaway train and he'd had to get off.

But God, he missed her.

His office door opened, and he looked up in irritation… didn't anyone knock anymore? When he saw it was Aurora, he bit back his annoyance. Snapping at her wouldn't do anyone any good.

"You're working late again."

"As are you, Maman. And you're supposed to be retired."

"No one is retired during the holiday season. Not in our business." She smiled at him, then came over and perched on the corner of his desk and reached out to smooth a piece of hair on his forehead. "Tell me where it hurts, *ma petite*."

She hadn't spoken to him like that in years, and his heart ached with it. It suddenly got difficult to swallow and his vision blurred. "I'm fine," he managed to say.

"No, you are not. I've seen this look on your face before, Christophe. Twice, to be exact. The first time was when we drove away from Orléans and brought you to Paris. The second was when I told you Cedric was gone." Her voice was soft but held a hint of steel. "Did she break your heart?"

He shook his head. "No, Maman. I broke hers."

Aurora sighed. "Oh, Christophe. I rather feared that was the case. You got scared and ran, didn't you?"

He looked up sharply, annoyed by how quickly she'd put that together. "Am I so transparent?"

"I've known you since you were a little boy. I will always maintain that bringing you to be part of our family was the best thing, for you and for us. But it is not without its scars. When I saw you with Sophie, I'd hoped you'd put those fears behind you."

"I don't know how to talk about this with you without seeming ungrateful."

She laughed, a small chuckle that was filled with affection. "Darling, I know you love me, just as I love you."

"You and Oncle Cedric…you raised me. You took me in when I wasn't wanted anywhere else."

"That is what you think? That we did it out of duty? Christophe. You were such a wonderful little boy. Your mother was struggling. She wouldn't let us help her, even though Cedric offered to. She was angry at me and angry at your father and at the world. We didn't 'take you in.' We saw an opportunity to give you the kind of life you deserved. We saw the opportunity to add to our family. I don't know how to explain it better than that. But you were wanted, Christophe."

Tears stung again. "I'm such a mess."

"We all are. We all have something. Bella's scars were on the outside. But so many of us…ours are on the inside. Facing them is torture. But happiness usually lies on the other side. You are miserable without her. The question is, does she love you?"

"She says she does."

"Why don't you believe her?"

He didn't answer at first. Then he reached over and took her hand. "I do believe her. But I'm afraid to hope. To trust. Because if she leaves me… I don't know if I can go through that."

"Not everyone leaves people." She reached out and touched his cheek. "If you marry her, you will be a father to her baby. Would you ever abandon him or her?"

"Of course not!" He was horrified at the thought.

"How do you know?"

He stared at her, confused.

"You trust yourself, but you don't trust someone else, and I understand why. You're willing to sit here right now and pledge that you would never abandon a child not your own flesh and blood. Not everyone is like your father, or even your mother, Christophe. But you will never know if you don't give them a chance, and you will never find happiness if you are determined to go through your life alone. If she loves you, and you love her, you're a fool to let her go." She lifted his chin. "And I did not raise you to be a fool."

"I'm still scared."

"Of course you are. It's a big thing, falling in love. Taking that leap." She frowned. "I just have one question. If you were this uncertain, why did you propose in the first place?"

"That is a question with a very long answer that will be a great anecdote someday."

They sat there for a long moment, and he was glad she was with him. Unconditionally. He looked up and his throat tightened again. "Thank you for being my mother," he said, his voice rough with emotion. "Sophie told me that a mother's love is unconditional, and she was right."

Aurora blinked rapidly and leaned over to kiss his forehead. "It is. Whatever you decide, I just want you to be happy. I saw you with Sophie at the château. It is extra special when you marry your best friend, Christophe. Don't throw that away because of fear. Work through it together. It's the only way your relationship will survive."

She left him sitting there and shut the door behind her as she left. Christophe stared at the spreadsheet but couldn't make heads nor tails of the columns and numbers. Instead, he searched his heart for the answers he needed. And when they came, he picked up his phone and called François.

Sophie stared at the email and felt an anger overcome her that was quite uncharacteristic. "Is he serious?" she asked the empty room. Empty except for Harry, who was perched on a cushion in the chair next to her. He looked up, gave a squeak, and put his head down again.

She stared at the email once more. What was his end-game? She hadn't heard a peep from him in two weeks. He'd walked out and…silence. Not that she'd expected anything. It had taken some serious verbal tap dancing around her parents to explain his absence. She'd framed it as both of them being extra busy during the holiday retail season, but it was hard to keep up the pretense of happiness. Harder to keep that up than the lie of the engagement.

Now he was making an offer on her jewelry collection. He'd sent through François's notes, too, and the CAD designs the designer had done of her drawings. He wanted them for a collection within the Aurora Gems line. And he wanted her to go to Paris for a meeting.

She hit the reply button and typed two words and then halted.

Aurora, Inc. would produce her collection using her name. It was a dream come true.

It was also a consolation prize, or at least it felt like it. As if he were saying "sorry, I don't have any love to give you, but here's a contract to make up for it." If she were going to sell the designs, she damned well wanted it to be on her own merit and not because Christophe felt guilty.

She fiddled with the ring on her finger. She'd been

wearing it to work to avoid questions, but suddenly now she wanted to take it off. Sophie twisted and pulled, but it stuck on her knuckle. "Oh, for God's sake!" she exploded, and then, for the millionth time since he'd walked out, she caught her lower lip wobbling.

It was hormones. It could only be hormones because she never let herself cry over a man like this.

When she composed herself again, she sent a quick email back. If he wanted to keep this business, so be it.

I'm interested in your proposal. Please send over the contract so I can review it, then I'll be in touch.

Short, to the point, no emotion. Perfect.

An hour later, she got an inbox notification. It was seven at night—eight in Paris. What was he still doing at work? Maybe, like her, he was working extra hours to fill the void.

We would prefer to meet in person before drawing up the contract. My assistant will contact you to set up a meeting at your convenience and will look after your travel arrangements for you. Best, Christophe

She briefly considered saying no, but as her mother would say, that would be cutting off her nose to spite her face, wouldn't it? If he could be utterly professional, then so could she. She'd show him that he might have broken her heart, but he hadn't broken her.

I'll look forward to her call.

CHAPTER SEVENTEEN

Sophie walked into the Aurora offices alone this time, and when she stopped at the front desk, she was greeted with a smile. "Oh, Ms. Waltham. We've been expecting you." Giselle's smile was wide. "Here's your card for the elevator. You remember the way to Monsieur Germain's office?"

"Oui, merci, Giselle." She offered a smile and fought of the sense of belonging that came over her when she entered the building. It wasn't right that she felt so at home here.

Maybe it was enough that her designs would be produced by Aurora. There was no better way to launch a career than with Aurora's backing. But not if Christophe was offering it as a token or to assuage some sort of guilt. He was a great one for gestures of that sort while refusing to accept anything in return. Well, not this time.

The elevator hummed quietly as she ascended to the executive offices. She pressed a hand to her stomach—it was growing by the day now, it seemed—and let out a breath to calm her jittery nerves. She had to keep her composure when she saw him again. Use her best poker face. She'd had enough practice the past month that it shouldn't be that hard, right?

She stepped off the elevator and went to main reception. "Ah, yes, Ms. Waltham. If you'll follow me. Monsieur

Germain has asked that you join him one floor down, actually. I'll take you there."

They went into the elevator again for the short trip, and the receptionist led her along the familiar hall. Perhaps they were meeting with François first? She should be glad; the designer would provide a welcome buffer during that first meeting.

A swipe of the key card and she was inside.

"Ah, Sophie! I heard you were on your way down." François approached, smiling broadly, and kissed her cheeks. "What did you think of the drawings?"

She was honest. "They turned out beautifully."

"I'm looking forward to working on them with you. Come with me."

He took her past his inner sanctum to a smaller office, set up similarly to his but on a smaller and neater scale. "What's this?"

"Your own space, for when you are here."

"François, I haven't signed anything."

"I know, *cherie*. The day is young."

"Where is Christophe?"

"Right here."

His voice came from behind her, in the doorway, and she spun around. He looked so good, so perfect, in a dark gray suit and pale blue shirt, open at the throat. She remembered how he hated ties, how he'd worn one to brunch and wrestled with the knot. She also remembered exactly how the hollow of his throat tasted. This had been a mistake. She should have insisted he send an agreement to her in London.

"This is kind of you, but I'll be working in London, remember? Waltham is there." Her anxiety kicked up a notch as she pointed out, "My baby's father is there."

"It is wonderful how convenient travel is between the

two cities," he pointed out. He stepped inside the room and François discreetly made himself scarce, leaving them alone. She realized belatedly that she'd mentioned the baby, something only his immediate family knew. "Don't worry about François. He adores you. He won't say a word."

She nodded and took a step back. "Do you have an offer for me? François didn't say which of the concepts you were interested in."

"Yes, I have an offer for you."

She waited, growing frustrated with his calm and patience. "Well?"

He took his hand out of his pockets and spread them out to his side a little. "Forever. My offer is forever, Sophie. If you can forgive me for being a total ass."

She stared. Surely she hadn't heard him right. "This isn't funny, Christophe. I came from London because you said you wanted to offer for my designs. Do you or don't you?"

"I do, and the paperwork is upstairs in my office. You're free to take it with you and have your lawyer look it over. The contract will stand no matter how you answer my next question."

She looked for signs he was joking, but there were none. No half smile, no teasing lift to his eyebrow. Instead, there was apology in his eyes, and something else, too. Something she'd wanted to see for a long time, only now she was too afraid to believe it was real.

"What's your next question, then?"

He didn't move. Just looked her square in the eye and said, "Will you marry me for real?"

It was amazing how she could stand so very still while inside it was all chaos. "I don't understand," she said slowly.

"You were right, about everything. About me being afraid. But I've come to understand that I am not my father or my mother. I would not abandon those whom I've claimed to love. And if I am not my parents, it is unfair for me to project my fears on you and expect you will leave me as they did. I was so afraid that I couldn't step back and see that for myself."

"What changed?"

"Aurora," he said simply. "Maman did what the best mothers do. She offered love and guidance…and a soft place to fall. I am blessed to have her. I only hope I am not too late with you. I never wanted to hurt you, Soph. I was just trying to protect myself."

"I know that," she said. "I could see it all along, but I didn't know how to get through to you."

"You couldn't. I had to figure it out myself. I would be a fool to throw away the love of my best friend. And I do love you, Sophie. I love you so much."

She'd never expected to hear those words in a hundred years, and she bit down on her lip because she didn't want to cry right now. "I was so mad at you for demanding I come here," she said. "Burning with rage because I thought you were offering me a consolation prize. A contract but no you. I was going to sign it just to spite you."

"And now?"

"Why would I want to spite my fiancé?"

His eyes widened. "Is that a yes?"

"Yes, Christophe. Yes, I'll marry you." She went to him and put her arms around his neck, holding him close. Oh, it felt so good to be in his arms again. Like coming home. "We have things to work out," she murmured, "but I really want us to do that together. The last two weeks have been horrible without you."

"For me, too. There were times I was fired up to get you back. And then other times I was sure it was for nothing and I'd lost you." He squeezed her tighter. "You're really here."

"Of course I am. I love you. Even when I'm furious with you."

He laughed then, and they pulled back to gaze at each other. His eyebrow twitched, and it gave her so much happiness she thought she might burst with it. "Are you planning to be furious with me often? It could be an interesting marriage."

"Only when you deserve it," she answered. Then she sobered and held his face between her hands. "Love means working through your problems and not walking away. I love you, Christophe. I know trust is so hard for you, so I'm just going to have to remind you every day that I'm not going anywhere."

"Nor am I," he replied, and he kissed her finally, long and deep, for the first time with their spoken feelings between them, and it was the sweetest thing she'd ever experienced.

Someone cleared their throat at the door and Sophie and Christophe broke apart. Her cheeks flushed as she saw François standing there with a lopsided grin on his face.

"Is there a reason you're interrupting me and my fiancée?" Christophe asked.

"Yes, sir. *Madame* herself is on the way down. I thought you might want to know before things got too…uh-huh." He wiggled his eyebrows and Sophie laughed.

"Thanks, François."

"We must look out for each other," he said wisely. "Welcome to the team, Sophie."

"Yeah," Christophe said, pulling her close to his side. "Welcome to the team."

Sophie couldn't believe she'd agreed to a Christmas Eve wedding. When Christophe had first suggested it, she had told him he was crazy, but it had taken maybe an hour for her to come around to the idea. The other alternative was the two of them spending the next several months traveling back and forth while her pregnancy progressed, and then trying to plan a wedding when the baby was small. Christophe's suggestion was to plan the wedding and then work out all the other logistics step by step: where they'd live, her role within Aurora and Waltham, and of course, shared parenting with Eric. They'd gone to see him together, and Christophe had asked his blessing. He'd even spoken to the other man about his childhood, and how he was determined that they all work together for this baby to feel loved and secure.

If she hadn't loved him completely before, that would have sealed it.

Her next step had been to sign the contract with Aurora. The Masterpiece Collection by Sophie Waltham was going to be a real thing.

Now she was standing in a guest room, wearing a stunning dress designed and tailored by Aurora's team. Christophe was down the hall in his own room, getting ready in his tuxedo. The wedding was going to take place in the grand hall downstairs, with only their families present…and François. He'd personally designed their wedding bands, and he'd come to mean a lot to her.

Bella and Gabi circled her, fluffing her skirt, smoothing a button. "You are stunning," Bella said, standing back and admiring.

"I feel like this is all a fairy tale and I'm going to wake up and find it's all been a dream," she admitted.

"Oh, it's real." Charlotte came in, beaming as usual. "Christophe is so smitten it's ridiculous. Never expected him to be the next to settle down." She sent a sarcastic look in Bella's direction. "Some people like long engagements, apparently."

Gabi laughed. "All right, Sophie. Here's your bouquet."
She handed over a bouquet of crimson roses. Sophie had
chosen it for its simplicity and for the season. The hall had
been decorated for weeks for the holiday. They'd hardly
had to do anything. Evergreen boughs and ribbon hung
from every banister and railing. Arrangements of flowers
and greens were everywhere, and white folding chairs had
been brought in for the guests. While the family tree was
in the drawing room, an arch had been constructed as an
altar for the ceremony in the grand hall. It had all been in
place when Sophie had left to get ready.

"We do need to get downstairs, girls," Gabi said, giving
Sophie's gown one last fluff. "Happy wedding day," she
whispered in Sophie's ear, giving her a little hug.

Sophie had quite fallen in love with the whole family
over the past few weeks, everyone chipping in to hastily
throw together the simple wedding—even the garrulous
Stephen, who seemed determined to retain his bachelor-
hood, despite the fact he was the heir and the oldest of
them all. He wasn't nearly as scary as he'd first appeared
and had told Christophe that he'd just acquired the most
precious gem in the Aurora dynasty. It was an uncharacteristically sentimental thing for him to say.

The sisters departed, and Sophie had a few moments to
herself. She took a large breath and went to stand in front
of the mirror. Her little bump didn't show in the empire-
waisted gown, which she adored. A low scoop neck showed
a hint of cleavage, but delicate cap sleeves gave the gown
an innocent look, and the lace overskirt was divine, ending
in a small train at the back. Aurora had loaned her a tiara,
too, the one that she had worn at her wedding to Cedric,
and Sophie had been particularly touched.

Christophe had even invited his mother, though she'd
declined the invitation. Sophie knew it had hurt him ter-

ribly, but she'd tried to make him see that his mother was the one losing out.

Either way, within the hour Sophie and Christophe would be husband and wife. He would be a father to her child. They would be…a family.

There was a knock on the door and her father peeked inside. "Are you ready, blossom? It's time."

"I am, Dad," she said, clutching her bouquet. She'd moved the diamond and ruby ring to her right hand for the ceremony, and just this morning Christophe had gifted her the matching necklace and earrings, which glittered at her throat and ears.

"I'm so happy for you, Sophie," he murmured, kissing her cheek. "I don't want to mess your makeup."

"You won't. We used setting spray." She laughed and kissed him on the cheek. "You and Mum…you like him, don't you?"

"We do. And he loves you, and that's all we ever want for our children." He stopped, choked up for a moment. "I didn't think it would be this hard, giving you away."

She got misty-eyed too, and took a moment to say, "Thank you, Dad. It's because of you and Mum that I know what love is, and why I wouldn't settle for less."

"Well, now that's done it." He reached inside his pocket for a handkerchief and wiped his eyes. "Sophie, one more thing you should know. Your mother and I have been talking, and it's unfair of us to expect you to take on Waltham when you have your own life to live. We're nowhere near ready to retire, mind you, but we'll support you in whatever future you choose. You have a family to consider now, after all. And family means everything."

"Oh, Dad." She sniffled and kissed his cheek. "I love you."

"I love you too, blossom. Come now, let's get you down the aisle."

They descended the stairs, Sophie careful to let her toe peek out from beneath her hem before taking each step. When they reached the end of the hall, every eye turned to look at her, but she had eyes only for Christophe. Pristine, black tuxedo with a white cravat and a red rose at his breast; curls freshly cut but barely tamed, and one damnable eyebrow lifted—the same one that had started all this trouble. A smile curved her lips as she made her way to him, growing the closer she got, until she reached his side, and they were both grinning like idiots.

To her right, Aurora gave a sniff and dabbed her eyes with a tissue.

The officiant took one look at them and declared, "I don't think I've ever seen a happier couple."

As Sophie looked into Christophe's eyes, she had a feeling the officiant was right. And after the vows were spoken and the rings exchanged, Christophe pointed to a spot above her head.

Mistletoe. He'd hung mistletoe from their bridal arch. And as they shared their first kiss as husband and wife, it was with the promise in her heart that each year they'd revisit this tradition and renew their vows to each other, no matter where the future took them. Whether it was Aurora or Waltham, Paris or London, it didn't matter. Their love was forever, and they would spend each and every day proving it.

* * * * *

COMING SOON!

We really hope you enjoyed reading this book.
If you're looking for more romance
be sure to head to the shops when
new books are available on

Thursday 16th January

To see which titles are coming soon, please visit

millsandboon.co.uk/nextmonth

MILLS & BOON

LET'S TALK
Romance

For exclusive extracts, competitions and special offers, find us online:

f MillsandBoon

X @MillsandBoon

⊙ @MillsandBoonUK

♪ @MillsandBoonUK

Get in touch on 01413 063 232

MILLS & BOON

MODERN

Power and Passion

Prepare to be swept off your feet by sophisticated, sexy and seductive heroes, in some of the world's most glamorous and romantic locations, where power and passion collide.

Eight Modern stories published every month, find them all at:

millsandboon.co.uk

MILLS & BOON

THE HEART OF ROMANCE

A ROMANCE FOR EVERY READER

MODERN

Prepare to be swept off your feet by sophisticated, sexy and seductive heroes, in some of the world's most glamourous and romantic locations, where power and passion collide.

HISTORICAL

Escape with historical heroes from time gone by. Whether your passion is for wicked Regency Rakes, muscled Vikings or rugged Highlanders, awaken the romance of the past.

MEDICAL

Set your pulse racing with dedicated, delectable doctors in the high-pressure world of medicine, where emotions run high and passion, comfort and love are the best medicine.

True Love

Celebrate true love with tender stories of heartfelt romance, from the rush of falling in love to the joy a new baby can bring, and a focus on the emotional heart of a relationship.

HEROES

The excitement of a gripping thriller, with intense romance at its heart. Resourceful, true-to-life women and strong, fearless men face danger and desire - a killer combination!

###

From showing up to glowing up, these characters are on the path to leading their best lives and finding romance along the way – with plenty of sizzling spice!

To see which titles are coming soon, please visit

millsandboon.co.uk/nextmonth

GET YOUR ROMANCE FIX!

Get the latest romance news,
exclusive author interviews, story
extracts and much more!

blog.millsandboon.co.uk